Beginning Arduino

Michael McRoberts

Apress®

Beginning Arduino

ISBN-13 (pbk): 978-1-4302-3240-7

ISBN-13 (electronic): 978-1-4302-3241-4

Printed and bound in the United States of America 9 8 7 6 5 4 3 2 1

President and Publisher: Paul Manning
Lead Editor: Michelle Lowman
Technical Reviewer: Josh Adams
Editorial Board: Steve Anglin, Mark Beckner, Ewan Buckingham, Gary Cornell, Jonathan Gennick, Jonathan Hassell, Michelle Lowman, Matthew Moodie, Duncan Parkes, Jeffrey Pepper, Frank Pohlmann, Douglas Pundick, Ben Renow-Clarke, Dominic Shakeshaft, Matt Wade, Tom Welsh
Coordinating Editor: Jennifer L. Blackwell
Copy Editor: Mary Behr
Production Support: Patrick Cunningham
Indexer: Julie Grady
Artist: April Milne
Cover Designer: Anna Ishchenko

Distributed to the book trade worldwide by Springer Science+Business Media, LLC., 233 Spring Street, 6th Floor, New York, NY 10013. Phone 1-800-SPRINGER, fax (201) 348-4505, e-mail orders-ny@springer-sbm.com, or visit www.springeronline.com.

For information on translations, please e-mail rights@apress.com, or visit www.apress.com.

Apress and friends of ED books may be purchased in bulk for academic, corporate, or promotional use. eBook versions and licenses are also available for most titles. For more information, reference our Special Bulk Sales–eBook Licensing web page at www.apress.com/info/bulksales.

The source code for this book is available to readers at www.apress.com.

I would like to dedicate this book to my mother for her encouragement throughout the book process and for being the best Mum anyone could ask for, and to my grandfather, Reginald Godfrey, for igniting the spark for science and electronics in me at a young age. Without all those kits from Radio Shack at Christmas I may never have reached the point where I ended up writing a book about microcontrollers and electronics. Thank you both.

Contents at a Glance

Contents

About the Author

Michael McRoberts discovered the Arduino in 2008 while looking for ways to connect a temperature sensor to a PC to make a Cloud Detector for his other hobby of astrophotography. After a bit of research, the Arduino seemed like the obvious choice, and the Cloud Detector was successfully made, quickly and cheaply. Mike's fascination with the Arduino had begun. Since then he has gone on to make countless projects using the Arduino. He had also founded an Arduino starter kit and component online business called Earthshine Electronics. His next project is to use an Arduino-based circuit to send a high altitude balloon up to the edge of space to take stills and video for the heck of it, with the help of the guys from UKHAS and CUSF.

Mike's hobby of electronics began as a child when the 100-in-1 electronics kits from Radio Shack made up his Christmas present list. He started programming as a hobby when he obtained a Sinclair ZX81 computer as a teenager. Since then, he's never been without a computer. Recently, he's become a Mac convert.

He is a member of London Hackspace and the Orpington Astronomical Society and can regularly be found contributing to the Arduino Forum. He also likes to lurk on IRC in the Arduino, high altitude and london-hack-space channels (as "earthshine"), and on Twitter as "TheArduinoGuy." When he is not messing around with Arduinos or running Earthshine Electronics, he likes to indulge in astronomy, astrophotography, motorcycling, and sailing.

About the Technical Reviewer

Josh Adams is a developer and architect with over nine years of professional experience building production-quality software and managing projects. He built a Tesla Coil for a high school science project that shot 27-inch bolts of lightning. As Isotope Eleven's lead architect, Josh is responsible for overseeing architectural decisions and translating customer requirements into working software. Josh graduated from the University of Alabama at Birmingham (UAB) with Bachelor of Science degrees in both Mathematics and Philosophy. In his free time (ha!), Josh provided the technical review for this book on programming with the Arduino microprocessor. When he's not working, Josh enjoys spending time with his family.

Acknowledgments

First of all, I'd like to thank my editors Michelle Lowman and Jennifer Blackwell from Apress, as without them this book would never have even got off the ground; my technical reviewer, Josh Adams, for patiently checking my code and circuit diagrams to get them right; and Nancy Wright for spotting all of the mistakes.

A huge thank you to all those people from Flickr and Wikimedia Commons who chose to put their image under a Creative Commons license and who gave me permission to use those images: Bruno Soares, Richard V. Gilbank, Inductiveload, Snorpey, Iain Fergusson, Patrick H. Lauke, cultured_society2nd, Cyril Buttay, Tony Jewell, Tod E. Kurt, Adam Grieg, David Stokes, Mike Prevette, David Mitchell, Aki Korhonen, Alex43223, Sparkfun, DFRobot, Adafruit Industries, Colin M.L. Burnett, David Batley, Jan-Piet Mens, Mercury13, Georg Wiora, and Timo Arnall.

Thanks to everyone who let me use or modify their code or Arduino libraries to create the projects and who gave technical assistance or advice: Michael Margolis, Usman Haque from Pachube, Georg Kaindl, Tom Pollard, Jim Studt, Miles Burton, Robin James, Paul Stoffregen, Conor, Tom Igoe, Tim Newsome, James Whiddon, Bill Greiman, Matt Joyce, D. Sjunnesson, David A. Mellis, Bob S. (Xtalker), Ian Baker, and NeoCat.

Thanks to Sparkfun and Adafruit Industries for providing me with parts and for letting me use their images. Thanks also to the Arduino core team without whom the fantastic Arduino and its community would not even exist: Massimo Banzi, Tom Igoe, David Cuartielles, Gianluca Martino, David Mellis, and Nicholas Zambetti.

Finally, thanks to all those people on the Arduino Forum, Arduino IRC channel, and Twitter for your help, advice, and encouragement throughout the book process and to London Hackspace for giving me a place to try out some experiments and to write the final chapter.

If I have missed anyone, my apologies and thanks to you, too.

Introduction

I first discovered the Arduino in 2008 when I was looking for ways to connect temperature sensors to my PC so I could make a Cloud Detector. I wanted to try out a cloud detection concept I'd read about on a weather forum, and as it was experimental, I didn't want to spend a lot of money on it in case it failed. There were many solutions on the market, but the Arduino appealed to me the most. Not only did it seem to be an easy and cheap way to connect the sensors I required but it could be used for other cool things. Thousands of projects in blogs, video sites, and forums showed the cool things people were doing with their Arduinos. There seemed to be a huge sense of community with everyone trying to help each other.

It was obvious that I could have a lot of fun with an Arduino. However, I didn't want to be trawling through websites for information. I wanted to buy a book on the subject, something I could hold in my hand and read on the train into work. After looking around, I found one book. Unfortunately, it was very basic and out of date. Worse, it didn't give me anything practical to do with the Arduino, and I didn't warm to the teaching style either. What I wanted was a hands-on book that taught me both programming and electronics as I built things instead of having to wade through pages of theory first. Such a book just didn't exist at the time.

Then I started Earthshine Electronics to sell kits based on the Arduino. To go with the kit, I produced a small tutorial booklet to get people started. This little booklet ended up being very popular, and I got hundreds of queries from people asking when I would be adding more projects or if I sold a printed version. In fact, I had already thought that it would be great to produce a comprehensive beginner's book, crammed with projects and written in the kind of easy-to-follow style. That is how this book came about.

I have written this book with the presumption that you have never done either computer programming or electronics before. I also presume you're not interested in reading lots of theory before you actually get down to making something with your Arduino. Hence, right from the start of the book, you will be diving right into making a simple project. From there, you will work through a total of 50 projects until you become confident and proficient at Arduino development. I believe that the best way to learn anything is by learning as you go and getting your hands dirty.

The book works like this: the first project introduces basic concepts about programming the Arduino and also about electronics. The next project builds on that knowledge to introduce a little bit more. Each project after that builds on the previous projects. By the time you have finished all 50 projects, you will be confident and proficient at making your own projects. You'll be able to adapt your new skills and knowledge to connect just about anything to your Arduino and thus make great projects for fun or to make your life easier.

Each project starts off with a list of required parts. I have chosen common parts that are easy to source. I also provide a circuit diagram showing exactly how to connect the Arduino and parts together using jumper wires and a breadboard. To create the parts images and breadboard diagrams for the book, I used the excellent open-source program Fritzing. The program allows designers to document their prototypes and then go on to create PCB layouts for manufacture. It is an excellent program and a brilliant way of demonstrating a breadboard circuit to others. Pop on over to http://fritzing.org and check it out.

After you have made your circuit, I supply a code listing to type into the Arduino's program editor (the IDE) which can then be uploaded to your Arduino to make the project work. You will very quickly have a fully working project. It is only after you have made your project and seen it working that I explain how it works. The hardware will be explained to you in such a way that you know how the component works and how to connect them to the Arduino correctly. The code will then be explained to you step by step so you understand exactly what each section of the code does. By dissecting the circuit and the code, you will understand how the whole project works and can then apply the skills and knowledge to later projects and then onto your own projects in the future.

The style of teaching is very easy to follow. Even if you have absolutely no experience of either programming or electronics, you will be able to follow along easily and understand the concepts as you go. More importantly, you will have fun. The Arduino is a great, fun, open source product. With the help of this book, you'll discover just how easy it is to get involved in physical computing to make your own devices that interact with their environment.

Mike McRoberts

CHAPTER 1

Introduction

Since the Arduino Project started back in 2005, over 150,000 boards have been sold worldwide to date. The number of unofficial clone boards sold no doubt outweighs the official boards, thus it's likely that over half a million Arduino boards and its variants are out in the wild. Its popularity is ever increasing as more and more people realize the amazing potential of this incredible open source project to create cool projects quickly and easily with a relatively shallow learning curve

The biggest advantage of the Arduino over other microcontroller development platforms is its ease of use; non-"techie" people can pick up the basics and be creating their own projects in a relatively short amount of time. Artists, in particular, seem to find it the ideal way to create interactive works of art quickly and without specialist knowledge of electronics. There is a huge community of people using Arduinos and sharing their code and circuit diagrams for others to copy and modify. The majority of this community is also very willing to help others. You'll find the Arduino Forum the place to go if you want answers quickly.

However, despite the huge amount of information available to beginners on the Internet, most of it is spread across various sources, making it tricky to track down the necessary information. This is where this book fits in. Within these pages are 50 projects that are all designed to take you step by step through programming your Arduino. When you first get an Arduino (or any new gadget, for that matter), you want to plug it in, connect an LED, and get it flashing right away. You don't want to read through pages of theory first. This author understands that excitement to "get going" and that is why you will dive right into connecting things to your Arduino, uploading code, and getting on with it. This is, I believe, the best way to learn a subject and especially a subject such as Physical Computing, which is what the Arduino is all about.

How to Use This Book

The book starts with an introduction to the Arduino, how to set up the hardware, install the software, upload your first sketch, and ensure that your Arduino and the software are working correctly. I then explain the Arduino IDE and how to use it before you dive right into projects progressing from very basic stuff through to advanced topics. Each project will start with a description of how to set up the hardware and what code is needed to get it working. I will then explain in some detail how the hardware and the code each work. Everything will be explained in clear and simple steps, with many diagrams and photographs to make it as easy as possible to check that you are following along with the project correctly.

You will come across some terms and concepts in the book that you may not understand at first. Don't worry; these will become clear as you work your way through the projects.

What You Will Need

To be able to follow along with the projects in this book, you will need various components. This could be expensive, so I suggest that you start off with purchasing the components for the projects in the first few chapters (the parts are listed at the start of the project pages). As you progress through the book, you can obtain the parts needed for subsequent projects.

There are a handful of other items you will need or may find useful. Of course, you will need to obtain an Arduino board or one of the many clone boards on the market such as the Freeduino, Seeeduino (yes it's really spelled that way), Boarduino, Sanguino, Roboduino, or any of the other "duino" variants. These are all fully compatible with the Arduino IDE, Arduino Shields, and everything else that you can use with an official Arduino Board. Remember that the Arduino is an open source project and therefore anyone is free to make a clone or other variant of the Arduino. However, if you wish to support the development team of the original Arduino board, get an official board from one of the recognized distributors. As of September 2010, the latest variant of the Arduino board is the Arduino Uno.

You will need access to the Internet to download the Arduino IDE (Integrated Development Environment—the software used to write your Arduino code) and to also download the code samples within this book (if you don't want to type them out yourself) and any code libraries that may be necessary to get your project working.

You will also need a well-lit table or other flat surface to lay out your components; this should be next to your desktop or laptop PC to enable you to upload the code to the Arduino. Remember that you are working with electricity (although low voltage DC); therefore, a metal surface will need to be covered in a non-conductive material, such as a tablecloth or paper, before laying out your materials. Also of some benefit, although not essential, may be a pair of wire cutters, a pair of long nosed pliers, and a wire stripper. A notepad and pen will come in handy for drawing out rough schematics, working out concepts and designs, etc.

Finally, the most important thing you will need is enthusiasm and a willingness to learn. The Arduino is designed as a simple and cheap way to get involved in microcontroller electronics and nothing is too hard to learn if you are willing to at least give it a go. This book will help you on that journey and introduce you to this exciting and creative hobby.

What Exactly is an Arduino?

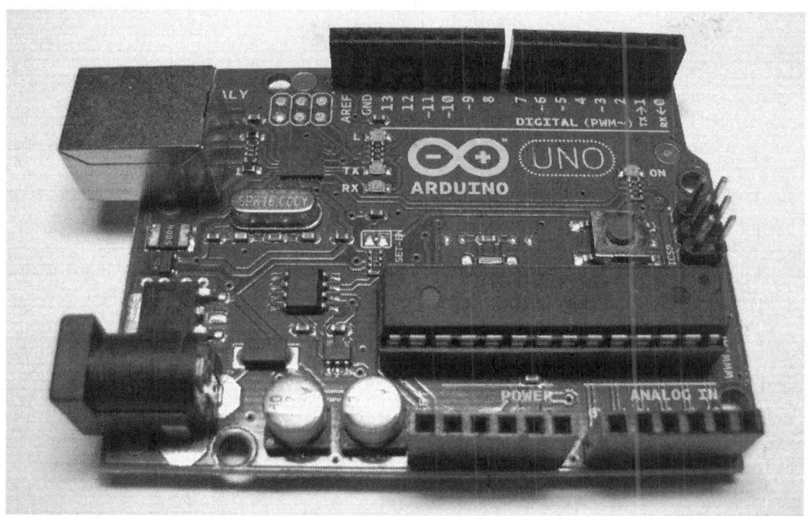

Figure 1-1. An Arduino Uno

Wikipedia states "*An Arduino is a single-board microcontroller and a software suite for programming it. The hardware consists of a simple open hardware design for the controller with an Atmel AVR processor and on-board I/O support. The software consists of a standard programming language and the boot loader that runs on the board.*"

To put that in layman's terms, an Arduino is a tiny computer that you can program to process inputs and outputs between the device and external components you connect to it (see Figure 1-1). The Arduino is what is known as a Physical or Embedded Computing platform, which means that it is an interactive system that can interact with its environment through the use of hardware and software. For example, a simple use of an Arduino would be to turn a light on for a set period of time, let's say 30 seconds, after a button has been pressed. In this example, the Arduino would have a lamp and a button connected to it. The Arduino would sit patiently waiting for the button to be pressed; once pressed, the Arduino would turn the lamp on and start counting. Once it had counted for 30 seconds, it would turn the lamp off and then wait for another button press. You could use this setup to control a lamp in an closet, for example.

You could extend this concept by connecting a sensor, such as a PIR, to turn the lamp on when it has been triggered. These are some simple examples of how you could use an Arduino.

The Arduino can be used to develop stand-alone interactive objects or it can be connected to a computer, a network, or even the Internet to retrieve and send data to and from the Arduino and then act on that data. In other words, it can send a set of data received from some sensors to a website, which can then be displayed in the form of a graph.

The Arduino can be connected to LEDs, dot matrix displays (see Figure 1-2), buttons, switches, motors, temperature sensors, pressure sensors, distance sensors, GPS receivers, Ethernet modules, or just about anything that outputs data or can be controlled. A look around the Internet will bring up a wealth of projects where an Arduino has been used to read data from or control an amazing array of devices.

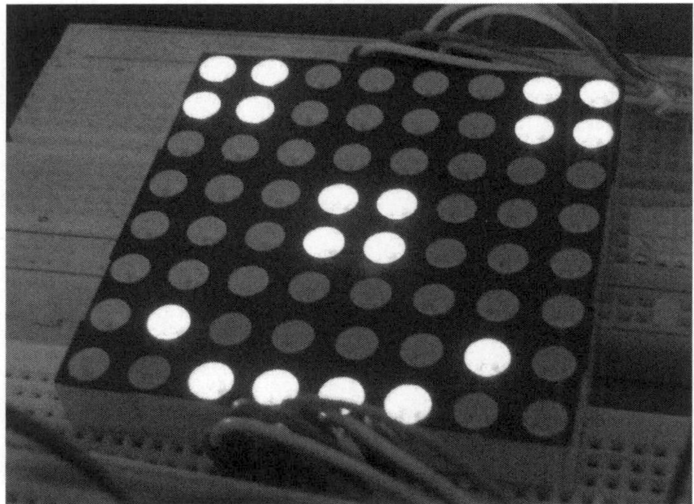

***Figure 1-2.** A dot matrix display controlled by an Arduino (image courtesy of Bruno Soares)*

The Arduino board is made up of an Atmel AVR Microprocessor, a crystal or oscillator (a crude clock that sends time pulses at a specified frequency to enable it to operate at the correct speed), and a 5-volt linear regulator. Depending on what type of Arduino you have, it may also have a USB socket to connect to a PC or Mac for uploading or retrieving data. The board exposes the microcontroller's I/O (input/output) pins so that you can connect those pins to other circuits or to sensors.

The latest Arduino board, the Uno, differs from the previous versions of the Arduino in that it does not use the FTDI USB-to-serial driver chip. Instead, it uses an Atmega8U2 programmed as a USB-to-serial converter. This gives the board several advantages over its predecessor, the Duemilanove. First, the Atmega chip is a lot cheaper than the FTDI chip, bringing the prices of the boards down. Secondly, and most importantly, it enables the USB chip to have its firmware reflashed to make the Arduino show up on your PC as another device, such as a mouse or game controller. This opens up a whole array of new uses for the Arduino. Unfortunately, moving over to this new USB chip has made it a lot more difficult for clone manufacturers to make Arduino Uno clones.

To program the Arduino (make it do what you want it to) you use the Arduino IDE (Integrated Development Environment), which is a piece of free software in which you write code in the language that the Arduino understands (a language called C). The IDE lets you to write a *computer program*, which is a set of step-by-step instructions that you then upload to the Arduino. Your Arduino will then carry out these instructions and interact with whatever you have connected to it. In the Arduino world, programs are known as *sketches*.

The Arduino hardware and software are both open source, which means that the code, schematics, design, etc. can be taken freely by anyone to do what they like with them. Hence, there are many clone boards and other Arduino-based boards available to purchase or to make from a schematic. Indeed, there is nothing stopping you from purchasing the appropriate components and making your own Arduino on a breadboard or on your own homemade PCB (Printed Circuit Board). The only caveat that the Arduino team imposes is that you cannot use the word "Arduino." This name is reserved for the official board. Hence, the clone boards have names such as Freeduino, Roboduino, etc.

As the designs are open source, any clone board is 100% compatible with the Arduino and therefore any software, hardware, shields, etc. will also be 100% compatible with a genuine Arduino.

The Arduino can also be extended with the use of *shields*, which are circuit boards containing other devices (e.g. GPS receivers, LCD Displays, Ethernet modules, etc.) that you can simply connect to the top of your Arduino to get extra functionality. Shields also extend the pins to the top of its own circuit board so you still have access to all of them. You don't have to use a shield if you don't want to; you can make the exact same circuitry using a breadboard, Stripboard, Veroboard, or by making your own PCB. Most of the projects in this book are made using circuits on a breadboard.

There are many different variants of the Arduino. The latest version is the Arduino Uno. The previous version, the very popular Duemilanove (Italian for 2009), is the board you will most likely see being used in the vast majority of Arduino projects across the Internet. You can also get Mini, Nano, and Bluetooth variations of the Arduino. Another new addition to the product line is the Arduino Mega 2560; it offers increased memory and number of I/O pins. The new boards use a new bootloader called Optiboot, which frees up another 1.5k of flash memory and enables faster boot up.

Probably the most versatile Arduino, and hence the reason it is the most popular, is the Uno, or its predecessor, the Duemilanove. This is because it uses a standard 28-pin chip attached to an IC (Integrated Circuit) socket. The beauty of this system is that if you make something with an Arduino and then want to turn it into something permanent, instead of using a relatively expensive Arduino board, you can simply pop the chip out of the board and place it into your own circuit board in your custom device. By doing so, you have made a custom embedded device, which is really cool.

Then, for a couple of quid or bucks, you can replace the AVR chip in your Arduino with a new one. Note that the chip must be pre-programmed with the Arduino Bootloader (software programmed onto the chip to enable it to be used with the Arduino IDE), but you can either purchase an AVR Programmer to burn the bootloader yourself or you can buy a chip ready programmed; most of the Arduino parts suppliers provide these. It is also possible to program a chip using a second Arduino; instructions are available online for this.

Figure 1-3. *Anthros art installation by Richard V. Gilbank controlled using an Arduino*

If you do a search on the Internet for "Arduino," you will be amazed at the large number of websites dedicated to the Arduino or that feature cool project created with an Arduino. The Arduino is an amazing device and will enable you to create anything from interactive works of art (see Figure 1-3) to robots. With a little enthusiasm for learning how to program an Arduino and make it interact with other components as well as a bit of imagination, you can build anything you can think of.

This book will give you the necessary skills needed to make a start in this exciting and creative hobby. Now that you know what an Arduino is, let's get one hooked up to your computer and start using it.

Getting Started

This section will explain how to set up your Arduino and the IDE for the first time. The instructions for Windows and Macs (running OSX 10.3.9 or later) are given. If you use Linux, refer to the Getting Started instructions on the Arduino website at www.arduino.cc.playground/Learning/Linux. I will also presume you are using an Arduino Uno. If you have a different type of board, such as the Duemilanove (see Figure 1-4), then refer to the corresponding page in the Getting Started guide of the Arduino website.

You will also need a USB cable (A to B plug type) which is the same kind of cable used for most modern USB printers. If you have an Arduino Nano, you will need a USB A to Mini-B cable instead. Do not plug in the Arduino just yet, wait until I tell you to do so.

Figure 1-4. *An Arduino Duemilanove (image courtesy of Snorpey)*

Next, download the Arduino IDE. This is the software you will use to write your programs (or sketches) and upload them to your board. For the latest IDE go to the Arduino download page at http://arduino.cc/en/Main/Software and obtain appropriate the version for your OS.

Windows XP Installation

Once you have downloaded the latest IDE, unzip the file and double-click the unzipped folder to open it. You will see the Arduino files and sub-folders inside. Next plug in your Arduino using the USB cable and ensure that the green power LED (labeled PWR) turns on. Windows will say "Found new hardware: Arduino Uno" and the Found New Hardware Wizard will appear. Click next and Windows will attempt to load the drivers. This process will fail. This is nothing to worry about; it's normal.

Next, right-click on the My Computer icon on your desktop and choose Manage. The Computer Management window will open up. Now go down to Event Manager in the System Tools list and click it. In the right hand window, you'll see a list of your devices. The Arduino Uno will appear on the list with a yellow exclamation mark icon over it to show that the device has not been installed properly. Right click on this and choose Update Driver. Choose "No, not this time" from the first page and click next. Then choose "Install from a list or specific location (Advanced)" and click next again. Now click the "Include this location in the search" and click Browse. Navigate to the Drivers folder of the unzipped Arduino IDE and click Next. Windows will install the driver and you can then click the Finish button.

The Arduino Uno will now appear under Ports in the device list and will show you the port number assigned to it (e.g. COM6). To open the IDE double-click the Arduino icon in its folder.

Windows 7 & Vista Installation

Once you have downloaded the latest IDE, unzip the file and double-click the unzipped folder to open it. You will see the Arduino files and sub-folders inside. Next, plug in your Arduino using the USB cable and ensure that the green power LED (labeled PWR) turns on. Windows will attempt to automatically install the drivers for the Arduino Uno and it will fail. This is normal, so don't worry.

Click the Windows Start button and then click Control Panel. Now click System and Security, then click System, and then click Device Manager from the list on the left hand side. The Arduino will appear in the list as a device with a yellow exclamation mark icon over it to show that it has not been installed properly. Right click on the Arduino Uno and choose "Update Driver Software."

Next, choose "Browse my computer for driver software" and on the next window click the Browse button. Navigate to the Drivers folder of the Arduino folder you unzipped earlier and then click OK and then Next. Windows will attempt to install the driver. A Windows Security box will open up and will state that "Windows can't verify the publisher of this driver software." Click "Install this driver software anyway." The Installing Driver Software window will now do its business. If all goes well, you will have another window saying "Windows has successfully updated your driver software. Finally click Close. To open the IDE double-click the Arduino icon in its folder.

Mac OSX Installation

Download the latest disk image (.dmg) file for the IDE. Open the .dmg file; it will appear like Figure 1-5.

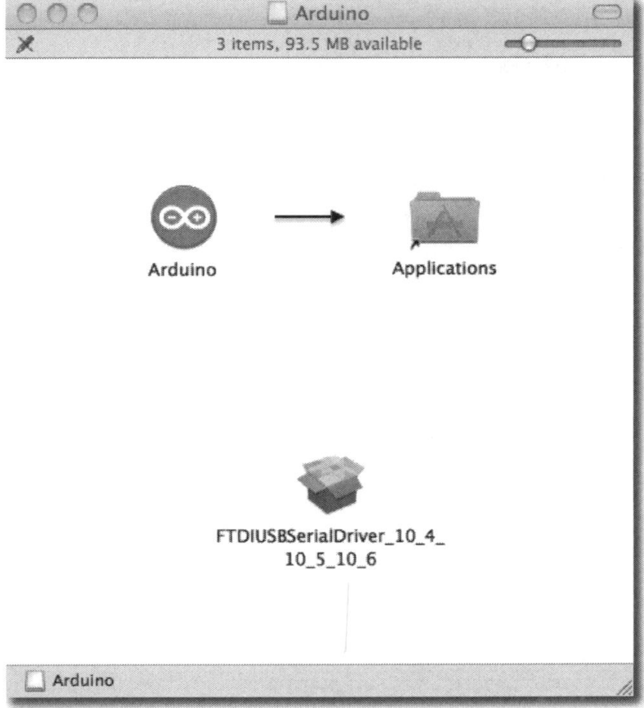

***Figure 1-5.** The Arduino .dmg file open in OSX*

Drag the Arduino icon over to the Applications folder and drop it in there. If are using an older Arduino, such as a Duemilanove, you will need to install the FTDI USB Serial Driver. Double-click the package icon and follow the instructions to do this. For the Uno and Mega 2560, there is no need to install any drivers.

To open the IDE, go into the Applications folder and click the Arduino icon.

Board and Port Selection

Once you open up the IDE, it will look similar to Figure 1-6.

Figure 1-6. The Arduino IDE when first opened

Now go to the menu and click Tools. Then click Board (See Figure 1-7).

Figure 1-7. The Arduino Tools menu

You will now be presented with a list of boards (See Figure 1-8). If you have an Uno, choose that. If you have a Duemilanove or another Arduino variant, choose the appropriate one from the list.

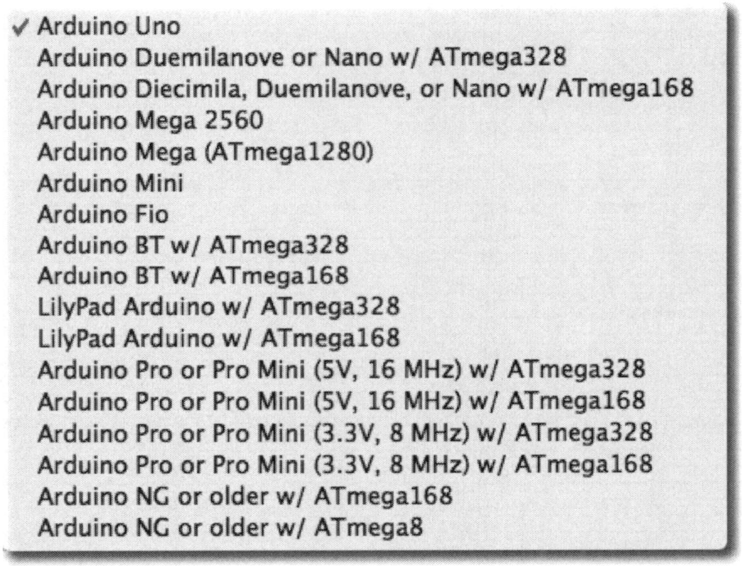

✓ Arduino Uno
Arduino Duemilanove or Nano w/ ATmega328
Arduino Diecimila, Duemilanove, or Nano w/ ATmega168
Arduino Mega 2560
Arduino Mega (ATmega1280)
Arduino Mini
Arduino Fio
Arduino BT w/ ATmega328
Arduino BT w/ ATmega168
LilyPad Arduino w/ ATmega328
LilyPad Arduino w/ ATmega168
Arduino Pro or Pro Mini (5V, 16 MHz) w/ ATmega328
Arduino Pro or Pro Mini (5V, 16 MHz) w/ ATmega168
Arduino Pro or Pro Mini (3.3V, 8 MHz) w/ ATmega328
Arduino Pro or Pro Mini (3.3V, 8 MHz) w/ ATmega168
Arduino NG or older w/ ATmega168
Arduino NG or older w/ ATmega8

Figure 1-8. *The Arduino Boards menu*

Next, click the Tools menu again, click Serial Port, and then choose the appropriate port from the list for your Arduino (Figure 1-9). You are now ready to upload an example sketch to test that the installation has worked.

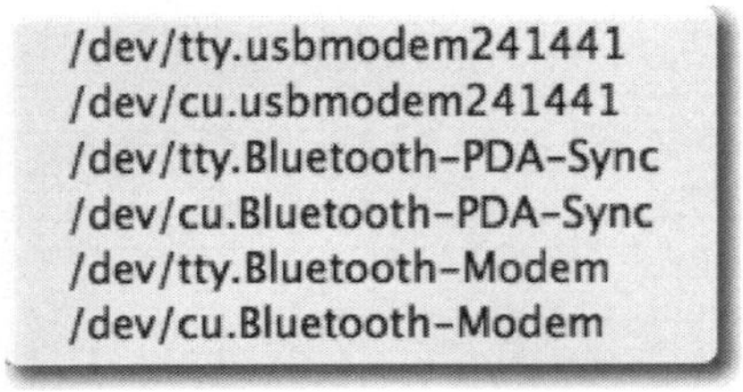

/dev/tty.usbmodem241441
/dev/cu.usbmodem241441
/dev/tty.Bluetooth-PDA-Sync
/dev/cu.Bluetooth-PDA-Sync
/dev/tty.Bluetooth-Modem
/dev/cu.Bluetooth-Modem

Figure 1-9. *The Serial Port list*

Upload Your First Sketch

Now that you have installed the drivers and the IDE and you have the correct board and ports selected, it's time to upload an example sketch to the Arduino to test that everything is working properly before moving on to the first project.

First, click the File menu (Figure 1-10) and then click Examples.

New ⌘N
Open... ⌘O
Sketchbook ▶
Examples ▶
Close ⌘W
Save ⌘S
Save As... ⇧⌘S
Upload to I/O Board ⌘U
Page Setup ⇧⌘P
Print ⌘P

Figure 1-10. The File menu

You will be presented with a huge list of examples to try out. Let's try a simple one. Click on Basics, and then Blink (Figure 1-11). The Blink sketch will be loaded into the IDE.

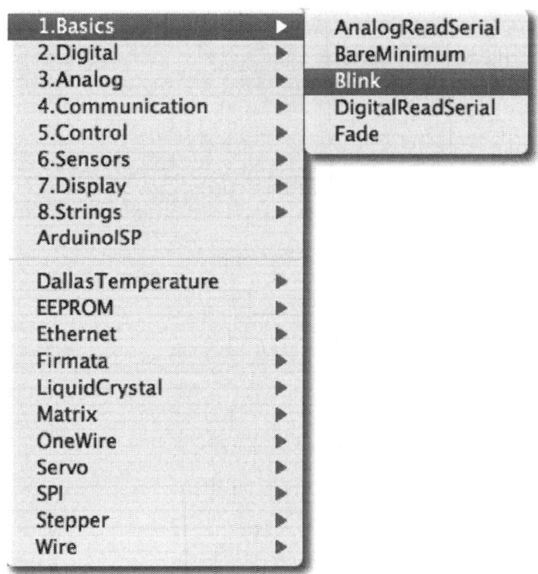

Figure 1-11. The Examples menu

Next, click the Upload button (sixth button from the left) and look at your Arduino. (If you have an Arduino Mini, NG, or other board, you may need to press the reset button on the board prior to pressing the Upload button.) The RX and TX lights should start to flash to show that data is being transmitted from your computer to the board. Once the sketch has successfully uploaded, the words "Done uploading" will appear in the IDE status bar and the RX and TX lights will stop flashing.

Figure 1-12. LED 13 blinking

After a few seconds, you should see the Pin 13 LED (the tiny LED next to the RX and TX LEDs) start to flash on and off at one second intervals. If it does, you have just successfully connected your Arduino, installed the drivers and software, and uploaded an example sketch. The Blink sketch is a very simple sketch that blinks LED 13 shown in Figure 1-12, the tiny green (or orange) LED soldered to the board (and also connected to Digital Pin 13 from the microcontroller).

Before you move onto Project 1, let's take a look at the Arduino IDE. I'll explain each part of the program.

The Arduino IDE

When you open up the Arduino IDE, it will look very similar to the image in Figure 1-13. If you are using Windows or Linux, there may be some slight differences but the IDE is pretty much the same no matter what OS you use.

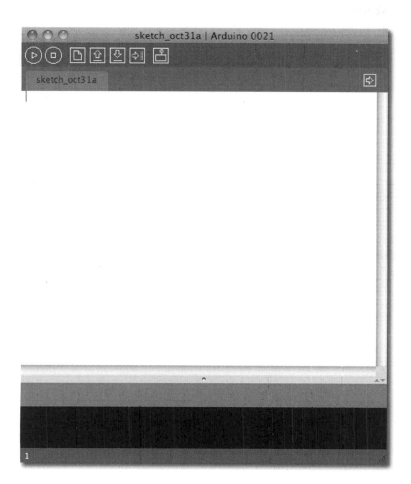

Figure 1-13. *What the IDE looks like when the application opens*

The IDE is split into three parts: the Toolbar across the top, the code or Sketch Window in the center, and the messages window in the bottom. The Toolbar consists of seven buttons. Underneath the Toolbar is a tab, or set of tabs, with the filename of the sketch within the tab. There is also one button on the far right hand side.

Along the top is the file menu with drop down menus labeled File, Edit, Sketch, Tools and Help. The buttons in the Toolbar (see Figure 1-14) provide convenient access to the most commonly used functions within this file menu.

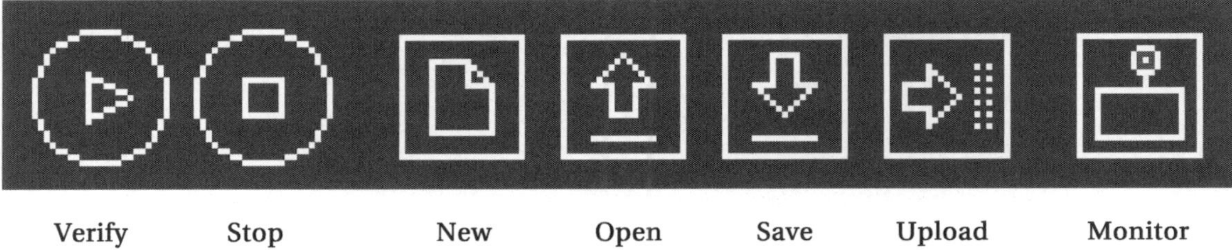

Figure 1-14. The Toolbar

The Toolbar buttons and their functions are listed in Table 1-1.

Table 1-1. The Toolbar button functions

Verify/Compile	Checks the code for errors
Stop	Stops the serial monitor, or un-highlights the other buttons
New	Creates a new blank sketch
Open	Shows a list of sketches in your Sketchbook to open
Save	Saves the current Sketch to your Sketchbook
Upload	Uploads the current Sketch to the Arduino
Serial Monitor	Displays serial data being sent from the Arduino

The Verify/Compile button is used to check that your code is correct and error free before you upload it to your Arduino board.

The Stop button stops the serial monitor from operating. It also un-highlights other selected buttons. While the serial monitor is operating, you can press the Stop button to obtain a snapshot of the serial data so far to examine it. This is particularly useful if you are sending data out to the Serial Monitor quicker than you can read it.

The New button creates a new and blank sketch ready for you to enter your code into. The IDE asks you to enter a name and a location for your sketch (try to use the default location if possible) and then gives you a blank Sketch ready to be coded. The tab at the top of the sketch shows the name you have given to your new sketch.

The Open button presents you with a list of sketches stored within your sketchbook as well as a list of example sketches that you can try out with various peripherals. The example sketches are invaluable for beginners to use as a foundation for their own sketches. Open the appropriate sketch for the device you are connecting and then modify the code for your own needs.

The Save button saves the code within the sketch window to your sketch file. Once complete, you will get a "Done Saving" message at the bottom of your code window.

The Upload to I/O Board button uploads the code within the current sketch window to your Arduino. Make sure that you have the correct board and port selected (in the Tools menu) before uploading. It is essential that you save your sketch before you upload it to your board in case a strange error causes your system to hang or the IDE to crash. It is also advisable to hit the Verify/Compile button before you upload to ensure there are no errors that need to be debugged first.

The serial monitor is a very useful tool, especially for debugging your code. The monitor displays serial data being sent out from your Arduino (USB or serial board). You can also send serial data back to the Arduino using the serial monitor. Clicking the Serial Monitor button results in a window like the one in Figure 1-15.

On the bottom right side, you can select the Baud Rate that the serial data is to be sent to/from the Arduino. The Baud Rate is the rate per second that state changes or bits (data) are sent to/from the board. The default setting is 9600 baud, which means that if you were to send a text novel over the serial communications line (in this case, your USB cable) then 1200 letters or symbols of the novel would be sent per second (9600 bits/8 bits per character = 1200 bytes or characters). Note that bits and bytes will be explained later.

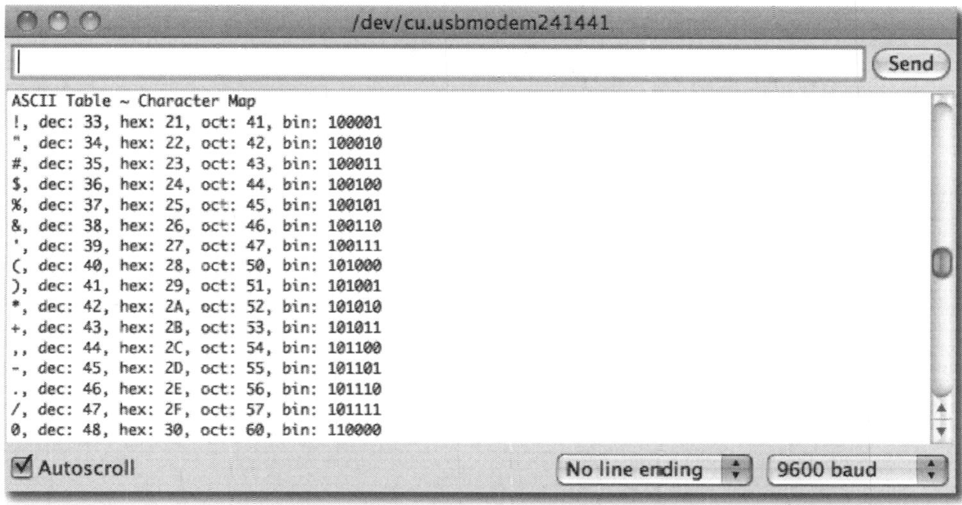

Figure 1-15. *The serial window in use*

At the top is a blank text box for you to enter text to send back to the Arduino and a Send button to make it happen. Note that the serial monitor can receive no serial data unless you have set up the code inside your sketch for it to do so. Similarly, the Arduino will not receive any data sent unless you have coded it to do so.

Finally, the black area is where your serial data will be displayed. In the image above, the Arduino is running the `ASCIITable` sketch (from the Communications example). This program outputs ASCII characters from the Arduino via serial (the USB cable) to the PC where the serial monitor then displays them.

To start the serial monitor, press the Serial Monitor button. To stop it, press the Stop button. On a Mac or in Linux, the Arduino board will reset itself (rerun the code from the beginning) when you click the Serial Monitor button.

Once you are proficient at communicating via serial to and from the Arduino, you can use other programs such as Processing, Flash, MaxMSP, etc. to communicate between the Arduino and your PC. You will make use of the serial monitor later when you read data from sensors and get the Arduino to send that data to the serial monitor in human readable form.

At the bottom of the IDE window is where you will see error messages (in red text) that the IDE will display when trying to connect to your board, upload code, or verify code. At the bottom left of the IDE you will see a number. This is the current location of the cursor within the program. If you have code in your window and you move down the lines of code (using the ↓ key on your keyboard), you will see the number increase as you move down the lines of code. This is useful for finding bugs highlighted by error messages.

Across the top of the IDE window (or across the top of your screen if you are using a Mac) you will see the various menus that you can click on to access more menu items (see Figure 1-16).

Arduino File Edit Sketch Tools Help

Figure 1-16. The IDE menus

The first menu is the Arduino menu (see Figure 1-17). The About Arduino option shows the current version number, a list of the people involved in making this amazing device, and some further information.

Figure 1-17. The Arduino menu

Underneath that is the Preferences option. This brings up the preferences window where you can change various IDE options, such as your default Sketchbook location, etc. The Quit option quits the program.

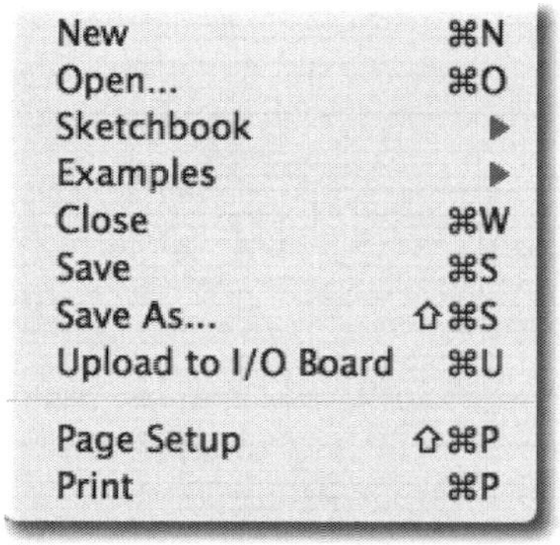

New	⌘N
Open...	⌘O
Sketchbook	▶
Examples	▶
Close	⌘W
Save	⌘S
Save As...	⇧⌘S
Upload to I/O Board	⌘U
Page Setup	⇧⌘P
Print	⌘P

Figure 1-18. *The File menu*

The File menu (see Figure 1-18) is where can access options to create a new sketch, take a look at sketches stored in your Sketchbook (as well as the example sketches), save your sketch or use the Save As option if you want to give it a different name, upload your sketch to the I/O Board (Arduino), or print out your code.

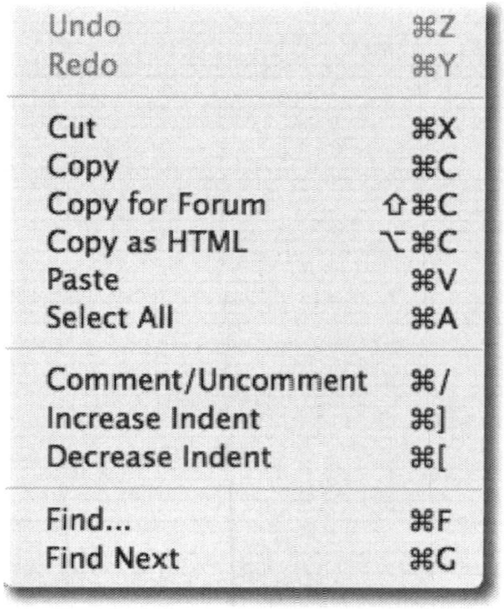

Undo	⌘Z
Redo	⌘Y
Cut	⌘X
Copy	⌘C
Copy for Forum	⇧⌘C
Copy as HTML	⌥⌘C
Paste	⌘V
Select All	⌘A
Comment/Uncomment	⌘/
Increase Indent	⌘]
Decrease Indent	⌘[
Find...	⌘F
Find Next	⌘G

Figure 1-19. *The Edit menu*

The Edit menu (see Figure 1-19) offers options to let you to cut, copy, and paste sections of code. You can also Select All of your code or Find certain words or phrases within the code. The useful Undo and Redo options come in handy when you make a mistake.

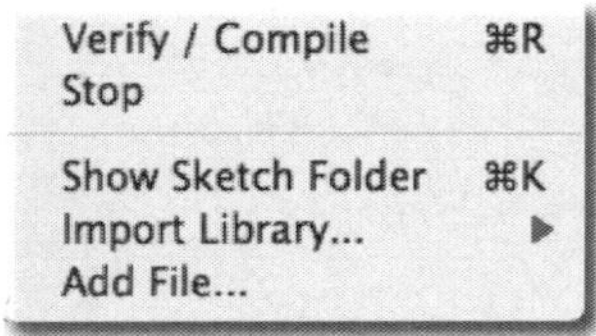

Figure 1-20. The Sketch menu

The Sketch menu (see Figure 1-20) contains the Verify/Compile functions and other useful functions including the Import Library option, which brings up a list of the available libraries stored within your libraries folder.

A *library* is a collection of code that you can include in your sketch to enhance the functionality of your project. It is a way of preventing you from re-inventing the wheel; instead, you can reuse code already written by someone else for various pieces of common hardware. For example, the Stepper library is a set of functions to control a stepper motor. Somebody else has kindly already created all of the functions necessary to control a stepper motor, so by including the Stepper library into your sketch, you can use those functions to control the motor. By storing commonly used code in a library, you can re-use that code over and over in different projects. You can also hide the complicated parts of the code from the user. I will go into greater detail concerning the use of libraries later on.

The Show Sketch Folder option opens the folder where your sketch is stored. The Add File option lets you to add another source file to your sketch, which allows you to split larger sketches into smaller files and then add them to the main sketch.

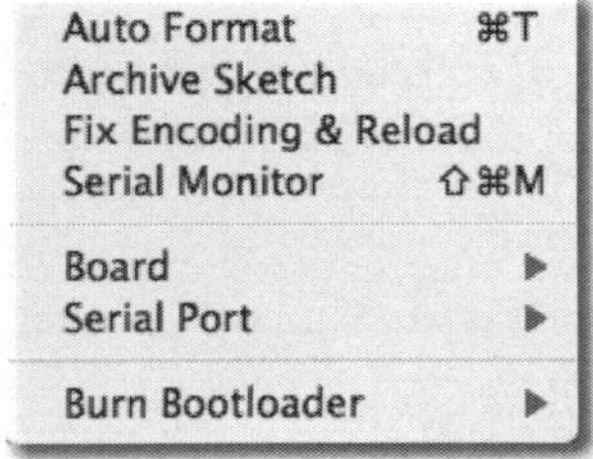

Figure 1-21. Tools menu

The Tools menu (see Figure 1-21) offers several options. You can select the Board and Serial Port, as you did when setting up the Arduino for the first time. The Auto Format function formats your code to make it look nicer. The Copy for Forum option copies the code within the sketch window, but in a format that, when pasted into the Arduino forum (or most other Forums for that matter), will show up the same as it is in the IDE, along with syntax coloring, etc. The Archive Sketch option lets you to compress your sketch into a ZIP file and will ask you where you want to store it. Finally, the Burn Bootloader option burns the Arduino Bootloader (the piece of code on the chip to make it compatible with the Arduino IDE) to the chip. This option can only be used if you have an AVR programmer and if you have replaced the chip in your Arduino or have bought blank chips to use in your own embedded project. Unless you plan on burning many chips, it's usually cheaper and easier to just buy an ATmega chip (see Figure 1-22) with the Arduino Bootloader already pre-programmed. Many online stores stock inexpensive pre-programmed chips.

Figure 1-22. *An Atmel ATmega chip, the heart of your Arduino. (image courtesy of Earthshine Electronics)*

The final menu, Help, is where you can find more information about the IDE or links to the reference pages of the Arduino website and other useful pages.

The Arduino IDE is pretty basic and you will learn how to use it quickly and easily as you work through the projects. As you become more proficient at using an Arduino and programming in C (the programming language used to code on the Arduino), you may find the Arduino IDE is too basic. If you want something with better functionality, you can try one of the professional IDE programs (some of which are free) such as Eclipse, ArduIDE, GNU/Emacs, AVR-GCC, AVR Studio, and even Apple's XCode.

Now that you have your Arduino software installed, the board connected and working, and you have a basic understanding of how to use the IDE, let's jump right in with Project 1 – LED Flasher.

CHAPTER 2

Light 'Em Up

You are now going to work your way through the first four projects. These projects all use LED lights in various ways. You will learn about controlling outputs from the Arduino as well as simple inputs such as button presses. On the hardware side, you will learn about LEDs, buttons, and resistors, including pull up and pull down resistors, which are important in ensuring that input devices are read correctly. Along the way, you will pick up the concepts of programming in the Arduino language. Let's start with a "Hello World" project that makes your Arduino flash an external LED.

Project 1 – LED Flasher

For the first project, you are going to repeat the LED blink sketch that you used during your testing stage. This time, however, you are going to connect an LED to one of the digital pins rather than using LED13, which is soldered to the board. You will also learn exactly how the hardware and the software for this project works, learning a bit about electronics and coding in the Arduino language (which is a variant of C) at the same time.

Parts Required

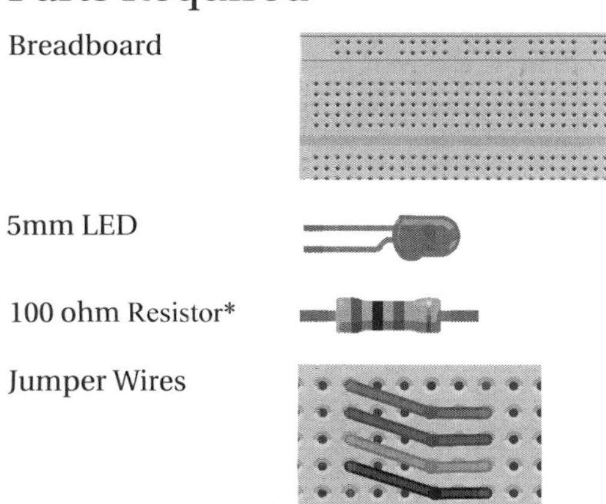

**This value may differ depending on what LED you use. The text will explain how to work it out.*

The best kind of breadboard for the majority of the projects in this book is an 840 tie-point breadboard. These are fairly standard sized breadboards, measuring approximately 16.5cm by 5.5cm and featuring 840 holes (or tie points) on the board. Usually, the boards have little dovetails on the side allowing you to connect several of them together to make larger breadboards; this is useful for more complex projects. For this project though, any sized breadboard will do.

The LED should be a 5mm one of any color. You will need to know the current and voltage (sometimes called forward current and forward voltage) of the LED so that you can calculate the resistor value needed—you will work out this value later in the project.

The jumper wires you use can either be commercially available jumper wires (usually with molded ends to make insertion into the breadboard easier) or you can make your own by cutting short strips of stiff single core wire and stripping away about 6mm from the end.

Connecting Everything

First, make sure your Arduino is powered off by unplugging it from the USB cable. Now, take your breadboard, LED, resistor, and wires and connect everything as shown in Figure 2-1.

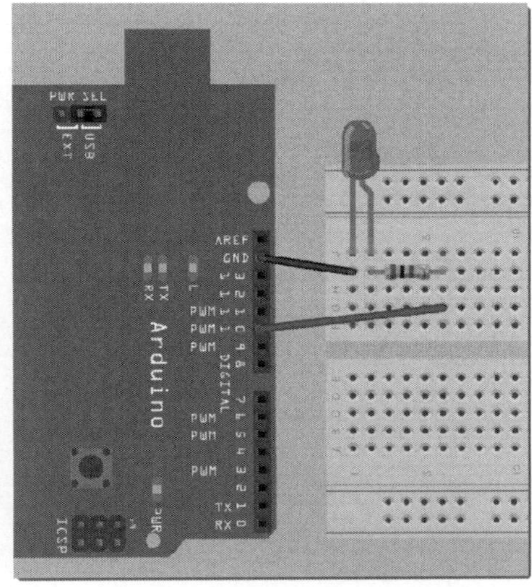

Figure 2-1. *The circuit for Project 1 – LED Flasher*

It doesn't matter if you use different colored wires or use different holes on the breadboard as long as the components and wires are connected in the same order as in the picture. Be careful when inserting components into the breadboard. If your breadboard is brand new, the grips in the holes will be stiff. Failure to insert components carefully could result in damage.

Make sure that your LED is connected correctly with the longer leg connected to Digital Pin 10. The long leg is the anode of the LED and must always go to the +5v supply (in this case, coming out of Digital Pin 10); the short leg is the cathode and must go to Gnd (ground).

When you are sure that everything is connected correctly, power up your Arduino and connect the USB cable.

Enter the Code

Open up your Arduino IDE and type in the code from Listing 2-1.

Listing 2-1. Code for Project 1

```
// Project 1 - LED Flasher
int ledPin = 10;
void setup() {
         pinMode(ledPin, OUTPUT);
}
void loop() {
        digitalWrite(ledPin, HIGH);
        delay(1000);
        digitalWrite(ledPin, LOW);
        delay(1000);
}
```

Press the Verify/Compile button at the top of the IDE to make sure there are no errors in your code. If this is successful, click the Upload button to upload the code to your Arduino. If you have done everything right, you should now see the red LED on the breadboard flashing on and off every second.

Let's take a look at the code and the hardware to find out how they both work.

Project 1 – LED Flasher – Code Overview

The first line of code for this project is:

```
// Project 1 - LED Flasher
```

This is just a *comment* in your code. You can tell it's a comment because it starts with // and any text that begins this way will be ignored by the compiler. Comments are essential in your code; they help you understand how your code works. As your projects get more complex and your code expands into hundreds or maybe thousands of lines, comments will be vital in making it easy for you to see how each section functions. You may come up with an amazing piece of code, but you can't count on remembering how it works when you revisit it several days, weeks, or months later. Comments, however, will remind you of its functionality. Also, if your code is meant to be seen by other people, comments will help that person understand what is going on in your code. The whole ethos of the Arduino, and indeed the whole Open Source community, is to share code and schematics. I hope that when you start making your own cool stuff with the Arduino you will be willing to share it with the world, too.

There is another format for making comments; it is a block statement bookended by /* and */ , like so:

```
/* All of the text within
the slash and the asterisks
is a comment and will be
ignored by the compiler */
```

The IDE will automatically turn the color of any commented text to grey. The next line of the program is

```
int ledPin = 10;
```

and this is what is known as a *variable*. A variable is a place to store data. In this case, you are setting up a variable of type int or integer. An *integer* is a number within the range of -32,768 to 32,767. Next, you have assigned that integer the name of ledPin and have given it a value of 10. (You didn't have to call it ledPin, you could have called it anything you wanted to. But you want your variable name to be descriptive, so you call it ledPin to show that this variable sets which pin on the Arduino you are going to use to connect your LED.) In this case, you are using Digital Pin 10. At the end of this statement is a semi-colon. This symbol tells the compiler that this statement is now complete.

Although you can call your variables anything, every variable name in C must start with a letter; the rest of the name can consist of letters, numbers, and underscore characters. Note that C recognizes upper and lower case characters as being different. Finally, you cannot use any of C's keywords like main, while, switch etc as variable names. Keywords are constants, variables, and function names that are defined as part of the Arduino language. To help you avoid naming a variable after a keyword, all keywords within the sketch will appear in red.

Imagine a variable as a small box where you can keep things. So in this sketch, you have set up an area in memory to store a number of type integer and have stored in that area the number 10.

Finally, a variable is called a variable because you can change it. Later, you will carry out mathematical calculations on variables to make your program do more advanced things.

Next is your `setup()` function:

```
void setup() {
        pinMode(ledPin, OUTPUT);
}
```

An Arduino sketch must have a `setup()` and `loop()` function, otherwise it will not work. The `setup()` function runs once and once only at the start of the program and is where you will issue general instructions to prepare the program before the main loop runs, such as setting up pin modes, setting serial baud rates, etc. Basically, a function is a bunch of code assembled into one convenient block. For example, if you created your own function to carry out a series of complicated mathematics that had many lines of code, you could run that code as many times as you liked simply by calling the function name instead of writing out the code again each time. You will go into functions in more detail later when you start to create your own. In the case of this program, however, the `setup()` function only has one statement to carry out. The function starts with

```
void setup()
```

This tells the compiler that your function is called setup, that it returns no data (void), and that you pass no parameters to it (empty parenthesis). If your function returned an integer value and you also had integer values to pass to it (e.g. for the function to process), it would look something like this:

```
int myFunc(int x, int y)
```

Here you have created a function (or a block of code) called myFunc. This function has been passed two integers called x and y. Once the function has finished, it will then return an integer value to the point after where your function was called in the program (hence `int` before the function name).

All of the code within the function is contained within the curly braces. A { symbol starts the block of code and a } symbol ends the block. Anything in between those two symbols is code that belongs to the function. (I will go into greater detail about functions later, so don't worry about them for now.)

In this program, you have two functions; the first function is called setup and its purpose is to setup anything necessary for your program to work before the main program loop runs:

```
void setup() {
        pinMode(ledPin, OUTPUT);
}
```

Your setup function only has one statement and that is pinMode, which telling the Arduino that you want to set the mode of one of your pins to be Output mode, rather than Input. Within the parenthesis, you put the pin number and the mode (OUTPUT or INPUT). Your pin number is ledPin, which has been previously set to the value 10. Therefore, this statement is simply telling the Arduino that Digital Pin 10 is to be set to OUTPUT mode. As the `setup()` function runs only once, you now move onto the main function loop:

```
void loop() {
        digitalWrite(ledPin, HIGH);
        delay(1000);
        digitalWrite(ledPin, LOW);
        delay(1000);
}
```

The `loop()` function is the main program function and runs continuously as long as the Arduino is turned on. Every statement within the `loop()` function (within the curly braces) is carried out, one by one, step by step, until the bottom of the function is reached, then the loop starts again at the top of the function, and so on forever or until you turn the Arduino off or press the Reset switch.

In this project, you want the LED to turn on, stay on for one second, turn off and remain off for one second, and then repeat. The commands to tell the Arduino to do this are contained within the `loop()` function because you wish them to repeat over and over. The first statement is

```
digitalWrite(ledPin, HIGH);
```

and this writes a HIGH or a LOW value to the pin within the statement (in this case ledPin, which is Digital Pin 10). When you set a pin to HIGH, you are sending out 5 volts to that pin. When you set it to LOW, the pin becomes 0 volts, or ground. This statement, therefore, sends out 5v to pin 10 and turns the LED on. After that is

```
delay(1000);
```

and this statement simply tells the Arduino to wait for 1000 milliseconds (there are 1000 milliseconds in a second) before carrying out the next statement of

```
digitalWrite(ledPin, LOW);
```

which will turn off the power going to Digital Pin 10 and therefore turn the LED off. Then there is another delay statement for another 1000 milliseconds and then the function ends. However, as this is your main `loop()` function, the function will start again at the beginning.

By following the program structure step by step again, you can see that it is very simple:

```
// Project 1 - LED Flasher
int ledPin = 10;
void setup() {
        pinMode(ledPin, OUTPUT);
}
void loop() {
        digitalWrite(ledPin, HIGH);
        delay(1000);
        digitalWrite(ledPin, LOW);
        delay(1000);
}
```

You start off by assigning a variable called ledPin, giving that variable a value of 10. Then you move on to the `setup()` function where you set the mode for Digital Pin 10 as an output. In the main program loop, you set Digital Pin 10 to high, sending out 5v. Then you wait for a second and then turn off the 5v to Digital Pin 10, before waiting another second. The loop then starts again at the beginning: the LED will turn on and off continuously for as long as the Arduino has power.

Now that you know this, you can modify the code to turn the LED on for a different period of time and turn it off for a different time period. For example, if you wanted the LED to stay on for 2 seconds, then go off for half a second, you could do the following:

```
void loop() {
        digitalWrite(ledPin, HIGH);
        delay(2000);
        digitalWrite(ledPin, LOW);
        delay(500);
}
```

If you would like the LED to stay off for 5 seconds and then flash briefly (250ms), like the LED indicator on a car alarm, you could do this:

```
void loop() {
        digitalWrite(ledPin, HIGH);
        delay(250);
        digitalWrite(ledPin, LOW);
        delay(5000);
}
```

To make the LED flash on and off very fast, try this:

```
void loop() {
        digitalWrite(ledPin, HIGH);
        delay(50);
        digitalWrite(ledPin, LOW);
        delay(50);
}
```

By varying the on and off times of the LED you create any effect you want (well, within the bounds of a single LED going on and off). Before you move onto something a little more exciting, let's take a look at the hardware and see how it works.

Project 1 – LED Flasher – Hardware Overview

The hardware used in Project 1:

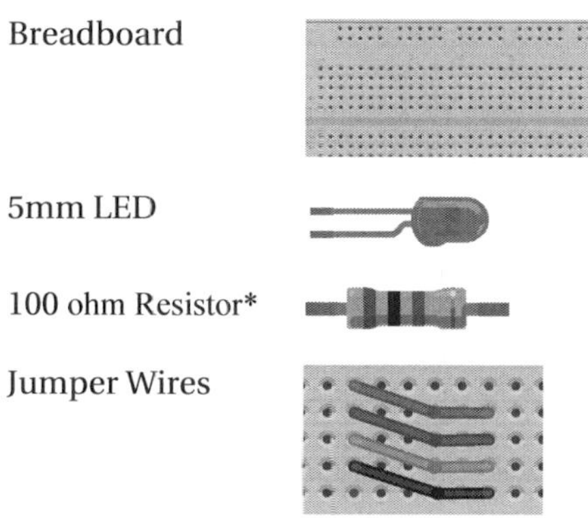

** or whatever value appropriate for your LED*

The breadboard is a reusable solderless device used to prototype an electronic circuit or for experimenting with circuit designs. The board consists of a series of holes in a grid; underneath the board these holes are connected by a strip of conductive metal. The way those strips are laid out is typically something like that in Figure 2-2.

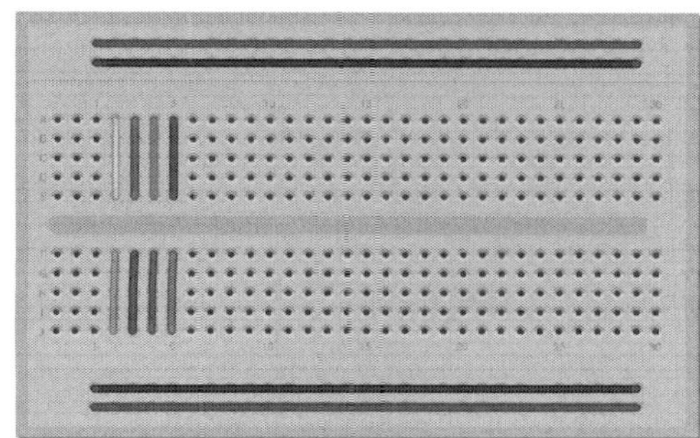

Figure 2-2. *How the metal strips in a breadboard are laid out*

The strips along the top and bottom run parallel to the board and are design to carry your power rail and your ground rail. The components in the middle of the board conveniently connect to either 5v (or whatever voltage you are using) and ground. Some breadboards have a red and a black line running parallel to these holes to show which is power (Red) and which is ground (Black). On larger breadboards, the power rail sometimes has a split, indicated by a break in the red line. This makes it possible to send different voltages to different parts of your board. If you are using just one voltage, a short piece of jumper wire can be placed across this gap to make sure that the same voltage is applied along the whole length of the rail.

The strips in the centre run at 90 degrees to the power and ground rails in short lengths and there is a gap in the middle to allow you to put Integrated Circuits across the gap so that each pin of the chip goes to a different set of holes and therefore a different rail (see Figure 2-3).

***Figure 2-3.** An Integrated Circuit (or chip) plugged across the gap in a breadboard*

The next component is a resistor. A *resistor* is a device designed to cause resistance to an electric current in order to cause a drop in voltage across its terminals. You can think of a resistor as a water pipe that is a lot thinner than the pipe connected to it. As the water (the electric current) comes into the resistor, the pipe gets thinner and the water volume (current) coming out of the other end is therefore reduced. You use resistors to decrease voltage or current to other devices.

The value of resistance is known as an Ohm and its symbol is a Greek Omega symbol Ω. In this case, Digital Pin 10 is outputting 5v DC at (according to the Atmega datasheet) 40mA (milliamps), and your LEDs require (according to their datasheet) a voltage of 2v and a current of 35mA. Therefore, you need a resistor that will reduce the 5v to 2v and the current from 40mA to 35mA if you want to display the LED at its maximum brightness. If you want the LED to be dimmer, you could use a higher value of resistance.

■ **Note** NEVER use a value of resistor that is LOWER than needed. You will put too much current through the LED and damage it permanently. You could also damage other parts of your circuit.

The formula to work out what resistor you need is

$R = (V_S - V_L) / I$

where V_S is the supply voltage, V_L is the LED voltage, and I is the LED current. Your example LED has a voltage of 2v and a current of 35mA connected to a digital pin from an Arduino, which gives out 5 volts, so the resistor value needed would be

$R = (5 - 2) / 0.035$

which gives a value of 85.71.

Resistors come in standard values and the closest common value would be 100 Ω. Always choose the next standard value resistor that is HIGHER than the value needed. If you choose a lower value, too much current will flow through the resistor and will damage it.

So how do you find a 100Ω resistor? A resistor is too small to contain easily readable labeling so resistors instead use a color code. Around the resistor you will typically find 4 colored bands; by using the color code in Table 2-1 you can find out the value of a resistor. Likewise, you can find the color code for a particular resistance.

Table 2-1. *Resistor color codes*

Color	1st Band	2nd Band	3rd Band (multiplier)	4th Band (tolerance)
Black 0		0	$x10^{0}$	
Brown 1		1	$x10^{1}$	±1%
Red 2		2	$x10^{2}$	±2%
Orange 3		3	$x10^{3}$	
Yellow 4		4	$x10^{4}$	
Green 5		5	$x10^{5}$	±0.5%
Blue 6		6	$x10^{6}$	±0.25%
Violet 7		7	$x10^{7}$	±0.1%
Grey 8		8	$x10^{8}$	±0.05%
White 9		9	$x10^{9}$	
Gold			$x10^{-1}$	±5%
Silver			$x10^{-2}$	±10%
None				±20%

According to the table, for a 100Ω resistor you need 1 in the first band, which is brown, followed by a 0 in the next band, which is black. Then you need to multiply this by 10^{1} (in other words add 1 zero), which results in brown for the third band. The final band indicates the tolerance of the resistor. If your resistor has a gold band, it has a tolerance of ±5 percent; this means the actual value of the resistor varies between 95Ω and 105Ω. Therefore, if you have an LED that requires 2 volts and 35mA, you need a resistor with a Brown, Black, Brown band combination.

If you need a 10K (or 10 kilo-ohm) resistor, you need a Brown, Black, Orange combination (1, 0, +3 zeros). If you need a 570K resistor, the colors would be Green, Violet, and Yellow.

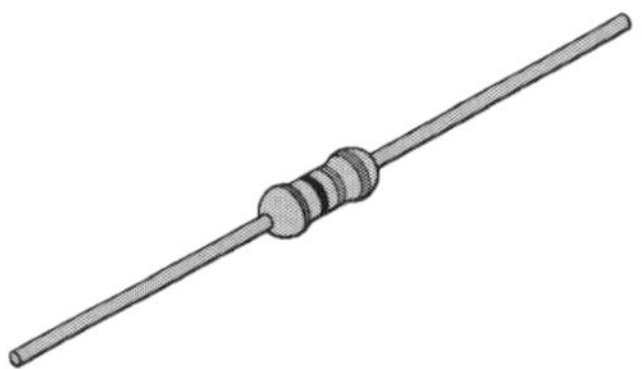

***Figure 2-4.** A 10KΩ resistor with a 5 percent tolerance*

In the same way, if you found a resistor and wanted to know its value, you would do the same in reverse. So if you found the resistor in Figure 2-4 and wanted to find its value so you could store it away in your nicely labeled resistor storage box, you could look at the table to see it has a value of 220Ω.

Now that you know how the color coding works, choose the correct resistance value for the LED you have purchased to complete this project.

The final component (other than the jumper wires, but I'm sure you can figure out what they do for yourself) is the LED, which stands for Light Emitting Diode. A diode is a device that permits current to flow in only one direction; it's just like a valve in a water system, but in this case it is letting electrical current to go in one direction. If the current tries to reverse and go back in the opposite direction, the diode stops it from doing so. Diodes can be useful to prevent someone from accidently connecting the power and ground to the wrong terminals in a circuit and damaging the components.

An LED is the same thing, but it also emits light. LEDs come in all kinds of different colors and levels of brightness, including the ultraviolet and infrared part of the spectrum (like in the LEDs in your TV remote control).

If you look carefully at an LED you will notice two things: the legs are of different lengths, and one side of the LED is flattened rather than cylindrical (see Figure 2-5). These are clues as to which leg is the Anode (positive) and which is the Cathode (negative): the longer leg (Anode) gets connected to the positive supply (3.3v) and the leg with the flattened side (Cathode) goes to ground.

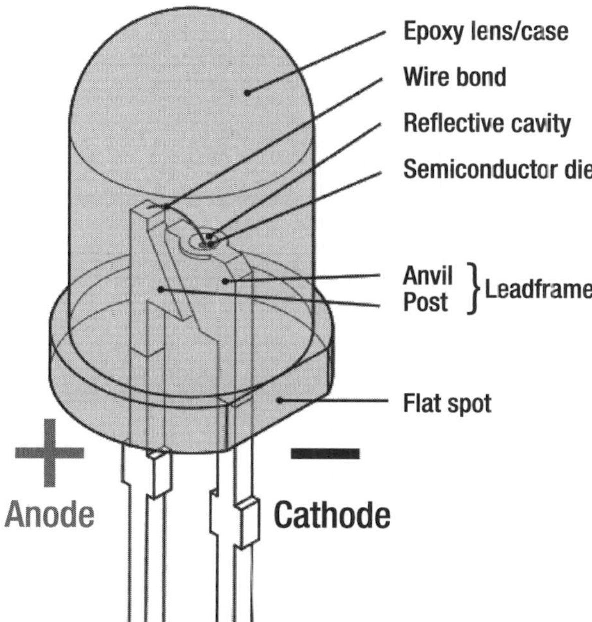

Figure 2-5. The parts of an LED (image courtesy of Inductiveload from Wikimedia Commons)

If you connect the LED the wrong way, it will not damage it (unless you put very high currents through it). However, it's essential that you always put a resistor in series with the LED to ensure that the correct current gets to the LED. You can permanently damage the LED if you fail to do this.

Note that you can also obtain bi-color and tri-color LEDs. These have several legs coming out of them. An RGB LED has a red, green, and blue (hence RGB) LED in one package. This LED has four legs; one will be a common anode or cathode (common to all three LEDs) and other legs will go to the anode or cathode of an individual LED. By adjusting the brightness values of the R, G and B channels of the RGB LED, you can get any color you want (the same effect can be obtained if you used three separate red, green and blue LEDs).

Now that you know how the components function and how the code in this project works, let's try something a bit more interesting.

Project 2 – S.O.S. Morse Code Signaler

For this project, you are going to reuse the circuit set up from Project 1 (so no need for a Hardware Overview), but you'll use different code to make the LED signal the letters S.O.S., which is the International Morse Code distress signal. Morse Code is a type of character encoding that transmits letters and numbers using patterns of on and off. It is therefore nicely suited to your digital system as you can turn an LED on and off in the necessary pattern to spell out a word or a series of characters. In this case, the S.O.S. pattern is three dits (short flash), followed by three dahs (long flash), followed by three dits again.

To flash the LED on and off in this pattern, signaling SOS, use the code in Listing 2-2.

Listing 2-2. Code for Project 2

```
// LED connected to pin 10
int ledPin = 10;

// run once, when the sketch starts
void setup()
{
        // sets the pin as output
        pinMode(ledPin, OUTPUT);
}

// run over and over again
void loop()
{
        // 3 dits
        for (int x=0; x<3; x++) {
                digitalWrite(ledPin, HIGH);   // sets the LED on
                delay(150);                  // waits for 150ms
                digitalWrite(ledPin, LOW);    // sets the LED off
                delay(100);                // waits for 100ms
        }

        // 100ms delay to cause slight gap betyouen letters
        delay(100);
        // 3 dahs
        for (int x=0; x<3; x++) {
                digitalWrite(ledPin, HIGH);   // sets the LED on
                delay(400);                  // waits for 400ms
                digitalWrite(ledPin, LOW);    // sets the LED off
                delay(100);                // waits for 100ms
        }

        // 100ms delay to cause slight gap betyouen letters
        delay(100);

  // 3 dits again
        for (int x=0; x<3; x++) {
                digitalWrite(ledPin, HIGH);   // sets the LED on
                delay(150);                  // waits for 150ms
                digitalWrite(ledPin, LOW);    // sets the LED off
                delay(100);                // waits for 100ms
        }

        // wait 5 seconds before repeating the SOS signal
        delay(5000);
}
```

Create a new sketch and then type in the code from Listing 2-2. Verify that your code is error free and then upload it to your Arduino. If all goes well, you will see the LED flash the Morse Code SOS signal, wait 5 seconds, then repeat.

If you were to rig up a battery operated Arduino to a very bright light and place the whole assembly into a waterproof and handheld box, it could be used to control an SOS emergency strobe light for used on boats, while mountain climbing, etc.

Let's figure out how this code works.

Project 2 – S.O.S. Morse Code Signaler – Code Overview

The first part of the code is identical to the last project where you initialize a variable and then set Digital Pin 10 to be an output. In the main code loop, you can see the same kind of statements to turn the LEDs on and off for a set period of time. This time, however, the statements are within three separate code blocks.

The first block is what outputs the three dits:

```
for (int x=0; x<3; x++) {
        digitalWrite(ledPin, HIGH);
        delay(150);
        digitalWrite(ledPin, LOW);
        delay(100);
  }
```

You can see that the LED is turned on for 150ms and then off for 100ms; you can also see that those statements are within a set of curly braces and are therefore in a separate code block. But, when you run the sketch you can see the light flashes three times, not just once.

This is done using the `for` loop:

```
for (int x=0; x<3; x++) {
```

This statement is what makes the code within the code block execute three times. There are three parameters you need to give to the `for` loop. These are initialization, condition, and increment. The **initialization** happens first and exactly once. Each time through the loop, the **condition** is tested; if it's true, the statement block and the **increment** is executed, then the **condition** is tested again. When the **condition** becomes false, the loop ends.

So, first you need to initialize a variable as the start number of the loop. In this case, you set up variable X and set it to zero:

```
int x=0;
```

You then set a condition to decide how many times the code in the loop will execute:

```
x<3;
```

In this case, the code will loop if x is smaller than (<) 3. The code within a `for` loop will always execute once no matter what the condition is set to.

The < symbol is what is known as a *comparison operator*. They are used to make decisions within your code and to compare two values. The symbols used are:

== (equal to)

!= (not equal to)

< (less than)

> (greater than)

<= (less than or equal to)

>= (greater than or equal to)

In your code, you are comparing x with the value of 3 to see if it is smaller than 3. If x is smaller than 3, the code in the block will repeat again.

The final statement

```
x++
```

is a statement to increase the value of x by 1. You could also have typed in x = x + 1, which would assign to x the value of x + 1. Note there is no need to put a semi-colon after this final statement in the `for` loop.

You can do simple mathematics by using the symbols +, -, * and / (addition, subtraction, multiplication and division). For example:

1 + 1 = 2

3 - 2 = 1

2 * 4 = 8

8 / 2 = 4

So, your `for` loop initializes the value of x to 0, then runs the code within the block (curly braces). It then increases the increment (in this case, adds 1 to x). Finally, it checks that the condition is met, which is that x is smaller than 3 and if so repeats.

Now that you know how the `for` loop works, you can see that there are three `for` loops in your code: one that loops three times and displays the dits, one that repeats three times and displays the dahs, and then there is a repeat of the dits again.

It must be noted that the variable x has a local *scope*, which means it can only be seen by the code within its own code block, unless you initialize it before the `setup()` function, in which case it has *global scope* and can be seen by the entire program. If you try to access x outside the `for` loop, you will get an error.

In between each `for` loop is a small delay to make a tiny visible pause between letters of SOS. Finally, the code waits for 5 seconds before the main program loop starts again from the beginning.

Now let's move onto using multiple LEDs.

Project 3 – Traffic Lights

You are now going to create a set of traffic lights that will change from green to red, via amber, and back again, after a set length of time using the four-state UK system. This project could be used to make a set of working traffic lights for a model railway or for a child's toy town. If you're not from the UK, you can modify the code and colors to make them work like the traffic lights in your own country. First, though, make the project as it is and change it once you know how it works.

Parts Required

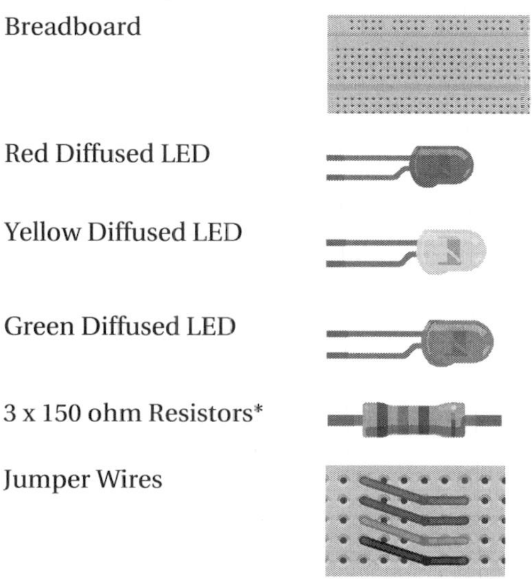

Breadboard

Red Diffused LED

Yellow Diffused LED

Green Diffused LED

3 x 150 ohm Resistors*

Jumper Wires

**or whatever value you require for your type of LED*

Connect It Up

Connect your circuit as shown in Figure 2-6. This time you connect three LEDs with the anode of each one going to Digital Pins 8, 9 and 10 via a 150Ω resistor (or whatever value you require) each.

Take a jumper wire from ground of the Arduino to the ground rail at the top of the breadboard; a ground wire goes from the Cathode leg of each LED to the common ground rail via a resistor—this time connected to the cathode. (For this simple circuit, it doesn't matter if the resistor is connected to the anode or cathode).

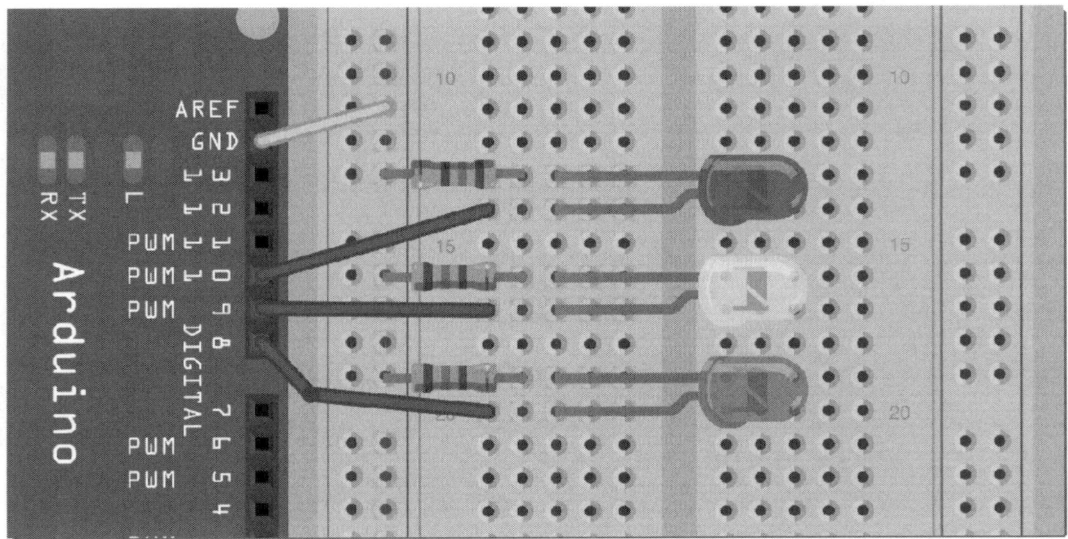

Figure 2-6. The circuit for Project 3 – Traffic Lights

Enter the Code

Enter the code from Listing 2-3, check it, and upload to your Arduino. The LEDs will now move through four states that simulate the UK traffic light system, as seen in Figure 2-7. If you have followed Projects 1 and 2, both the code and the hardware for Project 3 will be self-explanatory. I shall leave you to examine the code and figure out how it works.

Listing 2-3. Code for Project 3

```
// Project 3 - Traffic Lights

int ledDelay = 10000; // delay in between changes
int redPin = 10;
int yellowPin = 9;
int greenPin = 8;

void setup() {
        pinMode(redPin, OUTPUT);
        pinMode(yellowPin, OUTPUT);
        pinMode(greenPin, OUTPUT);
}
```

```
void loop() {

        digitalWrite(redPin, HIGH); // turn the red light on
        delay(ledDelay); // wait 5 seconds

        digitalWrite(yellowPin, HIGH); // turn on yellow
        delay(2000); // wait 2 seconds

        digitalWrite(greenPin, HIGH); // turn green on
        digitalWrite(redPin, LOW); // turn red off
        digitalWrite(yellowPin, LOW); // turn yellow off
        delay(ledDelay); // wait ledDelay milliseconds

        digitalWrite(yellowPin, HIGH); // turn yellow on
        digitalWrite(greenPin, LOW); // turn green off
        delay(2000); // wait 2 seconds

        digitalWrite(yellowPin, LOW); // turn yellow off
        // now our loop repeats

}
```

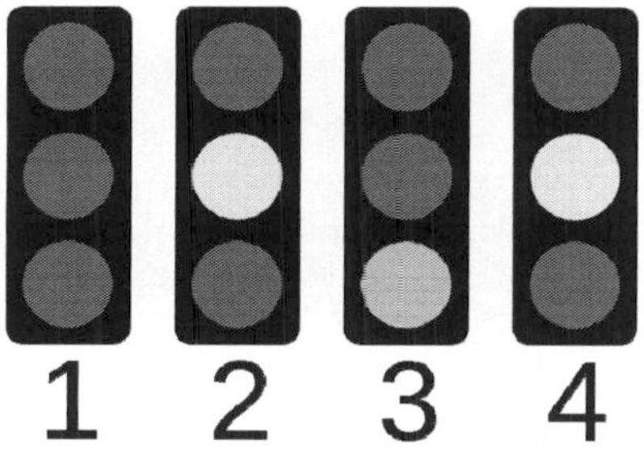

1 2 3 4

Figure 2-7. *The four states of the UK traffic light system (image by Alex43223 from WikiMedia)*

Project 4 – Interactive Traffic Lights

This time you are going to extend the previous project to include a set of pedestrian lights and a pedestrian push button to request to cross the road. The Arduino will react when the button is pressed by changing the state of the lights to make the cars stop and allow the pedestrian to cross safely.

This is the first time you are going to interact with the Arduino and cause it to do something when you change the state of a button that the Arduino is watching. In this project, you will also learn how to create your own functions in code.

From now on, I will no longer list the breadboard and jumper wires in the parts required list. Note that you will always need these basic components.

Parts Required

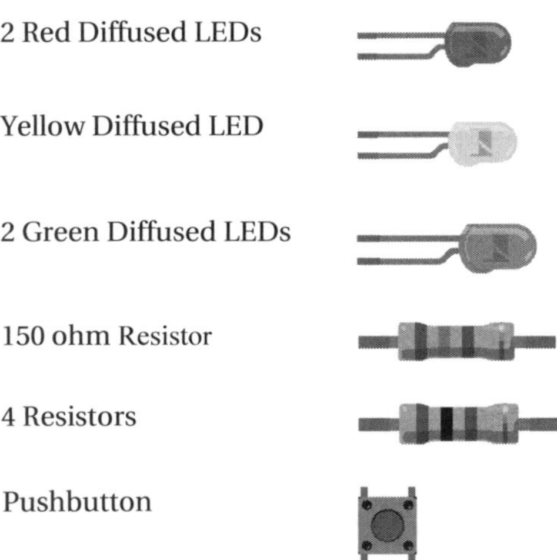

Choose the appropriate value resistor for the LEDs you are using in your project. The 150Ω resistor is for the pushbutton; it's known as a *pull down resistor* (which I will define later). The pushbutton is sometimes referred to by suppliers as a *tactile switch* and is ideal for breadboard use.

Connect It Up

Connect your circuit as shown in Figure 2-8. Double-check your wiring before providing any power to your Arduino. Remember to have your Arduino disconnected to the power while wiring up the circuit.

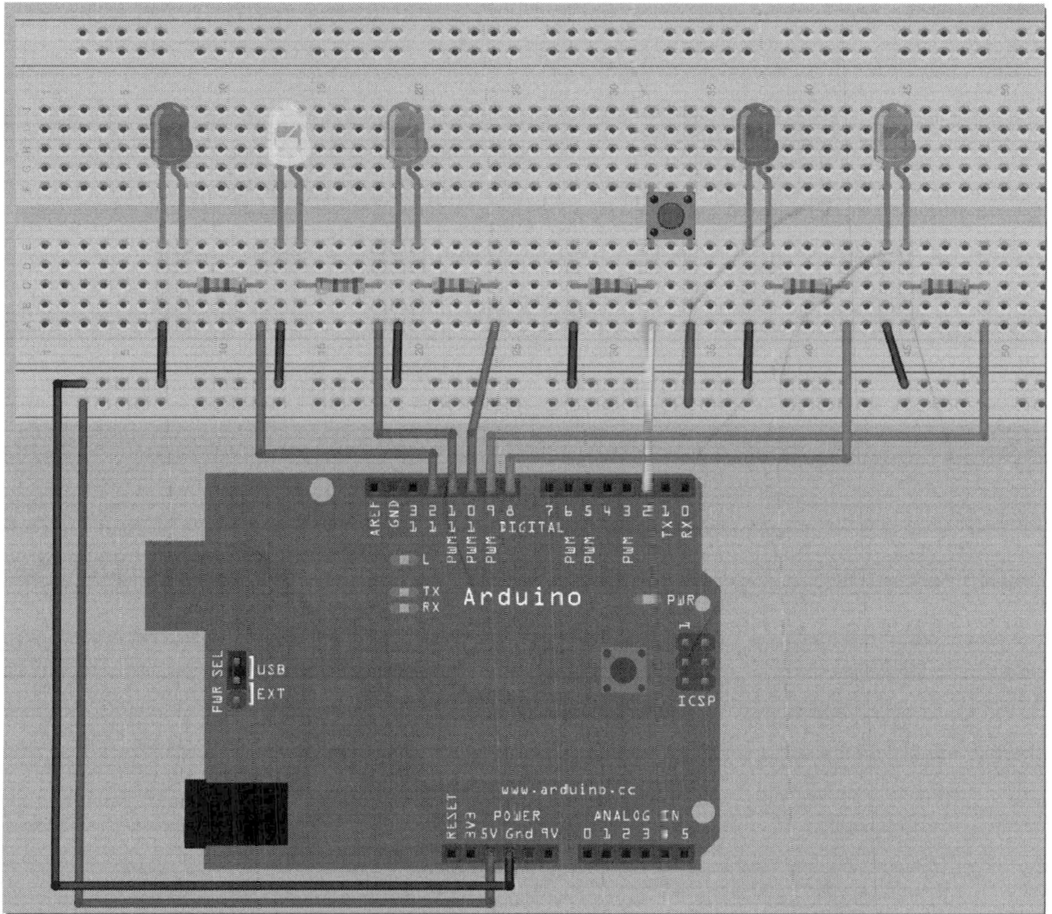

Figure 2-8. The circuit for Project 4 - Traffic light system with pedestrian crossing and request button

Enter the Code

Enter the code in Listing 2-4, verify, and upload it. When you run the program, it begins with the car traffic light on green to allow cars to pass and the pedestrian light on red.

When you press the button, the program checks that at least 5 seconds have gone by since the last time the lights changed (to allow traffic to get moving), and if so, passes code execution to the function you have created called `changeLights()`. In this function, the car lights go from green to amber to red, and then the pedestrian lights go green. After the period of time set in the variable crossTime (time enough to allow the pedestrians to cross), the green pedestrian light flash on and off as a warning to the pedestrians to hurry because the lights are about to change to red. Then the pedestrian light changes to red, the vehicle lights go from red to amber to green, and the traffic flow resumes.

Listing 2-4. Code for Project 4

```
// Project 4 - Interactive Traffic Lights

int carRed = 12; // assign the car lights
int carYellow = 11;
int carGreen = 10;
int pedRed = 9; // assign the pedestrian lights
int pedGreen = 8;
int button = 2; // button pin
int crossTime = 5000; // time alloyoud to cross
unsigned long changeTime; // time since button pressed

void setup() {
        pinMode(carRed, OUTPUT);
        pinMode(carYellow, OUTPUT);
        pinMode(carGreen, OUTPUT);
        pinMode(pedRed, OUTPUT);
        pinMode(pedGreen, OUTPUT);
        pinMode(button, INPUT); // button on pin 2
        // turn on the green light
        digitalWrite(carGreen, HIGH);
        digitalWrite(pedRed, HIGH);
}

void loop() {
        int state = digitalRead(button);
        /* check if button is pressed and it is over 5 seconds since last button press */
        if (state == HIGH && (millis() - changeTime) > 5000) {
                // Call the function to change the lights
                changeLights();
        }
}


void changeLights() {
        digitalWrite(carGreen, LOW); // green off
        digitalWrite(carYellow, HIGH); // yellow on
        delay(2000); // wait 2 seconds

        digitalWrite(carYellow, LOW); // yellow off
        digitalWrite(carRed, HIGH); // red on
        delay(1000); // wait 1 second till its safe

        digitalWrite(pedRed, LOW); // ped red off
        digitalWrite(pedGreen, HIGH); // ped green on
        delay(crossTime); // wait for preset time period
```

```
        // flash the ped green
        for (int x=0; x<10; x++) {
                digitalWrite(pedGreen, HIGH);
                delay(250);
                digitalWrite(pedGreen, LOW);
                delay(250);
        }
        // turn ped red on
        digitalWrite(pedRed, HIGH);
        delay(500);

        digitalWrite(carYellow, HIGH); // yellow on
        digitalWrite(carRed, LOW); // red off
        delay(1000);
        digitalWrite(carGreen, HIGH);
        digitalWrite(carYellow, LOW); // yellow off

        // record the time since last change of lights
        changeTime = millis();
        // then return to the main program loop
}
```

Project 4 – Code Overview

You will understand and recognize most of the code in this project from previous projects. I'll just point out the new keywords and concepts:

```
unsigned long changeTime;
```

Here is a new data type for a variable. Previously, you created integer data types, which can store a number between -32,768 and 32,767. This time you created a data type of *long*, which can store a number from -2,147,483,648 to 2,147,483,647. However, you have specified an *unsigned long*, which means the variable cannot store negative numbers, so the range is from 0 to 4,294,967,295. If you use an integer to store the length of time since the last change of lights, you would only get a maximum time of 32 seconds before the integer variable reached a number higher than it could store.

As a pedestrian crossing is unlikely to be used every 32 seconds, you don't want your program crashing due to your variable "overflowing" when it tries to store a number too high for the variable data type. So you use an unsigned long data type to get a huge length of time in between button presses:

4294967295 * 1ms = 4294967 seconds

4294967 seconds = 71582 minutes

71582 minutes - 1193 hours

1193 hours - 49 days

It's pretty inevitable that a pedestrian crossing button will be pressed at least once in 49 days, so you shouldn't have a problem with this data type.

So why isn't there just one data type that can store huge numbers all the time? Well, because variables take up space in memory; the larger the number, the more memory is used up for storing variables. On your home PC or laptop, you won't have to worry about it much at all, but on a small microcontroller like the Arduino's Atmega32, it's essential that you use only the smallest variable data type necessary for your purpose.

Table 2-2 lists the various data types you can use in your sketches.

Table 2-2. Data types

Data type	RAM	Number Range
void keyword	N/A	N/A
boolean	1 byte	0 to 1 (True or False)
byte	1 byte	0 to 255
char	1 byte	-128 to 127
unsigned char	1 byte	0 to 255
int	2 byte	-32,768 to 32,767
unsigned int	2 byte	0 to 65,535
word	2 byte	0 to 65,535
long	4 byte	-2,147,483,648 to 2,147,483,647
unsigned long	4 byte	0 to 4,294,967,295
float	4 byte	-3.4028235E+38 to 3.4028235E+38
double	4 byte	-3.4028235E+38 to 3.4028235E+38
string	1 byte + x	Arrays of chars
array	1 byte + x	Collection of variables

Each data type uses up a certain amount of memory: some variables use only 1 byte of memory and others use 4 or more (don't worry about what a byte is for now; I will discuss this later). Note that you can't copy data from one data type to another. In other words, if x was an int and y was a string, x = y would not work because the two data types are different.

The Atmega168 has 1Kb (1000 bytes) and the Atmega328 has 2Kb (2000 bytes) of SRAM; this is not a lot of memory. In large programs with lots of variables, you could easily run out of memory if you do not optimize your usage of the correct data types. As you have used int (which uses up 2 bytes and can store a number up to 32,767) to store the number of your pin, which will only go as high as 13 on your Arduino (and up to 54 on the Arduino Mega), you have used up more memory than was necessary. You could have saved memory by using the *byte* data type, which can store a number between 0 and 255—more than enough to store the number of an I/O pin.

Next you have

```
pinMode(button, INPUT);
```

which tells the Arduino that you want to use Digital Pin 2 (button = 2) as an INPUT. You are going to use Digital Pin 2 to listen for button presses so its mode needs to be set to input.

In the main program loop, you check the state of pin 2 with this statement:

```
int state = digitalRead(button);
```

This initializes an integer (yes, it's wasteful and you should use a boolean) called state and then sets the value of state to be the value of Digital Pin 2. The `digitalRead` statement reads the state of the pin within the parenthesis and returns it to the integer you have assigned it to. You can then check the value in state to see if the button has been pressed or not:

```
if (state == HIGH && (millis() - changeTime) > 5000) {
   // Call the function to change the lights
   changeLights();
 }
```

The `if` statement is an example of a control structure and its purpose is to check if a certain condition has been met or not. If so, it executes the code within its code block. For example, if you wanted to turn an LED on if a variable called x rose above the value of 500, you could write the following:

```
if (x>500) {digitalWrite(ledPin, HIGH);
```

When you read a pin using the `digitalRead` command, the state of the pin will either be `HIGH` or `LOW`. So the `if` command in your sketch looks like this:

```
if (state == HIGH && (millis() - changeTime) > 5000)
```

What you are doing here is checking that two conditions have been met. The first is that the variable called state is high. If the button has been pressed, state will be high because you have already set it to be the value read in from Digital Pin 2. You are also checking that the value of `millis()`-changeTime is greater than 5000 (using the logical AND command &&). The `millis()` function is one built into the Arduino language, and it returns the number of milliseconds since the Arduino started to run the current program. Your changeTime variable will initially hold no value, but after the changeLights) function runs, you set it at the end of that function to the current `millis()` value.

By subtracting the value in the changeTime variable from the current `millis()` value, you can check if 5 seconds have passed since changeTime was last set. The calculation of `millis()`- changeTime is put inside its own set of parenthesis to ensure that you compare the value of state and the result of this calculation, and not the value of `millis()` on its own.

The symbol && in between

```
state == HIGH
```

and the calculation is an example of a Boolean Operator. In this case, it means AND. To see what this means, let's take a look at all of the Boolean Operators:

&& - Logical AND

|| - Logical OR

! - NOT

These are logic statements and can be used to test various conditions in `if` statements.

&& means true if both operands are true, so this `if` statement will run its code only if x is 5 and y is 10:

```
if (x==5 && y==10)  {....
```

|| means true if either operand is true; for example, this `if` statement will run if x is 5 or if y is 10:

```
if (x==5 || y==10) {.....
```

The ! or NOT statement means true if the operand is false, so this `if` statement will run if x is false, i.e. equals zero:

```
if (!x) {.......
```

You can also *nest* conditions with parenthesis, for example:

```
if (x==5 && (y==10 || z==25)) {.......
```

In this case, the conditions within the parenthesis are processed separately and treated as a single condition and then compared with the second condition. So, if you draw a simple truth table (see Table 2-3) for this statement, you can see how it works.

Table 2-3. *Truth table for the condition (x==5 && (y==10 || z==25))*

x	y	z	True/False?
4	9	25	FALSE
5	10	24	TRUE
7	10	25	FALSE
5	10	25	TRUE

The command within the `if` statement is

```
changeLights();
```

and this is an example of a function call. A *function* is simply a separate code block that has been given a name. However, functions can be passed parameters and/or return data, too. In this case, you have not passed any data to the function nor have you had the function return any date. I will go into more detail later on about passing parameters and returning data from functions.

When `changeLights()` is called, the code execution jumps from the current line to the function, executes the code within that function, and then returns to the point in the code after where the function was called.

In this case, if the conditions in the if statement are met, then the program executes the code within the function and returns to the next line after `changeLights()` in the if statement.

The code within the function simply changes the vehicles lights to red, via amber, then turns on the green pedestrian light. After a period of time set by the variable crossTime, the light flashes a few time to warn the pedestrian that his time is about to run out, then the pedestrian light goes red and the vehicle light goes from red to green, via amber, thus returning to its normal state.

The main program loop simply checks continuously if the pedestrian button has been pressed or not, and, if it has and (&&) the time since the lights last changed is greater than 5 seconds, it calls the `changeLights()` function again.

In this program, there was no benefit from putting the code into its own function, apart from making the code look cleaner and to explain the concept of functions. It is only when a function is passed parameters and/or returns data that their true benefits come to light; you will take a look at that later when you use functions again.

Project 4 – Interactive Traffic Lights - Hardware Overview

The new piece of hardware introduced in Project 4 is the button, or tactile switch. As you can see by looking at the circuit, the button is not directly connected between the power line and the input pin; there is a resistor going between the button and the ground rail. This is what is known as a pull-down resistor and it is essential to ensure the button works properly. I will take a little diversion to explain pull-up and pull-down resistors.

Logic States

A *logic circuit* is one designed to give an output of either on or off, which are represented by the binary numbers 1 and 0. The off (or zero) state is a voltage near to zero volts at the output; a state of on (or 1) is represented by a higher level, closer to the supply voltage. The simplest representation of a logic circuit is a switch (see Figure 2-9).

Figure 2-9. *The electronic symbol for a switch*

When the switch is open, no current can flow through it and no voltage can be measured at the output. When you close the switch, the current can flow through it, thus a voltage can be measured at the output. The open state can be thought of as a 0 and the closed state as a 1 in a logic circuit.

In a logic circuit, if the expected voltage to represent the on (or 1) state is 5v, it's important that when the circuit outputs a 1 that the voltage is as close to 5v as possible. Similarly, when the output is a zero (or off), it is important that the voltage is as close to zero volts as possible. If you do not ensure that the states are close to the required voltages, that part of the circuit may be considered to be *floating* (it is neither in a high or low state). The floating state is also known as electrical noise, and noise in a digital circuit may be interpreted as random 1's and 0's.

This is where pull up or pull down resistors can be used to ensure the state is high or low. If you let that node in the circuit float, it may be interpreted as either a zero or a one, which is not desirable. It's better to force it towards a desired state.

Pull-Down Resistors

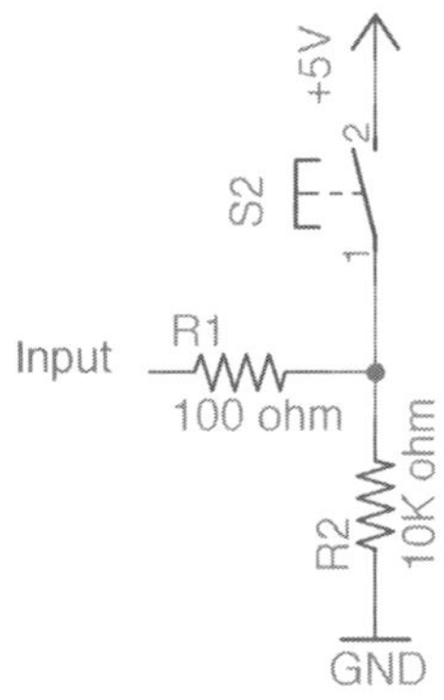

***Figure 2-10.** A pull-down resistor circuit*

Figure 2-10 shows a schematic where a pull-down resistor being used. If the button is pressed, the electricity takes the path of least resistance and moves between the 5v and the input pin (there is a 100 ohm resistor on the input pin and a 10K ohm resistor on ground). However, when the button is not pressed, the input is connected to the 100K ohm resistor and is pulled towards ground. Without this pull to ground, the pin would not be connected to anything when the button was not depressed, thus it would float between zero and 5v. In this circuit, the input will always be pulled to ground, or zero volts, when the button is not pressed and it will be pulled towards 5v when the button is pressed. In other words, you have ensured that the pin is not floating between two values. Now look at Figure 2-11.

Pull-Up Resistors

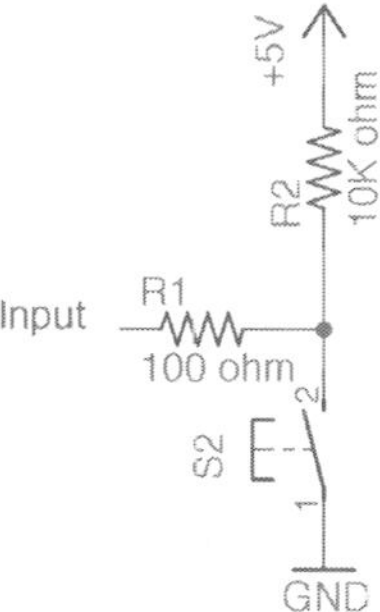

***Figure 2-11.** A pull-up resistor circuit*

In this circuit, you have swapped the pull-down resistor and the switch. The resistor now becomes a pull-up resistor. As you can see, when the button is not pressed, the input pin is pulled towards the 5v, so it will always be high. When the button is pressed, the path of least resistance is towards the ground and so the pin is pulled to ground or the low state. Without the resistor between 5v and ground, it would be a short circuit, which would damage your circuit or power supply. Thanks to the resistor, it is no longer a short circuit as the resistor limits the amount of current. The pull-up resistor is used more commonly in digital circuits.

With the use of simple pull-up or pull-down resistors you can ensure that the state of an input pin is always either high or low, depending on your application.

In Project 4, you use a pull-down resistor to ensure a button press will register correctly by the Arduino. Let's take a look at the pull-down resistor in that circuit again (see Figure 2-12).

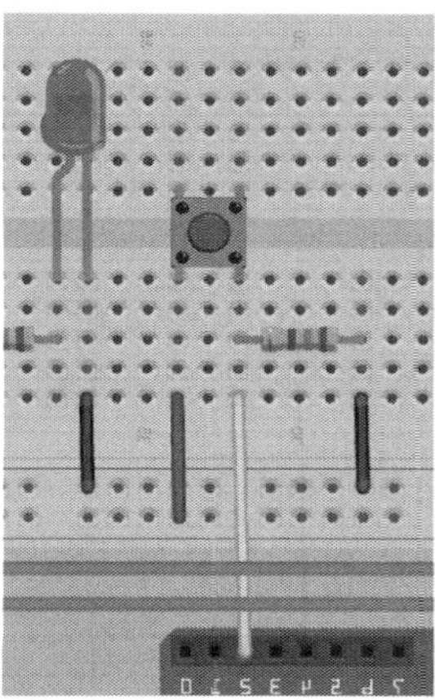

***Figure 2-12.** A pull-down resistor from Project 4*

This circuit contains a push button. One pin of the button is connected directly to 5v and the other is connected directly to Digital Pin 2. It is also connected directly to ground via a pull-down resistor. This means that when the button is not pushed, the pin is pulled to ground and therefore reads a zero or low state. When the button is pressed, 5 volts flows into the pin and it is read as a 1 or a high state. By detecting if the input is high or low, you can detect if the button is pressed or not. If the resistor was not present, the input pin wire would not be connected to anything and would be floating. The Arduino could read this as either a HIGH or a LOW state, which might result in it registering false button presses.

Pull-up resistors are often used in digital circuits to ensure an input is kept high. For example, the 74HC595 Shift Register IC (Integrated Circuit) that you will be using later on in the book has a Master Reset pin. This pin resets the chip when it is pulled low. As a result, it's essential that this pin is kept high at all times, unless you specifically want to do a reset; you can hold this pin high by using a pull-up resistor at all times. When you want to reset it, you pull it low using a digital output set to LOW; at all other times, it will remain high. Many other IC's have pins that must be kept high for most of the time and only pulled low for various functions to be activated.

The Arduino's Internal Pull-Up Resistors

Conveniently, the Arduino contains pull-up resistors that are connected to the pins (the analog pins have pull-up resistors also). These have a value of 20K ohms and need to be activated within software to use them. To activate an internal pull-up resistor on a pin, you first need to change the `pinMode` of the pin to an INPUT and then write a HIGH to that pin using a `digitalWrite` command:

```
pinMode(pin, INPUT);
digitalWrite(pin, HIGH);
```

If you change the pinMode from INPUT to OUTPUT after activating the internal pull-up resistors, the pin will remain in a HIGH state. This also works in reverse: an output pin that was in a HIGH state and is subsequently switched to an INPUT mode will have its internal pull-up resistors enabled.

Summary

Your first four projects covered a lot of ground. You now know the basics of reading inputs and turning LEDs on and off. You are beginning to build your electronic knowledge by understanding how LEDs and resistors work, how resistors can be used to limit current, and how they can be used to pull an input high or low according to your needs. You should also now be able to pick up a resistor and work out its value in ohms just by looking at its colored bands. Your understanding of the Arduino programming language is well underway and you have been introduced to a number of commands and concepts.

The skills learned in Chapter 2 are the foundation for even the most complex Arduino project. In Chapter 3, you will continue to use LEDs to create various effects, and in doing so will learn a huge number of commands and concepts. This knowledge will set you up for the more advanced subjects covered later in the book.

Subjects and Concepts Covered in Chapter 2:

- The importance of comments in code
- Variables and their types
- The purpose of the `setup()` and `loop()` functions
- The concept of functions and how to create them
- Setting the pinMode of a digital pin
- Writing a HIGH or LOW value to a pin
- How to create a delay for a specified number of milliseconds
- Breadboards and how to use them
- What a resistor is, its value of measurement, and how to use it to limit current
- How to work out the required resistor value for an LED
- How to calculate a resistor's value from its colored bands
- What an LED is and how it works
- How to make code repeat using a `for` loop
- The comparison operators
- Simple mathematics in code
- The difference between local and global scope
- Pull up and pull down resistors and how to use them
- How to read a button press
- Making decisions using the `if` statement
- Changing a pins mode between INPUT and OUTPUT
- The `millis()` function and how to use it
- Boolean operators and how to use them to make logical decisions

CHAPTER 3

LED Effects

In Chapter 2 you learned the basics of input and output, some rudimentary electronics, and a whole bunch of coding concepts. In this chapter, you're going to continue with LEDs, making them produce some very fancy effects. This chapter doesn't focus much on electronics; instead, you will be introduced to many important coding concepts such as arrays, mathematic functions, and serial communications that will provide the necessary programming skills to tackle the more advanced projects later in this book.

Project 5 – LED Chase Effect

You're going to use a string of LEDs (10 in total) to make an LED chase effect, similar to that used on the car KITT on Knight Rider or on the face of the Cylons in Battlestar Galactica. This project will introduce the concept of arrays.

Parts Required

10 5mm RED LEDs

10 Current Limiting Resistors

Connect It Up

First, make sure your Arduino is powered off by unplugging it from the USB cable. Now, use your breadboard, LEDs, resistors, and wires to connect everything as shown in Figure 3-1. Check your circuit thoroughly before connecting the power back to the Arduino.

Figure 3-1. The circuit for Project 5 – LED Chase Effect

Enter the Code

Open up your Arduino IDE and type in the code from Listing 3-1.

Listing 3-1. Code for Project 5

```
// Project 5 - LED Chase Effect
byte ledPin[] = {4, 5, 6, 7, 8, 9, 10, 11, 12, 13};    // Create array for LED pins
int ledDelay(65);  // delay between changes
int direction = 1;
int currentLED = 0;
unsigned long changeTime;

void setup() {
        for (int x=0; x<10; x++) {      // set all pins to output
                pinMode(ledPin[x], OUTPUT); }
        changeTime = millis();
}
```

```
void loop() {
        if ((millis() - changeTime) > ledDelay) {      // if it has been ledDelay ms since
last change
                changeLED();
                changeTime = millis();
        }
}

void changeLED() {
        for (int x=0; x<10; x++) {                // turn off all LED's
                digitalWrite(ledPin[x], LOW);
        }
        digitalWrite(ledPin[currentLED], HIGH);           // turn on the current LED
        currentLED += direction;         // increment by the direction value
        // change direction if we reach the end
        if (currentLED == 9) {direction = -1;}
        if (currentLED == 0) {direction = 1;}
}
```

Press the Verify/Compile button at the top of the IDE to make sure there are no errors in your code. If this is successful, click the Upload button. If you have done everything right, the LEDs will appear to move along the line then bounce back to the start.

I haven't introduced any new hardware in this project so there's no need to take a look at that. However, I have introduced a new concept in the code for this project in the form of arrays. Let's take a look at the code for Project 5 and see how it works.

Project 5 – LED Chase Effect – Code Overview

The first line in this sketch

```
byte ledPin[] = {4, 5, 6, 7, 8, 9, 10, 11, 12, 13};
```

is a declaration of a variable of data type array. An array is a collection of variables that are accessed using an index number. In your sketch, you declare an array of data type byte and called it `ledPin`. Then, you initialize the array with 10 values (Digital Pins 4 through to 13). To access an element of the array, you simply refer to the index number of that element. Arrays are zero indexed, which means that the first index starts at zero and not 1. So, in your 10 element array, the index numbers are 0 to 9.In this case, element 3 (`ledPin[2]`) has the value of 6 and element 7 (`ledPin[6]`) has a value of 10.

You have to tell the size of the array if you don't initialize it with data first. In your sketch, you didn't explicitly choose a size because the compiler is able to count the values you have assigned to the array to work out that the size is 10 elements. If you had declared the array but not initialized it with values at the same time, you would need to declare a size. For example, you could have done this

```
byte ledPin[10];
```

and then loaded data into the elements later. To retrieve a value from the array, you would do something like this:

```
x = ledpin[5];
```

In this example, x would now hold a value of 8.

To get back to your program, you have started off by declaring and initializing an array that stores 10 values, which are the digital pins used for the outputs to your 10 LEDs.

In your main loop, you check that at least **ledDelay** milliseconds have passed since the last change of LEDs; if so, it passes control to your function. The reason you pass control to the **changeLED()** function in this manner, rather than using **delay()** commands, is to allow other code to run in the main program loop, if needed (as long as that code takes less than **ledDelay** to run).

The function you create is

```
void changeLED() {
        // turn off all LED's
        for (int x=0; x<10; x++) {
                digitalWrite(ledPin[x], LOW);
         }
        // turn on the current LED
        digitalWrite(ledPin[currentLED], HIGH);
        // increment by the direction value
        currentLED += direction;
        // change direction if we reach the end
        if (currentLED == 9) {direction = -1;}
        if (currentLED == 0) {direction = 1;}
}
```

and the job of this function is to turn all LEDs off and then turn on the current LED (this is done so fast you will not see it happening), which is stored in the variable **currentLED**.

This variable then has direction added to it. As direction can only be either a 1 or a -1, the number will either increase (+1) or decrease by one (**currentLED** +(-1)).

Then there's an `if` statement to see if you have reached the end of the row of LEDs; if so, you reverse the direction variable.

By changing the value of **ledDelay** you can make the LED ping back and forth at different speeds. Try different values to see what happens.

Note that you have to stop the program, manually change the value of **ledDelay,** and then upload the amended code to see any changes. Wouldn't it be nice to be able to adjust the speed while the program is running? Yes, it would, so let's do exactly that in the next project. You'll learn how to interact with the program and adjust the speed using a potentiometer.

Project 6 – Interactive LED Chase Effect

Leave your circuit board intact from Project 5. You're just going to add a potentiometer to this circuit, which will allow you to change the speed of the lights while the code is running.

Parts Required

All of the parts for Project 5 plus....

4.7KΩ Rotary Potentiometer

Image courtesy of Iain Fergusson.

Connect It Up

First, make sure your Arduino is powered off by unplugging it from the USB cable. Now, add the potentiometer to the circuit so it is connected as shown in Figure 3-2 with the left leg going to the 5v on the Arduino, the middle leg going to Analog Pin 2, and the right leg going to ground.

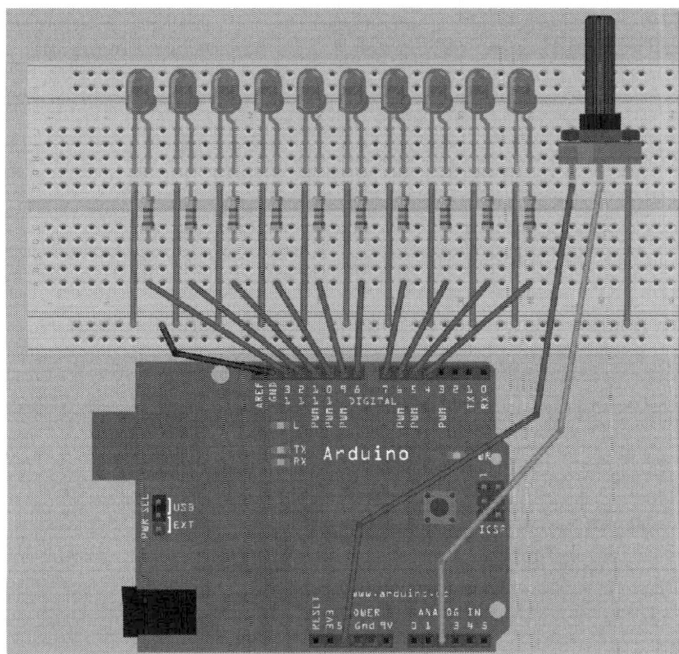

Figure 3-2. *The circuit for Project 6 – Interactive LED Chase Effect*

Enter The Code

Open up your Arduino IDE and type in the code from Listing 3-2.

Listing 3-2. Code for Project 6

```
byte ledPin[] = {4, 5, 6, 7, 8, 9, 10, 11, 12, 13};     // Create array for LED pins
int ledDelay; // delay between changes
int direction = 1;
int currentLED = 0;
unsigned long changeTime;
int potPin = 2;    // select the input pin for the potentiometer

void setup() {
for (int x=0; x<10; x++) {   // set all pins to output
                pinMode(ledPin[x], OUTPUT); }
        changeTime = millis();
}

void loop() {
ledDelay = analogRead(potPin); // read the value from the pot
        if ((millis() - changeTime) > ledDelay) {      // if it has been ledDelay ms since
                                                          last change
                changeLED();
                changeTime = millis();
        }
}

void changeLED() {
        for (int x=0; x<10; x++) {   // turn off all LED's
                digitalWrite(ledPin[x], LOW);
        }
        digitalWrite(ledPin[currentLED], HIGH); // turn on the current LED
        currentLED += direction; // increment by the direction value
        // change direction if we reach the end
        if (currentLED == 9) {direction = -1;}
        if (currentLED == 0) {direction = 1;}
}
```

When you verify and upload your code, you should see the lit LED appear to bounce back and forth between each end of the string of lights as before. But, by turning the knob of the potentiometer, you will change the value of `ledDelay` and speed up or slow down the effect.

Let's take a look at how this works and find out what a potentiometer is.

Project 6 – Interactive LED Chase Effect – Code Overview

The code for this Project is almost identical to the previous project. You have simply added a potentiometer to your hardware and the code additions enable it to read the values from the potentiometer and use them to adjust the speed of the LED chase effect.

You first declare a variable for the potentiometer pin

```
int potPin = 2;
```

because your potentiometer is connected to Analog Pin 2. To read the value from an analog pin, you use the analogRead command. The Arduino has six analog input/outputs with a 10-bit analog to digital convertor (I will discuss *bits* later). This means the analog pin can read in voltages between 0 to 5 volts in integer values between 0 (0 volts) and 1,023 (5 volts). This gives a resolution of 5 volts / 1024 units or 0.0049 volts (4.9mV) per unit.

Set your delay using the potentiometer so that you can use the direct values read in from the pin to adjust the delay between 0 and 1023 milliseconds (or just over 1 second). You do this by directly reading the value of the potentiometer pin into `ledDelay`. Notice that you don't need to set an analog pin to be an input or output (unlike with a digital pin):

```
ledDelay = analogRead(potPin);
```

This is done during your main loop and therefore it is constantly being read and adjusted. By turning the knob, you can adjust the delay value between 0 and 1023 milliseconds (or just over a second) and thus have full control over the speed of the effect.

Let's find out what a potentiometer is and how it works.

Project 6 – Interactive LED Chase Effect – Hardware Overview

The only additional piece of hardware used in this project is the 4K7 (4700Ω) potentiometer.

You know how resistors work. Well, the potentiometer is simply an adjustable resistor with a range from 0 to a set value (written on the side of the pot). In this project, you're using a 4K7 (4,700Ω) potentiometer, which means its range is from 0 to 4700 Ohms.

The potentiometer has three legs. By connecting just two legs, the potentiometer becomes a variable resistor. By connecting all three legs and applying a voltage across it, the pot becomes a voltage divider. The latter is how you going to use it in your circuit. One side is connected to ground, the other to 5v, and the center leg to your analog pin. By adjusting the knob, a voltage between 0 and 5v will be leaked from the center pin; you can read the value of that voltage on Analog Pin 2 and use it to change the delay rate of the light effect.

The potentiometer can be very useful in providing a means of adjusting a value from 0 to a set amount, e.g. the volume of a radio or the brightness of a lamp In fact, dimmer switches for your home lamps are a kind of potentiometer.

EXERCISES

You have all the necessary knowledge so far to adjust the code to enable you to do the following:

- Exercise 1: Get the LEDs at BOTH ends of the strip to start as on, then move towards each other, appear to bounce off each other, and then move back to the end.
- Exercise 2: Make a bouncing ball effect by turning the LEDs so they are vertical, then make an LED start at the bottom, then "bounce" up to the top LED, then back to the bottom, then only up to the 9th LED, then back down, then up to the 8th, and so on to simulate a bouncing ball losing momentum after each bounce.

Project 7 – Pulsating Lamp

You are now going try a more advanced method of controlling LEDs. So far, you have simply turned the LED on or off. Would you like to adjust the brightness of an LED? Can you do that with an Arduino? Yes, you can.

Time to go back to basics.

Parts Required

Green Diffused 5mm LED	
Current Limiting Resistor	

Connect It Up

The circuit for this project is simply a green LED connecting, via a current limiting resistor, between ground and Digital Pin 11 (see Figure 3-3).

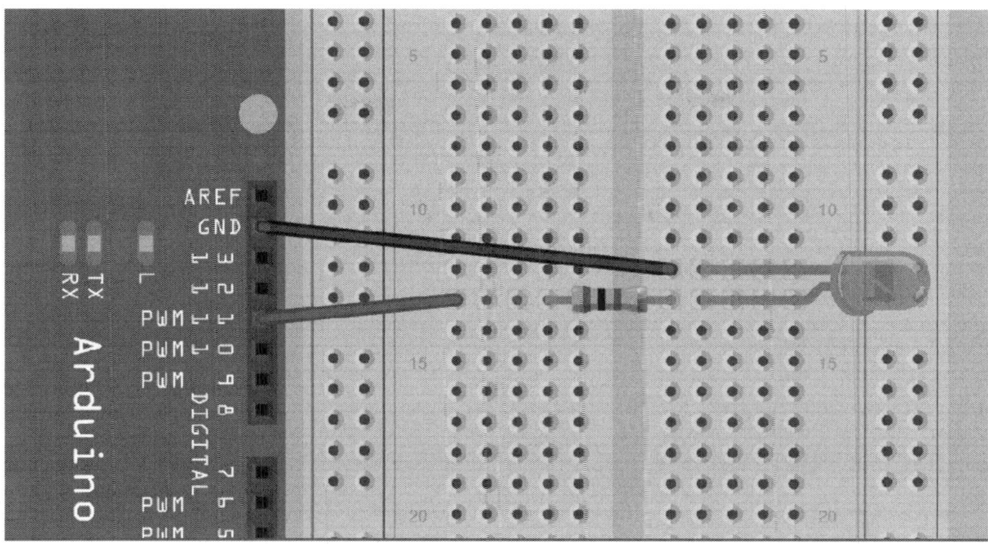

Figure 3-3. The circuit for Project 7 – Pulsating Lamp

Enter the Code

Open up your Arduino IDE and type in the code from Listing 3-3.

Listing 3-3. Code for Project 7

```
// Project 7 - Pulsating lamp
int ledPin = 11;
float sinVal;
int ledVal;

void setup() {
        pinMode(ledPin, OUTPUT);
}

void loop() {
        for (int x=0; x<180; x++) {
        // convert degrees to radians then obtain sin value
        sinVal = (sin(x*(3.1412/180)));
        ledVal = int(sinVal*255);
        analogWrite(ledPin, ledVal);
        delay(25);
        }
}
```

Verify and upload. You will see your LED pulsate on and off steadily. Instead of a simple on/off state, however, you're going to adjust the brightness. Let's find out how this works.

Project 7 – Pulsating Lamp – Code Overview

The code for this project is very simple, but it requires some explanation.

First, you set the variables for the LED Pin, a float (floating point data type) for a sine wave value, and `ledVal` which will hold the integer value to send out to Digital PWM Pin 11.

The concept here is that you are creating a sine wave and having the brightness of the LED follow the path of that wave. This is what makes the light pulsate instead of just flare to full brightness and fade back down again.

You use the sin() function, which is a mathematical function, to work out the sine of an angle. You need to give the function the degree in radians. So, you have a `for` loop that goes from 0 to 179; you don't want to go past halfway as this will take you into negative values and the brightness value can only be from 0 to 255.

The sin() function requires the angle to be in radians and not degrees so the equation of x*(3.1412/180) will convert the degree angle into radians. You then transfer the result to `ledVal`, multiplying it by 255 to get the value. The result from the `sin()` function will be a number between -1 and 1, so multiply it by 255 for the maximum brightness. You *cast* the floating point value of `sinVal` into an integer by the use of `int()` in the following statement:

```
ledVal = int(sinVal*255);
```

Then you send that value out to Digital PWM Pin 11 using the statement:

```
analogWrite(ledPin, ledVal);
```

Casting means you have converted the floating point value into an integer (effectively throwing away whatever is after the decimal point). But, how can you send an analog value to a digital pin? Well, take a look at your Arduino. If you examine the digital pins, you can see that six of them (3, 5, 6, 9, 10 & 11) have PWM written next to them. These pins differ from the remaining digital pins in that they are able to send out a PWM signal.

PWM stands for Pulse Width Modulation, which is a technique for getting analog results from digital means. On these pins, the Arduino sends out a square wave by switching the pin on and off very fast. The pattern of on/offs can simulate a varying voltage between 0 and 5v. It does this by changing the amount of time that the output remains high (on) versus off (low). The duration of the on time is known as the *pulse width.*

For example, if you were to send the value 0 out to Digital PWM Pin 11 using `analogWrite()`, the ON period would be zero, or it would have a 0 percent duty cycle. If you were to send a value of 64 (25 percent of the maximum of 255) the pin would be ON for 25 percent of the time and OFF for 75 percent of the time. The value of 191 would have a duty cycle of 75 percent; a value of 255 would have a duty cycle of 100 percent. The pulses run at a speed of approximately 500Hz or 2 milliseconds each.

So, in your sketch, the LED is being turned on and off very fast. If the Duty Cycle was 50 percent (a value of 127), the LED would pulse on and off at 500Hz and would display at half the maximum brightness. This is basically an illusion that you can use to your advantage by allowing the digital pins to output a simulated analog value to your LEDs.

Note that even though only six of the pins have the PWM function, you can easily write software to give a PWM output from all of the digital pins if you wish.

Later, you'll revisit PWM to create audible tones using a piezo sounder.

Project 8 – RGB Mood Lamp

In the last project, you learned how to adjust the brightness of an LED using the PWM capabilities of the Atmega chip. You'll now take advantage of this capability by using a red, green, and blue LED and mixing these colors to create any color you wish. From that, you'll create a mood lamp similar to those seen in stores nowadays.

Parts Required

This time you are going to use three LEDs: one red, one green, and one blue.

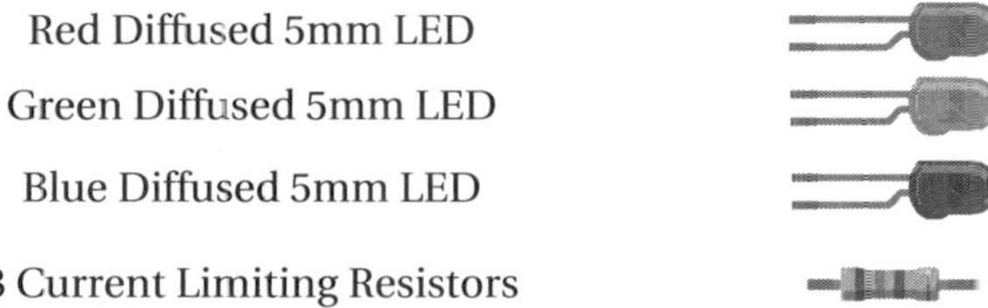

Connect It Up

Connect the three LEDs as shown in Figure 3-4. Get a piece of letter-size paper, roll it into a cylinder, and tape it to secure it. Place the cylinder over the top of the three LEDs. This will diffuse the light from each LED and merge the colors into one.

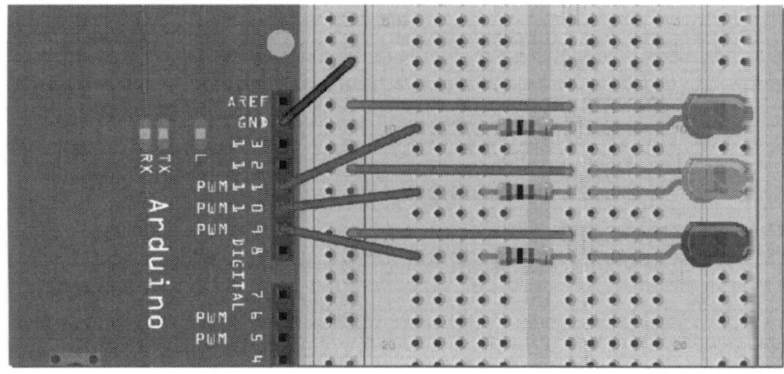

Figure 3-4. *The circuit for Project 8 – RGB Mood Lamp*

Enter the Code

Open up your Arduino IDE and type in the code from Listing 3-4.

Listing 3-4. Code for Project 8

```
// Project 8 - Mood Lamp
float RGB1[3];
float RGB2[3];
float INC[3];

int red, green, blue;

int RedPin = 11;
int GreenPin = 10;
int BluePin = 9;

void setup()
{
        randomSeed(analogRead(0));

        RGB1[0] = 0;
        RGB1[1] = 0;
        RGB1[2] = 0;

        RGB2[0] = random(256);
        RGB2[1] = random(256);
        RGB2[2] = random(256);
}

void loop()
{
        randomSeed(analogRead(0));

        for (int x=0; x<3; x++) {
                INC[x] = (RGB1[x] - RGB2[x]) / 256; }

        for (int x=0; x<256; x++) {
                red = int(RGB1[0]);
                green = int(RGB1[1]);
                blue = int(RGB1[2]);

                analogWrite (RedPin, red);
                analogWrite (GreenPin, green);
                analogWrite (BluePin, blue);
                delay(100);

                RGB1[0] -= INC[0];
                RGB1[1] -= INC[1];
                RGB1[2] -= INC[2];
        }
```

```
        for (int x=0; x<3; x++) {
                RGB2[x] = random(556)-300;
                RGB2[x] = constrain(RGB2[x], 0, 255);
                delay(1000);
        }
}
```

When you run this, you will see the colors slowly change. You've just made your own mood lamp!

Project 8 – RGB Mood Lamp – Code Overview

The LEDs that make up the mood lamp are red, green, and blue. In the same way that your computer monitor is made up of tiny red, green, and blue (RGB) dots, you can generate different colors by adjusting the brightness of each of the three LEDs in such a way to give you a different RGB value.

Alternatively, you could have used an RGB LED. This is a single 5mm LED, with 4 legs (some have more). One leg is either a common anode (positive) or common cathode (negative); the other three legs go to the opposite terminal of the red, green, and blue LEDs inside the lamp. It is basically three colored LEDs squeezed into a single 5mm LED. These are more compact, but more expensive.

An RGB value of 255, 0, 0 is pure red. A value of 0, 255, 0 is pure green and 0, 0, 255 is pure blue. By mixing these, you can get any color. This is the additive color model (see Figure 3-5). Note that if you were just turning the LEDs ON or OFF (i.e. not trying out different brightness) you would still get different colors.

Table 3-5. *Colors available by turning LEDs ON or OFF in different combinations*

Red	Green	Blue	Color
255 0		0	Red
0 255		0	Green
0 0 255			Blue
255 255	0		Yellow
0 255		255	Cyan
255 0		255	Magenta
255 255	255		White

Diffusing the light with the paper cylinder mixes the colors nicely. The LEDs can be placed into any object that will diffuse the light; another option is to bounce the light off a reflective diffuser. Try putting the lights inside a ping-pong ball or a small white plastic bottle (the thinner the plastic the better).

By adjusting the brightness using PWM, you can get every other color in between, too. By placing the LEDs close together and mixing their values, the light spectra of the three colors added together make a single color (see Figure 3-5). The total range of colors available using PWM with a range of 0 to 255 is 16,777,216 colors (256x256x256).

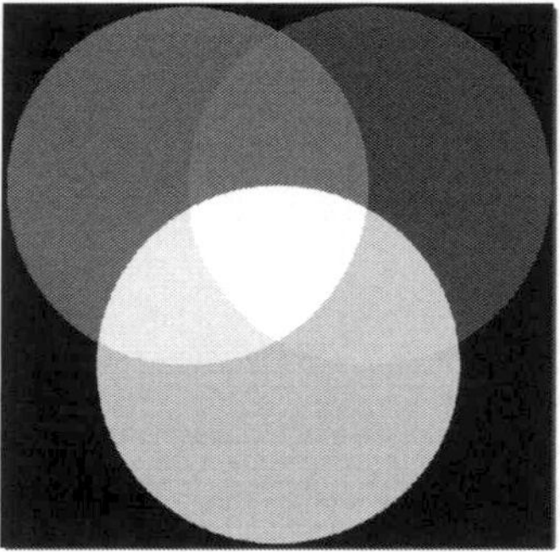

***Figure 3-5.** Mixing R, G, and B to get different colors*

In the code, you begin by declaring some floating point arrays and some integer variables to store your RGB values as well as an increment value, like so:

```
float RGB1[3];
float RGB2[3];
float INC[3];

int red, green, blue;
```

In the setup function, you have the following:

```
randomSeed(analogRead(0));
```

The randomSeed command creates random (actually pseudo-random) numbers. A computer chip is not able to produce truly random numbers so it looks at data in a part of its memory that may differ or it looks at a table of different values and uses those as pseudo-random numbers. By setting a *seed*, you can tell the computer where in memory or in that table to start counting from. In this case, the value you assign to randomSeed is a value read from Analog Pin 0. Because there's nothing connected to Analog Pin 0, all it will read is a random number created by analog noise.

Once you have set a seed for your random number, you can create one using the `random()` function. You then have two sets of RGB values stored in a three element array. RGB1 contains the RGB values you want the lamp to start with (in this case, all zeros, or off):

```
  RGB1[0] = 0;
  RGB1[1] = 0;
  RGB1[2] = 0;
```

The RGB2 array is a set of random RGB values that you want the lamp to transition to:

```
  RGB2[0] = random(256);
  RGB2[1] = random(256);
  RGB2[2] = random(256);
```

In this case, you have set them to a random number set by random(256) which will give you a number between 0 and 255 inclusive (as the number will always range from zero upwards).

If you pass a single number to the random() function, it will return a value between 0 and 1 less than the number, e.g. random(1000) will return a number between 0 and 999. If you supply two numbers as the parameters, it will return a random number between the lower number inclusive and the maximum number (-1), e.g. random(10,100) will return a random number between 10 and 99.

In the main program loop, you first take a look at the start and end RGB values and work out what value is needed as an increment to progress from one value to the other in 256 steps (as the PWM value can only be between 0 and 255). You do this with the following:

```
for (int x=0; x<3; x++) {
       INC[x] = (RGB1[x] - RGB2[x]) / 256; }
```

This `for` loop sets the INCrement values for the R, G and B channels by working out the difference between the two brightness values and dividing that by 256.

You have another `for` loop

```
for (int x=0; x<256; x++) {

       red = int(RGB1[0]);
       green = int(RGB1[1]);
       blue = int(RGB1[2]);

       analogWrite (RedPin, red);
       analogWrite (GreenPin, green);
       analogWrite (BluePin, blue);
       delay(100);

       RGB1[0] -= INC[0];
       RGB1[1] -= INC[1];
       RGB1[2] -= INC[2];
 }
```

that sets the red, green, and blue values to the values in the RGB1 array; writes those values to Digital Pins 9, 10 and 11; deducts the increment value; and repeats this process 256 times to slowly fade from one random color to the next. The delay of 100ms in between each step ensures a slow and steady progression. You can, of course, adjust this value if you want it slower or faster; you can also add a potentiometer to allow the user to set the speed.

After you have taken 256 slow steps from one random color to the next, the RGB1 array will have the same values (nearly) as the RGB2 array. You now need to decide upon another set of three random values ready for the next time. You do this with another `for` loop:

```
for (int x=0; x<3; x++) {
       RGB2[x] = random(556)-300;
       RGB2[x] = constrain(RGB2[x], 0, 255);
       delay(1000);
}
```

The random number is chosen by picking a random number between 0 and 556 (256+300) and then deducting 300. In this manner, you are trying to force primary colors from time to time to ensure that you don't always just get pastel shades. You have 300 chances out of 556 in getting a negative number and therefore forcing a bias towards one or more of the other two color channels. The next command makes sure that the numbers sent to the PWM pins are not negative by using the `constrain()` function.

The `constrain()` function requires three parameters: x, a, and b where x is the number you want to constrain, a is the lower end of the range, and b is the higher end. So, the `constrain()` function looks at the value of x and makes sure it is within the range of a to b. If it is lower than a, it sets it to a; if it is higher than b, it sets it to b. In your case, you make sure that the number is between 0 and 255 which is the range of your PWM output.

As you use random(556)-300 for your RGB values, some of those values will be lower than zero; the constrain function makes sure that the value sent to the PWM is not lower than zero.

EXERCISE

See if you can change the code to make the colors cycle through the colors of the rainbow rather than between random colors.

Project 9 – LED Fire Effect

Project 9 will use LEDs and a flickering random light effect, via PWM again, to mimic the effect of a flickering flame. If you place these LEDs inside a house on a model railway, for example, you can make it look like the house is on fire, or you can use it in a fireplace in your house instead of wood logs. This is a simple example of how LEDs can be used to create special effects for movies, stage plays, model dioramas, model railways, etc.

Parts Required

This time we are going to use three LEDs: one red and two yellow.

Red Diffused 5mm LED

2 Yellow Diffused 5mm LED

3 Current Limiting Resistor

Connect It Up

Power down your Arduino, then connect your three LEDs as shown in Figure 3-6. This is essentially the same circuit as in Project 8, but using one red and two yellow LEDs instead of a red, green, and blue. Again, the effect is best seen when the light is diffused using a cylinder of paper, or when bounced off a white card or mirror onto another surface.

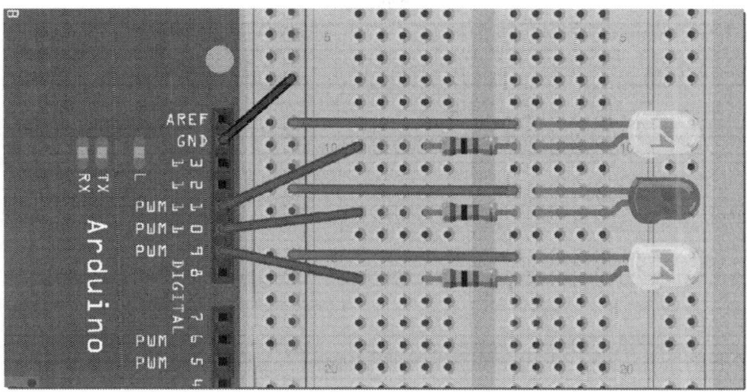

Figure 3-6. The circuit for Project 9 – LED Fire Effect

Enter the Code

Open up your Arduino IDE and type in the code from Listing 3-5.

Listing 3-5. Code for Project 9

```
// Project 9 - LED Fire Effect
int ledPin1 = 9;
int ledPin2 = 10;
int ledPin3 = 11;

void setup()
{
        pinMode(ledPin1, OUTPUT);
        pinMode(ledPin2, OUTPUT);
        pinMode(ledPin3, OUTPUT);
}

void loop()
{
        analogWrite(ledPin1, random(120)+135);
        analogWrite(ledPin2, random(120)+135);
        analogWrite(ledPin3, random(120)+135);
delay(random(100));
}
```

Press the Verify/Compile button at the top of the IDE to make sure there are no errors in your code. If this is successful, click the Upload button.

If you have done everything right, the LEDs will flicker in a random manner to simulate a flame or fire effect.

Project 9 – LED Fire Effect – Code Overview

Let's take a look at the code for this project. First, you declare and initialize some integer variables that will hold the values for the digital pins you are connecting your LEDs to:

```
int ledPin1 = 9;
int ledPin2 = 10;
int ledPin3 = 11;
```

Then, set them to be outputs:

```
pinMode(ledPin1, OUTPUT);
pinMode(ledPin2, OUTPUT);
pinMode(ledPin3, OUTPUT);
```

The main program loop sends out a random value between 0 and 120; add 135 to it to get full LED brightness for the PWM Pins 9, 10, and 11:

```
analogWrite(ledPin1, random(120)+135);
analogWrite(ledPin2, random(120)+135);
analogWrite(ledPin3, random(120)+135);
```

Lastly, you have a random delay between ON and 100ms:

```
delay(random(100));
```

The main loop then starts again, causing the flicker effect. Bounce the light off a white card or a mirror onto your wall and you will see a very realistic flame effect.

The hardware is simple and you should understand it by now, so let's move on to Project 10.

EXERCISE

Try out the following two exercises:

- Exercise 1: Using a blue and/or white LED or two, see if you can recreate the effect of the flashes of light from an arc welder.
- Exercise 2: Using blue and red LEDs, recreate the effect of the lights of an emergency vehicle.

Project 10 – Serial Controlled Mood Lamp

For Project 10, you will revisit the circuit from Project 8 — RGB Mood Lamp, but you'll now delve into the world of serial communications. You'll control your lamp by sending commands from the PC to the

Arduino using the Serial Monitor in the Arduino IDE. Serial communication is the process of sending data one bit at a time across a communication link.

This project also introduces how to manipulate text strings. So, set up the hardware as you did in Project 8 and enter the new code.

Enter the Code

Open up your Arduino IDE and type in the code from Listing 3-6.

Listing 3-6. *Code for Project 10*

```
// Project 10 - Serial controlled mood lamp
char buffer[18];
int red, green, blue;

int RedPin = 11;
int GreenPin = 10;
int BluePin = 9;

void setup()
{
        Serial.begin(9600);
        Serial.flush();
        pinMode(RedPin, OUTPUT);
        pinMode(GreenPin, OUTPUT);
        pinMode(BluePin, OUTPUT);
}

void loop()
{
        if (Serial.available() > 0) {
                int index=0;
                delay(100); // let the buffer fill up
                int numChar = Serial.available();
                if (numChar>15) {
                        numChar=15;
                 }
                while (numChar--) {
                        buffer[index++] = Serial.read();
                }
                splitString(buffer);
        }
}

void splitString(char* data) {
        Serial.print("Data entered: ");
        Serial.println(data);
        char* parameter;
        parameter = strtok (data, " ,");
        while (parameter != NULL) {
```

```
                setLED(parameter);
                parameter = strtok (NULL, " ,");
}

         // Clear the text and serial buffers
        for (int x=0; x<16; x++) {
                buffer[x]='\0';
         }
        Serial.flush();
}

void setLED(char* data) {
        if ((data[0] == 'r') || (data[0] == 'R')) {
                int Ans = strtol(data+1, NULL, 10);
                Ans = constrain(Ans,0,255);
                analogWrite(RedPin, Ans);
                Serial.print("Red is set to: ");
                Serial.println(Ans);
        }
        if ((data[0] == 'g') || (data[0] == 'G')) {
                int Ans = strtol(data+1, NULL, 10);
                Ans = constrain(Ans,0,255);
                analogWrite(GreenPin, Ans);
                Serial.print("Green is set to: ");
                Serial.println(Ans);
        }
        if ((data[0] == 'b') || (data[0] == 'B')) {
                int Ans = strtol(data+1, NULL, 10);
                Ans = constrain(Ans,0,255);
                analogWrite(BluePin, Ans);
                Serial.print("Blue is set to: ");
                Serial.println(Ans);
        }
}
```

Once you've verified the code, upload it to your Arduino.

Note when you upload the program nothing seems to happen. This is because the program is waiting for your input. Start the Serial Monitor by clicking its icon in the Arduino IDE taskbar.

In the Serial Monitor text window, you'll enter the R, G, and B values for each of the three LEDs manually. The LEDs will change to the color you have input.

If you enter R255, the Red LED will display at full brightness. If you enter R255, G255, both the red and green LEDs will display at full brightness. Now enter R127, G100, B255. You get a nice purplish color. Typing r0, g0, b0 will turn off all of the LEDs.

The input text is designed to accept a lowercase or uppercase R, G, and B and then a value from 0 to 255. Any value over 255 will be dropped down to 255 by default. You can enter a comma or a space between parameters and you can enter one, two, or three LED values at any once; for example:

```
r255 b100

r127 b127 g127

G255, B0

B127, R0, G255
```

Project 10 – Serial Controlled Mood Lamp – Code Overview

This project introduces a several new concepts, including serial communication, pointers, and string manipulation. Hold on to your hat; this will take a lot of explaining.

First, you set up an array of char (characters) to hold your text string that is 18 characters long, which is longer than the maximum of 16 allowed to ensure that you don't get "buffer overflow" errors.

```
char buffer[18];
```

You then set up the integers to hold the red, green, and blue values as well as the values for the digital pins:

```
int red, green, blue;

int RedPin = 11;
int GreenPin = 10;
int BluePin = 9;
```

In your setup function, you set the three digital pins to be outputs. But, before that, you have the Serial.begin command:

```
void setup()
{
        Serial.begin(9600);
        Serial.flush();
        pinMode(RedPin, OUTPUT);
        pinMode(GreenPin, OUTPUT);
        pinMode(BluePin, OUTPUT);
}
```

Serial.begin tells the Arduino to start serial communications; the number within the parenthesis (in this case, 9600) sets the baud rate (symbols or pulses per second) at which the serial line will communicate.

The Serial.flush command will flush out any characters that happen to be in the serial line so that it is empty and ready for input/output.

The serial communications line is simply a way for the Arduino to communicate with the outside world, which, in this case, is to and from the PC and the Arduino IDE's Serial Monitor.

In the main loop, you have an `if` statement

```
if (Serial.available() > 0) {
```

that is using the Serial.available command to check to see if any characters have been sent down the serial line. If any characters have been received, the condition is met and the code within the `if` statements code block is executed:

```
if (Serial.available() > 0) {
        int index=0;
        delay(100); // let the buffer fill up
        int numChar = Serial.available();
        if (numChar>15) {
                numChar=15;
        }
        while (numChar--) {
                buffer[index++] = Serial.read();
        }
        splitString(buffer);
}
```

An integer called index is declared and initialized as zero. This integer will hold the position of a pointer to the characters within the char array.

You then set a delay of 100. The purpose of this is to ensure that the serial buffer (the place in memory where the received serial data is stored prior to processing) is full before you process the data. If you don't do that, it's possible that the function will execute and start to process the text string before you have received all of the data. The serial communications line is very slow compared to the execution speed of the rest of the code. When you send a string of characters, the Serial.available function will immediately have a value higher than zero and the `if` function will start to execute. If you didn't have the `delay(100)` statement, it could start to execute the code within the `if` statement before all of the text string had been received, and the serial data might only be the first few characters of the line of text entered.

After you have waited for 100ms for the serial buffer to fill up with the data sent, you then declare and initialize the numChar integer to be the number of characters within the text string.

So, if we sent this text in the Serial Monitor

```
R255, G255, B255
```

the value of numChar would be 17. It is 17, and not 16, because at the end of each line of text there is an invisible character called a NULL character that tells the Arduino when it has reached the end of the line of text.

The next `if` statement checks if the value of numChar is greater than 15; if so, it sets it to be 15. This ensures that you don't overflow the array char buffer[18].

Next is a `while` command. This is something you haven't come across before, so let me explain.

You have already used the `for` loop, which will loop a set number of times. The `while` statement is also a loop, but one that executes only while a condition is true.

The syntax is as follows:

```
while(expression) {
        // statement(s)
}
```

In your code, the `while` loop is:

```
while (numChar--) {
      buffer[index++] = Serial.read();
    }
```

The condition it is checking is numChar. In other words, it is checking that the value stored in the integer numChar is not zero. Note that numChar has -- after it. This is a post-decrement: the value is decremented *after* it is used. If you had used –numChar, the value in numChar would be decremented (have one subtracted from it) before it was evaluated. In your case, the `while` loop checks the value of numChar and then subtracts 1 from it. If the value of numChar was not zero before the decrement, it then carries out the code within its code block.

numChar is set to the length of the text string that you have entered into the Serial Monitor window. So, the code within the `while` loop will execute that many times.

The code within the `while` loop is

```
buffer[index++] = Serial.read();
```

and this sets each element of the buffer array to each character read in from the Serial line. In other words, it fills up the buffer array with the letters you entered into the Serial Monitor's text window.

The `Serial.read()` command reads incoming serial data, one byte at a time. So now that your character array has been filled with the characters you entered in the Serial Monitor, the `while` loop will end once numChar reaches zero (i.e. the length of the string).

After the `while` loop you have

```
splitString(buffer);
```

which is a call to one of the two functions you created and called `splitString()`. The function looks like this:

```
void splitString(char* data) {
        Serial.print("Data entered: ");
        Serial.println(data);
        char* parameter;
        parameter = strtok (data, " ,");
        while (parameter != NULL) {
                setLED(parameter);
                parameter = strtok (NULL, " ,");
        }

        // Clear the text and serial buffers
        for (int x=0; x<16; x++) {
                buffer[x]='\0';
        }
        Serial.flush();
}
```

The function returns no data, hence its data type has been set to void. You pass the function one parameter, a char data type that you call data. However, in the C and C++ programming languages, you are not allowed to send a character array to a function. You get around that limitation by using a pointer. You know it's a pointer because an asterisk has been added to the variable name *data.

Pointers are an advanced subject in C, so I won't go into too much detail about them. If you need to know more, refer to a book on programming in C. All you need to know for now is that by declaring data as a pointer, it becomes a variable that points to another variable.

You can either point it to the address at which the variable is stored within memory by using the & symbol, or in your case, to the value stored at that memory address using the * symbol. You have used it to cheat the system, because, as mentioned, you aren't allowed to send a character array to a function. However, you are allowed to send a pointer to a character array to your function. So, you have declared a variable of data type Char and called it data, but the * symbol before it means that it is pointing to the value stored within the buffer variable.

When you call `splitString()`, you sent it the contents of buffer (actually a pointer to it, as you saw above):

```
splitString(buffer);
```

So you have called the function and passed it the entire contents of the buffer character array.

The first command is

```
Serial.print("Data entered: ");
```

and this is your way of sending data back from the Arduino to the PC. In this case, the print command sends whatever is within the parentheses to the PC, via the USB cable, where you can read it in the Serial Monitor window. In this case, you have sent the words "Data entered: ". Note that text must be enclosed within quotes. The next line is similar

```
Serial.println(data);
```

and again you have sent data back to the PC. This time, you send the char variable called data, which is a copy of the contents of the buffer character array that you passed to the function. So, if your text string entered is

```
R255 G127 B56
```

then the

```
Serial.println(data);
```

command will send that text string back to the PC and print it out in the Serial Monitor window. (Make sure you have enabled the Serial Monitor window first.)

This time the print command has ln on the end to make it println. This simply means "print with a linefeed."

When you print using the print command, the cursor (the point at where the next symbol will appear) remains at the end of whatever you printed. When you use the println command, a linefeed command is issued, so the text prints and then the cursor drops down to the next line:

```
Serial.print("Data entered: ");
Serial.println(data);
```

So if you look at your two print commands, the first one prints out "Data entered: " and then the cursor remains at the end of that text. The next print command will print data (which is the contents of the array called buffer) and then issue a linefeed, which drops the cursor down to the next line. If you issue another print or println statement after this, whatever is printed in the Serial Monitor window will appear on the next line.

You then create a new char data type called parameter

```
Char* parameter;
```

and as you are using this variable to access elements of the data array, it must be the same type, hence the * symbol. You cannot pass data from one data type variable to another; the data must be converted first. This variable is another example of one that has *local scope*. It can be seen only by the code within this function. If you try to access the parameter variable outside of the `splitString()` function, you will get an error.

You then use a strtok command, which is a very useful command for manipulating text strings. Strtok gets its name from String and Token because its purpose is to split a string using tokens. In your case, the token it is looking for is a space or a comma; it's being used to split text strings into smaller strings.

You pass the data array to the strtok command as the first argument and the tokens (enclosed within quotes) as the second argument. Hence

```
parameter = strtok (data, " ,");
```

and it splits the string at that point, which is a space or a comma.

So, if your text string is

```
R127 G56 B98
```

then after this statement the value of parameter will be

```
R127
```

because the strtok command splits the string up to the first occurrence of a space of a comma.

After you have set the d variable parameter to the part of the text string you want to strip out (i.e. the bit up to the first space or comma), you then enter a while loop with the condition that the parameter is not empty (i.e. you haven't reached the end of the string):

```
while (parameter != NULL) {
```

Within the loop we call our second function:

```
setLED(parameter);
```

(We will look at this one in detail later.) Then you set the variable parameter to the next part of the string up to the next space or comma. You do this by passing to strtok a NULL parameter, like so:

```
parameter = strtok (NULL, " ,");
```

This tells the strtok command to carry on where it last left off.

So this whole part of the function

```
char* parameter;
parameter = strtok (data, " ,");
while (parameter != NULL) {
        setLED(parameter);
        parameter = strtok (NULL, " ,");
  }
```

is simply stripping out each dpart of the text string that is separated by spaces or commas and sending that part of the string to the next function called `setLED()`.

The final part of this function simply fills the buffer array with NULL character, which is done with the /0 symbol, and then flushes the serial data out of the serial buffer so that it's ready for the next set of data to be entered:

```
// Clear the text and serial buffers
for (int x=0; x<16; x++) {
     buffer[x]='\0';
}
Serial.flush();
```

The `setLED()` function is going to take each part of the text string and set the corresponding LED to the color you have chosen. So, if the text string you enter is

```
G125 B55
```

the `splitString()`function splits that into the two separate components

```
G125
B55
```

and send that shortened text string onto the `setLED()` function, which will read it, decide what LED you have chosen, and set it to the corresponding brightness value.

Let's go back to the second function called `setLED()`:

```
void setLED(char* data) {
        if ((data[0] == 'r') || (data[0] == 'R')) {
                int Ans = strtol(data+1, NULL, 10);
                Ans = constrain(Ans,0,255);
                analogWrite(RedPin, Ans);
                Serial.print("Red is set to: ");
                Serial.println(Ans);
        }
        if ((data[0] == 'g') || (data[0] == 'G')) {
                int Ans = strtol(data+1, NULL, 10);
                Ans = constrain(Ans,0,255);
                analogWrite(GreenPin, Ans);
                Serial.print("Green is set to: ");
                Serial.println(Ans);
        }
```

```
        if ((data[0] == 'b') || (data[0] == 'B')) {
                int Ans = strtol(data+1, NULL, 10);
                Ans = constrain(Ans,0,255);
                analogWrite(BluePin, Ans);
                Serial.print("Blue is set to: ");
                Serial.println(Ans);
        }
}
```

This function contains three similar `if` statements, so let's pick one to examine:

```
if ((data[0] == 'r') || (data[0] == 'R')) {
    int Ans = strtol(data+1, NULL, 10);
    Ans = constrain(Ans,0,255);
    analogWrite(RedPin, Ans);
    Serial.print("Red is set to: ");
    Serial.println(Ans);
  }
```

The `if` statement checks that the first character in the string data[0] is either the letter r or R (upper case and lower case characters are totally different as far as C is concerned. You use the logical OR command (the symbol is ||) to check if the letter is an r OR an R, as either will do.

If it is an r or an R, the `if` statement knows you wish to change the brightness of the red LED, and the code within executes. First, you declare an integer called Ans (which has scope local to the setLED function only) and use the strtol (String to long integer) command to convert the characters after the letter R to an integer. The strtol command takes three parameters: the string you are passing it, a pointer to the character after the integer (which you won't use because you have already stripped the string using the strtok command and hence pass a NULL character), and the base (in your case, it's base 10 because you are using normal decimal numbers as opposed to binary, octal or hexadecimal, which would be base 2, 8 and 16 respectively). In summary, you declare an integer and set it to the value of the text string after the letter R (or the number bit).

Next, you use the constrain command to make sure that Ans goes from 0 to 255 and no more. You then carry out an analogWrite command to the red pin and send it the value of Ans. The code then sends out "Red is set to: " followed by the value of Ans back to the Serial Monitor. The other two `if` statements do exactly the same but for the green and blue LEDs.

You have covered a lot of ground and many new concepts in this project. To make sure you understand exactly what is going on in this code, I have set the project code (which is in C, remember) side by side with pseudo-code (essentially, the computer language described in more detail via whole words and thoughts). See Table 3-7 for the comparison.

Table 3-7. An explanation for the code in Project 10 using pseudo-code

The C Programming Language	Pseudo-Code
`// Project 10 - Serial controlled RGB Lamp`	A comment with the project number and name
`char buffer[18];`	Declare a character array of 18 letters
`int red, green, blue;`	Declare 3 integers called red, green and blue
`int RedPin = 11;`	An integer assigning a certain pin to the Red LED
`int GreenPin = 10;`	An integer assigning a certain pin to the Green LED
`int BluePin = 9;`	An integer assigning a certain pin to the Blue LED
`void setup()` `{`	The setup function
`Serial.begin(9600);`	Set serial comms to run at 9600 chars per second
`Serial.flush();`	Flush the serial line
`pinMode(RedPin, OUTPUT);`	Set the red led pin to be an output pin
`pinMode(GreenPin, OUTPUT);`	Same for green
`pinMode(BluePin, OUTPUT);` `}`	And blue
`void loop()` `{`	The main program loop
`if (Serial.available() > 0) {`	If data is sent down the serial line...
`int index=0;`	Declare integer called index and set to 0
`delay(100); // let the buffer fill up`	Wait 100 millseconds
`int numChar = Serial.available();`	Set numChar to the incoming data from serial
`if (numChar>15) {`	If numchar is greater than 15 characters...
`numChar=15;` `}`	Make it 15 and no more
`while (numChar--) {`	While numChar is not zero (subtract 1 from it)
`buffer[index++] = Serial.read();` `}`	Set element[index] to value read in (add 1)
`splitString(buffer);` `}` `}`	Call splitString function and send it data in buffer
`void splitString(char* data) {`	The splitstring function references buffer data
`Serial.print("Data entered: ");`	Print "Data entered: "
`Serial.println(data);`	Print value of data and then drop down a line
`char* parameter;`	Declare char data type parameter
`parameter = strtok (data, " ,");`	Set it to text up to the first space or comma
`while (parameter != NULL) {`	While contents of parameter are not empty..
`setLED(parameter);`	Call the setLED function
`parameter = strtok (NULL, " ,");` `}`	Set parameter to next part of text string
`// Clear the text and serial buffers`	Another comment
`for (int x=0; x<16; x++) {`	Do the next line 16 times
`buffer[x]='\0';` `}` `Serial.flush();` `}`	

```
void setLED(char* data) {
  if ((data[0] == 'r') || (data[0] == 'R')) {
         int Ans = strtol(data+1, NULL, 10);
         Ans = constrain(Ans,0,255);
         analogWrite(RedPin, Ans);
         Serial.print("Red is set to: ");
         Serial.println(Ans);
  }
  if ((data[0] == 'g') || (data[0] == 'G')) {
         int Ans = strtol(data+1, NULL, 10);
         Ans = constrain(Ans,0,255);
         analogWrite(GreenPin, Ans);
         Serial.print("Green is set to: ");
         Serial.println(Ans);
  }
  if ((data[0] == 'b') || (data[0] == 'B')) {
         int Ans = strtol(data+1, NULL, 10);
         Ans = constrain(Ans,0,255);
         analogWrite(BluePin, Ans);
         Serial.print("Blue is set to: ");
         Serial.println(Ans);
  }
}
```

```
Set each element of buffer to NULL (empty)


Flush the serial comms


A function called setLED is passed buffer
If first letter is r or R...
Set integer Ans to number in next part of text
Make sure it is between 0 and 255
Write that value out to the red pin
Print out "Red is set to: "
And then the value of Ans

If first letter is g or G...
Set integer Ans to number in next part of text
Make sure it is between 0 and 255
Write that value out to the green pin
Print out "Green is set to: "
And then the value of Ans

If first letter is b or B...
Set integer Ans to number in next part of text
Make sure it is between 0 and 255
Write that value out to the blue pin
Print out "Blue is set to: "
And then the value of Ans
```

Hopefully, the pseudo-code will help you understand exactly what is going on within the code.

Summary

Chapter 3 introduced many new commands and concepts in programming. You've learned about arrays and how to use them, how to read analog values from a pin, how to use PWM pins, and the basics of serial communications. Knowing how to send and read data across a serial line means you can use your Arduino to communicate with all kinds of serial devices and other devices with simple communication protocols. You will revisit serial communications later in this book.

Subjects and concepts covered in Chapter 3:

- Arrays and how to use them
- What a potentiometer (or variable resistor) is and how to use it
- Reading voltage values from an analog input pin
- How to use the mathematical sine (`sin`) function
- Converting degrees to radians
- The concept of casting a variable to a different type
- Pulse Width Modulation (PWM) and how to use it with `analogWrite()`

- Creating colored lights using different RGB values
- Generating random numbers using `random()` and `randomSeed()`
- How various lighting effects can be generated with the same circuit but different code
- The concept of serial communications
- Setting the serial baud rate using `Serial.begin()`
- Sending commands using the Serial Monitor
- Using an array to create text strings
- Flushing the serial buffer using `Serial.flush`
- Checking if data is sent over the serial line using `Serial.available`
- Creating a loop while a condition is met with the `while()` command
- Reading data from the serial line using `Serial.read()`
- The basic concept of pointers
- Sending data to the Serial Monitor using `Serial.print()` or `Serial.println()`
- Manipulating text strings using the `strtok()` function
- Converting a string to a long integer using `strtol()`
- Constraining a variables value using the `constrain()` function

CHAPTER 4

■ ■ ■

Simple Sounders and Sensors

This chapter is going to get noisy. You're going to attach a piezo sounder to your Arduino in order to add alarms, warning beeps, alert notifications, etc. to the device you are creating. As of version 0018 of the Arduino IDE, tones can be added easily thanks to a new command. You will also find out how to use the piezo as a sensor and learn how to read voltages from it. Finally, you'll learn about light sensors.

Let's start with a simple car alarm and the `tone()` command to make sounds from your Arduino.

Project 11 – Piezo Sounder Alarm

By connecting a piezo sounder to a digital output pin, you can create a wailing alarm sound. It's the same principle that you used in Project 7 when creating a pulsating lamp via a sine wave, but this time you replace the LED with a piezo sounder or piezo disc.

Parts Required

Piezo Sounder (or piezo disc)

2-Way Screw Terminal

Connect It Up

First, make sure your Arduino is powered off by unplugging it from the USB cable. Now take the piezo sounder and screw its wires into the screw terminal. Connect the screw terminal to the breadboard and then connect it to the Arduino, as in Figure 4-1. Now, connect your Arduino back to the USB cable and power it up.

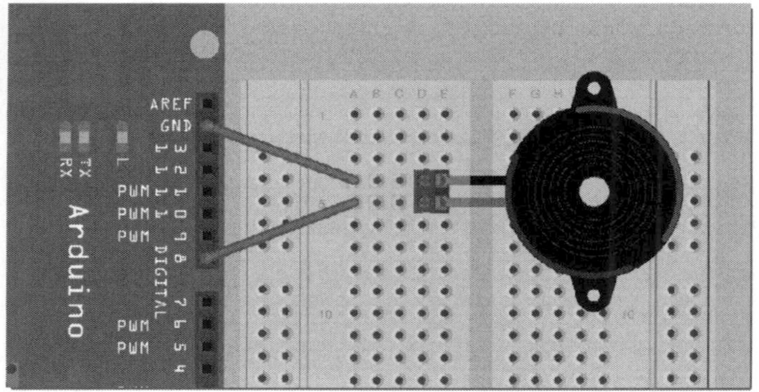

Figure 4-1. The circuit for Project 11 – Piezo Sounder Alarm

Enter the Code

Open up your Arduino IDE and type in the code from Listing 4-1.

Listing 4-1. Code for Project 11

```
// Project 11 - Piezo Sounder Alarm

float sinVal;
int toneVal;

void setup() {
        pinMode(8, OUTPUT);
}

void loop() {
        for (int x=0; x<180; x++) {
                // convert degrees to radians then obtain sin value
                sinVal = (sin(x*(3.1412/180)));
                // generate a frequency from the sin value
                toneVal = 2000+(int(sinVal*1000));
                tone(8, toneVal);
                delay(2);
        }
}
```

After you upload the code, there will be a slight delay and then your piezo will start emitting sounds. If everything is working as planned, you'll hear a rising and falling siren type alarm, similar to a car alarm. The code for Project 11 is almost identical to the code for Project 7; let's see how it works.

Project 11 – Piezo Sounder Alarm – Code Overview

First, you set up two variables:

```
float sinVal;
int toneVal;
```

The `sinVal` float variable holds the sin value that causes the tone to rise and fall in the same way that the lamp in Project 7 pulsated. The `toneVal` variable takes the value in `sinVal` and converts it to the frequency you require.

In the setup function, you set Digital Pin 8 to an output:

```
void setup() {
        pinMode(8, OUTPUT);
}
```

In the main loop, you set a `for` loop to run from 0 to 179 to ensure that the sin value does not go into the negative (as you did in Project 7):

```
for (int x=0; x<180; x++) {
```

You convert the value of x into radians (again, as in Project 7):

```
sinVal = (sin(x*(3.1412/180)));
```

Then that value is converted into a frequency suitable for the alarm sound:

```
toneVal = 2000+(int(sinVal*1000));
```

You take 2000 and add the sinVal multiplied by 1000. This supplies a good range of frequencies for the rising and falling tone of the sine wave.

Next, you use the `tone()` command to generate the frequency at the piezo sounder:

```
tone(8, toneVal);
```

The `tone()` command requires either two or three parameters, thus:

```
tone(pin, frequency)
tone(pin, frequency, duration)
```

The pin is the digital pin being used to output to the piezo and the frequency is the frequency of the tone in hertz. There is also the optional duration parameter in milliseconds for the length of the tone. If no duration is specified, the tone will keep on playing until you play a different tone or you use the `noTone(pin)` command to cease the tone generation on the specified pin.

Finally, you run a delay of 2 milliseconds between the frequency changes to ensure the sine wave rises and falls at the speed you require:

```
delay(2);
```

If you are wondering why you didn't put the 2 milliseconds into the duration parameter of the `tone()` command like this

```
tone(8, toneVal, 2);
```

it's because the `for` loop is so short that it will change the frequency in less than 2 milliseconds anyway, thus rendering the duration parameter useless. Therefore, a delay of 2 milliseconds is put in after the tone is generated to ensure that it plays for at least 2 milliseconds before the `for` loop repeats and the tone changes again.

You could use this alarm generation principle later when you learn how to connect sensors to your Arduino. Then you could activate an alarm when a sensor threshold has been reached, such as if someone gets too close to an ultrasonic detector or if a temperature gets too high.

If you change the values of 2000 and 1000 in the `toneVal` calculation and the length of the delay, you can generate different alarm sounds. Have some fun and see what sounds you can make!

Project 11 – Piezo Sounder Alarm – Hardware Overview

There are two new components in this project: a screw terminal and a piezo sounder. You use the screw terminal because the wires from your piezo sounder or disc are too thin and soft to insert into the breadboard. The screw terminal has pins on it that allow you to push it into a breadboard.

The piezo sounder or piezo disc (see Figure 4-2) is a simple device made up of a thin layer of ceramic bonded to a metallic disc.

Figure 4-2. *A piezo disc and Arduino (Image courtesy of Patrick H. Lauke/splintered.co.uk)*

Piezoelectric materials, which are made up of crystals and ceramics, have the ability to produce electricity when mechanical stress is applied to them. The effect finds useful applications such as the production and detection of sound, generation of high voltages, electronic frequency generation, microbalances, and ultra fine focusing of optical assemblies.

The effect is also reversible; if an electric field is applied across the piezoelectric material, it will cause the material to change shape (by as much as 0.1 percent in some cases).

To produce sounds from a piezo disc, an electric field is turned on and off very fast to make the material change shape; this causes an audible "click" as the disc pops out and back in again (like a tiny drum). By changing the frequency of the pulses, the disc will deform hundreds or thousands of times per second, causing the buzzing sound. By changing the frequency of the clicks and the time in between them, specific notes can be produced.

You can also use the piezo's ability to produce an electric field to measure movement or vibrations. In fact, piezo discs are used as contact microphones for guitars or drum kits. You will use this feature of a piezo disc in Project 13 when you make a knock sensor.

Project 12 – Piezo Sounder Melody Player

Rather than using the piezo to make annoying alarm sounds, why not use it to play a melody? You are going to get your Arduino to play the chorus of "Puff the Magic Dragon." Leave the circuit exactly the same as in Project 11; you are just changing the code.

Enter the Code

Open up your Arduino IDE and type in the code from Listing 4-2.

Listing 4-2. *Code for Project 12*

```
// Project 12 - Piezo Sounder Melody Player

#define NOTE_C3  131
#define NOTE_CS3 139
#define NOTE_D3  147
#define NOTE_DS3 156
#define NOTE_E3  165
#define NOTE_F3  175
#define NOTE_FS3 185
#define NOTE_G3  196
#define NOTE_GS3 208
#define NOTE_A3  220
#define NOTE_AS3 233
#define NOTE_B3  247
#define NOTE_C4  262
#define NOTE_CS4 277
#define NOTE_D4  294
#define NOTE_DS4 311
#define NOTE_E4  330
#define NOTE_F4  349
#define NOTE_FS4 370
#define NOTE_G4  392
#define NOTE_GS4 415
```

```
#define NOTE_A4  440
#define NOTE_AS4 466
#define NOTE_B4  494

#define WHOLE 1
#define HALF 0.5
#define QUARTER 0.25
#define EIGHTH 0.125
#define SIXTEENTH 0.0625

int tune[] = { NOTE_C4, NOTE_C4, NOTE_C4, NOTE_C4, NOTE_C4, NOTE_B3, NOTE_G3, NOTE_A3,↵
 NOTE_C4, NOTE_C4, NOTE_G3, NOTE_G3, NOTE_F3, NOTE_F3, NOTE_G3, NOTE_F3, NOTE_E3, NOTE_G3,↵
 NOTE_C4, NOTE_C4, NOTE_C4, NOTE_C4, NOTE_A3, NOTE_B3, NOTE_C4, NOTE_D4};

float duration[] = { EIGHTH, QUARTER+EIGHTH, SIXTEENTH, QUARTER, QUARTER, HALF, HALF,↵
 HALF, QUARTER, QUARTER, HALF+QUARTER, QUARTER, QUARTER, QUARTER, QUARTER+EIGHTH, EIGHTH,↵
 QUARTER, QUARTER, QUARTER, EIGHTH, EIGHTH, QUARTER, QUARTER, QUARTER, QUARTER,↵
 HALF+QUARTER};

int length;

void setup() {
        pinMode(8, OUTPUT);
        length = sizeof(tune) / sizeof(tune[0]);
}

void loop() {
        for (int x=0; x<length; x++) {
                tone(8, tune[x]);
                delay(1500 * duration[x]);
                noTone(8);
        }
        delay(5000);
}
```

After you upload the code, there will be a slight delay and then your piezo will start to play a tune. Hopefully you will recognize it as part of the chorus of "Puff the Magic Dragon." Now, let's look at the new concepts from this project.

Project 12 – Piezo Sounder Melody Player – Code Overview

The first thing you see when looking at the code for Project 12 is the long list of define directives. The *define directive* is very simple and very useful. **#define** simply defines a value and its token. For example,

```
#define PI 3.14159265358979323846264338327950288419716939937510
```

will allow you to substitute PI in any calculation instead of having to type out pi to 50 decimal places. Another example,

```
#define TRUE  1
#define FALSE 0
```

means that you can put a TRUE or FALSE into your code instead of a 0 or a 1. This makes logical statements easier for a human to read.

Let's say that you wrote some code to display shapes on an LED dot matrix display and the resolution of the display was 8 x 32. You could create define directives for the height and width of the display thus:

```
#define DISPLAY_HEIGHT 8
#define DISPLAY_WIDTH 32
```

Now, whenever you refer to the height and width of the display in your code you can put DISPLAY_HEIGHT and DISPLAY_WIDTH instead of the numbers 8 and 32.

There are two main advantages to doing this instead of simply using the numbers. Firstly, the code becomes a lot easier to understand as you have changed the height and width values of the display into tokens that make these numbers clearer to a third party. Secondly, if you change your display at a later date to a larger resolution, say a 16 × 64 display, all you need to do is changed the two values in the define directives instead of having to change numbers in what could be hundreds of lines of code. By changing the values in the define directive at the start of the program the new values are automatically used throughout the rest of the code.

In Project 12, you create a whole set of define directives where the tokens are the notes C3 through to B4 and the values are the frequencies required to create that note. The first note of your melody is C4 and its corresponding frequency is 262 Hz. This is middle C on the musical scale. (Not all of the notes defined are used in your melody, but I have included them in case you wish to write your own tune.)

The next five define directives are for the note lengths. The notes can be a whole bar, half, quarter, eighth, or a sixteenth of a bar in length. The numbers are what we will use to multiply the length of the bar in milliseconds to get the length of each note. For example, a quarter note is 0.25 (or one quarter of one); therefore, multiply the length of the bar (in this case, 1500 milliseconds) by 0.25 to get the length of a quarter note:

1500 × QUARTER = 375 milliseconds

Define directives can also be used for creating macros; more on macros in a later chapter.

Next, you define an integer array called tune[] and fill it with the notes for "Puff the Magic Dragon" like so:

```
int tune[] = { NOTE_C4, NOTE_C4, NOTE_C4, NOTE_C4, NOTE_C4, NOTE_B3, NOTE_G3, NOTE_A3,↩
 NOTE_C4, NOTE_C4, NOTE_G3, NOTE_G3, NOTE_F3, NOTE_F3, NOTE_G3, NOTE_F3, NOTE_E3, NOTE_G3,↩
 NOTE_C4, NOTE_C4, NOTE_C4, NOTE_C4, NOTE_A3, NOTE_B3, NOTE_C4, NOTE_D4};
```

After that, you create another array, a float that will hold the duration of the each note as it is played:

```
float duration[] = { EIGHTH, QUARTER+EIGHTH, SIXTEENTH, QUARTER, QUARTER, HALF, HALF,↩
 HALF, QUARTER, QUARTER, HALF+QUARTER, QUARTER, QUARTER, QUARTER, QUARTER+EIGHTH, EIGHTH,↩
 QUARTER, QUARTER, QUARTER, EIGHTH, EIGHTH, QUARTER, QUARTER, QUARTER, QUARTER,↩
 HALF+QUARTER};
```

As you can see by looking at these arrays, the use of the define directives to define the notes and the note lengths makes reading and understanding the array a lot easier than if it were filled with a series of numbers. You then create an integer called length

```
int length;
```

which will be used to calculate and store the length of the array (i.e. the number of notes in the tune).

In your setup routine, you set Digital Pin 8 to an output

```
pinMode(8, OUTPUT);
```

then initialize the integer length with the number of notes in the array using the `sizeof()` function:

```
length = sizeof(tune) / sizeof(tune[0]);
```

The sizeof function returns the number of bytes in the parameter passed to it. On the Arduino, an integer is made up of two bytes. A *byte* is made up of 8 bits. (This is delving into the realm of binary arithmetic and for this project you do not need to worry about bits and bytes. You will come across them later in the book and all will be explained.) Your tune just happens to have 26 notes in it, so the `tunes[]` array has 26 elements. To calculate that we get the size (in bytes) of the entire array

```
sizeof(tune)
```

and divide that by the number of bytes in a single element

```
sizeof(tune[0])
```

which, in this case, this is equivalent to

```
26 / 2 = 13
```

If you replace the tune in the project with one of your own, length will be calculated as the number of notes in your tune.

The `sizeof()` function is useful in working out the lengths of different data types and is particularly useful if you were to port your code over to another device where the length of the datatypes may differ from those on the Arduino.

In the main loop, you set up a `for` loop that iterates the number of times there are notes in the melody

```
for (int x=0; x<length; x++) {
```

then play the next note in the `tune[]` array on Digital Pin 8

```
tone(8, tune[x]);
```

then wait the appropriate amount of time to let the note play

```
delay(1500 * duration[x]);
```

The delay is 1500 milliseconds multiplied by the note length (0.25 for a quarter note, 0.125 for an eighth note, etc.).

Before the next note is played you cease the tone generated on Digital Pin 8:

```
noTone(8);
```

This is to ensure that when two identical notes are played back to back they can be distinguished as individual notes. Without the `noTone()` function, the notes would merge into one long note instead.

Finally, after the `for` loop is complete, you run a delay of 5 seconds before repeating the melody over again:

```
delay(5000);
```

To create the notes for this tune, I found some public domain sheet music for "Puff the Magic Dragon" on the Internet and typed the notes into the `tune[]` array, followed by the note lengths in the `duration[]` array. Note that I have added note lengths to get dotted notes (e.g. `QUARTER+EIGHTH`). By doing something similar you can create any tune you want.

If you wish to speed up or slow down the pace of the tune, change the value of 1500 in the delay function to something higher or lower.

You can also replace the piezo in the circuit with a speaker or headphones, as long as you put a resistor in series with it to ensure that the maximum current for the speaker is not exceeded.

You are going to use the piezo disc for another purpose—its ability to produce a current when the disc is squeezed or knocked. Utilizing this feature, you are going to make a Knock Sensor in Project 13.

Project 13 – Piezo Knock Sensor

A piezo disc works when an electric current is passed over the ceramic material in the disc, causing it to change shape and hence make a sound (a click). The disc also works in reverse: when the disc is knocked or squeezed, the force on the material causes the generation of an electric current. You can read that current using the Arduino and you are going to do that now by making a Knock Sensor.

Parts Required

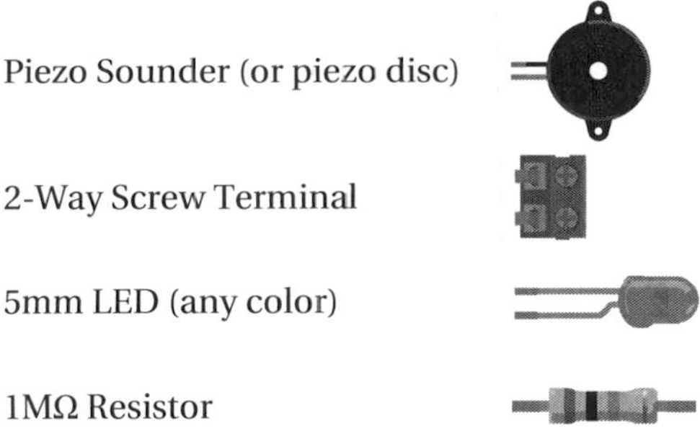

Connect It Up

First, make sure your Arduino is powered off by unplugging it from the USB cable. Then connect up your parts so you have the circuit in Figure 4-3. Note that a piezo disc works better for this project than a piezo sounder.

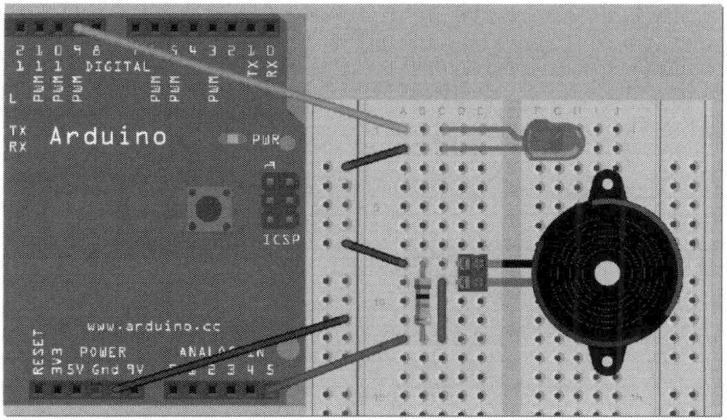

Figure 4-3. *The circuit for Project 13 – Piezo Knock Sensor*

Enter the Code

Open up your Arduino IDE and type in the code from Listing 4-3.

Listing 4-3. *Code for Project 13*

```
// Project 13 - Piezo Knock Sensor

int ledPin = 9; // LED on Digital Pin 9
int piezoPin = 5; // Piezo on Analog Pin 5
int threshold = 120; // The sensor value to reach before activation
int sensorValue = 0;  // A variable to store the value read from the sensor
float ledValue = 0; // The brightness of the LED


void setup() {
        pinMode(ledPin, OUTPUT); // Set the ledPin to an OUTPUT
        // Flash the LED twice to show the program has started
        digitalWrite(ledPin, HIGH); delay(150); digitalWrite(ledPin, LOW); delay(150);
        digitalWrite(ledPin, HIGH); delay(150); digitalWrite(ledPin, LOW); delay(150);
}
```

```
void loop() {
        sensorValue = analogRead(piezoPin);  // Read the value from the sensor
        if (sensorValue >= threshold) { // If knock detected set brightness to max
                ledValue = 255;
        }
        analogWrite(ledPin, int(ledValue) ); // Write brightness value to LED
        ledValue = ledValue - 0.05; // Dim the LED slowly
        if (ledValue <= 0) { ledValue = 0;}  // Make sure value does not go below zero
}
```

After you have uploaded your code, the LED will flash quickly twice to indicate that the program has started. You can now knock the sensor (place it flat on a surface first) or squeeze it between your fingers. Every time the Arduino detects a knock or squeeze, the LED will light up and then gently fade back down to off. (Note that the threshold value in the code was set for the specific piezo disc I used when building the project. You may need to set this to a higher or lower value depending on the type and size of piezo you have used for your project. Lower is more sensitive and higher is less.)

Project 13 – Piezo Knock Sensor – Code Overview

There aren't any new code commands in this project, but I'll go over how it works anyway.

First, set up the necessary variables for your program; these are self explanatory:

```
int ledPin = 9; // LED on Digital Pin 9
int piezoPin = 5; // Piezo on Analog Pin 5
int threshold = 120; // The sensor value to reach before activation
int sensorValue = 0;  // A variable to store the value read from the sensor
float ledValue = 0; // The brightness of the LED
```

In the setup function, the ledPin is set to an output and, as noted, the LED is flashed quickly twice as a visual indication that the program has started working:

```
void setup() {
        pinMode(ledPin, OUTPUT);
        digitalWrite(ledPin, HIGH); delay(150); digitalWrite(ledPin, LOW); delay(150);
        digitalWrite(ledPin, HIGH); delay(150); digitalWrite(ledPin, LOW); delay(150);
}
```

In the main loop, you first read the analog value from Analog Pin 5, which the piezo is attached to:

```
sensorValue = analogRead(piezoPin);
```

Then the code checks if that value is greater than or equal to (>=) the threshold you have set, i.e. if it really is a knock or squeeze. (The piezo is very sensitive as you will see if you set the threshold to a very low value). If yes, then it sets ledValue to 255, which is the maximum voltage out of Digital PWM Pin 9:

```
if (sensorValue >= threshold) {
        ledValue = 255;
}
```

You then write that value to Digital PWM Pin 9. Because **ledValue** is a float, you cast it to an integer, as the analogWrite function can only accept an integer and not a floating value

```
analogWrite(ledPin, int(ledValue) );
```

and then reduce the value of **ledValue**, which is a float, by 0.05

```
ledValue = ledValue - 0.05;
```

You want the LED to dim gently, hence you use a float instead of an integer to store the brightness value of the LED. This way you can deduct its value by a small amount (in this case 0.05), so it will take a little while as the main loop repeats for the value of **ledValue** to reach zero. If you want the LED to dim slower or faster, increase or decrease this value.

Finally, you don't want **ledValue** to go below zero as Digital PWM Pin 9 can only output a value from 0 to 255, so you check if it is smaller or equal to zero, and if so, change it back to zero:

```
if (ledValue <= 0) { ledValue = 0;}
```

The main loop then repeats, dimming the LED slightly each time until the LED goes off or another knock is detected and the brightness is set back to maximum.

Now let's introduce a new sensor, the Light Dependent Resistor or LDR.

Project 14 – Light Sensor

This project introduces a new component known as a Light Dependent Resistor, or LDR. As the name implies, the device is a resistor that depends on light. In a dark environment, the resistor has a very high resistance. As photons (light) land on the detector, the resistance decreases. The more light, the lower the resistance. By reading the value from the sensor, you can detect if it is light, dark, or anywhere between. In this project, you use an LDR to detect light and a piezo sounder to give audible feedback of the amount of light detected.

This setup could be used as an alarm that indicates when a door has been opened, for example. Alternatively, you could use it to create a musical instrument similar to a theremin.

Parts Required

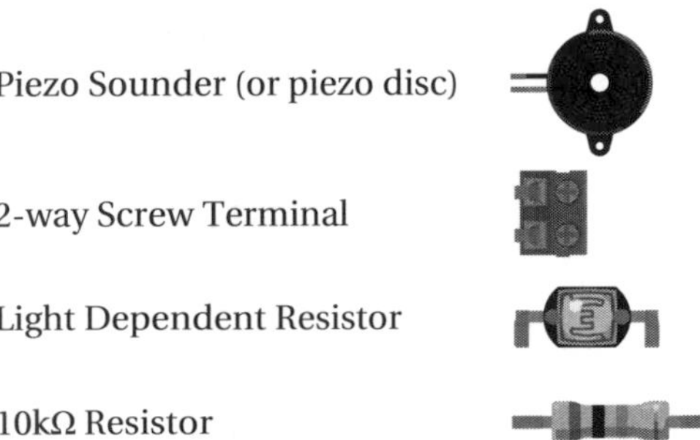

Connect It Up

First, make sure your Arduino is powered off by unplugging it from the USB cable. Then connect up your parts so you have the circuit shown in Figure 4-3. Check all of your connections before reconnecting the power to the Arduino.

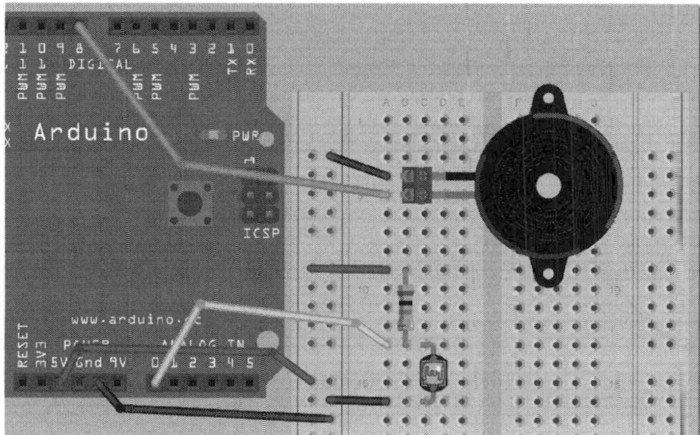

Figure 4-4. *The circuit for Project 14 – Light Sensor*

The LDR can be inserted any way because it does not have polarity. I found a 10kΩ resistor worked well for my LDR but you may need to try different resistor settings until you find one suitable for your LDR. A value between 1kΩ and 10kΩ should do the trick. Having a selection of different common resistor values in your component box will always come in handy.

Enter the Code

Now fire up your Arduino IDE and enter the short and simple code in Listing 4-4.

Listing 4-4. *Code for Project 13*

```
// Project 14 - Light Sensor

int piezoPin = 8;  // Piezo on Pin 8
int ldrPin = 0;    // LDR on Analog Pin 0
int ldrValue = 0;  // Value read from the LDR

void setup() {
  // nothing to do here
}
```

```
void loop() {
        ldrValue = analogRead(ldrPin); // read the value from the LDR
        tone(piezoPin,1000); // play a 1000Hz tone from the piezo
        delay(25);  // wait a bit
        noTone(piezoPin);  // stop the tone
        delay(ldrValue); // wait the amount of milliseconds in ldrValue
}
```

When you upload this code to the Arduino, the Arduino makes short beeps. The gap between the beeps will be long if the LDR is in the shade and will be short if bright light shines on the LDR, giving it a Geiger counter type effect. You may find it more practical to solder a set of long wires to the LDR to allow you to keep your breadboard and Arduino on the table while moving the LDR around to point it at dark and light areas. Alternatively, shine a flashlight on the sensor and move it around.

The code for Project 14 is very simple and you should be able to work out how it works yourself without any help. I will, however, show you how an LDR works and why the additional resistor is important.

Project 14 – Light Sensor – Hardware Overview

The new component in this project is a Light Dependent Resistor (LDR), otherwise known as a CdS (Cadmium-Sulfide) or a photoresistor. LDRs come in and shapes and sizes (see Figure 4-5) and in different ranges of resistance.

Figure 4-5. *Different kinds of LDR (image by cultured_society2nd)*

Each of the legs on the LDR goes to an electrode. Between a darker material, making a squiggly line between the electrodes, is the photoconductive material. The component has a transparent plastic or glass coating. When light hits the photoconductive material, it loses its resistance, allowing more current to flow between the electrodes. LDRs can be used in all kinds of interesting projects; for example, you could fire a laser into an LDR and detect when a person breaks the beam, triggering an alarm or a shutter on a camera.

The next new concept in your circuit is a voltage divider (also known as a potential divider). This is where the resistor comes in. By using two resistors and taking the voltage across just one of them you can reduce the voltage going into the circuit. In your case, you have a resistor of a fixed value (10kΩ or thereabouts) and variable resistor in the form of a LDR. Let's take a look at a standard voltage divider circuit using resistors and see how it works. Figure 4-6 shows a voltage divider using two resistors.

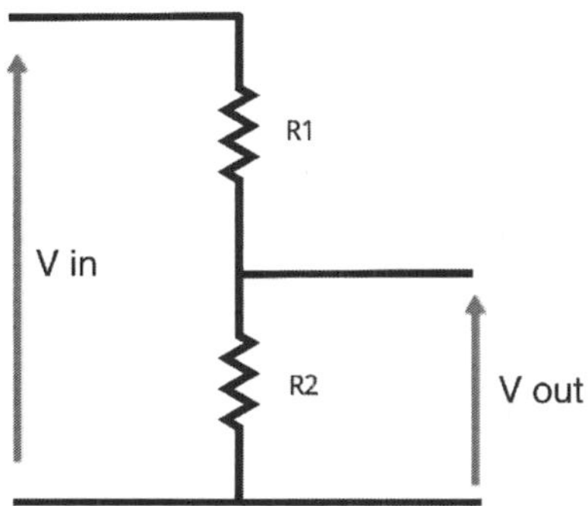

Figure 4-6. *A voltage divider*

The voltage in (Vin) is connected across both resistors. When you measure the voltage across one of the resistors (Vout) it will be less (divided). The formula for working out what the voltage at Vout comes out when measured across R2 is:

$$\text{Vout} = \frac{R2}{R2 + R1} \times \text{Vin}$$

So, if you have 100Ω resistors (or 0.1kΩ) for both R1 and R2 and 5v going into Vin, your formula is:

$$\frac{0.1}{0.1 + 0.1} \times 5 = 2.5 \text{ volts}$$

Let's do it again with 470Ω resistors:

$$\frac{0.47}{0.47 + 0.47} \times 5 = 2.5 \text{ volts}$$

Again, you get 2.5 volts. This demonstrates that the value of the resistors is not important, but the ratio between them is. Let's try a 1kΩ and a 500Ω resistor:

$$\frac{0.5}{0.5 + 1} \times 5 = 1.66 \text{ volts}$$

With the bottom resistor half the value of the top one, you get 1.66 volts, which is a third of the voltage going in. Let's make the bottom resistor twice the value of the top at 2kΩ

$$\frac{2}{2+1} \times 5 = 3.33 \text{ volts}$$

which is two-thirds of the voltage going in. So, let's apply this to the LDR. You can presume that the LDR has a range of around 10kΩ when in the dark and 1kΩ in bright light. Table 4-1 shows what voltages you will get out of your circuit as the resistance changes.

Table 4-1. *Vout values for a LDR with 5v as Vin*

R1	R2 (LDR)	Vout	Brightness
10kΩ	100kΩ	4.54v Dark	est
10kΩ	73kΩ	4.39v 25%	
10kΩ	45kΩ	4.09v 50%	
10kΩ	28kΩ	3.68v 75%	
10kΩ	10kΩ	2.5v Bri	ghtest

As you can see, as the brightness increases, the voltage at Vout decreases. As a result, the value you read at the sensor gets less and the delay after the beep gets shorter, causing the beeps to occur more frequently. If you were to switch the resistor and LDR, the voltage would increase as more light fell onto the LDR. Either way will work; it just depends how you want your sensor to be read.

Summary

In Chapter 6, you learned how to make music, alarm sounds, warning beeps, etc, from your Arduino. These sounds have many useful applications. You can, for example, make your own alarm clock. By using a piezo sounder in reverse to detect voltages from it and use that effect to detect a knock or pressure on the disc, you can make a musical instrument. Finally, by using an LDR to detect light, you can turn on a night light when ambient light falls below a certain threshold.

Subjects and Concepts covered in Chapter 4:

- What a piezoelectric transducer is and how it works
- How to create sounds using the `tone()` function
- How to stop tone generation using the `noTone()` function
- The `#define` command and how it makes code easier to debug and understand
- Obtaining the size of an array (in bytes) using the `sizeof()` function
- What an LDR (Light Dependent Resistor) is, how it works, and how to read values from it
- The concept of voltage dividers and how to use them

CHAPTER 5

■ ■ ■

Driving a DC Motor

Now it's time to control a DC motor. If you ever plan on building a robot or any moving device, the skills you are about to learn will be essential. Driving a motor requires currents higher than the Arduino can safely provide from its outputs, so you will need to make use of transistors to ensure that you have enough current for the motor and diodes for protection of the Arduino. The hardware overview will explain how these work.

For your first project, you will control a motor using a very simple method. Then you'll go on to use the very popular L293D Motor Driver chip. Later in the book you'll learn how to use these to control a stepper motor.

Project 15 – Simple Motor Control

First, you're going to simply control the speed of a DC motor in one direction, using a power transistor, diode, external power supply (to power the motor), and a potentiometer (to control the speed). Any suitable NPN power transistor designed for high current loads can replace the TIP120 transistor.

The external power supply can be a set of batteries or a "wall wart" style external DC power supply. The power source must have enough voltage and current to drive the motor. The voltage must not exceed that required by the motor. For my testing purposes, I used a DC power supply that provided 5v at 500mA, which was enough for the 5v DC motor I was using. Note that if you use a power supply with voltage higher than the motor can handle, you may damage it permanently.

Parts Required

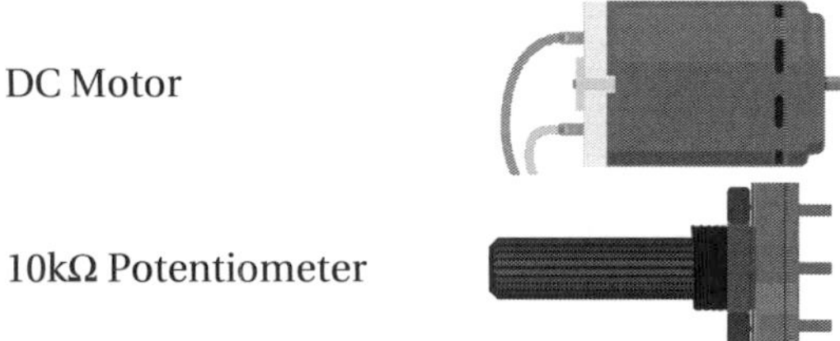

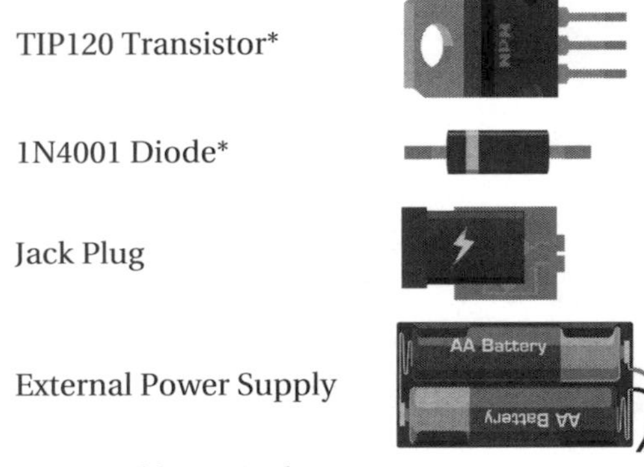

**or suitable equivalent*

Connect It Up

First, make sure your Arduino is powered off by unplugging it from the USB cable. Now, take the required parts and connect them as shown in Figure 5-1. It is essential that you check and double check that all of your connections are as they should be before supplying power to the circuit. Failure to do so may result in damage to the components or the Arduino. The diode plays an essential role in protecting the Arduino from back EMF, which I will explain later.

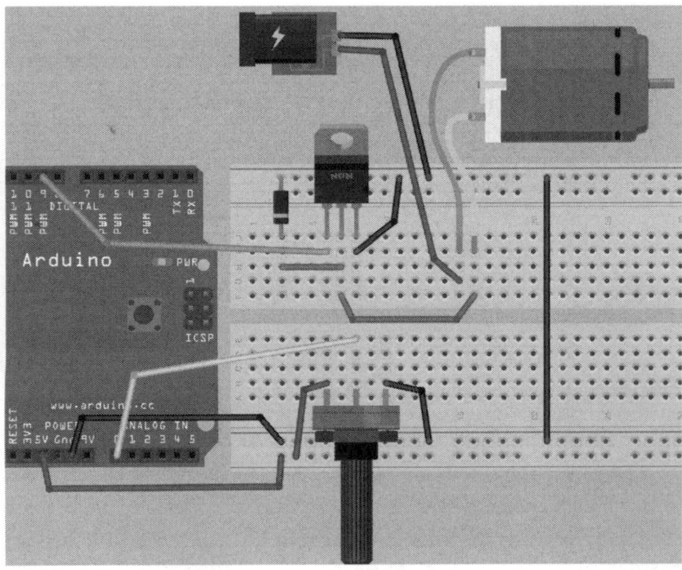

Figure 5-1. *The circuit for Project 15 – Simple Motor Control*

Enter The Code

Open up your Arduino IDE and type in the code from Listing 5-1. Before uploading your code, disconnect the external power supply to the motor and ensure the potentiometer is turned clockwise all the way. Now upload the code to the Arduino.

***Listing 5-1.** Code for Project 15*

```
// Project 15 - Simple Motor Control

int potPin = 0;           // Analog in 0 connected to the potentiometer
int transistorPin = 9;     // PWM Pin 9 connected to the base of the transistor
int potValue = 0;         // value returned from the potentiometer

void setup() {
  // set  the transistor pin as output:
  pinMode(transistorPin, OUTPUT);
}

void loop() {
  // read the potentiometer, convert it to 0 - 255:
  potValue = analogRead(potPin) / 4;
  // use that to control the transistor:
  analogWrite(transistorPin, potValue);
}
```

Once the code is uploaded, connect the external power supply. You can now turn the potentiometer to control the speed of the motor.

Project 15 – Simple Motor Control – Code Overview

First, declare the three variables that will hold the value for the Analog Pin connected to the potentiometer, the PWM pin connected to the base of the transistor, and one to hold the value read back from the potentiometer from Analog Pin 0:

```
int potPin = 0;           // Analog in 0 connected to the potentiometer
int transistorPin = 9     // PWM Pin 9 connected to the base of the transistor
int potValue = 0;         // value returned from the potentiometer
```

In the `setup()` function, you set the pinmode of the transistor pin to output:

```
void setup() {
  // set  the transistor pin as output:
  pinMode(transistorPin, OUTPUT);
}
```

In the main loop, potValue is set to the value read in from Analog Pin 0 (the potPin) and then divided by 4:

```
potValue = analogRead(potPin) / 4;
```

You need to divide the value read in by 4 as the analog value will range from 0 for 0 volts to 1023 for 5 volts. The value you need to write out to the transistor pin can only range from 0 to 255, so you divide the value of analog pin 0 (max 1023) by 4 to give the maximum value of 255 for setting the Digital Pin 9 (using analogWrite, as you are using PWM).

The code then writes out to the transistor pin the value of the pot:

```
analogWrite(transistorPin, potValue);
```

In other words, when you rotate the potentiometer, different values ranging from 0 to 1023 are read in; these are converted to the range 0 to 255. Then that value is written out (via PWM) to Digital Pin 11, which changes the speed of the DC motor. Turn the pot all the way to the right and the motor goes off, turn it to the left and it speeds up until it reaches maximum speed. The code is very simple and you have learned nothing new.

Let's now take a look at the hardware used in this project and see how it all works.

Project 15 – Simple Motor Control – Hardware Overview

The circuit is essentially split into two sections. Section 1 is the potentiometer, which is connected to 5v and Ground with the centre pin going into Analog Pin 0. As the potentiometer is rotated, the resistance changes to allow voltages from 0 to 5v to come out of the centre pin, where the value is read using Analog Pin 0.

The second section is what controls the power to the motor. The digital pins on the Arduino give out a maximum of 40mA (milliamps). A DC Motor may require around 500mA to operate at full speed; this is obviously too much for the Arduino. If you were to try to drive the motor directly from a pin on the Arduino, serious and permanent damage could occur.

Therefore, you need to find a way to supply it with a higher current. The answer is to take power from an external power supply, which will supply enough current to power the motor. You could use the 5v output from the Arduino, which can provide up to 800mA when connected to an eternal power supply. However, Arduino boards are expensive and it is all too easy to damage them when connecting them up to high current sources such as DC motors. So play it safe and use an external power supply. Also, your motor may require 9v or 12v or higher amperages and this is beyond anything the Arduino can supply.

Note also that this project controls the speed of the motor, so you need a way to control that voltage to speed up or slow down the motor. This is where the TIP-120 transistor comes in.

Transistors

A transistor is essentially a digital switch. It can also be used as a power amplifier. In your circuit, you'll use it as a switch. The electronic symbol for a transistor looks like Figure 5-2.

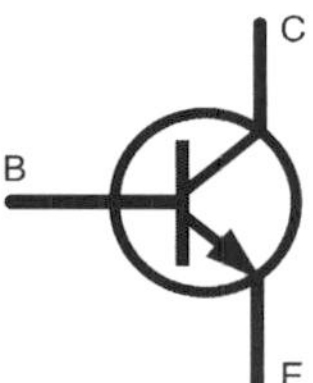

***Figure 5-2.** The symbol for an NPN transistor*

The transistor has 3 legs: the Base, the Collector, and the Emitter. These are marked as C, B and E on the diagram. In your circuit, you have up to 5 volts going into the Base via Digital Pin 9. The Collector is connected to one terminal on the motor. The Emitter is connected to Ground. Whenever you apply a voltage to the Base via Digital Pin 9, the transistor turns on, allowing current to flow through it between the Emitter and Collector and thus powering the motor that is connected in series with this circuit. By applying a small current at the Base, you can control a larger current between Emitter and Collector.

Transistors are the key components in just about any piece of modern electronic equipment. Many people consider transistors to be the greatest invention of the twentieth century. Desktop PC and laptop processors have between 300 million and 1 billion transistors.

In your case, you have used the transistor as a switch to turn on and off a higher voltage and current. When a current is applied at the base, the voltage applied at the Collector is turned on and allowed to flow between the Collector and Emitter. As you are pulsing your signal, the transistor is turned on and off many times per second; it is this pulsed current that controls the speed of the motor.

Motors

A motor is an electromagnet, and it has a magnetic field while power is supplied to it. When the power is removed, the magnetic field collapses; this collapsing field can produce a reverse voltage that goes back up its wiring. This could seriously damage your Arduino, and this is why the diode has been placed the wrong way around on the circuit. The white stripe on the diode normally goes to ground. Power will flow from the positive side to the negative side. As you have it the wrong way around, no power will flow down it at all. However, if the motor were to produce a "back EMF" (electromotive force) and send current back down the wire, the diode would act as a valve to prevent it from doing so. The diode in your circuit is therefore put in place to protect your Arduino.

If you were to connect a DC motor directly to a multimeter with no other components connected to it and then spin the shaft of the motor, you would see that the motor generates a current. This is exactly how wind turbines work. When you have the motor powered up and spinning and you then remove the power, the motor will keep on spinning under its own inertia until it comes to a stop. In that short time while the motor is spinning without power applied, it is generating a current. This is the aforementioned "back EMF." Again, the diode acts as a valve and ensures that the electricity does not flow back to the circuit and damage other components.

Diodes

Diodes are one-way valves. In exactly the same way that a non-return valve in a water pipe will allow water to flow in one direction but not in the other, the diode allows a current to flow in one direction but not the other. You came across diodes when you used LEDs. An LED has a polarity. You connect the positive terminal of the power to the long lead on the LED to make the LED turn on. By turning the LED around, the LED will not only fail to illuminate but will also prevent electricity from flowing across its terminals. The diode has a white band around it next to the negative lead. Imagine the white band as being a barrier. Electricity flows through the diode from the terminal that has no barrier. When you reverse the voltage and try to make it flow through the side that has the white band, the current will be stopped.

Diodes are essential in protecting circuits from a reverse voltage, such as if you connecting a power supply the wrong way around or if a voltage is reversed such as the back EMF in your circuit. Therefore, always try to use them in your circuits wherever there is a danger of the power being reversed either by user error or via phenomena such as back EMF.

Project 16 – Using an L293D Motor Driver IC

In the previous project, you used a transistor to control the motor. In this project, you are going to use a very popular motor driver IC called an L293D. The advantage of using this chip is that you can control two motors at the same time, plus you can control their direction. The chip can also be used to control a stepper motor, as you will find out in Project 28. (You can also use a pin-for-pin compatible chip known as the SN754410, which has a higher current rating.) Notice anything missing from the parts list? Diodes, perhaps? Not to worry; the IC has its own internal diodes, so you do not need one for this project.

Parts Required

Connect It Up

First, make sure your Arduino is powered off by unplugging it from the USB cable. Now, take the required parts and connect them as shown in Figure 5-3. Again, check the circuit thoroughly before powering it up. The L293D gets VERY hot when in use. Therefore, a heatsink is essential. Glue the heatsink to the top of the chip using a strong epoxy glue. The larger the heatsink, the better. Be warned that the temperature can get hot enough to melt the plastic on a breadboard or any wires touching it. Do not touch the heatsink as you may burn yourself. Do not leave the circuit powered up and unattended in case it overheats. It may be prudent to use stripboard instead of a breadboard for this project to save damaging your breadboard due to heat.

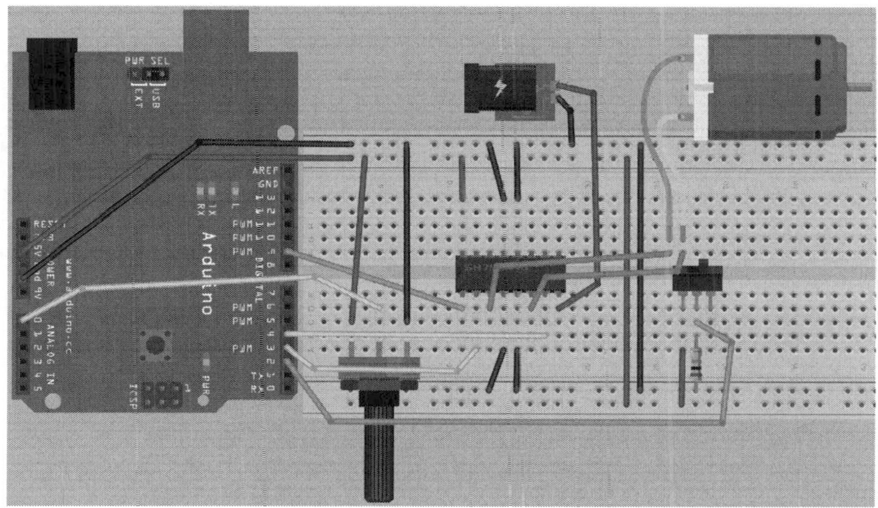

Figure 5-3. *The circuit for Project 16*

Enter the Code

Once you are satisfied that your circuit is connected correctly, upload the code in Listing 5-2. Do not connect the external power supply at this stage.

Listing 5-2. *Code for Project 16*

```
// Project 16 - Using an L293D Motor Driver IC
#define switchPin 2 // switch input
#define motorPin1 3 // L293D Input 1
#define motorPin2 4 // L293D Input 2
#define speedPin 9 // L293D enable Pin 1
#define potPin 0 // Potentiometer on Analog Pin 0
int Mspeed = 0;  // a variable to hold the current speed value
```

```
void setup() {
//set switch pin as INPUT
pinMode(switchPin, INPUT);

// set remaining pins as outputs
pinMode(motorPin1, OUTPUT);
pinMode(motorPin2, OUTPUT);
pinMode(speedPin, OUTPUT);
}

void loop() {
  Mspeed = analogRead(potPin)/4; // read the speed value from the potentiometer
  analogWrite(speedPin, Mspeed); // write speed to Enable 1 pin
  if (digitalRead(switchPin)) { // If the switch is HIGH, rotate motor clockwise
    digitalWrite(motorPin1, LOW); // set Input 1 of the L293D low
    digitalWrite(motorPin2, HIGH); // set Input 2 of the L293D high
  }
  else {  // if the switch is LOW, rotate motor anti-clockwise
    digitalWrite(motorPin1, HIGH); // set Input 1 of the L293D low
    digitalWrite(motorPin2, LOW); // set Input 2 of the L293D high
  }
}
```

Once the code has finished uploading, set the potentiometer at its midpoint and plug in the external power supply. The motor will now rotate; you can adjust its speed by turning the potentiometer. To change direction of the motor, first set the speed to minimum, then flick the toggle switch. The motor will now rotate in the opposite direction. Again, be careful of that chip as it will get very hot once powered up.

Project 16 – Using an L293D Motor Driver IC – Code Overview

The code for this project is very simple. First, you define the pins you are going to put to use on the Arduino:

```
#define switchPin 2 // switch input
#define motorPin1 3 // L293D Input 1
#define motorPin2 4 // L293D Input 2
#define speedPin 9 // L293D enable Pin 1
#define potPin 0 // Potentiometer on Analog Pin 0
```

Then, set an integer to hold the speed value read from the potentiometer:

```
int Mspeed = 0;  // a variable to hold the current speed value
```

In the setup function, you then set the appropriate pins to either inputs or outputs:

```
pinMode(switchPin, INPUT);

pinMode(motorPin1, OUTPUT);
pinMode(motorPin2, OUTPUT);
pinMode(speedPin, OUTPUT);
```

In the main loop, you first read in the value from the potentiometer connected to Analog Pin 0 and store it in Mspeed:

```
Mspeed = analogRead(potPin)/4; // read the speed value from the potentiometer
```

Then you set the PWM value on PWM Pin 9 to the appropriate speed:

```
analogWrite (speedPin, Mspeed); // write speed to Enable 1 pin
```

Then you have an if statement to decide if the value read in from the switch pin is either HIGH or LOW. If it is HIGH, then output 1 on the L293D is set to LOW and output 2 is set to HIGH. This will be the same as output 2 having a positive voltage and output 1 being ground, causing the motor to rotate in one direction:

```
if (digitalRead(switchPin)) { // If the switch is HIGH, rotate motor clockwise
    digitalWrite(motorPin1, LOW); // set Input 1 of the L293D low
    digitalWrite(motorPin2, HIGH); // set Input 2 of the L293D high
  }
```

If the switch pin is LOW, then output 1 is set to HIGH and output 2 is set to LOW, reversing the direction of the motor:

```
  else {  // if the switch is LOW, rotate motor anti-clockwise
    digitalWrite(motorPin1, HIGH); // set Input 1 of the L293D low
    digitalWrite(motorPin2, LOW); // set Input 2 of the L293D high
  }
```

The loop will repeat, checking for a new speed value or a new direction and setting the appropriate speed and direction pins. As you can see, using the motor driver IC is not at all as daunting as you might have thought at first. In fact, it has made your life a lot easier. Trying to recreate the above circuit and code without it would have been far more complex. Never be intimidated by ICs! A slow and careful read of their datasheets will reveal their secrets. Let's see how the new component introduced in this project works.

Project 16 – Using an L293D Motor Driver IC – Hardware Overview

The new component in Project 16 is the Motor Driver IC. This will be either the L293D or the SN754410, depending on what you have chosen (there are other chips available and a little research on the internet will find other pin compatible motor drivers).

The L293D is what is known as a Dual H-Bridge. A H-Bridge is a useful but simple electronic concept (see Figure 5-4).

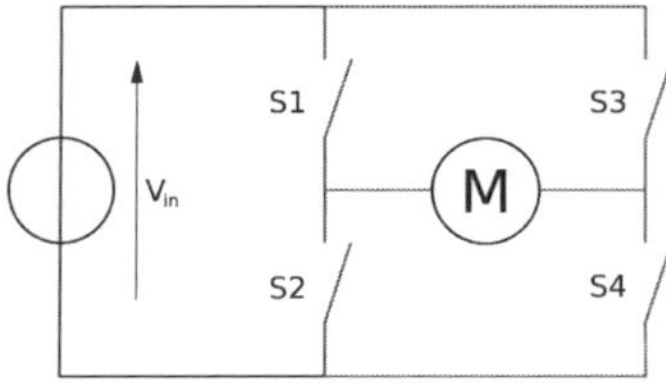

Figure 5-4. *A H-Bridge made of switches (image by Cyril Buttay)*

In Figure 5-4, a motor is connected to four switches. The configuration is called a H-Bridge as it resembles a letter H with the load bridge the centre. Now take a look at Figure 5-5.

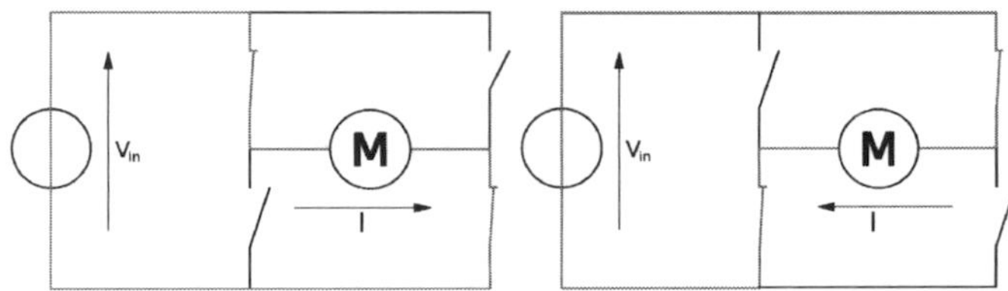

Figure 5-5. *Changing motor direction on the H-Bridge (image by Cyril Buttay)*

On the left hand side, the top left and the bottom right switches are closed. By doing so, the current will flow across the motor from left to right and the motor will rotate. If you open those switches and close the top right and bottom left switches instead, the current will flow across the motor in the opposite direction and hence cause it to rotate in the opposite direction. This is how an H-Bridge works.

The Motor driver IC is made up of two H-Bridges. Instead of switches, it uses transistors. In the same way that the transistor in Project 15 was used as a switch, the transistors inside the H-Bridge switch on and off in the same configuration as Figure 5-5 to make your motor rotate in either direction. The chip is a Dual H-Bridge because it has two H-Bridges inside it. Thus you are able to control two motors and their directions at the same time.

Note that you could make your own H-Bridge out of transistors and diodes, and it would do the same job as the L293D. The L293D has the advantage of being tiny and having all those transistors and diodes packaged up inside a small space.

EXERCISE

Now try out the following exercise.

Exercise 1: Instead of just one motor, try connecting up two, with two direction switches and potentiometers to control the direction and speed. Figure 5-6 shows the pinouts of the chip.

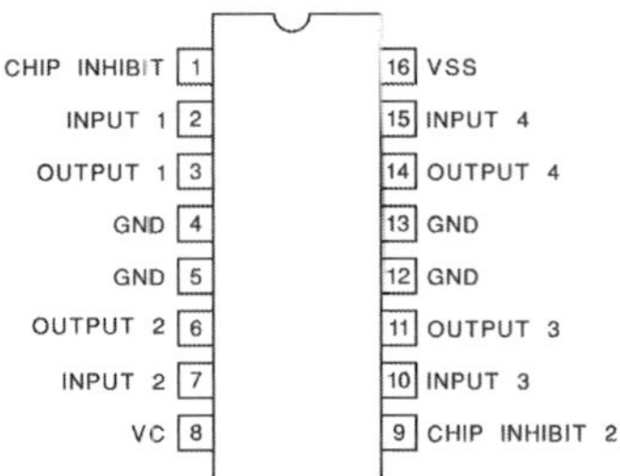

Figure 5-6. *The pinouts for the L293D (or SN754410)*

Summary

Chapter 5 showed you how to use motors in your projects. It also introduced you to the important concepts concerning transistors and diodes; you will use both of these components a lot in your projects, especially if you are controlling devices that require larger voltages or currents than the Arduino can supply.

You now also know how to construct a H-Bridge and how to use it to change the direction of a motor. You have also used the popular L293D Motor Driver IC; you will work with this chip later on in the book when you look at a different kind of motor. The skills required to drive a motor are vital if you are going to build a robot or a radio controlled vehicle of any kind using an Arduino.

Subjects and concepts covered in Chapter 5

- Using a transistor to power high power devices
- Controlling a motor's speed using PWM
- The current supplied by an Arduino digital pin
- Using an external power supply is essential for high power devices
- The concept of transistors and how they work
- Motors and how they work

- Using a diode to avoid back EMF
- How a diode works
- How motors can be used to generate power
- How vital diodes can be in protecting a circuit
- How to power a motor with an L293D Motor Driver IC
- Why heatsinks are essential for dissipating heat from ICs
- The concept of a H-Bridge and how it can be used to change motor direction

CHAPTER 6

Binary Counters

You are now going to go back to controlling LEDs. This time, however, you won't be driving them directly from the Arduino. Instead, you're going to use a fantastic little chip known as a *shift register*. These ICs (Integrated Circuits) will let you control eight separate LEDs using just three pins from the Arduino. But wait, there's more: in Project 18, you'll control a total of 16 LEDs, again using just three pins from the Arduino.

To demonstrate the way the data is output from these chips, you are going to create two binary counters, first using a single shift register and then moving onto two chips cascaded (you will learn what cascading is in the aforementioned Project 18). Chapter 6 is going to delve into some pretty advanced stuff so you might want to pour yourself a stiff drink before going any further.

Project 17 – Shift Register 8-Bit Binary Counter

In this project, you're going to use additional ICs (Integrated Circuits) in the form of shift registers in order to drive LEDs to count in binary (I will explain what binary is soon). Specifically, you will drive eight LEDs independently using just three output pins from the Arduino.

Parts Required

1 × 74HC595 Shift Register IC

8 × 220Ω Resistors*

8 × 5mm LEDs

**or suitable equivalent*

Connect It Up

Examine the diagram carefully. Connect the 3.3V to the top rail of your breadboard and the Ground to the bottom. The chip has a small dimple on one end; this dimple goes to the left. Pin 1 is below the dimple, Pin 8 is at bottom right, Pin 9 is at top right, and Pin 16 is at top left.

You now need wires to go from the 3.3V supply to Pins 10 and 16, and wires from Ground to Digital Pins 8 and 13. A wire goes from Digital Pin 8 to Pin 12 on the IC. Another one goes from Digital Pin 12 to Pin 14 on the IC and finally one from Digital Pin 11 to Pin 11 on the IC.

The eight LEDs have a 220 ohm resistor between the cathode and ground, then the anode of LED 1 goes to Pin 15. The anode of LEDs 2 through 8 goes to Pins 1 to 7 on the IC.

Once you have connected everything, check again that your wiring is correct and that the IC and LEDs are the right way around.

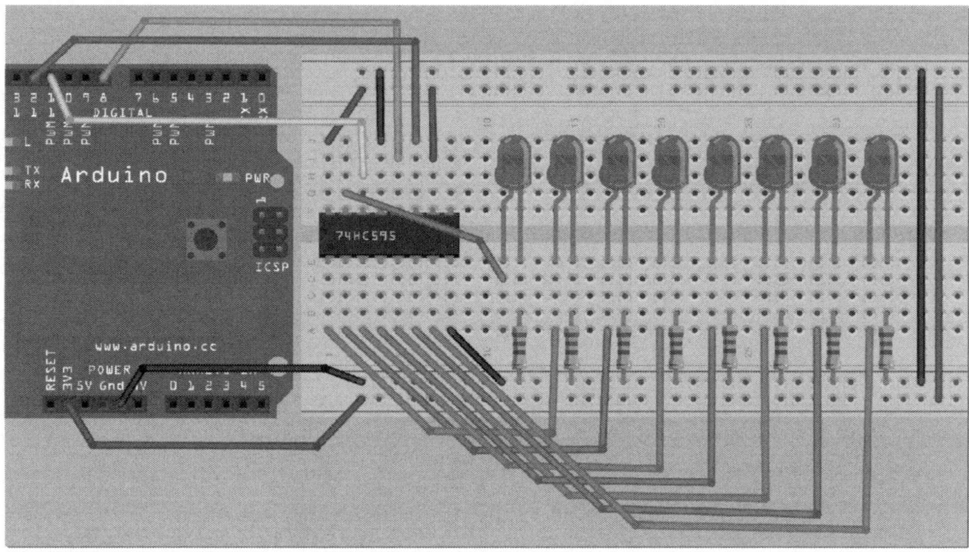

Figure 6-1. The circuit for Project 17 – Shift Register 8-Bit Binary Counter

Enter The Code

Enter the following code in Listing 6-1 and upload it to your Arduino. Once the code is run, you will see the LEDs turn on and off individually as they count up in binary every second from 0 to 255, then start again.

Listing 6-1. Code for Project 17

```
// Project 17

int latchPin = 8; //Pin connected to Pin 12 of 74HC595 (Latch)
int clockPin = 12; //Pin connected to Pin 11 of 74HC595 (Clock)
int dataPin = 11; //Pin connected to Pin 14 of 74HC595 (Data)
```

```
void setup() {
        //set pins to output
        pinMode(latchPin, OUTPUT);
        pinMode(clockPin, OUTPUT);
        pinMode(dataPin, OUTPUT);
}

void loop() {
        //count from 0 to 255
        for (int i = 0; i < 256; i++) {
                //set latchPin low to allow data flow
                digitalWrite(latchPin, LOW);
                shiftOut(i);
                //set latchPin to high to lock and send data
                digitalWrite(latchPin, HIGH);
                delay(1000);
        }
}

void shiftOut(byte dataOut) {
        // Shift out 8 bits LSB first, on rising edge of clock
        boolean pinState;
        digitalWrite(dataPin, LOW); //clear shift register ready for sending data
        digitalWrite(clockPin, LOW);

        for (int i=0; i<=7; i++)  { // for each bit in dataOut send out a bit
                digitalWrite(clockPin, LOW); //set clockPin to LOW prior to sending bit

                // if the value of DataOut and (logical AND) a bitmask
                // are true, set pinState to 1 (HIGH)
                if ( dataOut & (1<<i) ) {
                        pinState = HIGH;
                }
                else {
                        pinState = LOW;
                }

                //sets dataPin to HIGH or LOW depending on pinState
                digitalWrite(dataPin, pinState); //send bit out on rising edge of clock
                digitalWrite(clockPin, HIGH);
        }
        digitalWrite(clockPin, LOW); //stop shifting out data
}
```

The Binary Number System

Before I dissect the code and the hardware for Project 17, let's look at the binary number system. It's essential to understand binary to be able to successfully program a microcontroller.

Human beings use a Base 10, or decimal number system, because we have 10 fingers on our hands. Computers do not have fingers, and so the best way for a computer to count is using its equivalent of fingers, which is a state of either ON or OFF (1 or 0). A logic device, such as a computer, can detect if a voltage is there (1) or if it is not (0) and so uses a binary, or base 2, number system as this number system can easily be represented in an electronic circuit with a high or low voltage state.

In our number system, base 10, we have 10 digits ranging from 0 to 9. When we count to the next digit after 9, the digit resets back to zero, but a 1 is incremented to the tens column to its left. Once the tens column reaches 9, incrementing this by 1 will reset it to zero, but add 1 to the hundreds column to its left, and so on:

```
000,001,002,003,004,005,006,007,008,009
010,011,012,013,014,015,016,017,018,019
020,021,023 .........
```

In the binary system, the exact same thing happens, except the highest digit is 1 so adding 1 to 1 results in the digit resetting to zero and 1 being added to the column to the left:

```
000, 001
010, 011
100, 101...
```

An 8 bit number (or a byte) is represented like in Table 6-1.

Table 6-1. *An 8-bit binary number*

2^7 128	2^6 64	2^5 32	2^4 16	2^3 8	2^2 4	2^1 2	2^0 1
0	1	0	0	1	0	1	1

The number above in Binary is 1001011, and in Decimal this is 75.

This is worked out like this:

$1 \times 1 = 1$
$1 \times 2 = 2$
$1 \times 8 = 8$
$1 \times 64 = 64$

Add that all together and you get 75. Table 6-2 shows some other examples.

Table 6-2. Binary number examples

Dec	2^7 128	2^6 64	2^5 32	2^4 16	2^3 8	2^2 4	2^1 2	2^0 1
75	0	1	0	0	1	0	1	1
1	0	0	0	0	0	0	0	1
2	0	0	0	0	0	0	1	0
3	0	0	0	0	0	0	1	1
4	0	0	0	0	0	1	0	0
12	0	0	0	0	1	1	0	0
27	0	0	0	1	1	0	1	1
100	0	1	1	0	0	1	0	0
127	0	1	1	1	1	1	1	1
255	1	1	1	1	1	1	1	1

...and so on.

■ **Tip** You can use Google to convert between a decimal and a binary number and vice versa.

So to convert 171 decimal to binary, type ***171 in binary*** into the Google search box which returns

171 = 0b10101011

The 0b prefix shows the number is a binary number and not a decimal number. So the answer is 10101011.

To convert a binary number to decimal, do the reverse. Enter ***0b11001100 in decimal*** into the search box, and it returns ***0b11001100 = 204***

So now that you understand binary, let's take a look at the hardware before looking at the code.

Project 17 – Shift Register 8-Bit Binary Counter - Hardware Overview

You are using a shift register, specifically the 74HC595. This type of shift register is an 8-bit serial-in, serial or parallel-out shift register with output latches. This means that you can send data in to the shift register in series and send it out in parallel. In series means 1 bit at a time. Parallel means lots of bits (in this case 8) at a time.

Data is entered when the LATCH is set to LOW (this allows data to be sent to the chip) and sent out when the LATCH is set to HIGH. So you give the shift register data (in the form of 1's and 0's) one bit at a time, then send out 8 bits all at the exact same time. Each bit is shunted along as the next bit is entered. If a 9th bit is entered before the Latch is set to HIGH, then the first bit entered will be shunted off the end of the row and be lost forever.

Shift registers are usually used for serial-to-parallel data conversion. In this case, the data that is output is 1's and 0's (or 0V and 3.3V), so you can use it to turn on and off a bank of eight LEDs.

The Shift Register for this project requires only three inputs from the Arduino. The outputs of the Arduino and the inputs of the 595 are shown in Table 6-3.

Table 6-3. *Pins used*

Arduino Pin	595 Pin	Description
8	12	Storage Register Clock Input
11	14	Serial Data Input
12	11	Shift Register Clock Input

Let's refer to Pin 12 as the Clock Pin, Pin 14 as the Data Pin, and Pin 11 as the Latch Pin.

Imagine the Latch as a gate that will allow data to escape from the 595. When the gate is lowered (LOW), the data in the 595 cannot get out, but data can be entered. When the gate is raised (HIGH), data can no longer be entered, but the data in the Shift register is released to the eight pins (QA-QH or Q0 to Q7, depending on your datasheet; see Figure 6-2). The Clock is simply a pulse of 0's and 1's, and the Data Pin is where you send data from the Arduino to the 595.

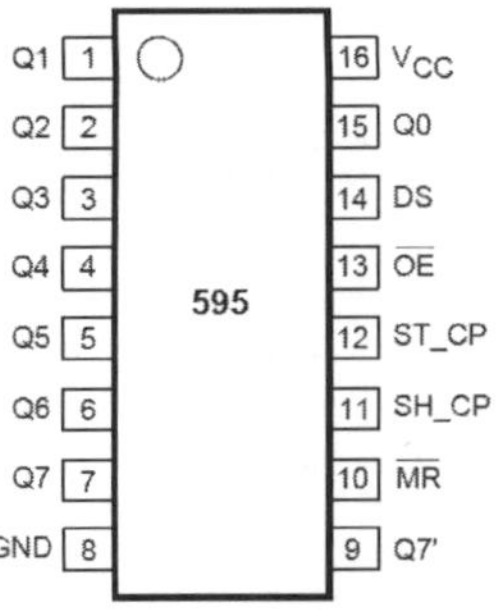

Figure 6-2. *Pin diagram of a 595 chip*

To use the shift register, the Latch Pin and Clock Pin must be set to LOW. The Latch Pin will remain at LOW until all 8 bits have been set. This allows data to be entered into the storage register (the storage register is simply a place inside the IC for storing a 1 or a 0). You then present either a HIGH or LOW signal at the Data Pin and then set the Clock Pin to HIGH. Setting the Clock Pin to HIGH stores the data presented at the Data Pin into the Storage Register. Once this is done, you set the Clock to LOW again, then present the next bit of data at the Data Pin. Once you have done this eight times, you have sent a full 8-bit number into the 595. The Latch Pin is now raised, which transfers the data from the storage register into the shift register and outputs it from Q0 to Q7 (Pin 15, 1 to 7).

This sequence of events is described in Table 6-4.

Table 6-4. *Sequence of events*

Pin	State	Description
Latch	LOW	Latch lowered to allow data to be entered
Data	HIGH	First bit of data (1)
Clock	HIGH	Clock goes HIGH. Data stored.
Clock	LOW	Ready for next Bit. Prevent any new data.
Data	HIGH	2nd bit of data (1)
Clock	HIGH	2nd bit stored
...	...	...
Data	LOW	8th bit of data (0)
Clock	HIGH	Store the data
Clock	LOW	Prevent any new data being stored
Latch	HIGH	Send 8 bits out in parallel

I connected a Logic Analyzer (a device that lets you see the 1's and 0's coming out of a digital device) to my 595 while this program was running; Figure 6-3 shows the output. You can see from this diagram that the binary number 0011011 (reading from right to left), or Decimal 55, has been sent to the IC.

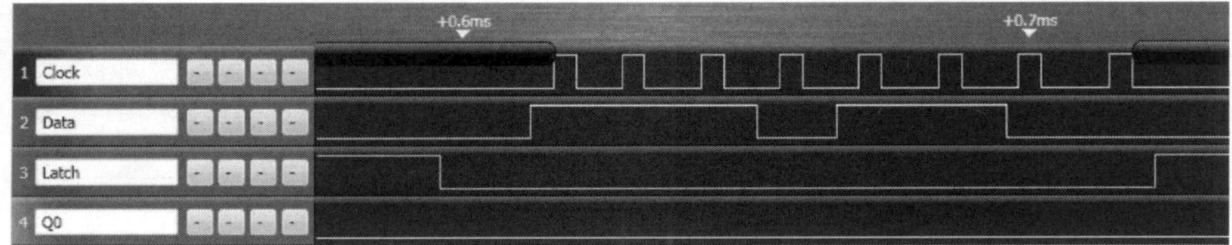

Figure 6-3. The output from the 595 shown in a Logic Analyzer

So to summarize the use of a single shift register in this project, you have eight LEDs attached to the eight outputs of the Register. The Latch is set to LOW to enable data entry. Data is sent to the Data Pin, one bit at a time, and the Clock Pin is set to HIGH to store that data, then back down to low ready for the next bit. After all eight bits have been entered, the latch is set to HIGH, which prevents further data entry and sets the eight output pins to either High (3.3V or LOW (0V), depending on the state of the register.

If you want to read more about shift registers, look at the serial number on the IC (e.g. 74HC595N or SN74HC595N, etc.) and type it into a search engine. You can then find the specific datasheet for that IC.

I'm a huge fan of the 595 chip. It is very versatile and can, of course, increase the number of digital output pins at your disposal. The standard Arduino has 19 Digital Outputs (the six Analog Pins can also be used as Digital Pins numbered 14 to 19). Using 8-bit shift registers, you can expand that to 49 (6 × 595's plus one spare pin left over). They also operate very fast, typically at 100MHz, which means that you can send data out at approximately 100 million times per second if you wanted to (and if the Arduino was capable of doing so). This means you can also send PWM signals via software to the ICs and enable brightness control of the LEDs, too.

As the output is simply the ON and OFF of an output voltage, it can also be used to switch other low powered devices (or even high powered devices with the use of transistors or relays) on and off or send data to devices (such as an old dot matrix printer or other serial device).

Note that the 595 shift registers from any manufacturer are just about identical to each other. There are also larger shift registers with 16 outputs or higher. Some ICs advertised as LED Driver Chips are, when you examine the datasheet, simply larger shift registers (e.g. the M5450 and M5451 from STMicroelectronics).

Project 17 – Shift Register 8-Bit Binary Counter – Code Overview

The code for Project 15 looks pretty daunting at first look. But when you break it down into its component parts, you'll see it's not as complex as it looks.

First, three variables are initialized for the three pins you are going to use:

```
int latchPin = 8;
int clockPin = 12;
int dataPin = 11;
```

Then, in setup, the pins are all set to outputs:

```
pinMode(latchPin, OUTPUT);
pinMode(clockPin, OUTPUT);
pinMode(dataPin, OUTPUT);
```

The main loop simply runs a for loop counting from 0 to 255. On each iteration of the loop, the latchPin is set to LOW to enable data entry, then the function called shiftOut is called, passing the value of *i* in the for loop to the function. Then the latchPin is set to HIGH, preventing further data entry and setting the outputs from the eight pins. Finally, there is a delay of half a second before the next iteration of the loop commences:

```
void loop() {
  //count from 0 to 255
  for (int i = 0; i < 256; i++) {
    //set latchPin low to allow data flow
    digitalWrite(latchPin, LOW);
    shiftOut(i);
    //set latchPin to high to lock and send data
    digitalWrite(latchPin, HIGH);
    delay(500);
  }
}
```

The shiftOut function receives as a parameter a Byte (8 bit number), which will be your number between 0 and 255. You have chosen a Byte for this usage as it is exactly 8 bits in length, and you need to send only 8 bits out to the shift register:

```
void shiftOut(byte dataOut) {
```

Then a Boolean variable called pinState is initialized. This will store the state you wish the relevant pin to be in when the data is sent out (1 or 0):

```
boolean pinState;
```

The Data and Clock pins are set to LOW to reset the data and clock lines ready for fresh data to be sent:

```
digitalWrite(dataPin, LOW);
digitalWrite(clockPin, LOW);
```

After this, you are ready to send the 8 bits in series to the 595, one bit at a time. A for loop that iterates eight times is set up:

```
for (int i=0; i<=7; i++)  {
```

The clock pin is set low prior to sending a Data bit:

```
digitalWrite(clockPin, LOW);
```

Now an if/else statement determines if the pinState variable should be set to a 1 or a 0:

```
if ( dataOut & (1<<i) ) {
      pinState = HIGH;
}
else {
      pinState = LOW;
}
```

The condition for the if statement is:

```
dataOut & (1<<i).
```

This is an example of what is called a *bitmask*, and you are now using bitwise operators. These are logical operators similar to the Boolean operators you used in previous projects. However, the bitwise operators act on number at the bit level.

In this case, you are using the bitwise AND (&) operator to carry out a logical operation on two numbers. The first number is dataOut and the second is the result of (1<<i). Before you go any further, let's take a look at the bitwise operators.

Bitwise Operators

The bitwise operators perform calculations at the bit level on variables. There are six common bitwise operators:

& Bitwise and

| Bitwise or

^ Bitwise xor

~ Bi twise not

<< Bitshift left

>> Bi tshift right

Bitwise operators can only be used between integers. Each operator performs a calculation based on a set of logic rules. Let's take a close look at the bitwise AND (&) operator first, followed by the other operators.

Bitwise AND (&)

The Bitwise AND operator acts according to this rule:

If both inputs are 1, the resulting outputs are 1, otherwise the output is 0.

Another way of looking at this is:

```
0 0 1 1    Operand1
0 1 0 1    Operand2
-------
0 0 0 1    (Operand1 & Operand2)
```

A type int is a 16-bit value, so using & between two int expressions causes 16 simultaneous AND operations to occur. In a section of code like this:

```
int x = 77;    //binary: 0000000001001101
int y = 121;   //binary: 0000000001111001
int z = x & y;//result: 0000000001001001
```

or in this case

77 & 121 = 73

Bitwise OR (|)

If either or both of the inputs is 1, the result is 1, otherwise it is 0.

```
0 0 1 1    Operand1
0 1 0 1    Operand2
-------
0 1 1 1    (Operand1 | Operand2)
```

Bitwise XOR (^)

If only 1 of the inputs is 1, then the output is 1. If both inputs are 1, then the output 0.

```
0 0 1 1    Operand1
0 1 0 1    Operand2
-------
0 1 1 0    (Operand1 ^ Operand2)
```

Bitwise NOT (~)

The Bitwise NOT Operator is applied to a single operand to its right.

The output becomes the opposite of the input.

```
0 0 1 1    Operand1
-------
1 1 0 0    ~Operand1
```

Bitshift Left (<<), Bitshift Right (>>)

The Bitshift operators move all of the bits in the integer to the left or right the number of bits specified by the right operand.

variable << number_of_bits

E.g.

```
byte x = 9 ;     // binary: 00001001
byte y = x << 3; // binary: 01001000 (or 72 dec)
```

Any bits shifted off the end of the row are lost forever. You can use the left bitshift to multiply a number by powers of 2 and the right bitshift to divide by powers of 2 (work it out).

Now that you have taken a look at the bitshift operators, let's return to the code.

Project 17 – Code Overview (continued)

The condition of the if/else statement was:

```
dataOut & (1 << i)
```

You now know this is a Bitwise AND (&) operation. The right hand operand inside the parenthesis is a left bitshift operation. This is a bitmask. The 74HC595 will only accept data one bit at a time. You therefore need to convert the 8-bit number in dataOut into a single bit number representing each of the 8 bits in turn. The bitmask allows you to ensure that the pinState variable is set to either a 1 or a 0, depending on the result of the bitmask calculation. The right hand operand is the number 1 bit shifted *i* number of times. As the `for` loop makes the value of i go from 0 to 7, you can see that 1 bitshifted *i* times, each time through the loop, will result in these binary numbers (see Table 6-5).

***Table 6-5.** The results of 1<<i*

Value of I	Result of (1<<i) in Binary
0	00000001
1	00000010
2	00000100
3	00001000
4	00010000
5	00100000

Value of I	Result of (1<<i) in Binary
6	01000000
7	10000000

So you can see that the 1 moves from right to left as a result of this operation.

Now, the AND operator's rule states that

If both inputs are 1, the resulting outputs are 1, otherwise the output is 0.

So, the condition of

```
dataOut & (1<<i)
```

will result in a 1 if the corresponding bit in the same place as the bitmask is a 1; otherwise it will be a zero. For example, if the value of dataOut was Decimal 139 or 10001011 binary, then each iteration through the loop will result in the values shown in Table 6-6.

Table 6-6. *The results of b10001011<<i*

Value of I	Result of b10001011(1<<i) in Binary
0	00000001
1	00000010
2	00000000
3	00001000
4	00000000
5	00000000
6	00000000
7	10000000

So every time there is a 1 in the I position (reading from right to left), the value comes out at higher than 1 (or TRUE) and every time there is a 0 in the I position, the value comes out at 0 (or FALSE).

The `if` condition will therefore carry out its code in the block if the value is higher than 0 (or in other words, if the bit in that position is a 1) or else (if the bit in that position is a 0) it will carry out the code in the else block.

So looking at the if/else statement once more

```
if ( dataOut & (1<<i) ) {
  pinState = HIGH;
}
else {
  pinState = LOW;
}
```

and cross referencing this with the truth table in Table 6-6, you can see that for every bit in the value of dataOut that has the value of 1, that pinState will be set to HIGH, and for every value of 0, it will be set to LOW.

The next piece of code writes either a HIGH or LOW state to the Data Pin and then sets the Clock Pin to HIGH to write that bit into the storage register:

```
digitalWrite(dataPin, pinState);
digitalWrite(clockPin, HIGH);
```

Finally, the Clock Pin is set to low to ensure no further bit writes:

```
digitalWrite(clockPin, LOW);
```

So, in simple terms, this section of code looks at each of the 8 bits of the value in dataOut one by one and sets the data pin to HIGH or LOW accordingly, then writes that value into the storage register.

This is simply sending the 8 bit number out to the 595 one bit at a time, and then the main loop sets the Latch Pin to HIGH to send out those 8 bits simultaneously to Pins 15 and 1 to 7 (QA to QH) of the shift register. The result is that your 8 LEDs show a visual representation of the binary number stored in the shift register.

Your brain may hurt after Project 17, so take a rest, stretch your legs, get another stiff drink before you dive into Project 18 where you will now use two shift registers daisy chained together.

Project 18 – Dual 8-Bit Binary Counters

In Project 18, you will daisy chain (or cascade) another 74HC595 IC onto the one used in Project 17 to create a dual binary counter.

Parts Required

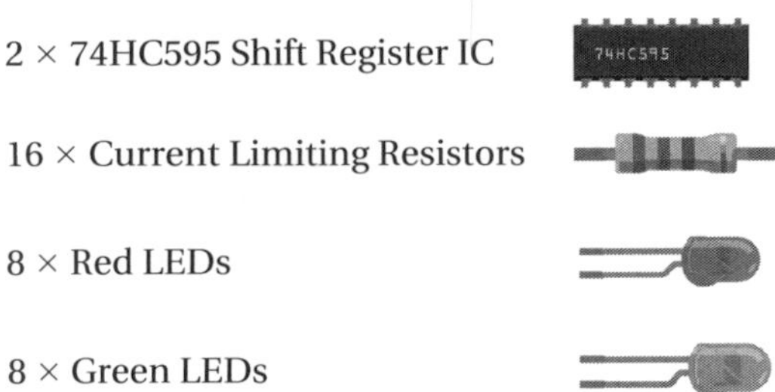

Connect It Up

The first 595 is wired the same as in Project 15.7 The second 595 has +5V and Ground wires going to the same pins as on the first 595. Then, add a wire from Pin 9 on IC 1 to Pin 14 on IC 2. Add another from Pin 11 on IC 1 to Pin 11 on IC 2, and Pin 12 on IC 1 to Pin 12 on IC 2.

The same outputs as on the first 595 going to the first set of LEDs go from the second IC to the second set of LEDs.

Examine the diagrams carefully in Figures 6-4 and 6-5.

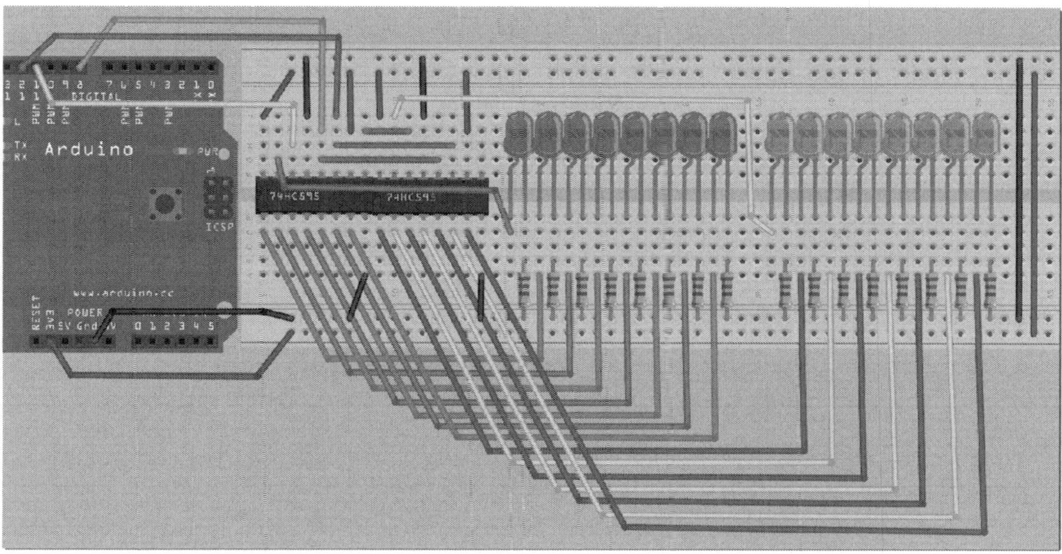

***Figure 6-4.** The circuit for Project 18*

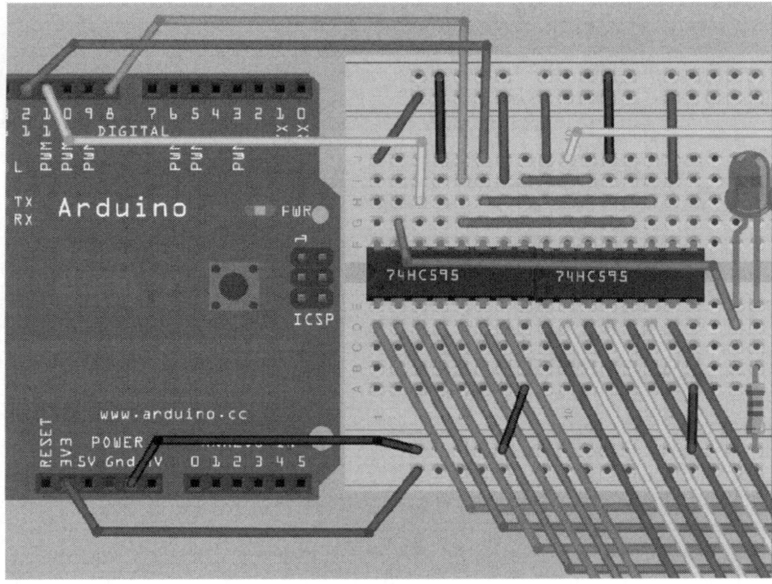

Figure 6-5. Close up of the wiring of the ICs for Project 18

Enter the Code

Enter the following code in Listing 6-2 and upload it to your Arduino. When you run this code, you will see the green set of LEDs count up (in binary) from 0 to 255 and the red LEDs count down from 255 to 0 at the same time.

Listing 6-2. Code for Project 18

```
// Project 18

int latchPin = 8;  //Pin connected to Pin 12 of 74HC595 (Latch)
int clockPin = 12; //Pin connected to Pin 11 of 74HC595 (Clock)
int dataPin = 11;  //Pin connected to Pin 14 of 74HC595 (Data)

void setup() {
        //set pins to output
        pinMode(latchPin, OUTPUT);
        pinMode(clockPin, OUTPUT);
        pinMode(dataPin, OUTPUT);
}
```

```
void loop() {
	for (int i = 0; i < 256; i++) {      //count from 0 to 255
		digitalWrite(latchPin, LOW); //set latchPin low to allow data flow
		shiftOut(i);
		shiftOut(255-i);
		//set latchPin to high to lock and send data
		digitalWrite(latchPin, HIGH);
		delay(250 );
	}
}

void shiftOut(byte dataOut) {
	boolean pinState; // Shift out 8 bits LSB first, on rising edge of clock

	digitalWrite(dataPin, LOW); //clear shift register ready for sending data
	digitalWrite(clockPin, LOW);

	for (int i=0; i<=7; i++)  {  // for each bit in dataOut send out a bit
	digitalWrite(clockPin, LOW); //set clockPin to LOW prior to sending bit

// if value of DataOut and (logical AND) a bitmask are true, set pinState to 1 (HIGH)
		if ( dataOut & (1<<i) ) {
			pinState = HIGH;
		}
		else {
			pinState = LOW;
		}

		//sets dataPin to HIGH or LOW depending on pinState
		digitalWrite(dataPin, pinState);

		digitalWrite(clockPin, HIGH); //send bit out on rising edge of clock
		digitalWrite(dataPin, LOW);
	}

	digitalWrite(clockPin, LOW); //stop shifting
}
```

Project 18 - Code & Hardware Overview

The code for Project 18 is identical to that in Project 17 apart from the addition of

```
shiftOut(255-i);
```

in the main loop. The shiftOut routine sends 8 bits to the 595. In the main loop, you have put two sets of calls to shiftOut, one sending the value of *i* and the other sending *255-i*. You call shiftOut twice before you set the latch to HIGH. This will send two sets of 8 bits, or 16 bits in total, to the 595 chips before the latch is set HIGH to prevent further writing to the registers and to output the contents of the shift register to the output pins, which in turn make the LEDs go on or off.

The second 595 is wired up exactly the same as the first one. The Clock and Latch pins are tied to the pins of the first 595. However, you have a wire going from Pin 9 on IC 1 to Pin 14 on IC 2. Pin 9 is the data output pin and Pin 14 is the data input pin.

The data is input to Pin 14 on the first IC from the Arduino. The second 595 chip is daisy chained to the first chip by Pin 9 on IC 1, which is outputting data into Pin 14 on the second IC, which is the data input.

As you enter a ninth bit and above, the data in IC 1 gets shunted out of its data pin and into the data pin of the second IC. So, once all 16 bits have been sent down the data line from the Arduino, the first 8 bits sent would have been shunted out of the first chip and into the second. The second 595 chip will contain the FIRST 8 bits sent out and the first 595 chip will contain bits 9 to 16.

An almost unlimited number of 595 chips can be daisy chained in this manner.

EXERCISE

Using the same circuit for Project 18 and all 16 LEDs, recreate the Knight Rider (or Cylon) light effect, making the LEDs bounce back and forth across all 16 LEDs.

Summary

Chapter 6 covered a lot of ground concerning the use of an external IC to supply extra output pins for the Arduino. Although you could have done these projects without the external IC, the shift registers have made life a lot easier. If you didn't use the shift registers, the code for these projects would be a lot more complex. The use of an IC designed to take serial data and output it in a parallel fashion is ideal for controlling lines of LEDs in this way.

Never be daunted by using external ICs. A slow and methodical read of the datasheets will reveal how they work. Datasheets at first glance look complicated, but once you strip out the irrelevant data, you'll be able to understand how the chip works.

In Chapter 7, you are going to continue to use shift registers, but this time you are going to use them to control LED Dot Matrix displays that contain at least 64 LEDs per unit. I will show you how to control a large number of LEDs at the same time using a great technique known as multiplexing.

Subjects and Concepts covered in Chapter 6

- The binary number system and how to convert to and from decimal
- How to use a shift register to input serial data and output parallel data
- Using an external IC to decrease the complexity of a project
- Sending a parameter to a function call
- Using variables of type Boolean
- The concept and use of bitwise operators
- Using bitwise operators to create a bitmask
- How to cascade (or daisy chain) two or more shift registers

CHAPTER 7

LED Displays

So far you have dealt with individual 5mm LEDs. LEDs can also be obtained in a package known as a dot matrix display, the most popular being a matrix of 8×8 LEDs or 64 LEDs in total. You can also obtain bi-color dot matrix displays (e.g. red and green) or even RGB dot matrix displays, which can display any color and contains a total of 192 LEDs in a single display package. In this chapter, you are going to deal with a standard single color 8×8 dot matrix display and show you how to display images and text. You will start off with a simple demonstration of creating an animated image on an 8×8 display and then move onto more complex display projects. Along the way, you will learn the very important concept of multiplexing.

Project 19 – LED Dot Matrix Display – Basic Animation

In this project, you shall again use two sets of shift registers. These will be connected to the rows and columns of the dot matrix display. You will then show a simple object, or sprite, on the display and animate it. The main aim of this project is to show you how a dot matrix display works and introduce the concept of multiplexing because this is an invaluable skill to have.

Parts Required

You will need two shift registers (74HC595) and eight current-limiting resistors. You also need to obtain a common anode (C+) dot matrix display and the datasheet for the display so you know which pin connects to which row or column.

2 × 74HC595 Shift Register IC 

8 × Current Limiting Resistors 

8×8 Dot Matrix Display (C+) 

Connect It Up

Examine the diagram carefully. It is important you do not connect the Arduino to the USB cable or power until the circuit is complete; you risk damaging the shift registers or the dot matrix display otherwise. This is a complicated wiring exercise so be careful. Make sure you connect things slowly and methodically.

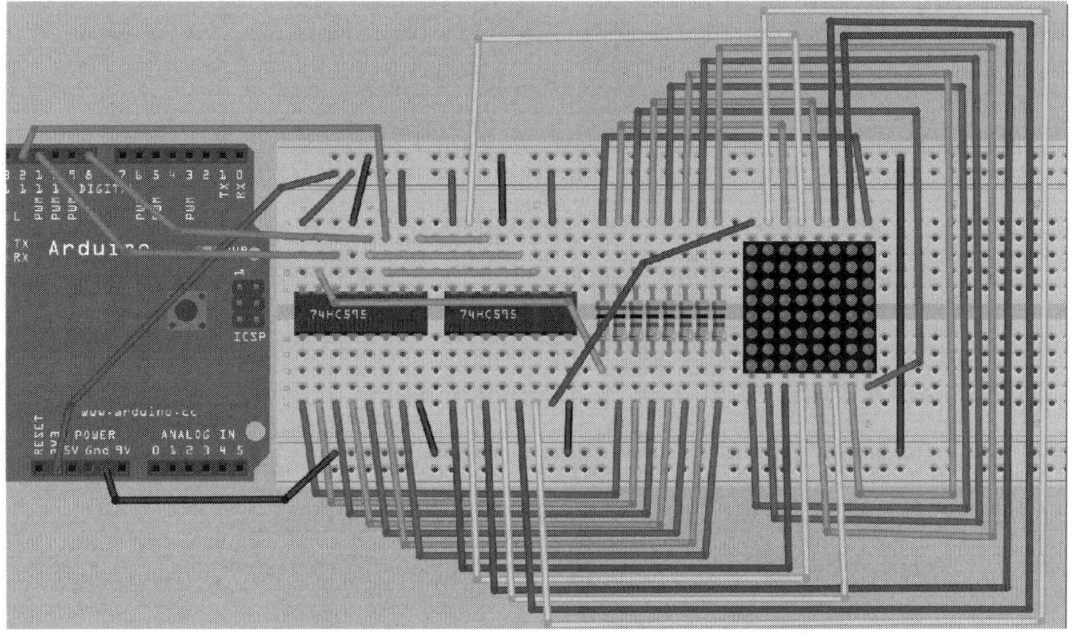

Figure 7-1. *The circuit for Project 19 – LED Dot Matrix – Basic Animation*

The wiring diagram in Figure 7-1 is relevant to the specific dot matrix unit that I used in creating this project, a mini 8×8 red dot matrix display unit. However, your display may (and quite likely will) have different pins than the one I used. You *must* read the datasheet of the unit you have bought to ensure that the correct output pins on the shift registers go to the correct pins on the dot matrix. For a good tutorial in PDF format on how to read a datasheet, go to www.egr.msu.edu/classes/ece480/goodman/read_datasheet.pdf.

To make this easier, Table 7-1 shows which pins from the shift registers need to go to which pins on the dot matrix display. Adjust the circuit accordingly so that it is correct for the type of display you have obtained.

Table 7-1. Pins required for the dot matrix display

	Shift Register 1	Shift Register 2
Row 1	Pin 15	
Row 2	Pin 1	
Row 3	Pin 2	
Row 4	Pin 3	
Row 5	Pin 4	
Row 6	Pin 5	
Row 7	Pin 6	
Row 8	Pin 7	
Column 1		Pin 15
Column 2		Pin 1
Column 3		Pin 2
Column 4		Pin 3
Column 5		Pin 4
Column 6		Pin 5
Column 7		Pin 6
Column 8		Pin 7

The schematic for the dot matrix display used to create this project is in Figure 7-2. As you can see, the rows and columns (anodes and cathodes) are not ordered logically. Using Table 7-1 and the schematic in Figure 7-2, you can see that pin 15 on shift register 1 needs to go to row 1 on the display and hence goes (via a resistor) to pin 9 on the display. Pin 1 on the shift register needs to go to row 2 and hence goes to pin 14 on the display, and so on.

You will need to read the datasheet of the display you have and go through a similar exercise to ascertain which pins from the shift register go to which pins on the LED display.

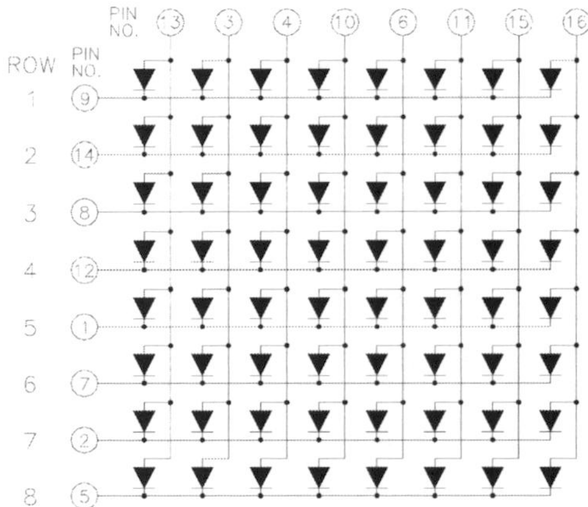

Figure 7-2. *A typical schematic for an 8×8 LED dot matrix display*

Enter the Code

Once you have confirmed that your wiring is correct, enter the code in Listing 7-1 and upload it to your Arduino. You will also need to download the TimerOne library. This can be downloaded from the Arduino website at www.arduino.cc/playground/Code/Timer1. Once you have downloaded the library, unzip it and put the entire TimerOne folder into the hardware/libraries folder inside the Arduino installation. This is an example of an external library. The Arduino IDE comes preloaded with many libraries, such as Ethernet, LiquidCrystal, Servo, etc. The TimerOne library is an external library, which you simply need to download and install in the libraries folder for it to work (you will need to restart your IDE before it will be recognized).

A library is simply a collection of code that someone else has written to give you functionality that would otherwise require you to write from scratch. This is code re-use and it helps to speed up your development process. After all, there is nothing to be gained from reinventing the wheel. If someone has already created some code to carry out a task and that code is out in the public domain, then make use of it.

Once the code is run, you will see a heart on the display. Approximately every half a second the display will invert to give a basic animated effect to the image.

Listing 7-1. *Code for Project 19*

```
// Project 19
#include <TimerOne.h>

int latchPin = 8; //Pin connected to Pin 12 of 74HC595 (Latch)
int clockPin = 12; //Pin connected to Pin 11 of 74HC595 (Clock)
int dataPin = 11; //Pin connected to Pin 14 of 74HC595 (Data)

byte led[8];  // 8 element unsigned integer array to store the sprite
```

```
void setup() {
        pinMode(latchPin, OUTPUT);  // set the 3 digital pins to outputs
        pinMode(clockPin, OUTPUT);
        pinMode(dataPin, OUTPUT);
        led[0] = B11111111;  // enter the binary representation of the image
        led[1] = B10000001;  // into the array
        led[2] = B10111101;
        led[3] = B10100101;
        led[4] = B10100101;
        led[5] = B10111101;
        led[6] = B10000001;
        led[7] = B11111111;
        // set a timer of length 10000 microseconds (1/100th of a second)
        Timer1.initialize(10000);
        // attach the screenUpdate function to the interrupt timer
        Timer1.attachInterrupt(screenUpdate);
}

void loop() {
        for (int i=0; i<8; i++) {
                led[i]= ~led[i]; // invert each row of the binary image
        }
        delay(500);
}

void screenUpdate() { // function to display image
        byte row = B10000000; // row 1
        for (byte k = 0; k < 9; k++) {
                digitalWrite(latchPin, LOW); // open latch ready to receive data
        shiftIt(~led[k] ); // shift out the LED array (inverted)
        shiftIt(row ); // shift out row binary number

        // Close the latch, sending the data in the registers out to the matrix
        digitalWrite(latchPin, HIGH);
        row = row << 1; // bitshift left
        }
}

void shiftIt(byte dataOut) {    // Shift out 8 bits LSB first, on rising edge of clock

        boolean pinState;
        digitalWrite(dataPin, LOW); //clear shift register read for sending data

        for (int i=0; i<8; i++)  {    // for each bit in dataOut send out a bit
                digitalWrite(clockPin, LOW); //set clockPin to LOW prior to sending bit

                // if the value of DataOut and (logical AND) a bitmask
                // are true, set pinState to 1 (HIGH)
                if ( dataOut & (1<<i) ) {
                        pinState = HIGH;
                }
```

```
                else {
                        pinState = LOW;
                }
                //sets dataPin to HIGH or LOW depending on pinState
                digitalWrite(dataPin, pinState);
                digitalWrite(clockPin, HIGH); //send bit out on rising edge of clock
                digitalWrite(dataPin, LOW);
        }
digitalWrite(clockPin, LOW); //stop shifting
}
```

Project 19 – LED Dot Matrix – Basic Animation – Hardware Overview

For this project, you'll take a look at the hardware before you look at how the code works. It will make the code easier to understand.

You learned how to use the 74HC595 in the previous projects. The only addition to the circuit this time is an 8×8 LED dot matrix unit.

Dot matrix units typically come in either a 5×7 or 8×8 matrix of LEDs. The LEDs are wired in the matrix such that either the anode or cathode of each LED is common in each row. In other words, in a common anode LED dot matrix unit, each row of LEDs would have all of their anodes in that row wired together. The cathodes of the LEDs would all be wired together in each column. The reason for this will become apparent soon.

A typical single color 8×8 dot matrix unit will have 16 pins, 8 for each row and 8 for each column. You can also obtain bi-color units (e.g. red and green) as well as full color RGB (red, green, and blue) units—the ones used in large video walls. Bi or Tri (RGB) color units have two or three LEDs in each pixel of the array. These are very small and next to each other.

By turning on different combinations of red, green, or blue in each pixel and by varying their brightnesses, any color can be obtained.

The reason the rows and columns are all wired together is to minimize the number of pins required. If this were not the case, a single color 8×8 dot matrix unit would need 65 pins, one for each LED and a common anode or cathode connector. By wiring the rows and columns together, only 16 pins are required.

However, this now poses a problem if you want a particular LED to light in a certain position. If, for example, you had a common anode unit and wanted to light the LED at X, Y position 5, 3 (5th column, 3rd row), then you would apply a current to the 3rd Row and ground the 5th column pin.

The LED in the 5th column and 3rd row would now light.

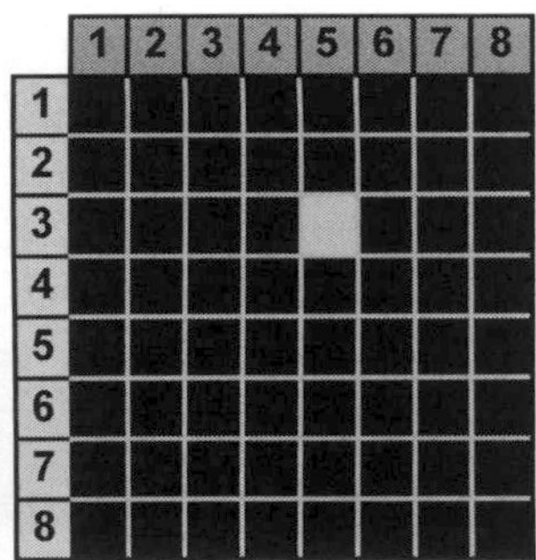

Now let's imagine that you want to also light the LED at column 3, row 6. So you apply a current to the 6th row and ground the 3rd column pin. The LED at column 3, row 6 now illuminates. But wait…the LEDs at column 3, row 6 and column 5, row 6 have also lit up.

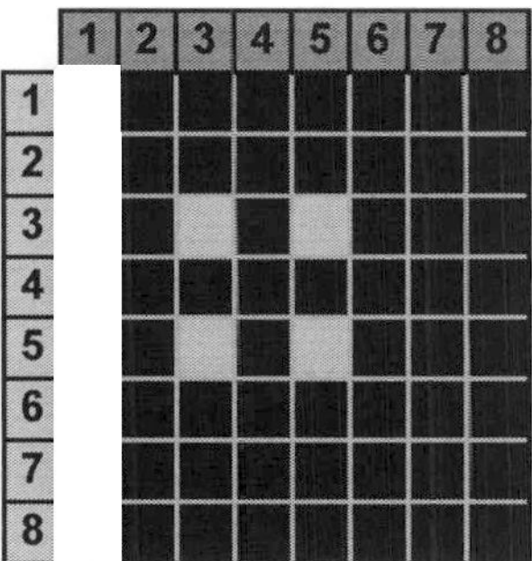

This is because you are applying power to row 3 and 6 and grounding columns 3 and 5. You can't turn off the unwanted LEDs without turning off the ones you want on. It would appear that there is no way you can light just the two required LEDs with the rows and columns wired together as they are. The only way this would work would be to have a separate pinout for each LED, meaning the number of pins would jump from 16 to 65. A 65-pin dot matrix unit would be very hard to wire up and control because you'd need a microcontroller with at least 64 digital outputs.

Is there a way to get around this problem? Yes there is, and it is called *multiplexing* (or *muxing*).

Multiplexing

Multiplexing is the technique of switching one row of the display on at a time. By selecting the column that contains the row that contains the LED that you want to be lit, and then turning the power to that row on (or the other way round for common cathode displays), the chosen LEDs in that row will illuminate. That row is then turned off and the next row is turned on, again with the appropriate columns chosen and the LEDs in the second row will now illuminate. Repeat with each row till you get to the bottom and then start again at the top.

If this is done fast enough (at more than 100Hz, or 100 times per second) then the phenomenon of *persistence of vision* (where an afterimage remains on the retina for approx 1/25th of a second) will mean that the display will appear to be steady, even though each row is turned on and off in sequence.

By using this technique, you get around the problem of displaying individual LEDs without the other LEDs in the same column or row also being lit.

For example, you want to display the following image on your display:

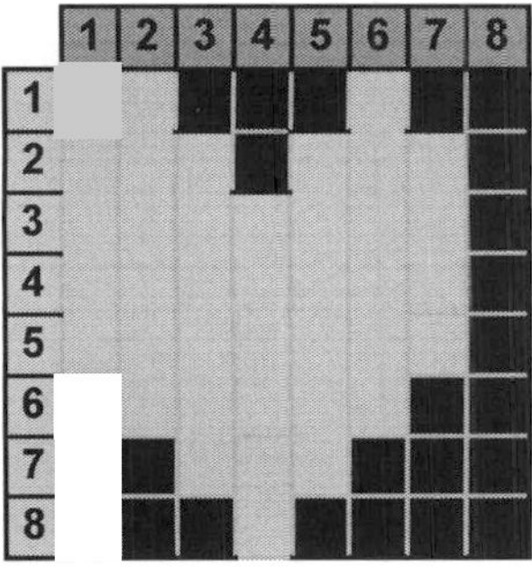

Then each row would be lit like so:

By scanning down the rows and illuminating the respective LEDs in each column of that row and doing this very fast (more than 100Hz) the human eye will perceive the image as steady and the image of the heart will be recognizable in the LED pattern.

You are using this multiplexing technique in the Project's code. That's how you're to display the heart animation without also displaying extraneous LEDs.

Project 19 – LED Dot Matrix – Basic Animation – Code Overview

The code for this project uses a feature of the ATmega chip called a Hardware Timer. This is essentially a timer on the chip that can be used to trigger an event. In your case, you're setting the ISR (Interrupt Service Routine) to fire every 10000 microseconds, which is every 100th of a second.

You make use of a library that enables easy use of interrupts, the TimerOne library. TimerOne makes creating an ISR very easy. You simply tell the function what the interval is (in this case, 10000 microseconds) and the name of the function you wish to activate every time the interrupt is fired (in this case, it's the `screenUpdate()` function).

TimerOne is an external library, so you need to include it in your code. This is easily done using the include command:

```
#include <TimerOne.h>
```

Next, the pins used to interface with the shift registers are declared:

```
int latchPin = 8; //Pin connected to Pin 12 of 74HC595 (Latch)
int clockPin = 12; //Pin connected to Pin 11 of 74HC595 (Clock)
int dataPin = 11; //Pin connected to Pin 14 of 74HC595 (Data)
```

Next, create an array of type byte that has eight elements. The led[8] array will be used to store the image you are going to display on the dot matrix display:

```
byte led[8];  // 8 element byte array to store the sprite
```

In the setup routine, you set the latch, clock, and data pins as outputs:

```
void setup() {
        pinMode(latchPin, OUTPUT);  // set the 3 digital pins to outputs
        pinMode(clockPin, OUTPUT);
        pinMode(dataPin, OUTPUT);
```

Once the pins have been set to outputs, the led array is loaded with the 8-bit binary images that will be displayed in each row of the 8×8 dot matrix display:

```
        led[0] = B11111111;  // enter the binary representation of the image
        led[1] = B10000001;  // into the array
        led[2] = B10111101;
        led[3] = B10100101;
        led[4] = B10100101;
        led[5] = B10111101;
        led[6] = B10000001;
        led[7] = B11111111;
```

By looking at the array above, you can make out the image that will be displayed, which is a box within a box. The 1s indicate where an LED will be lit and the 0s where it will be off. You can, of course, adjust the 1s and 0s yourself to make any 8×8 sprite you wish.

After this, the `Timer1` function is used. First, the function needs to be initialized with the frequency it will be activated at. In this case, you set the period to 10000 microseconds, or 1/100th of a second. Once the interrupt has been initialized, you need to attach to the interrupt a function that will be executed every time the time period is reached. This is the `screenUpdate()` function which will fire every 1/100th of a second:

```
// set a timer of length 10000 microseconds (1/100th of a second)
Timer1.initialize(10000);
// attach the screenUpdate function to the interrupt timer
Timer1.attachInterrupt(screenUpdate);
```

In the main loop, a `for` loop cycles through each of the eight elements of the led array and inverts the contents using the ~ or NOT bitwise operator. This simply turns the binary image into a negative of itself by turning all 1s to 0s and all 0s to 1s. Then it waits 500 milliseconds before repeating.

```
for (int i=0; i<8; i++) {
led[i]= ~led[i]; // invert each row of the binary image
}
delay(500);
```

You now have the `screenUpdate()` function. This is the function that the interrupt is activating every 100th of a second. This whole routine is very important because it is responsible for ensuring the LEDs in the dot matrix array are lit correctly and displaying the image you wish to convey. It's a very simple but effective function.

```
void screenUpdate() { // function to display image
byte row = B10000000; // row 1
 for (byte k = 0; k < 9; k++) {
     // Open up the latch ready to receive data
       digitalWrite(latchPin, LOW); // open latch ready to receive data

       shiftIt(~led[k] ); // LED array (inverted)
       shiftIt(row); // row binary number
       // Close the latch, sending the data in the registers out to the matrix
       digitalWrite(latchPin, HIGH);
       row = row >> 1; // bitshift right
       }
}
```

A byte called `row` is declared and initialized with the value B10000000:

```
byte row = B10000000; // row 1
```

You now cycle through the led array and send that data out to the shift registers (which is processed with the bitwise NOT ~ to make sure the columns you want to display are turned off, or grounded), followed by the row:

```
for (byte k = 0; k < 9; k++) {
        digitalWrite(latchPin, LOW); // open latch ready to receive data
shiftIt(~led[k] ); // LED array (inverted)
shiftIt(row); // row binary number
```

Once you have shifted out that current row's 8 bits, the value in row is bit shifted right one place so that the next row is displayed (i.e. the row with the 1 in it gets displayed only). You learned about the `bitshift` command in Chapter 6.

```
row = row >> 1; // bitshift right
```

Remember from the hardware overview that the multiplexing routine is only displaying one row at a time, turning it off and then displaying the next row. This is done at 100Hz which is too fast for the human eye to see the flicker.

Finally, you have a `shiftIt` function, the same as in the previous shift register-based projects, which sends the data out to the 74HC595 chips:

```
void shiftIt(byte dataOut)
```

So, the basic concept here is that you have an interrupt routine that executes every 100th of a second. In that routine, you simply take a look at the contents of a screen buffer array (in this case, `led[]`) and display it on the dot matrix unit one row at a time, but do this so fast that to the human eye it all seems to be lit at once.

The main loop of the program is simply changing the contents of the screen buffer array and letting the ISR do the rest.

The animation in this project is very simple, but by manipulating the 1s and 0s in the buffer you can make anything you like, from shapes to scrolling text, appear on the dot matrix unit. Let's try a variation on this in the next project; you'll create an animated scrolling sprite.

Project 20 – LED Dot Matrix Display – Scrolling Sprite

You're going to use the same circuit, but with a slight variation in the code to create a multi-frame animation that also scrolls from right to left. In doing so, you will be introduced to the concept of multi-dimensional arrays. You'll also learn a little trick to get bitwise rotation (or circular shift). To start, you'll use the exact same circuit as in Project 19.

Enter the Code

Enter and upload the code in Listing 7-2.

Listing 7-2. Code for Project 20

```
// Project 20
#include <TimerOne.h>

int latchPin = 8; //Pin connected to Pin 12 of 74HC595 (Latch)
int clockPin = 12; //Pin connected to Pin 11 of 74HC595 (Clock)
```

```
int dataPin = 11; //Pin connected to Pin 14 of 74HC595 (Data)
byte frame = 0;  // variable to store the current frame being displayed

byte led[8][8] = { {0, 56, 92, 158, 158, 130, 68, 56}, // 8 frames of an animation
                   {0, 56, 124, 186, 146, 130, 68, 56},
                   {0, 56, 116, 242, 242, 130, 68, 56},
                   {0, 56, 68, 226, 242, 226, 68, 56},
                   {0, 56, 68, 130, 242, 242, 116, 56},
                   {0, 56, 68, 130, 146, 186, 124, 56},
                   {0, 56, 68, 130, 158, 158, 92, 56},
                   {0, 56, 68, 142, 158, 142, 68, 56} };

void setup() {
        pinMode(latchPin, OUTPUT);  // set the 3 digital pins to outputs
        pinMode(clockPin, OUTPUT);
        pinMode(dataPin, OUTPUT);

        Timer1.initialize(10000); // set a timer of length 10000 microseconds
        Timer1.attachInterrupt(screenUpdate); // attach the screenUpdate function
}

void loop() {
        for (int i=0; i<8; i++) { // loop through all 8 frames of the animation
                for (int j=0; j<8; j++) { // loop through the 8 rows per frame
                        led[i][j]= led[i][j] << 1 | led[i][j] >> 7; // bitwise rotation
                }
        }
        frame++; // go to the next frame in the animation
        if (frame>7) { frame =0;} // make sure we go back to frame 0 once past 7
        delay(100); // wait a bit between frames
}

void screenUpdate() { // function to display image
        byte row = B10000000; // row 1
        for (byte k = 0; k < 9; k++) {
                digitalWrite(latchPin, LOW); // open latch ready to receive data

                shiftIt(~led[frame][k] ); // LED array (inverted)
                shiftIt(row); // row binary number

                // Close the latch, sending the data in the registers out to the matrix
                digitalWrite(latchPin, HIGH);
                row = row >> 1; // bitshift right
        }
}

void shiftIt(byte dataOut) {
        // Shift out 8 bits LSB first, on rising edge of clock

        boolean pinState;
```

```
        //clear shift register read for sending data
        digitalWrite(dataPin, LOW);

        // for each bit in dataOut send out a bit
        for (int i=0; i<8; i++)  {
                //set clockPin to LOW prior to sending bit
                digitalWrite(clockPin, LOW);

                // if the value of DataOut and (logical AND) a bitmask
                // are true, set pinState to 1 (HIGH)
                if ( dataOut & (1<<i) ) {
                        pinState = HIGH;
                }
                else {
                        pinState = LOW;
                }

                //sets dataPin to HIGH or LOW depending on pinState
                digitalWrite(dataPin, pinState);
                //send bit out on rising edge of clock
                digitalWrite(clockPin, HIGH);
                digitalWrite(dataPin, LOW);
        }

digitalWrite(clockPin, LOW); //stop shifting
}
```

When you run Project 20, you will see an animated wheel rolling along. The hardware hasn't changed so I don't need to discuss that. Let's see how this code works.

Project 20 – LED Dot Matrix – Scrolling Sprite – Code Overview

Again, you load the TimerOne library and set the three pins that control the shift registers:

```
#include <TimerOne.h>

int latchPin = 8; //Pin connected to Pin 12 of 74HC595 (Latch)
int clockPin = 12; //Pin connected to Pin 11 of 74HC595 (Clock)
int dataPin = 11; //Pin connected to Pin 14 of 74HC595 (Data)
```

Then you declare a variable of type byte and initialize it to zero. This will store the number of the currently displayed frame of the eight-frame animation:

```
byte frame = 0;  // variable to store the current frame being displayed
```

Next, you set up a two dimensional array of type **byte**:

```
byte led[8][8] = { {0, 56, 92, 158, 158, 130, 68, 56}, // 8 frames of an animation
                   {0, 56, 124, 186, 146, 130, 68, 56},
                   {0, 56, 116, 242, 242, 130, 68, 56},
                   {0, 56, 68, 226, 242, 226, 68, 56},
                   {0, 56, 68, 130, 242, 242, 116, 56},
                   {0, 56, 68, 130, 146, 186, 124, 56},
                   {0, 56, 68, 130, 158, 158, 92, 56},
                   {0, 56, 68, 142, 158, 142, 68, 56} };
```

Arrays were introduced in Chapter 3. An array is a collection of variables that are accessed using an index number. This array differs in that it has two sets of numbers for the elements. In Chapter 3 you declared a one-dimensional array like this:

```
byte ledPin[] = {4, 5, 6, 7, 8, 9, 10, 11, 12, 13};
```

Here you have to create a two-dimensional array with two sets of index numbers. In this case, your array is 8 X 8, or 64 elements in total. A two-dimensional array is pretty much the same as a two-dimensional table in that you can access a single cell by referencing the row and column number accordingly. Table 7-2 shows you how to access the elements in your array.

Table 7-2. *The Elements in Your Array*

	0	1	2	3	4	5	6	7
0	0	56	92 158		158	130 68		56
1	0	56	124 186	146		130	68	56
2	0	56	116 242	242		130	68	56
3	0	56	68 226		242	226 68		56
4	0	56	68	130 242		242 116		56
5	0	56	68	130 146		186 124		56
6	0	56	68 130		158	158 92		56
7	0	56	68 142		158	142 68		56

The rows represent the first number of the array index, i.e. `byte led[8][..]` and the columns represent the second number of the array index, i.e. `byte led[..][8]`. To access the number 158 in the 6th row and 4th column, you would use `byte led[6][4]`.

Notice that when you declared the array, you initialized it with data at the same time. To do this with a two-dimensional array, you put the entire data within curly brackets and each set of data from the second index into its own curly bracket with a comma after it, like so:

```
byte led[8][8] = { {0, 56, 92, 158, 158, 130, 68, 56},
                   {0, 56, 124, 186, 146, 130, 68, 56},
                   {0, 56, 116, 242, 242, 130, 68, 56}, // etc, etc.
```

The two dimensional array will store the eight frames of your animation. The first index of the array will reference the frame of the animation and the second index which of the 8 rows of 8 bit numbers make up the pattern of LEDs to turn on and off. To save space in the code, the numbers have been converted from binary to decimal. If you were to see the binary numbers, you would make out the following animation in Figure 7-3.

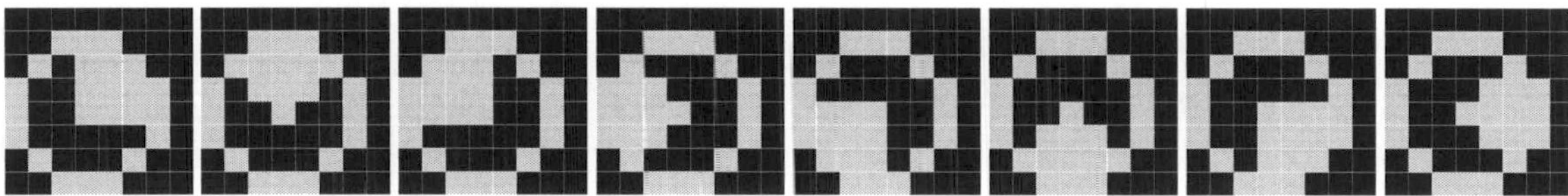

Figure 7-3. *The rolling wheel animation*

Of course, you can change this animation to anything you want and increase or decrease the number of frames, too. Draw out your animation on graph paper and then convert the rows to 8-bit binary numbers and put them into your array.

In the setup loop, you set the three pins to output again, create a timer object with a length of 10000 microseconds, and attach the `screenUpdate()` function to the interrupt:

```
void setup() {
        pinMode(latchPin, OUTPUT);  // set the 3 digital pins to outputs
        pinMode(clockPin, OUTPUT);
        pinMode(dataPin, OUTPUT);

        Timer1.initialize(10000); // set a timer of length 10000 microseconds
        Timer1.attachInterrupt(screenUpdate); // attach the screenUpdate function
}
```

In the main loop, as in Project 19, you loop through the eight rows of the sprite. However, this loop is inside another loop that repeats eight times and this loop controls which frame you wish to display:

```
void loop() {
        for (int i=0; i<8; i++) { // loop through all 8 frames of the animation
                for (int j=0; j<8; j++) { // loop through the 8 rows per frame
```

Next, you get every element in the array, one by one, and bitshift the value left by one. However, using a neat little logic trick, you ensure that whatever bit is shifted off the left hand side rolls around back to the right hand side. This is done with the following command:

```
led[i][j]= led[i][j] << 1 | led[i][j] >> 7; // bitwise rotation
```

What is happening here is that the current element of the array, chosen by the integers i and j, is shifted one place to the left. However, you then take that result and logic OR the number with the value of `led[i][j]` that has been bit shifted seven places to the right. Let's take a look at how that works.

Let's say the current value of led[i][j] is 156. This is the binary number 10011100. If this number gets bit shifted left by one, you end up with 00111000. You now take the same number, 156, and bit shift it right seven times. You now have 00000001. In other words, you have shifted the far left binary digit from the left hand side to the right hand side. You now carry out a logical OR bitwise operation on the two numbers. Remember that the bitwise OR calculation will produce a one if there is a one in either digit, like so:

00111000 |
00000001 =

____

00111001

So, you have shifted the number left one place, and OR'ed that with the same number shifted right seven places. As you can see above, the result is the same as shifting the number left by one and shifting any digit that has shifted off the left back to the right hand side. This is known as a *bitwise rotation* or a *circular shift*, and this technique is frequently used in digital cryptography. You can carry out a bitwise rotation on any length binary digit using the calculation

```
i << n | i >> (a - n);
```

where n is the number of digits you wish to rotate the number by and a is the length, in bits, of your original digit.

Next, you increase the frame value by one, check it isn't greater than seven, and if so, set it back to zero again. This will cycle through each of the eight frames of the animation one by one until you reach the end of the frames and then repeat. Finally, there is a delay of 100 milliseconds.

```
frame++; // go to the next frame in the animation
if (frame>7) { frame =0;} // make sure we go back to frame 0 once past 7
delay(100); // wait a bit between frames
```

You then run the `screenUpdate()` and `shiftIt` functions as you did in the previous shift register-based projects. In the next project, you'll be using an LED dot matrix again, but this time you won't be using shift registers. Instead, you'll use the popular MAX7219 chip.

Project 21 – LED Dot Matrix Display – Scrolling Message

There are many different ways to drive LEDs. Using shift registers is one way and they have their advantages. However, there are lots of ICs available that are specifically designed to drive LED displays and make life a lot easier for you. One of the most popular LED Driver ICs in the Arduino community is the MAX7219 serial interfaced, 8-digit LED Display Driver chips made by Maxim. These chips are designed to control 7-segment numeric LED displays of up to 8 digits, bar graph displays, or 8×8 LED dot matrix displays, which is what you will be using them for. The Arduino IDE comes with a library called Matrix plus some example code that was specifically written for the MAX7219 chips. Using this library will make using these chips a breeze. However, in this project you are not going to use any external libraries. Instead, you are going to do things the hard way and write every piece of code yourself. That way, you will learn exactly how the MAX7219 chip works, and you can transfer these skills to utilizing any other LED driver chip you wish.

Parts Required

You will need a MAX7219 LED Driver IC. Alternatively, you can use an Austria Microsystems AS1107, which is pretty much identical to the MAX7219 and will work with no changes to your code or circuit. The 8×8 dot matrix display needs to be of the Common Cathode variety this time as the MAX chip will not work with a Common Anode display.

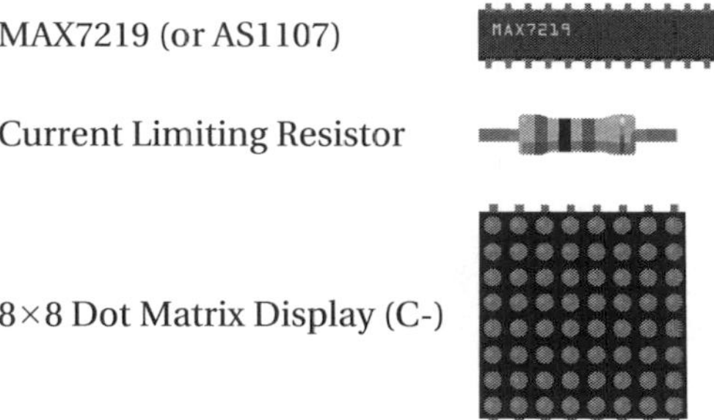

Connect It Up

Examine the diagram carefully in Figure 7-4. Make sure your Arduino is powered off while connecting the wires. The wiring from the MAX7219 to the dot matrix display in Figure 7-4 is set up for the display unit I used for creating this project. The pins on your display may differ. This isn't relevant, just wire up the pins coming out of the MAX7219 to the appropriate column and row pins on your display (see Table 7-3 for the pinouts). Reading horizontally will show which two devices are connected and to what pins. On the display, the columns are the cathodes and the rows are the anodes. On my display, I found Row 1 was at the bottom and Row 8 the top. You may need to reverse the order on your own display if you find your letters are upside down or back to front. Connect the 5V from the Arduino to the positive rail of the breadboard and the ground to the ground rail.

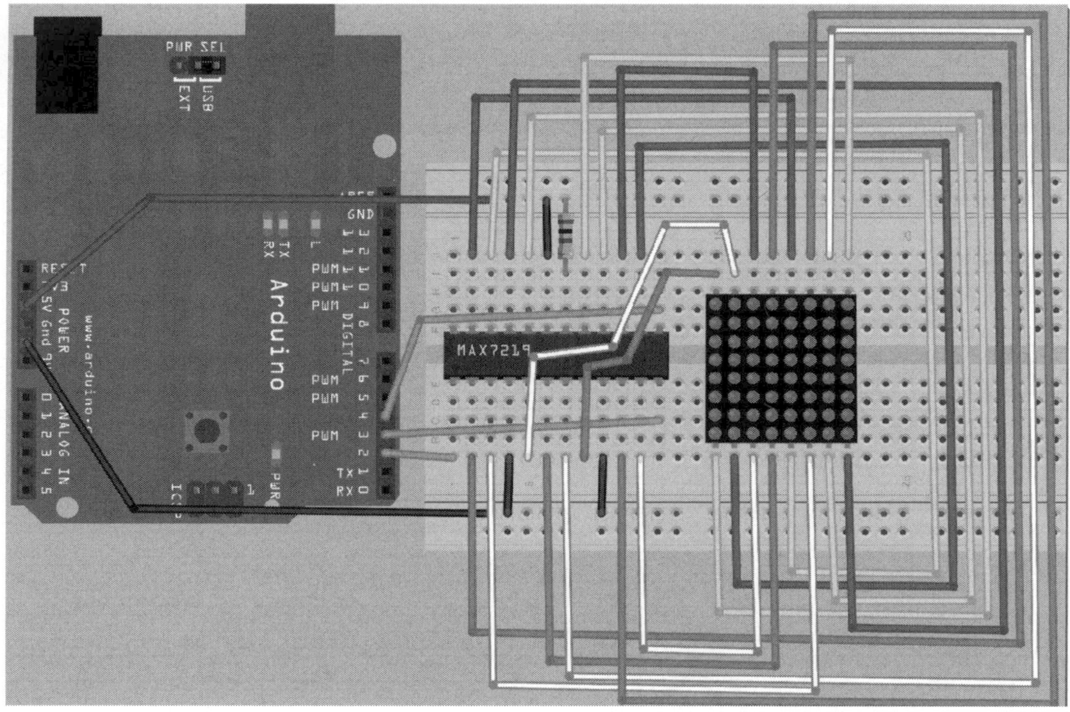

Figure 7-4. The circuit for Project 21

Table 7-3. Pinouts between the Arduino, IC, and the Dot Matrix Display

Arduino	MAX7219	Display	Other
Digital 2	1 (DIN)		
Digital 3	12 (LOAD)		
Digital 4	13 (CLK)		
4,	9		Gnd
19			+5v
	18 (ISET)		Resistor to +5v
	2 (DIG 0)	Column 1	

Arduino	MAX7219	Display	Other
	11 (DIG 1)	Column 2	
	6 (DIG 2)	Column 3	
	7 (DIG 3)	Column 4	
	3 (DIG 4)	Column 5	
	10 (DIG 5)	Column 6	
	5 (DIG 6)	Column 7	
	8 (DIG 7)	Column 8	
	22 (SEG DP)	Row 1	
	14 (SEG A)	Row 2	
	16 (SEG B)	Row 3	
	20 (SEG C)	Row 4	
	23 (SEG D)	Row 5	
	21 (SEG E)	Row 6	
	15 (SEG F)	Row 7	
	17 (SEG G)	Row 8	

Check your connections before powering up the Arduino.

Enter the Code

Enter and upload the code in Listing 7-3.

Listing 7-3. Code for Project 21

```
#include <avr/pgmspace.h>
#include <TimerOne.h>

int DataPin = 2; // Pin 1 on MAX
int LoadPin = 3; // Pin 12 on MAX
```

```
int ClockPin = 4; // Pin 13 on MAX
byte buffer[8];

static byte font[][8] PROGMEM = {
// The printable ASCII characters only (32-126)
{B00000000, B00000000, B00000000, B00000000, B00000000, B00000000, B00000000, B00000000},
{B00000100, B00000100, B00000100, B00000100, B00000100, B00000100, B00000000, B00000100},
{B00001010, B00001010, B00001010, B00000000, B00000000, B00000000, B00000000, B00000000},
{B00000000, B00001010, B00011111, B00001010, B00011111, B00001010, B00011111, B00001010},
{B00000111, B00001100, B00010100, B00001100, B00000110, B00000101, B00000110, B00011100},
{B00011001, B00011010, B00000010, B00000100, B00000100, B00001000, B00001011, B00010011},
{B00000110, B00001010, B00010010, B00010100, B00001001, B00010110, B00010110, B00001001},
{B00000100, B00000100, B00000100, B00000000, B00000000, B00000000, B00000000, B00000000},
{B00000010, B00000100, B00001000, B00001000, B00001000, B00001000, B00000100, B00000010},
{B00001000, B00000100, B00000010, B00000010, B00000010, B00000010, B00000100, B00001000},
{B00010101, B00001110, B00011111, B00001110, B00010101, B00000000, B00000000, B00000000},
{B00000000, B00000000, B00000100, B00000100, B00011111, B00000100, B00000100, B00000000},
{B00000000, B00000000, B00000000, B00000000, B00000000, B00000110, B00000100, B00001000},
{B00000000, B00000000, B00000000, B00000000, B00001110, B00000000, B00000000, B00000000},
{B00000000, B00000000, B00000000, B00000000, B00000000, B00000000, B00000000, B00000100},
{B00000001, B00000010, B00000010, B00000100, B00000100, B00001000, B00001000, B00010000},
{B00001110, B00010001, B00010011, B00010001, B00010101, B00010001, B00011001, B00001110},
{B00000100, B00001100, B00010100, B00000100, B00000100, B00000100, B00000100, B00011111},
{B00001110, B00010001, B00010001, B00000010, B00000100, B00001000, B00010000, B00011111},
{B00001110, B00010001, B00000001, B00001110, B00000001, B00000001, B00010001, B00001110},
{B00010000, B00010000, B00010100, B00010100, B00011111, B00000100, B00000100, B00000100},
{B00011111, B00010000, B00010000, B00011110, B00000001, B00000001, B00000001, B00011110},
{B00000111, B00001000, B00010000, B00011110, B00010001, B00010001, B00010001, B00001110},
{B00011111, B00000001, B00000001, B00000001, B00000010, B00000100, B00001000, B00010000},
{B00001110, B00010001, B00010001, B00001110, B00010001, B00010001, B00010001, B00001110},
{B00001110, B00010001, B00010001, B00001111, B00000001, B00000001, B00000001, B00000001},
{B00000000, B00000100, B00000100, B00000000, B00000000, B00000100, B00000100, B00000000},
{B00000000, B00000100, B00000100, B00000000, B00000000, B00000100, B00000100, B00001000},
{B00000001, B00000010, B00000100, B00001000, B00001000, B00000100, B00000010, B00000001},
{B00000000, B00000000, B00000000, B00011110, B00000000, B00011110, B00000000, B00000000},
{B00010000, B00001000, B00000100, B00000010, B00000010, B00000100, B00001000, B00010000},
{B00001110, B00010001, B00010001, B00000010, B00000100, B00000100, B00000000, B00000100},
{B00001110, B00010001, B00010001, B00010101, B00010101, B00010001, B00010001, B00011110},
{B00001110, B00010001, B00010001, B00010001, B00011111, B00010001, B00010001, B00010001},
{B00011110, B00010001, B00010001, B00011110, B00010001, B00010001, B00010001, B00011110},
{B00000111, B00001000, B00010000, B00010000, B00010000, B00010000, B00001000, B00000111},
{B00011100, B00010010, B00010001, B00010001, B00010001, B00010001, B00010010, B00011100},
{B00011111, B00010000, B00010000, B00011110, B00010000, B00010000, B00010000, B00011111},
{B00011111, B00010000, B00010000, B00011110, B00010000, B00010000, B00010000, B00010000},
{B00001110, B00010001, B00010000, B00010000, B00010111, B00010001, B00010001, B00001110},
{B00010001, B00010001, B00010001, B00011111, B00010001, B00010001, B00010001, B00010001},
{B00011111, B00000100, B00000100, B00000100, B00000100, B00000100, B00000100, B00011111},
{B00011111, B00000100, B00000100, B00000100, B00000100, B00000100, B00010100, B00001000},
{B00010001, B00010010, B00010100, B00011000, B00010100, B00010010, B00010001, B00010001},
{B00010000, B00010000, B00010000, B00010000, B00010000, B00010000, B00010000, B00011111},
{B00010001, B00011011, B00011111, B00010101, B00010001, B00010001, B00010001, B00010001},
{B00010001, B00011001, B00011001, B00010101, B00010101, B00010011, B00010011, B00010001},
```

```
{B00001110, B00010001, B00010001, B00010001, B00010001, B00010001, B00010001, B00001110},
{B00011110, B00010001, B00010001, B00011110, B00010000, B00010000, B00010000, B00010000},
{B00001110, B00010001, B00010001, B00010001, B00010001, B00010101, B00010011, B00001111},
{B00011110, B00010001, B00010001, B00011110, B00010100, B00010010, B00010001, B00010001},
{B00001110, B00010001, B00010000, B00001000, B00000110, B00000001, B00010001, B00001110},
{B00011111, B00000100, B00000100, B00000100, B00000100, B00000100, B00000100, B00000100},
{B00010001, B00010001, B00010001, B00010001, B00010001, B00010001, B00010001, B00001110},
{B00010001, B00010001, B00010001, B00010001, B00010001, B00010001, B00001010, B00000100},
{B00010001, B00010001, B00010001, B00010001, B00010001, B00010101, B00010101, B00001010},
{B00010001, B00010001, B00001010, B00000100, B00000100, B00001010, B00010001, B00010001},
{B00010001, B00010001, B00001010, B00000100, B00000100, B00000100, B00000100, B00000100},
{B00011111, B00000001, B00000010, B00000100, B00001000, B00010000, B00010000, B00011111},
{B00001110, B00001000, B00001000, B00001000, B00001000, B00001000, B00001000, B00001110},
{B00010000, B00001000, B00001000, B00000100, B00000100, B00000010, B00000010, B00000001},
{B00001110, B00000010, B00000010, B00000010, B00000010, B00000010, B00000010, B00001110},
{B00000100, B00001010, B00010001, B00000000, B00000000, B00000000, B00000000, B00000000},
{B00000000, B00000000, B00000000, B00000000, B00000000, B00000000, B00000000, B00011111},
{B00001000, B00000100, B00000000, B00000000, B00000000, B00000000, B00000000, B00000000},
{B00000000, B00000000, B00000000, B00001110, B00010010, B00010010, B00010010, B00001111},
{B00000000, B00010000, B00010000, B00010000, B00011100, B00010010, B00010010, B00011100},
{B00000000, B00000000, B00000000, B00001110, B00010000, B00010000, B00010000, B00001110},
{B00000000, B00000001, B00000001, B00000001, B00000111, B00001001, B00001001, B00000111},
{B00000000, B00000000, B00000000, B00011100, B00010010, B00011110, B00010000, B00001110},
{B00000000, B00000011, B00000100, B00000100, B00000110, B00000100, B00000100, B00000100},
{B00000000, B00001110, B00001010, B00001010, B00001110, B00000010, B00000010, B00001100},
{B00000000, B00010000, B00010000, B00010000, B00011100, B00010010, B00010010, B00010010},
{B00000000, B00000000, B00000100, B00000000, B00000100, B00000100, B00000100, B00000100},
{B00000000, B00000010, B00000000, B00000010, B00000010, B00000010, B00000010, B00001100},
{B00000000, B00010000, B00010000, B00010100, B00011000, B00011000, B00010100, B00010000},
{B00000000, B00010000, B00010000, B00010000, B00010000, B00010000, B00010000, B00001100},
{B00000000, B00000000, B00000000, B00001010, B00010101, B00010001, B00010001, B00010001},
{B00000000, B00000000, B00000000, B00010100, B00011010, B00010010, B00010010, B00010010},
{B00000000, B00000000, B00000000, B00001100, B00010010, B00010010, B00010010, B00001100},
{B00000000, B00011100, B00010010, B00010010, B00011100, B00010000, B00010000, B00010000},
{B00000000, B00001110, B00010010, B00010010, B00001110, B00000010, B00000010, B00000001},
{B00000000, B00000000, B00000000, B00001010, B00001100, B00001000, B00001000, B00001000},
{B00000000, B00000000, B00001110, B00010000, B00001000, B00000100, B00000010, B00011110},
{B00000000, B00010000, B00010000, B00011100, B00010000, B00010000, B00010000, B00001100},
{B00000000, B00000000, B00000000, B00010010, B00010010, B00010010, B00010010, B00001100},
{B00000000, B00000000, B00000000, B00010001, B00010001, B00010001, B00001010, B00000100},
{B00000000, B00000000, B00000000, B00010001, B00010001, B00010001, B00010101, B00001010},
{B00000000, B00000000, B00000000, B00010001, B00001010, B00000100, B00001010, B00010001},
{B00000000, B00000000, B00010001, B00001010, B00000100, B00001000, B00001000, B00010000},
{B00000000, B00000000, B00000000, B00011111, B00000010, B00000100, B00001000, B00011111},
{B00000010, B00000100, B00000100, B00000100, B00001000, B00000100, B00000100, B00000010},
{B00000100, B00000100, B00000100, B00000100, B00000100, B00000100, B00000100, B00000100},
{B00001000, B00000100, B00000100, B00000100, B00000010, B00000100, B00000100, B00001000},
{B00000000, B00000000, B00000000, B00001010, B00011110, B00010100, B00000000, B00000000}
};
```

```
void clearDisplay() {
	for (byte x=0; x<8; x++) {
		buffer[x] = B00000000;
	}
	screenUpdate();
}

void initMAX7219() {
	pinMode(DataPin, OUTPUT);
	pinMode(LoadPin, OUTPUT);
	pinMode(ClockPin, OUTPUT);
	clearDisplay();
	writeData(B00001011, B00000111); // scan limit set to 0:7
	writeData(B00001001, B00000000); // decode mode off
	writeData(B00001100, B00000001); // Set shutdown register to normal operation
	intensity(15); // Values 0 to 15 only (4 bit)
}

void intensity(int intensity) {
	writeData(B00001010, intensity); //B0001010 is the Intensity Register
}

void writeData(byte MSB, byte LSB) {
	byte mask;
	digitalWrite(LoadPin, LOW); // set loadpin ready to receive data
	// Send out MSB
	for (mask = B10000000; mask>0; mask >>= 1) { //iterate through bit mask
		digitalWrite(ClockPin, LOW);
		if (MSB & mask){ // if bitwise AND resolves to true
			digitalWrite(DataPin,HIGH); // send 1
		}
		else{ //if bitwise and resolves to false
			digitalWrite(DataPin,LOW); // send 0
		}
		digitalWrite(ClockPin, HIGH); // clock high, data gets input
	}
	// send out LSB for data
	 for (mask = B10000000; mask>0; mask >>= 1) { //iterate through bit mask
		digitalWrite(ClockPin, LOW);
		if (LSB & mask){ // if bitwise AND resolves to true
			digitalWrite(DataPin,HIGH); // send 1
		}
		else{ //if bitwise and resolves to false
			digitalWrite(DataPin,LOW); // send 0
		}
		digitalWrite(ClockPin, HIGH); // clock high, data gets input
	}
	digitalWrite(LoadPin, HIGH); // latch the data
	digitalWrite(ClockPin, LOW);
}
```

```
void scroll(char myString[], int speed) {
        byte firstChrRow, secondChrRow;
        byte ledOutput;
        byte chrPointer = 0; // Initialise the string position pointer
        byte Char1, Char2; // the two characters that will be displayed
        byte scrollBit = 0;
        byte strLength = 0;
        unsigned long time;
        unsigned long counter;

        // Increment count till we reach the string
        while (myString[strLength]) {strLength++;}

        counter = millis();

        while (chrPointer < (strLength-1)) {
                time = millis();
                if (time > (counter + speed)) {
                        Char1 = myString[chrPointer];
                        Char2 = myString[chrPointer+1];
                        for (byte y= 0; y<8; y++) {
                                firstChrRow = pgm_read_byte(&font[Char1 - 32][y]);
                                secondChrRow = (pgm_read_byte(&font[Char2 - 32][y])) << 1;
                                ledOutput = (firstChrRow << scrollBit) | (secondChrRow >>↵
 (8 - scrollBit) );
                                buffer[y] = ledOutput;
                        }
                        scrollBit++;
                        if (scrollBit > 6) {
                        scrollBit = 0;
                        chrPointer++;
                        }
                        counter = millis();
                }
        }
}

void screenUpdate() {
        for (byte row = 0; row < 8; row++) {
                writeData(row+1, buffer[row]);
        }
}

void setup() {
        initMAX7219();
        Timer1.initialize(10000);         // initialize timer1 and set interrupt period
        Timer1.attachInterrupt(screenUpdate);
}
```

```
void loop() {
        clearDisplay();
        scroll("   BEGINNING ARDUINO   ", 45);
        scroll("   Chapter 7 - LED Displays   ", 45);
        scroll("   HELLO WORLD!!!  :)   ", 45);
}
```

When you upload the code, you will see a message scroll across the display.

Project 21 – LED Dot Matrix – Scrolling Message – Hardware Overview

Again, to make it easier to understand the code you will need to know how the MAX7219 chip works first so let's look at the hardware before the code.

The MAX7219 operates very similarly to the shift registers in that you have to enter data in a serial fashion, bit by bit. A total of 16 bits must be loaded into the device at a time. The chip is easy to use, and it uses just three pins from the Arduino. Digital Pin 2 goes to Pin 1 on the MAX, which is the Data In. Digital Pin 3 goes to Pin 12 on the MAX, which is LOAD and finally, Digital Pin 4 goes to Pin 13 on the MAX, which is the clock. See Figure 7-5 for the pinouts of the MAX7219.

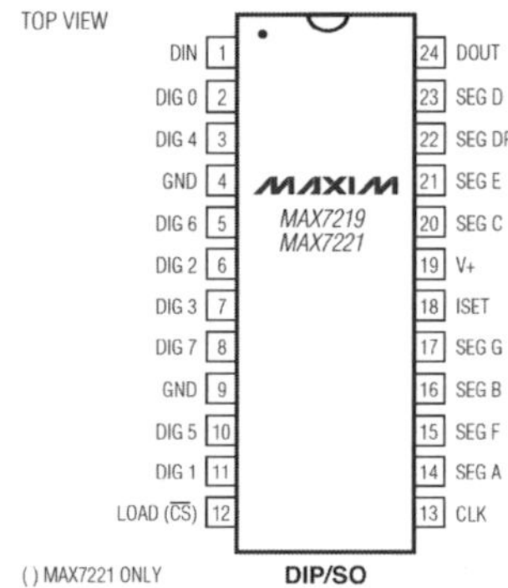

Figure 7-5. *Pin diagram for the MAX7219*

The LOAD pin is pulled low and the first bit of the data is set as either HIGH or LOW at the DIN pin. The CLK pin is set to oscillate between LOW and HIGH. On the rising edge of the clock pulse, the bit at the DIN pin is shifted into the internal register. The clock pulse then falls to LOW and the next data bit is set at the DIN pin before the process repeats. After all 16 bits of data have been pushed into the register as the clock falls and rises 16 times, the LOAD pin is finally set to HIGH and this latches the data into the register. Figure 7-6 is the timing diagram from the MAX7219 datasheet and shows how the three pins are manipulated to send data bits D0 to D15 into the device. The DOUT pin, which is pin 24, is not used in this project. But, if you had more than one MAX7219 chip daisy chained together, the DOUT of the first chip is connected to the DIN of the second and so on. Data is clocked out of the DOUT pin on the falling edge of the clock cycle.

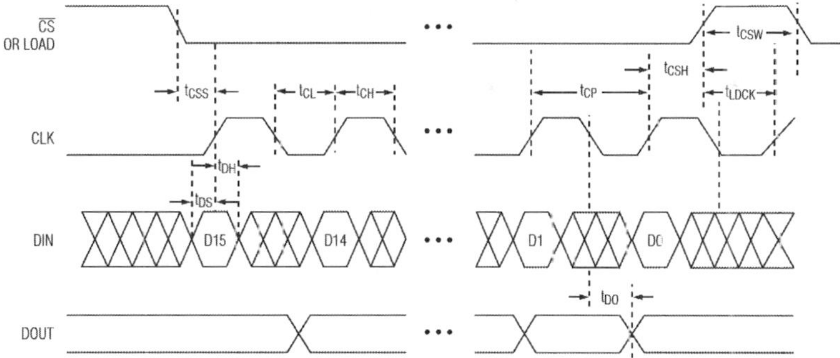

Figure 7-6. *Timing diagram for the MAX7219*

You need to recreate this timing sequence in your code to be able to send the appropriate codes to the chip. The chip can source a current of up to 100mA, which is more than enough for most dot matrix displays. If you wish to read the datasheet for the MAX7219, you can download it from Maxim at `http://datasheets.maxim-ic.com/en/ds/MAX7219-MAX7221.pdf`

The device accepts data in 16 bits. D15 or the msb (most significant bit) is sent first so the order goes from D15 down to D0. The first 4 bits are "don't care" bits, i.e. they are not used by the IC so they can be anything. The next 4 bits make up the register address and then the final 8 bits make up the data. Table 7-4 shows the serial data format and Table 7-5 shows the Register Address Map.

Table 7-4. *Serial Data Format (16 bits) of the MAX7219*

D15	D14	D13	D12	D11	D10	D9	D8	D7	D6	D5	D4	D3	D2	D1	D0
X X X X				ADDRESS				MSB			DATA X X X X X X X				LSB

Table 7-5. Register Address Map of the MAX7219

REGISTER	ADDRESS					HEX CODE
	D15-D12	D11	D10	D9	D8	
No-Op	X	0 0		0 0		0xX0
Digit 0	X	0 0		0 1		0xX1
Digit 1	X	0 0		1 0		0xX2
Digit 2	X	0 0		1 1		0xX3
Digit 3	X	0 1		0 0		0xX4
Digit 4	X	0 1		0 1		0xX5
Digit 5	X	0 1		1 0		0xX6
Digit 6	X	0 1		1 1		0xX7
Digit 7	X	1 0		0 0		0xX8
Decode Mode	X	1 0		0 1		0xX9
Intensity	X	1 0		1 0		0xXA
Scan Limit	X	1 0		1 1		0xXB
Shutdown	X	1 1		0 0		0xXC
Display Test	X	1 1		1 1		0xXF

For example, as you can see from the register address map in Table 7-5, the address for the intensity register is 1010 binary. The intensity register sets the brightness of the display with values from the dimmest at 0 to the brightest at 15 (B000 to B1111). To set the intensity to 15 (maximum), you would send the following 16 bits with the most significant bit (the bit on the far left) being sent first and the least significant bit (the bit at the far right) being sent last (i.e. the number is in reverse bit order):

```
0000101000001111
```

The 4 lowest significant bits of the first 8 bits is the value of B1111, which is the address of the intensity register. The 4 most significant bits of the first 8 bits is "don't care" so you send B0000. The LSB of the second 8 bits is the data being sent to the register. In this case, you want the value B1111 to go to the intensity register. The first 4 bits are again "don't care" so you send B0000. By sending out these 16 bits to the device, you set the display intensity to maximum. The entire 16 bit value you want to send is

B00010100 001111, but as it is sent msb (most significant bit) first and lsb (least significant bit) last, the number is sent in reverse bit order, i.e. B111100000101000.

Another address you will be using is the scan limit. Remember that the MAX7219 is designed to work with 7-segment LED displays (see Figure 7-7).

Figure 7-7. *7-segment LED display (image by Tony Jewell)*

The scan limit decides how many of the 8 digits are to be lit. In your case, you are not using 7-segment displays, but 8×8 dot matrix displays. The digits correspond to the columns in your display. You want all 8 columns to be enabled at all times, hence the scan limit register will be set to B00000111 (digits are 0 to 7 and 7 in binary is B111).

The decode mode register is only relevant if you are using 7-segment displays, so it will be set to B00000000 to turn decode off.

Finally, you will set the shutdown register to B00000001 to ensure it is in normal operation and not shutdown mode. If you set the shutdown register to B00000000, then the current sources are all pulled to ground which then blanks the display.

For further information about the MAX7219 IC, read the datasheet. Just read the parts of the datasheet that are relevant to your project and you will see that it is a lot easier to understand than it appears at first.

Now that you (hopefully) understand how the MAX7219 works, let's take a look at the code and see how to make it display scrolling text.

Project 21 – LED Dot Matrix – Scrolling Message – Code Overview

The first thing you do at the start of the sketch is to load in the two libraries that you will be utilizing in the code:

```
#include <avr/pgmspace.h>
#include <TimerOne.h>
```

The first library is the `pgmspace` or Program Space utilities. The functions in this library allow your program to access data stored in program space or flash memory. The Arduino with the ATmega328 chip has 32KB of flash memory (2KB of this is used by the bootloader, so 30KB is available). The Arduino Mega has 128KB of flash memory, 4KB of which is used by the bootloader. The program space is exactly that, the space that your program will be stored in. You can utilize the free unused space in the flash memory by using the Program Space utilities. This is where you will store the extremely large 2D array that will hold the font for your characters.

The second library is the `TimerOne` library that was first used in Project 19. Next, the three Digital Pins that will interface with the MAX7219 are declared:

```
int DataPin = 2; // Pin 1 on MAX
int LoadPin = 3; // Pin 12 on MAX
int ClockPin = 4; // Pin 13 on MAX
```

Then you create an array of type buffer with 8 elements:

```
byte buffer[8];
```

This array will store the pattern of bits that will decide what LEDs are on or off when the display is active.

Next comes a large 2D array of type byte:

```
static byte font[][8] PROGMEM = {
// The printable ASCII characters only (32-126)
{B00000000, B00000000, B00000000, B00000000, B00000000, B00000000, B00000000, B00000000},
{B00000100, B00000100, B00000100, B00000100, B00000100, B00000100, B00000000, B00000100},
..etc
```

This array is storing the pattern of bits that make up the font you will use to show text on the display. It is a two dimensional array of type `static byte`. You have also added after the array declaration the command `PROGMEM`. This is a function from the Program Space utilities and it tells the compiler to store this array in the flash memory instead of the SRAM (Static Random Access memory).

SRAM is the memory space on the ATmega chip that is normally used to store the variables and character strings used in your sketch. They are copied from program space and into SRAM when used. However, the array used to store the font is made up of 96 characters made up of eight bytes each. The array is 96 x 8 elements which is 768 elements in total, and each element is a byte (8 bits). The font therefore takes up around 768 bytes in total. The ATmega328 has only 2KB, or approx 2000 bytes of memory space for variables. Once you add to that the other variables and strings of text used in the program, you run the risk of running out of memory fast.

The Arduino has no way of warning you that it is running out of memory. Instead it just crashes. To prevent this from happening, you are storing this array in the flash memory instead of SRAM, as it has much more space for you to play with. The sketch is around 2800 bytes and the array is just under 800 bytes, so you have used about 3.6KB out of the 30KB flash memory available to you.

Then you start to create the various functions you will require for the program. The first one will simply clear the display. Whatever bits are stored in the buffer array will be displayed on the matrix. The `clearDisplay()` function simply cycles through all eight elements of the array and sets their values to zero so that no LEDs are lit and the display is blank. It then calls the `screenUpdate()` function that displays the pattern stored in the buffer[] array on the matrix. In this case, as the buffer contains nothing but zeros, nothing will be displayed.

```
void clearDisplay() {
        for (byte x=0; x<8; x++) {
                buffer[x] = B00000000;
        }
        screenUpdate();
}
```

The next function, `initMAX7219()`, has the job of setting up the MAX7219 chip ready for use. First, the three pins are set to OUTPUT:

```
void initMAX7219() {
        pinMode(DataPin, OUTPUT);
        pinMode(LoadPin, OUTPUT);
        pinMode(ClockPin, OUTPUT);
```

The display is then cleared:

```
clearDisplay();
```

The scan limit is set to 7, decode mode is turned off, and the shutdown register is set to normal operation:

```
writeData(B00001011, B00000111); // scan limit set to 0:7
writeData(B00001001, B00000000); // decode mode off
writeData(B00001100, B00000001); // Set shutdown register to normal operation
```

Then the intensity is set to maximum by calling the `intensity()` function:

```
intensity(15); // Values 0 to 15 only (4 bit)
```

Next comes the `intensity()` function itself, which simply takes the value passed to it and writes it to the intensity register by calling the `writeData` function:

```
void intensity(int intensity) {
        writeData(B00001010, intensity); //B0001010 is the Intensity Register
}
```

The next function does most of the hard work. Its job is to write the data out to the MAX7219 one bit at a time. The function requires two parameters, both bytes, and these make up the Most Significant Byte (not bit) and Least Significant Byte of the 16-bit number:

```
void writeData(byte MSB, byte LSB) {
```

A variable of type byte called mask is declared:

```
byte mask;
```

This will be used as a bitmask (introduced in Project 17) for choosing the correct bit to send out.

Next, the loadPin is set to LOW. This unlatches the data in the IC's register ready to receive new data:

```
digitalWrite(LoadPin, LOW); // set loadpin ready to receive data
```

Now you need to send out the Most Significant Byte of the 16-bit number to the chip with the leftmost (msb) bit sent first. To do this, you use two sets of `for` loops, one for the MSB and one for the LSB. The loop uses a bitmask to cycle through all 8 bits. Using a bitwise AND (&) function decides if the current bit is a 1 or a 0 and sets the dataPin to HIGH or LOW, accordingly. The clockPin is set to LOW, and the HIGH or LOW value is written to the dataPin:

```
// Send out MSB
for (mask = B10000000; mask>0; mask >>= 1) { //iterate through bit mask
        digitalWrite(ClockPin, LOW);
        if (MSB & mask){ // if bitwise AND resolves to true
                digitalWrite(DataPin,HIGH); // send 1
        }
        else{ //if bitwise and resolves to false
                digitalWrite(DataPin,LOW); // send 0
        }
        digitalWrite(ClockPin, HIGH); // clock high, data gets input
}
// send out LSB for data
 for (mask = B10000000; mask>0; mask >>= 1) { //iterate through bit mask
        digitalWrite(ClockPin, LOW);
        if (LSB & mask){ // if bitwise AND resolves to true
                digitalWrite(DataPin,HIGH); // send 1
        }
        else{ //if bitwise and resolves to false
                digitalWrite(DataPin,LOW); // send 0
        }
        digitalWrite(ClockPin, HIGH); // clock high, data gets input
}
```

Finally, the loadPin is set to HIGH to ensure the 16 bits are latched into the chips register and the clockPin is set to LOW as the last pulse was high (the clock must oscillate between HIGH and LOW for data to be pulsed successfully):

```
digitalWrite(LoadPin, HIGH); // latch the data
digitalWrite(ClockPin, LOW);
```

Next is the `scroll()` function, which is what displays the appropriate characters of the text string on the display. The function accepts two parameters, the first being the text string you wish to display and the second is the speed in which you wish the scrolling to occur in milliseconds between refreshes:

```
void scroll(char myString[], int speed) {
```

Then two variables of type byte are set up. These will store one of the eight rows of bit patterns that make up the particular character being displayed:

```
byte firstChrRow, secondChrRow;
```

Another byte is declared and called `ledOutput`. This will store the result of a calculation on the first bit pattern and second bit pattern of the characters, and it will decide which LEDs are on or off (this will be explained shortly):

```
byte ledOutput;
```

Another variable of type byte is declared called `chrPointer` and initialized to zero. chrPointer will store the current position in the text string being displayed, starting at zero and incrementing up to the length of the string:

```
byte chrPointer = 0; // Initialise the string position pointer
```

Another two bytes are declared. These will hold the current character and the next one in the string:

```
byte Char1, Char2; // the two characters that will be displayed
```

These differ from `firstChrRow` and `secondChrRow` in that they store the ASCII (American Standard Code for Information Interchange) value of the character to be displayed and the next one in the string. `firstChrRow` and `secondChrRow` store the pattern of bits that make up the letters to be displayed.

All letters, numbers, symbols, etc. that can be displayed on a computer screen or sent via serial have an ASCII code. This is simply an index number to state which character it is in the ASCII table. Characters 0 to 31 are control codes, and you will not be using those as they cannot be displayed on your dot matrix display. You will use ASCII characters 32 to 196 which are the 95 printable characters. These start at number 32, which is a space, and go up to 126, which is the tilde (~) symbol. The printable ASCII characters are listed in Table 7-6.

Table 7-6. *The Printable ASCII Characters*

```
 !"#$%&'()*+,-./0123456789:;⇔?@
ABCDEFGHIJKLMNOPQRSTUVWXYZ[\]^_`
abcdefghijklmnopqrstuvwxyz{|}~
```

Another byte is declared and initialized to zero. This will store how many bits the character pattern of the current set of letters need to be shifted to give the impression of scrolling from right to left:

```
byte scrollBit = 0;
```

Another byte will hold the length of the string of characters. This is initialized to zero:

```
byte strLength = 0;
```

Then two variables of type unsigned long are declared and these will store the current time in milliseconds since the Arduino chip was booted up or reset and another one to store the same value, but this time after a `while` routine has ran. Together these will ensure that the bits are shifted only after a specified time, in milliseconds, so it scrolls at a readable speed:

```
unsigned long time;
unsigned long counter;
```

You now need to find out how many characters are in the string. There are several ways of doing this, but in your case you simply set up a `while` loop that checks if there is data in the current array index, which is `strLength` (initialized to zero), and if so, increments the `strLength` variable by one. The loop then repeats until the condition of `myString[strLength]` is false, i.e. there are no more characters in the string, and then `strLength`, which has been incremented by one on each iteration, will now hold the length of the string:

```
while (myString[strLength]) {strLength++;}
```

Next, you set the value of counter to the value of `millis()`. You came across `millis()` in Project 4. It stores the value, in milliseconds, since the Arduino was turned on or reset:

```
counter = millis();
```

A `while` loop will now run on the condition that the current character position is smaller than the string length minus one:

```
while (chrPointer < (strLength-1)) {
```

The variable `time` is set to the current value of `millis()`:

```
time = millis();
```

An `if` statement then checks if the current time is greater than the last time stored plus the value in speed, i.e. 45 milliseconds, and if so, runs the code block within it:

```
if (time > (counter + speed)) {
```

`Char1` is loaded with the ASCII character value of the character at `chrPointer` in the `myString` array and `Char2` with the one after that:

```
Char1 = myString[chrPointer];
Char2 = myString[chrPointer+1];
```

A `for` loop now iterates through each of the eight rows:

```
for (byte y= 0; y<8; y++) {
```

You now read the font array and put the bit pattern in the current row of eight into `firstChrRow` and the second into `secondChrRow`. Remember that the font array is storing the bit patterns that make up the characters in the ASCII table, but only the printable ones from 32 to 126. The first element of the array is the ASCII code of the character (minus 32, as you are not using characters 0 to 31) and the second element of the array stores the eight rows of bit patterns that make up that character. For example, the letters A and Z are ASCII characters 65 and 90 respectively. You deduct 32 from these numbers to give you your array index.

So the letter A, which is ASCII code 65, is stored in array element 33 (65-32) and the second dimension of the array at that index stores the eight bit patterns that make up the letter. The letter Z is ASCII code 90, which is index number 58 in the array. The data in font[33][0…8], for the letter A, is

```
{B00001110, B00010001, B00010001, B00010001, B00011111, B00010001, B00010001, B00010001},
```

If you put that data on top of each other so you can see it clearer, you have

```
B00001110
B00010001
B00010001
B00010001
B00011111
B00010001
B00010001
B00010001
```

and if you look closely, you will see the following pattern which makes up the letter A:

For the letter Z, the data in the array is

```
B00011111
B00000001
B00000010
B00000100
B00001000
B00010000
B00010000
B00011111
```

which corresponds with the LED bit pattern of

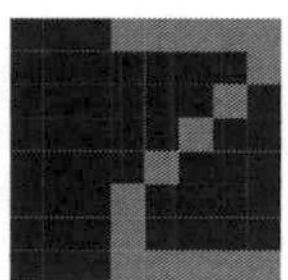

To read the bit pattern, you need to access the font, which is stored in program space and not SRAM as normal. To do this, you need to make use of one of the utilities from the pgmspace library, `pgm_read_byte`.

```
firstChrRow = pgm_read_byte(&font[Char1 - 32][y]);
secondChrRow = (pgm_read_byte(&font[Char2 - 32][y])) << 1;
```

When you access program space, you are obtaining data held in the flash memory. To do so, you need to know the address in memory where the data is stored (each storage location in memory has a unique address number).

To do that, you use the & symbol in front of a variable. When you do that, you do not read the data in that variable, you read the address where the data is stored instead. The `pgm_read_byte` command needs to know the flash memory address of the data you want to retrieve, so you put a & symbol in front of `font[Char1 - 32][y]` to make `pgm_read_byte(&font[Char1 - 32][y])`. This simply means that you read the byte in program space stored at the address of `font[Char1 - 32][y]`.

The value of `secondChrRow` is bitshifted left one simply to make the gap between letters smaller, thereby making them more readable on the display. This is because there are no bits used to the left of all characters for three spaces. You could bitshift it left by two to bring them closer but it starts to become hard to read if you do.

The next line loads the bit pattern for the relevant row into `ledOutput`:

```
ledOutput = (firstChrRow << scrollBit) | (secondChrRow >> (8 - scrollBit) );
```

As you want the letters to scroll from right to left, you bitshift left the first letter by `scrollBit` amount of times and the second letter by 8 – `scrollBit` amount of times. You then logical OR the results together to merge them into the 8-bit pattern required to display. For example, if the letters you were displaying were A and Z, then the patterns for both would be

```
B00001110 B00011111
B00010001 B00000001
B00010001 B00000010
B00010001 B00000100
B00011111 B00001000
B00010001 B00010000
B00010001 B00010000
B00010001 B00011111
```

So, the calculation above on the top row, when `scrollBit` is set to 5, i.e. the letters have scrolled five pixels to the left, would be

B11000000 B00000011

which is the top row of the A bitshifted left 5 times and the top row of the Z bitshifted right 3 times (8-5). You can see that the left hand pattern is what you get when the letter A is scrolled left by five pixels and the right hand pattern is what you get if the letter Z was scrolled in from the right hand side by 5 pixels. The logical OR, which is the | symbol, has the effect of merging these two patterns together to create

B11000011

which is what you would get if the letter A and Z were next to each other and scrolled left five pixels.

The next line loads that pattern of bits in to the appropriate row of the screen buffer:

```
buffer[y] = ledOutput;
```

The scrollBit is increased by one:

```
scrollBit++;
```

Then an `if` statement checks if the `scrollBit` value has reached 7. If so, it sets it back to zero and increases the `chrPointer` by one so the next time the function is called, it will display the next two sets of characters:

```
if (scrollBit > 6) {
        scrollBit = 0;
        chrPointer++;
}
```

Finally, the value of counter is updated to the latest `millis()` value:

```
counter = millis();
```

The `screenUpdate()` function simply takes the eight rows of bit patterns you have loaded into the eight element buffer array and writes it to the chip, which in turn displays it on the matrix:

```
void screenUpdate() {
        for (byte row = 0; row < 8; row++) {
                writeData(row+1, buffer[row]);
        }
}
```

After setting up these six functions, you finally reach the `setup()` and `loop()` functions of the program. In `setup()`, the chip is initialized by calling `initMax7219()`, a timer is created and set to a refresh period of 10000 microseconds, and the `screenUpdate()` function attached. As before, this ensures the `screenUpdate()` function is activated every 10000 microseconds no matter what else is going on.

```
void setup() {
        initMAX7219();
        Timer1.initialize(10000);         // initialize timer1 and set interrupt period
        Timer1.attachInterrupt(screenUpdate);
}
```

Finally, the main loop of the program simply has four lines. The first clears the display and then the next three call the scroll routine to display the three lines of text and set them scrolling across the display.

```
void loop() {
        clearDisplay();
        scroll("   BEGINNING ARDUINO   ", 45);
        scroll("   Chapter 7 - LED Displays   ", 45);
        scroll("   HELLO WORLD!!!  :)   ", 45);
}
```

You can, of course, change the text in the code so that the display says anything you wish. Project 21 was pretty complex as far as the code goes. As I said at the start, all of this hard work could have been avoided if you had simply used some of the pre-existing LED matrix libraries that are available in the public domain. But in doing so, you would not have learnt how the MAX7219 chip works. By doing things the hard way, you should now have a good understand of the MAX7219 chip and how to control it. These skills can be ported to operate just about any other external IC as the principles are pretty much the same.

In the next project, you will make use of these libraries so you can see how they make life easier for you. Let's take your display and have a bit of fun with it.

Project 22 – LED Dot Matrix Display – Pong Game

Project 21 was hard going and a lot to take in. So, for Project 22 you are going to create a simple game with simple code using the dot matrix display and a potentiometer. This time you are going to use one of the many available libraries for controlling LED dot matrix displays to see how much easier it can make your life when coding.

Parts Required

The parts required are the same as Project 21 with the addition of a 10KΩ Potentiometer

Same as Project 21 plus....

10KΩ Potentiometer 

Connect It Up

Leave the circuit the same as in Project 21 and add a potentiometer. The left and right pins go to Ground and +5V, respectively, and the center pin goes to Analog Pin 5.

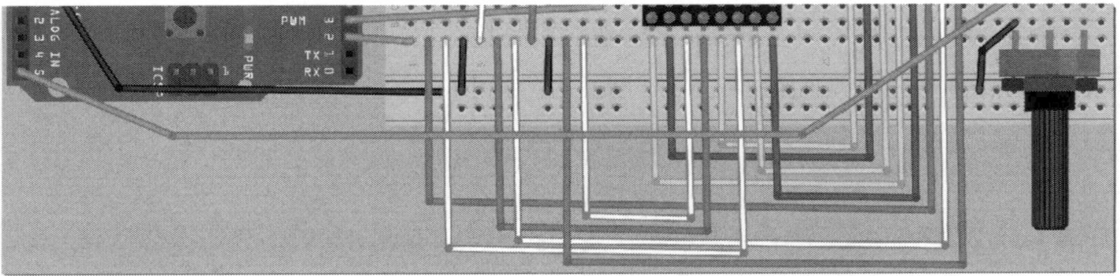

Figure 7-8. Add a potentiometer to the Project 21 circuit

Upload the Code

Upload the code from Listing 7-4. When the program is run, a ball will start from a random location on the left and head towards the right. Using the potentiometer, control the paddle to bounce the ball back towards the wall. As time goes by, the speed of the ball will increase faster and faster until you will not be able to keep up with it.

When the ball bounces past the paddle, the screen will flash and the game will restart. See how long you can go for before the game resets.

Listing 7-4. Code for Project 21

```
//Project 22
#include "LedControl.h"

LedControl myMatrix = LedControl(2, 4, 3, 1); // create an instance of a Matrix

int column = 1, row = random(8)+1; // decide where the ball will start
int directionX = 1, directionY = 1; // make sure it heads from left to right first
int paddle1 = 5, paddle1Val; // Pot pin and value
int speed = 300;
int counter = 0, mult = 10;

void setup()
{
        myMatrix.shutdown(0, false); // enable display
        myMatrix.setIntensity(0, 8); //  Set the brightness to medium
        myMatrix.clearDisplay(0); // clear the display
        randomSeed(analogRead(0));
}

void loop()
{
        paddle1Val = analogRead(paddle1);
        paddle1Val = map(paddle1Val, 200, 1024, 1,6);
        column += directionX;
        row += directionY;
        if (column == 6 && directionX == 1 && (paddle1Val == row || paddle1Val+1 ==↵
 row || paddle1Val+2 == row)) {directionX = -1;}
        if (column == 0 && directionX == -1 ) {directionX = 1;}
        if (row == 7 && directionY == 1 ) {directionY = -1;}
 if (row == 0 && directionY == -1 ) {directionY = 1;}
        if (column == 7) { oops();}
        myMatrix.clearDisplay(0); // clear the screen for next animation frame
        myMatrix.setLed(0, column, row, HIGH);
        myMatrix.setLed(0, 7, paddle1Val, HIGH);
        myMatrix.setLed(0, 7, paddle1Val+1, HIGH);
        myMatrix.setLed(0, 7, paddle1Val+2, HIGH);
        if (!(counter % mult)) {speed -= 5; mult * mult;}
        delay(speed);
        counter++;
}
```

```
void oops() {
        for (int x=0; x<3; x++) {
        myMatrix.clearDisplay(0);
        delay(250);
                for (int y=0; y<8; y++) {
                        myMatrix.setRow(0, y, 255);
                }
                delay(250);
        }
        counter=0; // reset all the values
        speed=300;
        column=1;
        row = random(8)+1; // choose a new starting location
}
```

Project 22 – LED Dot Matrix – Pong Game

The code for Project 22 is really simple. After all, you are taking a break from the hard work done in Project 21!

First, the LedControl.h library is included in the sketch. You will need to download the library and install it in the libraries folder as before. The library, as well as further information, can be found at `www.arduino.cc/playground/Main/LedControl`

```
#include "LedControl.h"
```

You then create an instance of an `LedControl` object like so

```
LedControl myMatrix = LedControl(2, 4, 3, 1); // create an instance of a Matrix
```

This creates an `LedControl` object called myMatrix. The `LedControl` object requires four parameters. The first three are the pin numbers for the MAX7219; the order is Data In, Clock, and Load. The final number is for the number of the chip (in case you are controlling more than one MAX7219 and display).

Then you decide which column and row the ball will start in. The row is decided using a random number.

```
int column = 1, row = random(8)+1; // decide where the ball will start
```

Now two integers are declared to decide the direction the ball will travel in. If the number is positive, it will head from left to right and bottom to top, respectively, and if negative, it will be in reverse.

```
int directionX = 1, directionY = 1; // make sure it heads from left to right first
```

You decide which pin is being used for the paddle (the potentiometer) and declare an integer to hold the value read from the analog pin:

```
int paddle1 = 5, paddle1Val; // Pot pin and value
```

The speed of the ball is declared in milliseconds:

```
int speed = 300;
```

Then you declare and initialize a counter to zero and its multiplier to 10:

```
int counter = 0, mult = 10;
```

The `setup()` function enables the display by ensuring that the powersaving mode is set to false. The intensity is set to medium and then the display is cleared in preparation for the game. Before you start, the `randomSeed` is set with a random value read from an unused analog pin.

```
void setup()
{
        myMatrix.shutdown(0, false); // enable display
        myMatrix.setIntensity(0, 8); //  Set the brightness to medium
        myMatrix.clearDisplay(0); // clear the display
        randomSeed(analogRead(0));
}
```

In the main loop, you start by reading the analog value from the paddle:

```
paddle1Val = analogRead(paddle1);
```

Then those values are mapped to between 1 and 6:

```
paddle1Val = map(paddle1Val, 200, 1024, 1,6);
```

The map command requires five parameters. The first is the number to map. Next are the low and high values of the number and the low high values you wish to map it to. In your case, you are taking the value in `paddle1Val`, which is the voltage read from Analog Pin 5. This value ranges from 0 at 0 volts to 1024 at 5 volts. You want those numbers mapped to read only between 1 and 6 as this is the row the paddle will be displayed on when drawn on the display.

The column and row coordinates are increased by the values in directionX and directionY:

```
column += directionX;
row += directionY;
```

You now need to decide if the ball has hit a wall or a paddle, and if so, bounce back (the exception being if it goes past the paddle0. The first `if` statement checks that the ball has hit the paddle. It does this by deciding if the column the ball is in is column 6 and (logical AND &&) is also heading left to right:

```
if (column == 6 && directionX == 1 && (paddle1Val == row || paddle1Val+1 == row ||
paddle1Val+2 == row)) {directionX = -1;}
```

There are three conditions that have to be met for the ball direction to change. The first is that the column is 6, second is that the direction is positive (i.e. left to right) and third is that the ball is on the same row that either of the 3 dots that make up the paddle is in. This is done by nesting a set of `or` (logical OR ||) commands inside brackets. The result of this calculation is checked first and then the result added to the three && statements in the first set of brackets.

The next three sets of `if` statements check if the ball has hit the top, bottom, or left side walls, and if so, reverses the ball direction:

```
if (column == 0 && directionX == -1 ) {directionX = 1;}
if (row == 7 && directionY == 1 ) {directionY = -1;}
if (row == 0 && directionY == -1 ) {directionY = 1;}
```

Finally, if the ball is in column 7, it has obviously not hit the paddle but has gone past it. If that is the case, call the `oops()` function to flash the display and reset the values:

```
if (column == 7) { oops();}
```

Next the display is cleared to erase any previous dots:

```
myMatrix.clearDisplay(0); // clear the screen for next animation frame
```

The ball is drawn at the column and row location. This is done with the `.setLed` command of the LedControl library:

```
myMatrix.setLed(0, column, row, HIGH);
```

The `.setLed` command requires four parameters. The first number is the address of the display, then the x and y (or column and row) co-ordinates and finally a HIGH or LOW for on and off. These are used again to draw the three dots that make up the paddle at column 7 and row `paddle1Val` (plus one above and one above that).

```
myMatrix.setLed(0, 7, paddle1Val, HIGH);
myMatrix.setLed(0, 7, paddle1Val+1, HIGH);
myMatrix.setLed(0, 7, paddle1Val+2, HIGH);
```

You then check if the modulo of `counter` % `mult` is NOT (logical NOT !) true, and if so, decrease the speed by five and multiply the multiplier by itself. Modulo is the remainder when you divide one integer by another. In your case, you divide counter by `mult` and check if the remainder is a whole number or not. This basically ensures that the speed is only increased after a set time and that the time increases proportionally to the decreasing delay.

```
if (!(counter % mult)) {speed -= 5; mult * mult;}
```

A delay in milliseconds of the value of speed is activated and then the counter value is increased by one:

```
delay(speed);
counter++;
}
```

Finally, the `oops()` function causes a `for` loop within a `for` loop to clear the display and then fills in all rows repeatedly with a 250 millisecond delay in between. This makes all LEDs flash on and off to indicate the ball has gone out of play and the game is about to reset. Then all of the values of counter, speed, and column are set to their starting positions and a new random value chosen for row.

```
void oops() {
for (int x=0; x<3; x++) {
myMatrix.clearDisplay(0);
delay(250);
```

```
            for (int y=0; y<8; y++) {
                    myMatrix.setRow(0, y, 255);
            }
            delay(250);
    }
    counter=0; // reset all the values
    speed=300;
    column=1;
    row = random(8)+1; // choose a new starting location
}
```

The `.setRow` command works by passing the address of the display, the row value, and then the binary pattern of which LEDs to turn on or off. In this case, you want them all on, which is binary 11111111 and decimal 255.

The purpose of Project 22 was to show how much easier it is to control an LED Driver chip if you use a ready-made library of code designed for the chip. In Project 21, you did it the hard way coding everything from scratch; in Project 22, the hard work was all done for you behind the scenes. There are other Matrix libraries available; in fact, the Arduino IDE comes with one called matrix. I had better luck with the LedControl.h library myself and so I chose that. You can use whichever library suits your needs best.

In the next chapter, you will look at a different type of dot matrix display, the LCD.

EXERCISE

Take the concepts from Projects 21 and 22 and combine them. Make a Pong Game but have the code keep a tab of the score (in milliseconds since the game started). When the ball goes out of play, use the scrolling text function to show the score of the game just played (milliseconds the player survived) and the highest score to date.

Summary

Chapter 7 introduced you to some pretty complex subjects, including the use of external ICs. You are not even half way through the projects yet and you already know how to control a dot matrix display using both shift registers and a dedicated LED driver IC. Also, you learned how to coding things the hard way and then how to code the easy way by incorporating a ready-made library designed for your LED Driver IC.

You have also learned the sometimes-baffling concept of multiplexing, a skill that will come in very handy for many other things as well as dot matrix displays.

Subjects and concepts covered in Chapter 7:

- How a dot matrix display is wired up
- How to install an external library
- The concept of multiplexing (or muxing)

- How to use multiplexing to turn on 64 LEDs individually using just 16 output pins
- The basic concept of timers
- How to use the TimerOne library to activate code no matter what else is going on
- How to include external libraries in your code using the #include directive
- How to use binary numbers to store LED images
- How to invert a binary number using a bitwise NOT ~
- How to take advantage of persistence of vision to trick the eye
- How to store animation frames in multidimensional arrays
- How to declare and initialize a multidimensional array
- Accessing data in a specific element in a two dimensional array
- How to do a bitwise rotation (aka circular shift)
- How to control LED dot matrix displays using shift registers
- How to control LED dot matrix displays using MAX7219 ICs
- How to time pulses correctly to load data in and out of external ICs
- How to store a character font in a two dimensional array
- How to read timing diagrams from datasheets
- How to use the registers in the MAX7219
- How to bypass the SRAM limits and store data in program space
- How to reverse the order of bits
- How to make text and other symbols scroll across a dot matrix display
- The concept of the ASCII character table
- Choosing a character from its ASCII code
- How to find out the length of a text string
- How to write to and read from program space
- How to obtain the address in memory of a variable using the & symbol
- How to use the LedControl.h library to control individual LEDs and rows of LEDs
- How to use the logical operators
- How to make life easier and code development faster using code libraries

CHAPTER 8

■ ■ ■

Liquid Crystal Displays

Let's investigate another popular method of displaying text and symbols, the LCD (Liquid Crystal Display). LCDs are the displays typically used in calculators and alarm clocks. Many Arduino projects involve LCDs, so it's essential that you know how to use them. LCD displays require driver chips to control them; these are built into the display. The most popular type of driver chip is the Hitachi HD44780 (or compatible).

Creating projects based around LCD displays is nice and easy thanks to an array of readily available LCD code libraries. The Arduino IDE comes with a library called LiquidCrystal.h that has a great list of features. You will be using this one in your projects.

Project 23 – Basic LCD Control

To start with, you will create a demonstration project that will show off most of the functions available in the LiquidCrystal.h library. To do so, you'll use a backlit 16×2 LCD Display.

Parts Required

You need to obtain an LCD Display that uses the HD44780 driver. There are many available and they come in all kinds of colors. As an amateur astronomer, I particularly like the red on black displays (red text on a black background) because they preserve your night vision if used in astronomy based projects. You can choose another color text and background but your display must have a backlight and be able to display sixteen columns and two rows of characters (often referred to as 16×2 LCD displays).

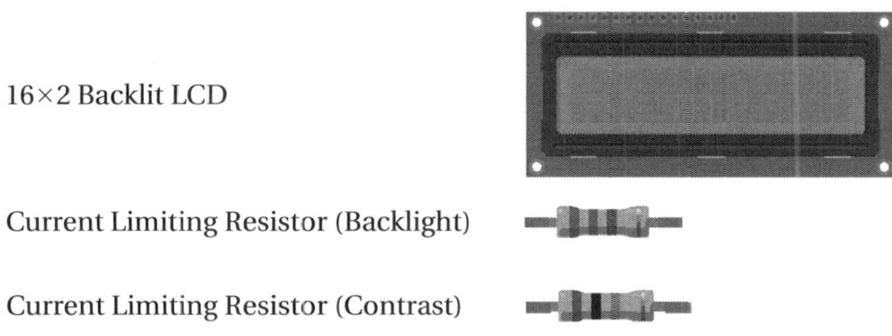

Connect It Up

The circuit for Project 23 is quite simple. Find the datasheet for the LCD you are using. The following pins (see Table 8-1) from the Arduino, +5v, and Ground need to go to the LCD.

Table 8-1. *Pins to use for the LCD*

Arduino	Other	Matrix
Digital 11		Enable
Digital 12		RS (Register Select)
Digital 5		DB4 (Data Pin 4)
Digital 4		DB5 (Data Pin 5)
Digital 3		DB6 (Data Pin 6)
Digital 2		DB7 (Data Pin 7)
Gnd		Vss (GND)
Gnd		R/W (Read/Write)
+5v		Vdd
	+5v via resistor	Vo (Contrast)
	+5v via resistor	A/Vee (Power for LED)
	Gnd	Gnd for LED

Data Pins 0 to 3 are not used because you are going to use what is known as 4-bit mode. For a typical LCD display the circuit in Figure 8-1 will be correct.

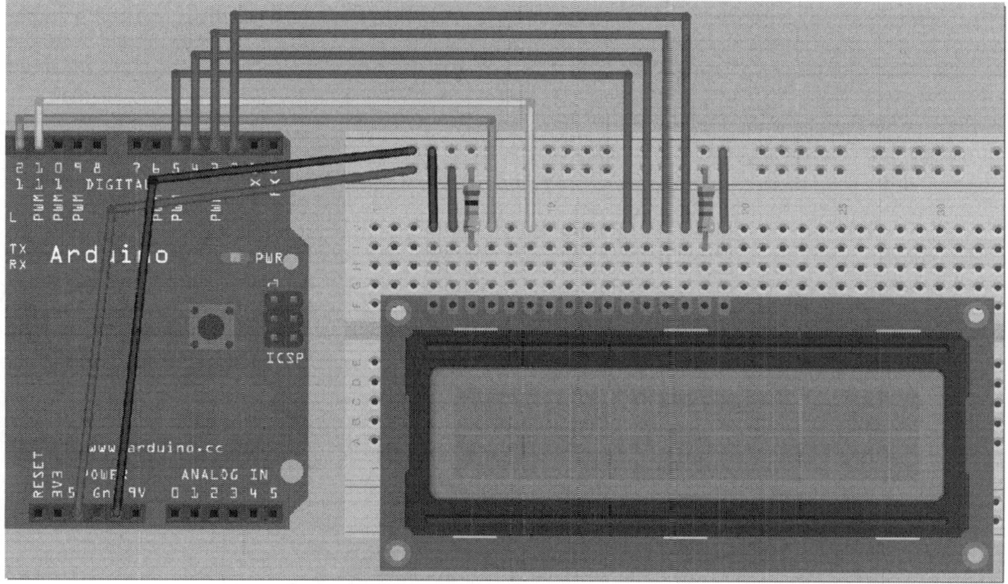

Figure 8-1. The circuit for Project 23 – Basic LCD Control

The contract adjustment pin on the LCD must be connected via a current limiting resistor in order to adjust the contrast the desired level. A value of around 10K ohm should suffice. If you find it difficult to get the right value, then connect a potentiometer (with value between about 4K ohm to 10K ohm) with the left leg to +5v, the right leg to ground, and the center leg to the contrast adjustment pin (Pin 3 on my test LCD). Now you can use the knob to adjust the contrast until you can see the display clearly.

The backlight on my test LCD required 4.2v, so I added the appropriate current limiting resistor between +5v and the LED power supply pin (Pin 15 on my LCD). You could connect the LED power pin to a PWM pin on the Arduino and use a PWM output to control the brightness of the backlight, but for simplicity's sake you won't use this method in this project. Once you're happy that you have the correct pins going between the Arduino, +5v, and Ground (according to the LCDs datasheet), you can enter the code

Enter The Code

Check your wiring, then upload the code from Listing 8-1.

Listing 8-1. Code for Project 23

```
// PROJECT 23
#include <LiquidCrystal.h>

// Initialize the library with the numbers of the interface pins
LiquidCrystal lcd(12, 11, 5, 4, 3, 2); // Create an lcd object and assign the pins
```

```
void setup() {
	lcd.begin(16, 2); // Set the display to 16 columns and 2 rows
}

void loop() {
	// Run the seven demo routines
	basicPrintDemo();
	displayOnOffDemo();
	setCursorDemo();
	scrollLeftDemo();
	scrollRightDemo();
	cursorDemo();
	createGlyphDemo();
}

void basicPrintDemo() {
	lcd.clear(); // Clear the display
	lcd.print("Basic Print"); // Print some text
	delay(2000);
}

void displayOnOffDemo() {
	lcd.clear(); // Clear the display
	lcd.print("Display On/Off"); // Print some text
	for(int x=0; x < 3; x++) { // Loop 3 times
		lcd.noDisplay(); // Turn display off
		delay(1000);
		lcd.display(); // Turn it back on again
		delay(1000);
	}
}

void setCursorDemo() {
	lcd.clear(); // Clear the display
	lcd.print("SetCursor Demo"); // Print some text
	delay(1000);
	lcd.clear(); // Clear the display
	lcd.setCursor(5,0); // Cursor at column 5 row 0
	lcd.print("5,0");
	delay(2000);
	lcd.setCursor(10,1); // Cursor at column 10 row 1
	lcd.print("10,1");
	delay(2000);
	lcd.setCursor(3,1); // Cursor at column 3 row 1
	lcd.print("3,1");
	delay(2000);
}
```

```
void scrollLeftDemo() {
        lcd.clear(); // Clear the display
        lcd.print("Scroll Left Demo");
        delay(1000);
        lcd.clear(); // Clear the display
        lcd.setCursor(7,0);
        lcd.print("Beginning");
        lcd.setCursor(9,1);
        lcd.print("Arduino");
        delay(1000);
        for(int x=0; x<16; x++) {
                lcd.scrollDisplayLeft(); // Scroll display left 16 times
                delay(250);
        }
}

void scrollRightDemo() {
        lcd.clear(); // Clear the display
        lcd.print("Scroll Right");
        lcd.setCursor(0,1);
        lcd.print("Demo");
        delay(1000);
        lcd.clear(); // Clear the display
        lcd.print("Beginning");
        lcd.setCursor(0,1);
        lcd.print("Arduino");
        delay(1000);
        for(int x=0; x<16; x++) {
                lcd.scrollDisplayRight(); // Scroll display right 16 times
                delay(250);
        }
}

void cursorDemo() {
        lcd.clear(); // Clear the display
        lcd.cursor(); // Enable cursor visible
        lcd.print("Cursor On");
        delay(3000);
        lcd.clear(); // Clear the display
        lcd.noCursor(); // Cursor invisible
        lcd.print("Cursor Off");
        delay(3000);
        lcd.clear(); // Clear the display
        lcd.cursor(); // Cursor visible
        lcd.blink(); // Cursor blinking
        lcd.print("Cursor Blink On");
        delay(3000);
        lcd.noCursor(); // Cursor invisible
        lcd.noBlink(); // Blink off
}
```

```
void createGlyphDemo() {
        lcd.clear();

        byte happy[8] = { // Create byte array with happy face
        B00000,
        B00000,
        B10001,
        B00000,
        B10001,
        B01110,
        B00000,
        B00000};

        byte sad[8] = { // Create byte array with sad face
        B00000,
        B00000,
        B10001,
        B00000,
        B01110,
        B10001,
        B00000,
        B00000};

        lcd.createChar(0, happy); // Create custom character 0
        lcd.createChar(1, sad); // Create custom character 1

        for(int x=0; x<5; x++) { // Loop animation 5 times
                lcd.setCursor(8,0);
                lcd.write(0); // Write custom char 0
                delay(1000);
                lcd.setCursor(8,0);
                lcd.write(1); // Write custom char 1
                delay(1000);
        }
}
```

Project 23 – Basic LCD Control – Code Overview

First you load in the library that you are going to use to control the LCD. There are many libraries and code examples available for different types of LCDs; you can find them all on the Arduino playground at www.arduino.cc/playground/Code/LCD. However, the Arduino IDE comes with a library called LiquidCrystal.h that is easy to understand and use:

```
#include <LiquidCrystal.h>
```

Now you need to create and LiquidCrystal object and set the appropriate pins:

```
LiquidCrystal lcd(12, 11, 5, 4, 3, 2); // Create an lcd object and assign the pins
```

So you have created a LiquidCrystal object and called it lcd. The first two parameters set the pins for RS (Register Select) and Enable. The last four parameters are Data Pins D4 to D7. As you are using 4-bit mode, you are only using four of the eight data pins on the display.

The difference between 4-bit and 8-bit modes is that in 8-bit mode you can send data one byte at a time whereas in 4-bit mode the 8 bits have to be split up into to 4-bit numbers (known as nibbles). This makes the code larger and more complex. However, you are using a readymade library, so you don't need to worry about that. If, however, you were writing space- or time-critical code, you would consider writing directly to the LCD in 8-bit mode. Using 4-bit mode has the advantage of saving four pins which is useful if you want to connect other devices at the same time.

In the `setup()` loop you initialize the display to the size required, which is 16 columns and 2 rows:

```
lcd.begin(16, 2); // Set the display to 16 columns and 2 rows
```

The main program loop simply runs seven different demo routines, one by one, before restarting. Each demo routine shows off one set of related routines in the LiquidCrystal.h library:

```
void loop() {
        // Run the seven demo routines
        basicPrintDemo();
        displayOnOffDemo();
        setCursorDemo();
        scrollLeftDemo();
        scrollRightDemo();
        cursorDemo();
        createGlyphDemo();
}
```

The first function is `basicPrintDemo()` and it is designed to show use of the `.print()` command. This demo simply clears the display using `lcd.clear()` and then prints to the display using `lcd.print()`. Note that if you had initialized your LiquidCrystal object and called it, for example, LCD1602, then these commands would be `LCD1602.clear()` and `LCD1602.print()` accordingly. In other words, the command comes after the name of the object, with a dot between them.

The `print()` command will print whatever is inside the brackets at the current cursor location. The default cursor location is always column 0 and row 0, which is the top right corner. After clearing the display, the cursor will be set to the default or home position.

```
void basicPrintDemo() {
        lcd.clear(); // Clear the display
        lcd.print("Basic Print"); // Print some text
        delay(2000);
}
```

The second function is designed to show off the `display()` and noDisplay() commands. These commands simply enable or disable the display. The routine prints out "Display On/Off" and then runs a loop three times to turn the display off, wait one second, turn it back on, wait another second, then repeat. Whenever you turn the display off, whatever was printed on the screen before it went off will be preserved when the display is re-enabled.

```
void displayOnOffDemo() {
        lcd.clear(); // Clear the display
        lcd.print("Display On/Off"); // Print some text
        for(int x=0; x < 3; x++) { // Loop 3 times
                lcd.noDisplay(); // Turn display off
                delay(1000);
                lcd.display(); // Turn it back on again
                delay(1000);
        }
}
```

The next function shows off the **setCursor()** command, which sets the cursor to the column and row location set within the brackets. The demonstration sets the cursor to three locations and prints that location in text on the display. The **setCursor()** command is useful for controlling the layout of your text and ensuring that your output goes to the appropriate part of the display screen.

```
void setCursorDemo() {
        lcd.clear(); // Clear the display
        lcd.print("SetCursor Demo"); // Print some text
        delay(1000);
        lcd.clear(); // Clear the display
        lcd.setCursor(5,0); // Cursor at column 5 row 0
        lcd.print("5,0");
        delay(2000);
        lcd.setCursor(10,1); // Cursor at column 10 row 1
        lcd.print("10,1");
        delay(2000);
        lcd.setCursor(3,1); // Cursor at column 3 row 1
        lcd.print("3,1");
        delay(2000);
}
```

There are two commands in the library for scrolling text: **scrollDisplayLeft()** and **scrollDisplayRight()**. Two demo routines show off these commands. The first prints "Beginning Arduino" on the right side of the display and scrolls it left 16 times, which will make it scroll off the screen:

```
void scrollLeftDemo() {
        lcd.clear(); // Clear the display
        lcd.print("Scroll Left Demo");
        delay(1000);
        lcd.clear(); // Clear the display
        lcd.setCursor(7,0);
        lcd.print("Beginning");
        lcd.setCursor(9,1);
        lcd.print("Arduino");
        delay(1000);
```

```
        for(int x=0; x<16; x++) {
                lcd.scrollDisplayLeft(); // Scroll display left 16 times
                delay(250);
        }
}
```

The next function acts similarly, starting with the text on the left and scrolling it right 16 times till it scrolls off the screen:

```
void scrollRightDemo() {
        lcd.clear(); // Clear the display
        lcd.print("Scroll Right");
        lcd.setCursor(0,1);
        lcd.print("Demo");
        delay(1000);
        lcd.clear(); // Clear the display
        lcd.print("Beginning");
        lcd.setCursor(0,1);
        lcd.print("Arduino");
        delay(1000);
        for(int x=0; x<16; x++) {
                lcd.scrollDisplayRight(); // Scroll display right 16 times
                delay(250);
        }
}
```

The cursor so far has been invisible—it's always there but just not seen. Whenever you clear the display, the cursor returns to the top left corner (column 0 and row 0). After printing some text, the cursor will sit just after the last character printed. The next function clears the display, then turns the cursor on with `cursor()` and prints some text. The cursor will be visible, just after this text, as an underscore (_) symbol:

```
void cursorDemo() {
        lcd.clear(); // Clear the display
        lcd.cursor(); // Enable cursor visible
        lcd.print("Cursor On");
        delay(3000);
```

The display is cleared again. This time the cursor is turned off, which is the default mode, using `noCursor()`. Now the cursor cannot be seen:

```
        lcd.clear(); // Clear the display
        lcd.noCursor(); // Cursor invisible
        lcd.print("Cursor Off");
        delay(3000);
```

Next, the cursor is enabled again. Blink mode is also enabled using **blink()**:

```
        lcd.clear(); // Clear the display
        lcd.cursor(); // Cursor visible
        lcd.blink(); // Cursor blinking
        lcd.print("Cursor Blink On");
        delay(3000);
```

This time the cursor will not only be visible, but will be blinking on and off. This mode is useful if you are waiting for some text input from a user. The blinking cursor will act as a prompt to enter some text.

Finally, the cursor and blink are turned off to put the cursor back into the default mode:

```
        lcd.noCursor(); // Cursor invisible
        lcd.noBlink(); // Blink off
}
```

The final function called **createGlyphDemo()** creates a custom character. Most LCDs let you program your own custom characters to them. The standard 16×2 LCD has space to store eight custom characters in memory. The characters are 5 pixels wide by 8 pixels high (a pixel is a picture element, i.e. the individual dots that make up a digital display). The display is cleared and then two arrays of type byte are initialized with the binary pattern of a happy and a sad face. The binary patterns are 5 bits wide.

```
void createGlyphDemo() {
        lcd.clear();

        byte happy[8] = { // Create byte array with happy face
        B00000,
        B00000,
        B10001,
        B00000,
        B10001,
        B01110,
        B00000,
        B00000};

        byte sad[8] = { // Create byte array with sad face
        B00000,
        B00000,
        B10001,
        B00000,
        B01110,
        B10001,
        B00000,
        B00000};
```

Then you create the two custom characters using the **createChar()** command. This requires two parameters: the first is the number of the custom character (0 to 7 in the case of my test LCD, which can store a maximum of 8), and the second is the name of the array that creates and stores the custom characters binary pattern in memory on the LCD:

```
        lcd.createChar(0, happy); // create custom character 0
        lcd.createChar(1, sad); // create custom character 1
```

A for loop will now loop through itself five times. On each iteration the cursor is set to column 8 and row 0, and the first custom character is written to that location using the write() command. This writes the custom character within the brackets to the cursor location. The first character, a happy face, is written to the cursor location; after a delay of one second the second character, a sad face, is then written to the same cursor location. This repeats five times to make a crude animation.

```
        for(int x=0; x<5; x++) { // loop animation 5 times
                lcd.setCursor(8,0);
                lcd.write(0); // write custom char 0
                delay(1000);
                lcd.setCursor(8,0);
                lcd.write(1); // write custom char 1
                delay(1000);
        }
}
```

Project 23 covered most of the popular commands within the LiquidCrystal.h library. There are several others to discover, however, and you can read about them in the Arduino Reference library at www.arduino.cc/en/Reference/LiquidCrystal.

Project 23 – Basic LCD Control – Hardware Overview

The new component in this project was obviously the LCD. A liquid crystal display works by using the light modulating properties of liquid crystals. The display is made up of pixels, each one filled with liquid crystals. These pixels are arrayed in front of a backlighting source or a reflector. The crystals are placed into layers sandwiched between polarizing filters. The two polarizing panels are aligned at 90 degrees to each other, which blocks light. The first polarizing filter will polarize the light waves so that they all run in one orientation only. The second filter, being at 90 degrees to the first, will block the light. In other words, imagine that the filter is made up of very thin slits going in one direction. Light polarized in one direction will go through slits in the same orientation, but when it reaches the second filter, which has its slits running the other way, it will not pass through. By running a current across the rows and columns of the layers, the crystals can be made to change orientation and line up with the electric field. This causes the light to twist 90 degrees, thus allowing it through the second filter. Hence, some displays are referred to as "Super-Twist."

The LCD is made up of a grid of pixels and these are arranged into smaller grids that make up the characters. A typical 16×2 LCD will have 16 character grids in two rows. Each character grid is made up of 5 pixels wide by 8 pixels high. If you turn the contrast up very high on your display, the 32 arrays of 5×7 pixels will become visible.

That is really all you need to know about how LCDs work. Let's now put the LCD to use by making a temperature display.

Project 24 – LCD Temperature Display

This project is a simple demonstration of using an LCD to present useful information to the user—in this case, the temperature from an analog temperature sensor. You will add a button to switch between displaying the in Celsius or Fahrenheit. Also, the maximum and minimum temperature will be displayed on the second row.

Parts Required

The parts required are the same as for Project 23, plus a button and an analogue temperature sensor. Make sure that the temperature sensor only outputs positive values.

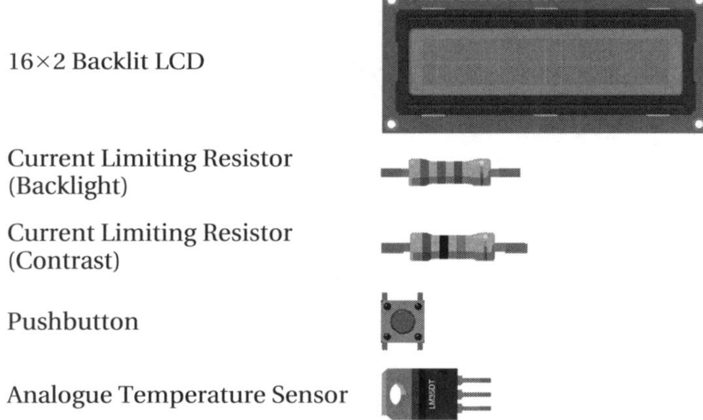

Connect It Up

Use the exact same circuit that you set up for Project 23. Then add a pushbutton and temperature sensor as shown in Figure 8-2.

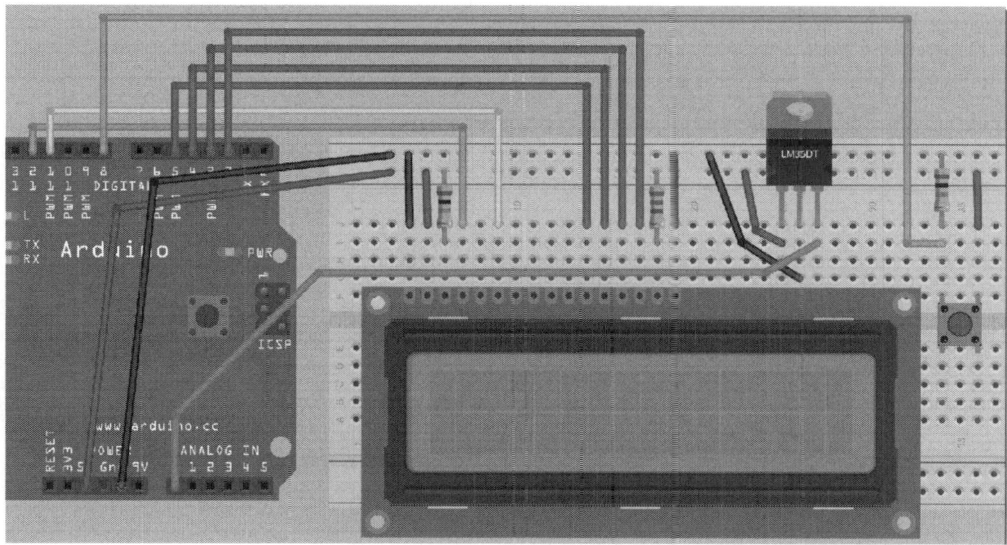

***Figure 8-2.** The circuit for Project 24 – LCD Temperature Display*

I have used an LM35DT temperature sensor, which has a range from 0ºC to 100ºC. You can use any analogue temperature sensor. The LM35 is rated from -55ºC to +150ºC. You will need to adjust your code accordingly (more on this later).

Enter The Code

Check your wiring, then upload the code from Listing 8-2.

***Listing 8-2.** Code for Project 24*

```
// PROJECT 24
#include <LiquidCrystal.h>

// Initialize the library with the numbers of the interface pins
LiquidCrystal lcd(12, 11, 5, 4, 3, 2); // Create an lcd object and assign the pins
int maxC=0, minC=100, maxF=0, minF=212;
int scale = 1;
int buttonPin=8;

void setup() {
        lcd.begin(16, 2); // Set the display to 16 columns and 2 rows
        analogReference(INTERNAL);
        pinMode(buttonPin, INPUT);
        lcd.clear();
}
```

```
void loop() {
        lcd.setCursor(0,0); // Set cursor to home position
        int sensor = analogRead(0); // Read the temp from sensor
        int buttonState = digitalRead(buttonPin); // Check for button press
        switch (buttonState) { // Change scale state if pressed
                case HIGH:
                        scale=-scale; // Invert scale
                        lcd.clear();
        }

        delay(250);
        switch (scale) { // Decide if C or F scale
                case 1:
                        celsius(sensor);
                        break;
                case -1:
                        fahrenheit(sensor);
        }
}

void celsius(int sensor) {
        lcd.setCursor(0,0);
        int temp = sensor * 0.09765625; // Convert to C
        lcd.print(temp);
        lcd.write(B11011111); // Degree symbol
        lcd.print("C  ");
        if (temp>maxC) {maxC=temp;}
        if (temp<minC) {minC=temp;}
        lcd.setCursor(0,1);
        lcd.print("H=");
        lcd.print(maxC);
        lcd.write(B11011111);
        lcd.print("C L=");
        lcd.print(minC);
        lcd.write(B11011111);
        lcd.print("C  ");
}

void fahrenheit(int sensor) {
        lcd.setCursor(0,0);
        float temp = ((sensor * 0.09765625) * 1.8)+32; // convert to F
        lcd.print(int(temp));
        lcd.write(B11011111); // Print degree symbol
        lcd.print("F ");
        if (temp>maxF) {maxF=temp;}
        if (temp<minF) {minF=temp;}
        lcd.setCursor(0,1);
        lcd.print("H=");
        lcd.print(maxF);
        lcd.write(B11011111);
```

```
        lcd.print("F L=");
        lcd.print(minF);
        lcd.write(B11011111);
        lcd.print("F ");
}
```

When you run the code the current temperature will be displayed on the top row of the LCD. The bottom row will display the maximum and minimum temperatures recorded since the Arduino was turned on or the program was reset. By pressing the button, you can change the temperature scale between Celsius and Fahrenheit.

Project 24 – LCD Temperature Display – Code Overview

As before, the LiquidCrystal library is loaded into your sketch:

```
#include <LiquidCrystal.h>
```

A LiquidCrystal object called lcd is initialized and the appropriate pins set:

```
LiquidCrystal lcd(12, 11, 5, 4, 3, 2); // Create an lcd object and assign the pins
```

Some integers to hold the maximum and minimum temperatures in degrees C and F are declared and initialized with impossible max and min values. These will be changed as soon as the program runs for the first time.

```
int maxC=0, minC=100, maxF=0, minF=212;
```

A variable called scale of type int is declared and initialized with 1. The scale variable will decide if you are using Celsius or Fahrenheit as your temperature scale. By default, it's set to 1, which is Celsius. You can change this to -1 for Fahrenheit.

```
int scale = 1;
```

An integer to store the pin being used for the button is declared and initialized:

```
int buttonPin=8;
```

In the `setup()` loop, you set the display to be 16 columns and 2 rows:

```
lcd.begin(16, 2); // Set the display to 16 columns and 2 rows
```

The reference for the analogue pin is then set to INTERNAL:

```
analogReference(INTERNAL);
```

This gives you a better range on the Arduino's ADC (Analogue to Digital Convertor). The output voltage of the LM35DT at 100°C is 1v. If you were using the default reference of 5 volts, then at 50°C, which is half of the sensors range, the reading on the ADC would be 0.5v = (0.5/5)*1023 = 102, which is only about 10% of the ADC's range. When using the internal reference voltage of 1.1 volts, the value at the analogue pin at 50°C is now 0.5v = (0.5/1.1)*1023 = 465.

As you can see, this is almost half way through the entire range of values that the analogue pin can read (0 to 1023), therefore the resolution and accuracy of the reading has increased, as has the sensitivity of the circuit.

The button pin is now set to an input and the LCD display cleared:

```
pinMode(buttonPin, INPUT);
lcd.clear();
```

In the main loop, the program starts off by setting the cursor to its home position:

```
lcd.setCursor(0,0); // Set cursor to home position
```

Then you read a value from the temperature sensor on Analogue Pin 0:

```
int sensor = analogRead(0); // Read the temp from sensor
```

Then you read the state of the button and store the value in buttonState:

```
int buttonState = digitalRead(buttonPin); // Check for button press
```

Now you need to know if the button has been pressed or not and if so, to change the scale from Celsius to Fahrenheit or vice-versa. This is done using a switch/case statement:

```
        switch (buttonState) { // change scale state if pressed
                case HIGH:
                        scale=-scale; // invert scale
                        lcd.clear();
        }
```

This is a new concept: The switch/case command controls the flow of the program by specifying what code should be run based on what conditions have been met. The switch/case statement compares the value of a variable with values in the case statements, and if true, runs the code after that case statement.

For example, if you had a variable called var and you wanted things to happen if its value was either 1, 2, or 3, then you could decide what to do for those values like so:

```
switch (var) {
        case 1:
                // run this code here if var is 1
                break;
        case 2:
                // run this code here if var is 2
                break;
        case 3:
                // run this code here if var is 3
                break;
        default:
                // if nothing else matches run this code here
        }
```

The switch/case statement will check the value of var. If it's 1, it will run the code within the case 1 block up to the break command. The break command is used to exit out of the switch/case statement. Without it, the code would carry on executing until a break command is reached or the end of the switch/case statement is reached. If none of the checked-for values are reached, then the code within the default section will run. Note that the default section is optional and not necessary.

In your case, you only check one case: if the buttonState is HIGH. If so, the value of scale is inverted (from C to F or vice-versa) and the display is cleared.

Next is a short delay:

```
delay(250);
```

Then another switch/case statement to check if the value of scale is either a 1 for Celsius or a -1 for Fahrenheit and if so to run the appropriate functions:

```
        switch (scale) { // decide if C or F scale
                case 1:
                        celsius(sensor);
                        break;
                case -1:
                        fahrenheit(sensor);
        }
}
```

Next you have the two functions to display the temperatures on the LCD. One is for working in Celsius and the other for Fahrenheit. The functions have a single parameter. You pass it an integer value that will be the value read from the temperature sensor:

```
void celsius(int sensor) {
```

The cursor is set to the home position:

```
lcd.setCursor(0,0);
```

Then you take the sensor reading and convert it to degrees Celsius by multiplying by 0.09765625:

```
int temp = sensor * 0.09765625; // convert to C
```

This factor is reached by taking 100, which is the range of the sensor and dividing it by the range of the ADC, which is 1024:

100/1024=0.09765625.

If your sensor had a range from -40 to +150 degrees Celsius, the calculation would be the following (presuming you had a sensor that did not output negative voltages):

190 / 1024 = 0.185546875

You then print that converted value to the LCD, along with char B11011111, which is a degree symbol, followed by a C to indicate that you are displaying the temperature in Celsius:

```
lcd.print(temp);
lcd.write(B11011111); // degree symbol
lcd.print("C  ");
```

Then the current temperature reading is checked to see if it is greater than the currently stored values of maxC and minC. If so, the values of maxC or minC are changed to the current value of temp. This will keep a running score of the highest or lowest temperatures read since the Arduino was turned on.

```
if (temp>maxC) {maxC=temp;}
if (temp<minC) {minC=temp;}
```

On the second row of the LCD you print H (for HIGH) and the value of maxC and then an L (for LOW) followed by the degree symbol and a letter C:

```
lcd.setCursor(0,1);
lcd.print("H=");
lcd.print(maxC);
lcd.write(B11011111);
lcd.print("C L=");
lcd.print(minC);
lcd.write(B11011111);
lcd.print("C  ");
```

The Fahrenheit function does exactly the same, except it converts the temperature in Celsius to Fahrenheit by multiplying it by 1.8 and adding 32:

```
float temp = ((sensor * 0.09765625) * 1.8)+32; // convert to F
```

Now that you know how to use an LCD to display useful information, you can create your own projects to display sensor data or to create a simple user interface.

Summary

In Chapter 8, you have explored the most popular functions in the LiquidCrystal.h library: clearing the display; printing text to specific locations on the screen; making the cursor visible, invisible, or blinking; and even how to make the text scroll to the left or the right. Project 24 was a simple application of these functions in a temperature sensor, an oversight of how an LCD could be used in a real project to display data.

Subjects and Concepts Covered in Chapter 8

- How to load the LiquidCrystal.h library
- How to wire an LCD up to an Arduino
- How to adjust the backlight brightness and display contrast using different resistor values

- How to control the backlight brightness from a PWM pin
- How to declare and initialize a LiquidCrystal object
- How to set the correct number of columns and rows on the display
- How to clear the LCD display using `.clear()`
- How to print to the cursor location using `.print()`
- How to turn the display on and off using `.display()` and `.noDisplay()`
- How to set the cursor location using `.setCursor(x, y)`
- How to scroll the display left using `.scrollDisplayLeft()`
- How to scroll the display right using `.scrollDisplayRight()`
- How to enable or disable the cursor using `.cursor()` and `noCursor()`
- How to make a visible cursor blink using `.blink()`
- How to create custom characters using `.createChar()`
- How to write a single character to the cursor location using `.write()`
- How an LCD display works
- How to read values from an analogue temperature sensor
- How to increase ADC resolution using an internal voltage reference
- Decision making using the switch/case statement
- How to convert ADC values to temperature readings in both Celsius and Fahrenheit
- How to convert the code to read from different temperature sensors with different ranges

CHAPTER 9

Servos

In this chapter, we are going to look at servos motors or servomechanisms. A servo is a motor with a feedback system that helps to control the position of the motor. Servos typically rotate through 180 degrees, although you can also buy continuous rotation servos or even modify a standard one for continuous rotation. If you have ever owned a Radio Controlled Airplane, you have come across servos; they are used to control the flight surfaces. RC cars use them for the steering mechanism, and RC boats use them to control the rudder. Likewise, they are often used as the moving joints in small robot arms and for controlling movement in animatronics. Perhaps by the end of this chapter you'll be inspired to put some servos inside a teddy bear or other toy to make it move. Figures 9-1 and 9-2 show other ways to use servos.

Figure 9-1. *A servo being used to control a meter (image by Tod E. Kurt)*

Servos are really easy to control thanks to the Servo.h library that comes with the Arduino IDE. The three projects in this chapter are all quite simple and small compared to some of the other projects in the book and yet are very effective. Let's start off with a really simple program to control one servo, then move onto two servos, and finish with two servos controlled by a joystick.

Figure 9-2. *Three servos controlling a head and eyeballs for a robot (image by Tod E. Kurt)*

Project 25 – Servo Control

In this very simple project you will control a single servo using a potentiometer.

Parts Required

You will need to obtain a standard RC servo; any of the small or mid-sized servos will do. Larger servos are not recommended because they require their own power supply as they consume a lot of current. Also, you'll need a potentiometer; pretty much any value rotary potentiometer will do. I used a 4.7K ohm one for testing. Note that you may also wish to connect your Arduino to an external DC power supply.

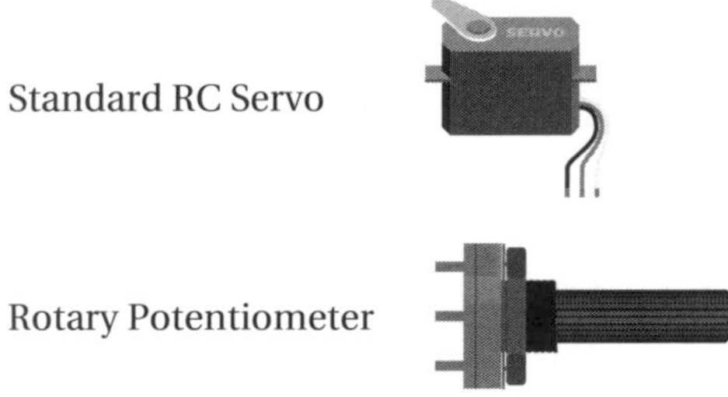

Connect It Up

The circuit for Project 25 is extremely simple. Connect it as shown in Figure 9-3.

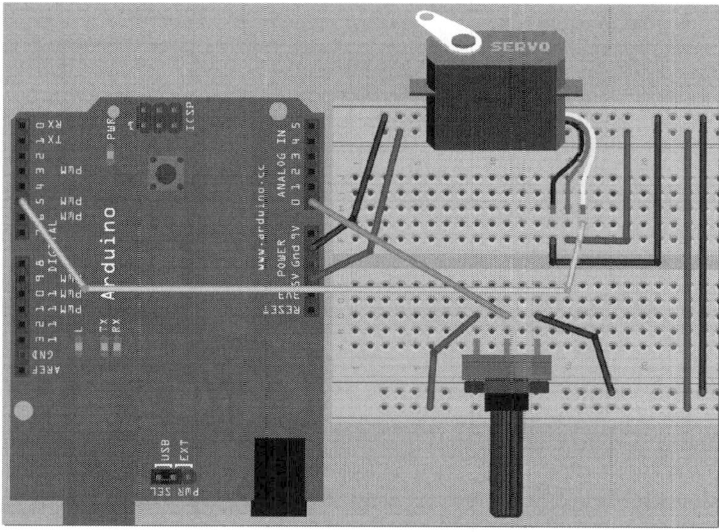

***Figure 9-3.** The circuit for Project 25 – Servo Control*

The servo has three wires coming from it. One will be red and will go to +5v. One will be black or brown and will go to Ground. The third will be white, yellow, or orange and will be connected to Digital Pin 5.

The rotary potentiometer has the outer pins connected to +5v and Ground and the middle pin to Analog Pin 0.

Once you are happy everything is connected as it should be, enter the code below.

Enter The Code

And now for one of the shortest programs in the book, see Listing 9-1!

***Listing 9-1.** Code for Project 25*

```
// Project 25
#include <Servo.h>

Servo servo1;  // Create a servo object
```

```
void setup()
{
        servo1.attach(5);  // Attaches the servo on Pin 5 to the servo object
}

void loop()
{
        int angle = analogRead(0); // Read the pot value
        angle=map(angle, 0, 1023, 0, 180); // Map the values from 0 to 180 degrees
        servo1.write(angle); // Write the angle to the servo
        delay(15); // Delay of 15ms to allow servo to reach position
}
```

Project 25 – Servo Control – Code Overview

First, the Servo.h library is included:

```
#include <Servo.h>
```

Then a Servo object called **servo1** is declared:

```
Servo servo1;  // Create a servo object
```

In the setup loop, you attach the servo you have just created to Pin 5:

```
servo1.attach(5);  // Attaches the servo on Pin 5 to the servo object
```

The attach command attaches a created servo object to a designated pin. The attach command can take either one parameter, as in your case, or three parameters. If three parameters are used, the first parameter is the pin, the second is the minimum (0 degree) angle in pulse width in microseconds (defaults to 544), and the third parameter is the maximum degree angle (180 degrees) in pulse width in microseconds (defaults to 2400). This will be explained in the hardware overview. For most purposes you can simply set the pin and ignore the optional second and third parameters.

You can connect up to 12 servos to an Arduino Duemilanove (or equivalent) and up to 48 on the Arduino Mega—perfect for robotic control applications!

Note that using this library disables the analogWrite (PWM) function on Pins 9 and 10. On the Mega you can have up to 12 motors without interfering with the PWM functions. The use of between 12 and 23 motors will disable the PWM functionality on Pins 11 and 12.

In the main loop, read the analog value from the potentiometer connected to Analog Pin 0:

```
int angle = analogRead(0); // Read the pot value
```

Then that value is mapped so the range is now between 0 and 180, which will correspond to the degree angle of the servo arm:

```
angle=map(angle, 0, 1023, 0, 180); // Map the values from 0 to 180 degrees
```

Then you take your servo object and write the appropriate angle, in degrees, to it (the angle must be between 0 and 180 degrees):

```
servo1.write(angle); // Write the angle to the servo
```

Finally, a delay of 15ms is programmed to allow the servo time to move into position:

```
delay(15); // Delay of 15ms to allow servo to reach position
```

You can also `detach()` a servo from a pin, which will disable it and allow the pin to be used for something else. Also, you can `read()` the current angle from the servo (this is the last value passed to the `write()` command).

You can read more about the Servo library on the Arduino website at `http://arduino.cc/en/Reference/Servo`.

Project 25 – Servo Control – Hardware Overview

A servo is a little box that contains a DC electric motor, a set of gears between the motor and an output shaft, a position sensing mechanism, and the control circuit. The position sensing mechanism feeds back the servo's position to the control circuitry, which uses the motor to adjust the servo arm to the position that the servo should be at.

Servos come in many sizes, speeds, strengths, and precisions. Some of them can be quite expensive. The more powerful or precise the servo is, the higher the price. Servos are most commonly used in radio controlled aircraft, cars, and boats.

The servo's position is controlled by providing a set of pulses. This is PWM, which you have come across before. The width of the pulses is measured in milliseconds. The rate at which the pulses are sent isn't particularly important; it's the width of the pulse that matters to the control circuit. Typical pulse rates are between 400Hz and 50Hz.

On a standard servo the center position is reached by providing pulses at 1.5 millisecond intervals, the -45 degree position by providing 0.6 millisecond pulses, and the +45 degree position by providing 2.4 millisecond pulses. You will need to read the datasheet for your servo to find the pulse widths required for the different angles. However, you are using the Servo.h library for this project, so you don't need to worry: the library provides the required PWM signal to the servo. Whenever you send a different angle value to the servo object, the code in the library takes care of sending the correct PWM signal to the servo.

Some servos provide continuous rotation. Alternatively, you can modify a standard servo relatively easily to provide continuous rotation.

***Figure 9-4.** Modifying a servo to provide continuous rotation (image by Adam Grieg)*

A continuous rotation servo is controlled in the same way, by providing an angle between 0 and 180 degrees. However, a value of 0 will provide rotation at full speed in one direction, a value of 90 will be stationary, and a value of 180 will provide rotation at full speed in the opposite direction. Values in-between these will make the servo rotate in one direction or the other and at different speeds. Continuous rotation servos are great for building small robots (see Figure 9-4). They can be connected to wheels to provide precise speed and direction control of each wheel.

There is another kind of servo known as a linear actuator that rotates a shaft to a desired position allowing you to push and pull items connected to the end of the shaft. These are used a lot in the TV program “Mythbusters” by their resident robotics expert, Grant Imahara.

Project 26 – Dual Servo Control

You’ll now create another simple project, but this time you’ll control two servos using commands from the serial monitor. You learned about serial control in Project 10 when you were changing the colors on an RGB lamp with serial commands. So let’s cannibalize the code from Project 10 to make this one.

Parts Required

This project requires two servos. You will not need the potentiometer.

Standard RC Servo × 2

Connect It Up

The circuit for Project 26 is again extremely simple. Connect it as shown in Figure 9-5. Basically, you remove the potentiometer from the last project and wire a second servo up to Digital Pin 6.

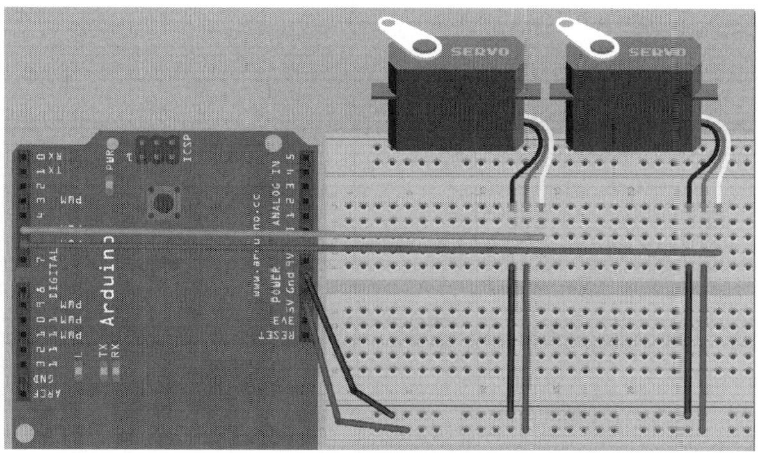

Figure 9-5. The circuit for Project 26 – Dual Servo Control

Enter The Code

Enter the code in Listing 9-2.

Listing 9-2. Code for Project 26

```
// Project 26
#include <Servo.h>

char buffer[10];
Servo servo1;  // Create a servo object
Servo servo2;  // Create a second servo object

void setup()
{
        servo1.attach(5);  // Attaches the servo on pin 5 to the servo1 object
        servo2.attach(6);  // Attaches the servo on pin 6 to the servo2 object
        Serial.begin(9600);
        Serial.flush();
        servo1.write(90);  // Put servo1 at home position
        servo2.write(90);  // Put servo2 at home postion
        Serial.println("STARTING...");
}

void loop()
{
        if (Serial.available() > 0) { // Check if data has been entered
                int index=0;
                delay(100); // Let the buffer fill up
                int numChar = Serial.available(); // Find the string length
```

```
                if (numChar>10) {
                numChar=10;
                }
                while (numChar--) {
                        // Fill the buffer with the string
                        buffer[index++] = Serial.read();
                }
                splitString(buffer); // Run splitString function
        }
}

void splitString(char* data) {
        Serial.print("Data entered: ");
        Serial.println(data);
        char* parameter;
        parameter = strtok (data, " ,"); //String to token
        while (parameter != NULL) { // If we haven't reached the end of the string...
                setServo(parameter); // ...run the setServo function
                parameter = strtok (NULL, " ,");
        }
        // Clear the text and serial buffers
        for (int x=0; x<9; x++) {
                buffer[x]='\0';
        }
        Serial.flush();
}


void setServo(char* data) {
        if ((data[0] == 'L') || (data[0] == 'l')) {
                int firstVal = strtol(data+1, NULL, 10); // String to long integer
                firstVal = constrain(firstVal,0,180); // Constrain values
                servo1.write(firstVal);
                Serial.print("Servo1 is set to: ");
                Serial.println(firstVal);
        }
        if ((data[0] == 'R') || (data[0] == 'r')) {
                int secondVal = strtol(data+1, NULL, 10); // String to long integer
                secondVal = constrain(secondVal,0,255); // Constrain the values
                servo2.write(secondVal);
                Serial.print("Servo2 is set to: ");
                Serial.println(secondVal);
        }
}
```

To run the code, open up the Serial Monitor window. The Arduino will reset, and the servos will move to their central locations. You can now use the Serial Monitor to send commands to the Arduino.

The left servo is controlled by sending an L and then a number between 0 and 180 for the angle. The right servo is controlled by sending an R and the number. You can send individual commands to each servo or send them both commands at the same time by separating the commands with a space or comma, like so:

```
L180
L45 R135
L180,R90
R77
R25 L175
```

This is a simple example of how you could send commands down a wire to an Arduino-controlled robot arm or an animatronic toy. Note that the serial commands don't have to come from the Arduino Serial Monitor. You can use any program that is capable of communicating over serial or write your own in Python or C++.

Project 26 – Dual Servo Control – Code Overview

The code for this project is basically unchanged from that of Project 10. I will therefore not go into each command in detail. Instead, I will give an overview if it is something already covered. Read up on Project 10 for a refresher on how the string manipulation commands work.

First the Servo.h library is included:

```
#include <Servo.h>
```

Then an array of type `char` is created to hold the text string you enter as a command into the serial monitor:

```
char buffer[10];
```

Two servo objects are created:

```
Servo servo1;  // Create a servo object
Servo servo2;  // Create a second servo object
```

In the setup routine, attach the servo objects to Pins 5 and 6:

```
servo1.attach(5);  // Attaches the servo on pin 5 to the servo1 object
servo2.attach(6);  // Attaches the servo on pin 6 to the servo2 object
```

Then begin serial communications and carry out a `Serial.flush()` command, which flushes any characters out of the serial buffer so it is empty and ready to receive commands for the servos:

```
Serial.begin(9600);
Serial.flush();
```

Both servos have a value of 90, which is the centre point, written to them so that they start off in the central position:

```
servo1.write(90);  // Put servo1 at home position
servo2.write(90);  // Put servo2 at home position
```

Then the word "STARTING......" is displayed in the Serial Monitor window so you know the device is ready to receive commands:

```
Serial.println("STARTING...");
```

In the main loop, check if any data has been sent down the serial line

```
if (Serial.available() > 0) { // check if data has been entered
```

and if so, let the buffer fill up and obtain the length of the string, ensuring it does not overflow above the maximum of 10 characters. Once the buffer is full, you call the `splitString` routine sending the buffer array to the function:

```
int index=0;
delay(100); // Let the buffer fill up
int numChar = Serial.available(); // Find the string length
if (numChar>10) {
        numChar=10;
}
while (numChar--) {
        // Fill the buffer with the string
        buffer[index++] = Serial.read();
}
splitString(buffer); // Run splitString function
```

The `splitString` function receives the buffer array, splits it into separate commands if more than one is entered, and calls the `setServo` routine with the parameter stripped from the command string received over the serial line:

```
void splitString(char* data) {
        Serial.print("Data entered: ");
        Serial.println(data);
        char* parameter;
        parameter = strtok (data, " ,"); //String to token
        while (parameter != NULL) { // If we haven't reached the end of the string...
                setServo(parameter); // ...run the setServo function
                parameter = strtok (NULL, " ,");
        }
        // Clear the text and serial buffers
        for (int x=0; x<9; x++) {
                buffer[x]='\0';
        }
        Serial.flush();
}
```

The setServo routine receives the smaller string sent from the `splitString` function and checks if an L or R is entered, and if so, moves either the left or right servo by the amount specified in the string:

```
void setServo(char* data) {
        if ((data[0] == 'L') || (data[0] == 'l')) {
                int firstVal = strtol(data+1, NULL, 10); // String to long integer
                firstVal = constrain(firstVal,0,180); // Constrain values
                servo1.write(firstVal);
                Serial.print("Servo1 is set to: ");
                Serial.println(firstVal);
        }
        if ((data[0] == 'R') || (data[0] == 'r')) {
                int secondVal = strtol(data+1, NULL, 10); // String to long integer
                secondVal = constrain(secondVal,0,255); // Constrain the values
                servo2.write(secondVal);
                Serial.print("Servo2 is set to: ");
                Serial.println(secondVal);
```

I've glossed over these last two functions as they are almost identical to those in Project 10. If you cannot remember what was covered in Project 10, feel free to go back and reread it.

Project 27 – Joystick Servo Control

For another simple project, let's use a joystick to control the two servos. You'll arrange the servos in such a way that you get a pan-tilt head, such as is used for CCTV cameras or for camera or sensor mounts on robots.

Parts Required

Leave the circuit as it was for the last project, and add either two potentiometers or a 2-axis potentiometer joystick.

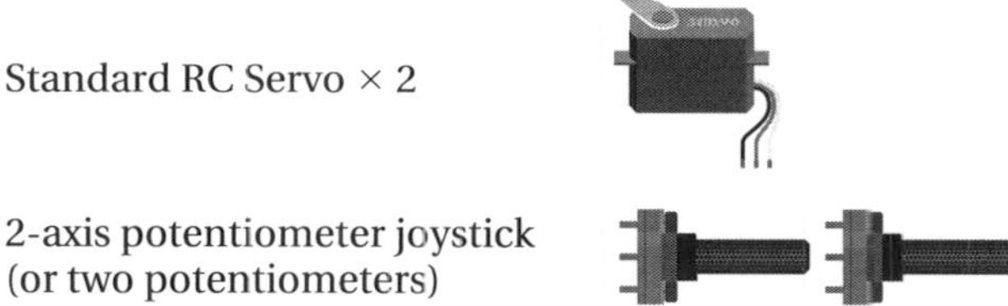

Standard RC Servo × 2

2-axis potentiometer joystick (or two potentiometers)

Connect It Up

The circuit for Project 27 is the same as for Project 26, with the addition of the joystick.

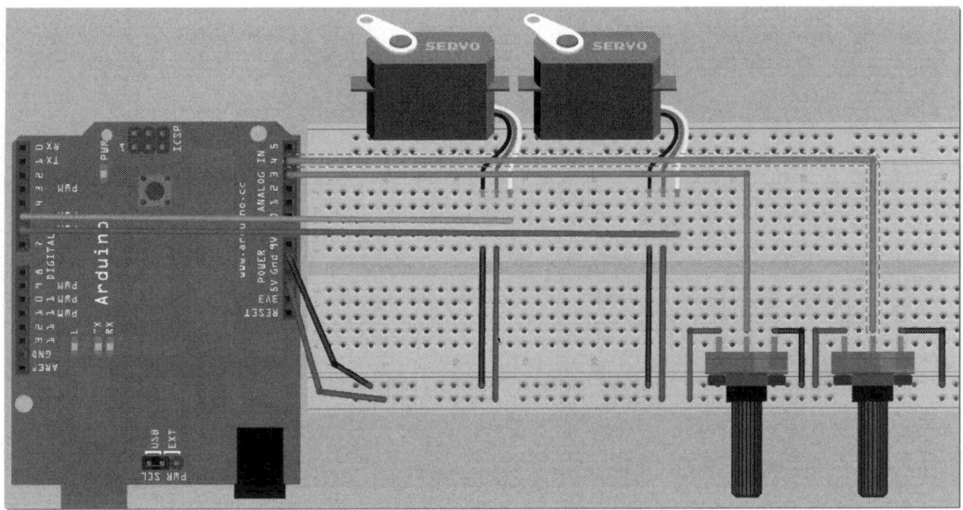

Figure 9-6. The circuit for Project 27 – Joystick Servo Control

A potentiometer joystick is simply that: a joystick made up of two potentiometers at right angles to each other. The axles of the pots are connected to a lever that is swung back and forth by the stick and returned to their centre positions thanks to a set of springs.

Connection is therefore easy: the outer pins of the two pots going to +5v and Ground and the centre pins going to Analog Pins 3 and 4. If you don't have a joystick, two potentiometers arranged at 90 degrees to each other will suffice.

Connect the two servos so that one has its axle vertical and the other horizontal at 90 degrees to the first servo and attached to the first servo's armature sideways. See Figure 9-7 for how to connect the servos. Some hot glue will do for testing. Use stronger glue for a permanent fixing.

Alternatively, get one of the ready-made pan and tilt servo sets you can buy for robotics. These can be picked up cheaply on eBay.

When the bottom servo moves it causes the top servo to rotate, and when the top servo moves its arm rocks back and forth. You could attach a webcam or an ultrasonic sensor to the arm, for example.

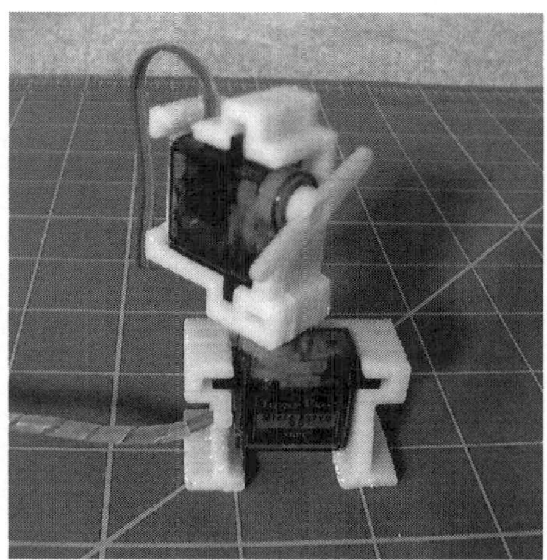

***Figure 9-7.** Mount one servo on top of the other (image by David Stokes)*

The joystick can be purchased from eBay or an electrical supplier. You could also find an old C64 or Atari joystick. However, there is a cheap alternative available called a PS2 controller; it contains two 2-axis potentiometer joysticks as well as a set of vibration motors and other buttons. These can be purchased on eBay very cheaply and are easily taken apart to access the parts within (see Figure 9-8). If you don't want to take the controller apart, you could access the digital code coming from the cable of the PS2 controller. In fact, there are Arduino libraries to enable you to do just this. This will give you full access to all of the joysticks and buttons on the device at once.

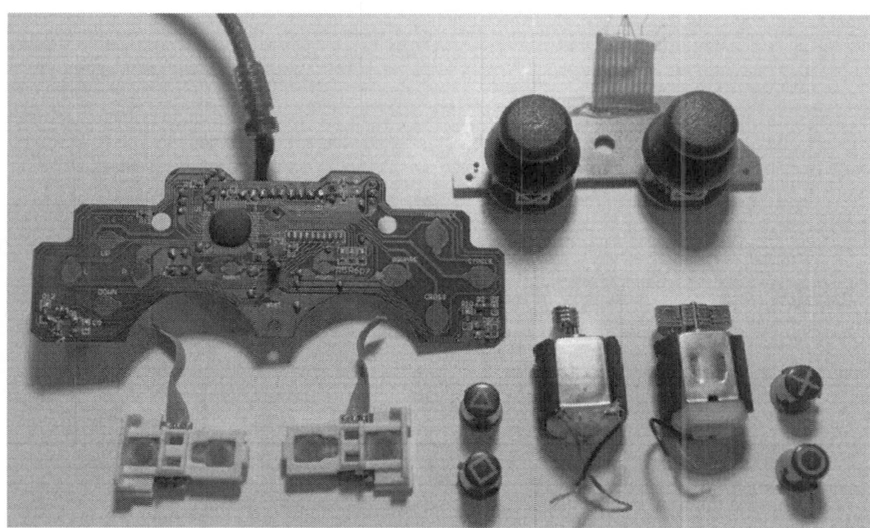

***Figure 9-8.** All the great parts available inside a PS2 Controller (image by Mike Prevette)*

Enter The Code

Enter the code in Listing 9-3.

Listing 9-3. Code for Project 27

```
// Project 27
#include <Servo.h>

Servo servo1;  // Create a servo object
Servo servo2;  // Create a second servo object
int pot1, pot2;

void setup()
{
  servo1.attach(5);  // Attaches the servo on pin 5 to the servo1 object
  servo2.attach(6);  // Attaches the servo on pin 6 to the servo2 object

  servo1.write(90);  // Put servo1 at home position
  servo2.write(90);  // Put servo2 at home postion

}

void loop()
{
  pot1 = analogRead(3); // Read the X-Axis
  pot2 = analogRead(4); // Read the Y-Axis
  pot1 = map(pot1,0,1023,0,180);
  pot2=map(pot2,0,1023,0,180);
  servo1.write(pot1);
  servo2.write(pot2);
  delay(15);
}
```

When you run this program you will be able to use the servos as a pan/tilt head. Rocking the joystick backwards and forwards will cause the top servo's armature to rock back and forth, and moving the joystick from side to side will cause the bottom servo to rotate.

If you find that the servos are going in the opposite direction from what you expected, then you have the outer pins of the appropriate servo connected the wrong way. Just swap them around.

Project 27 – Joystick Servo Control – Code Overview

Again, this is a very simple project, but the effect of the two servos moving is quite compelling.

The Servo library is loaded:

```
#include <Servo.h>
```

Two servo objects are created and two sets of integers hold the values read from the two potentiometers inside the joystick:

```
Servo servo1;  // Create a servo object
Servo servo2;  // Create a second servo object
int pot1, pot2;
```

The setup loop attaches the two servo objects to Pins 5 and 6 and moves the servos into the central positions:

```
servo1.attach(5);  // Attaches the servo on Pin 5 to the servo1 object
servo2.attach(6);  // Attaches the servo on Pin 6 to the servo2 object

servo1.write(90);  // Put servo1 at home position
servo2.write(90);  // Put servo2 at home postion
```

In the main loop, the analog values are read from both the X and Y axis of the joystick:

```
pot1 = analogRead(3); // Read the X-Axis
pot2 = analogRead(4); // Read the Y-Axis
```

Those values are then mapped to be between 0 and 180 degrees

```
pot1 = map(pot1,0,1023,0,180);
pot2 = map(pot2,0,1023,0,180);
```

and then sent to the two servos

```
servo1.write(pot1);
servo2.write(pot2);
```

The range of motion available with this pan/tilt rig is amazing, and you can make the rig move in a very humanlike way. This kind of servo setup is often made to control a camera for aerial photography (see Figure 9-9).

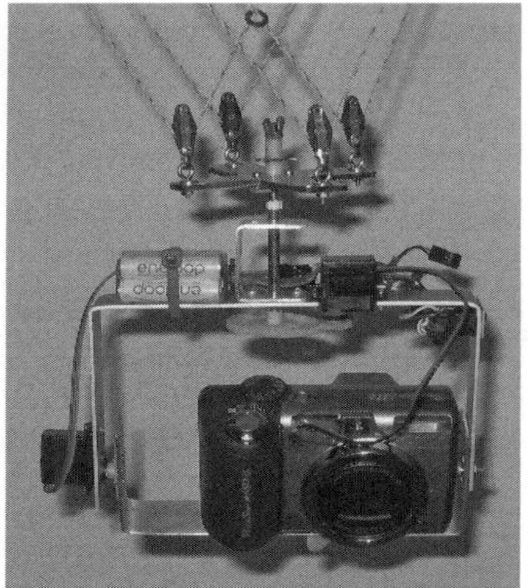

Figure 9-9. *A pan/tilt rig made for a camera using two servos (image by David Mitchell)*

Summary

In Chapter 9, you worked your way through three very simple projects that show how easily servos can be controlled using the servo.h library. You can easily modify these projects to add up to 12 servos to make a toy dinosaur, for example, move around in a realistic manner.

Servos are great for making your own RC vehicle or for controlling a robot. Furthermore, as seen in Figure 9-9, you can make a pan/tilt rig for camera control. A third servo could even be used to push the shutter button on the camera.

Subjects and Concepts Covered in Chapter 9

- The many potential uses for a servo
- How to use the Servo.h library to control between 1 and 12 servos
- How to use a potentiometer as a controller for a servo
- How a servo works
- How to modify a servo to provide continuous rotation
- How to control a set of servos using serial commands
- How to use an analog joystick for dual axis servo control
- How to arrange two servos to create a pan/tilt head
- How a PS2 Controller makes a great source for joystick and button parts

CHAPTER 10

■ ■ ■

Steppers and Robots

You are now going to take a quick look at a new type of motor called a stepper motor. Project 28 is a simple project to show you how to control the stepper, make it move a set distance, and change the speed and direction. Stepper motors are different than standard motors in that their rotation is divided up into a series of steps. By making the motor rotate a set number of steps, you can control the speed of the motor and how much it turns fairly precisely. Stepper motors come in different shapes and sizes and have four, five, or six wires.

Stepper motors have many uses; they are used in flatbed scanners to position the scanning head and in inkjet printers to control the location of the print head and paper.

Another project in this chapter has you using a motor shield with geared DC motors to control a robot base. You'll end up getting the robot to follow a black line drawn on the floor!

Project 28 – Basic Stepper Control

In this very simple project, you will connect up a stepper motor and then get the Arduino to control it in different directions and at different speeds for a set number of steps.

Parts Required

You will need either a bipolar or a unipolar DC stepper motor. I used a Sanyo 103H546-0440 unipolar stepper motor in the testing of this project.

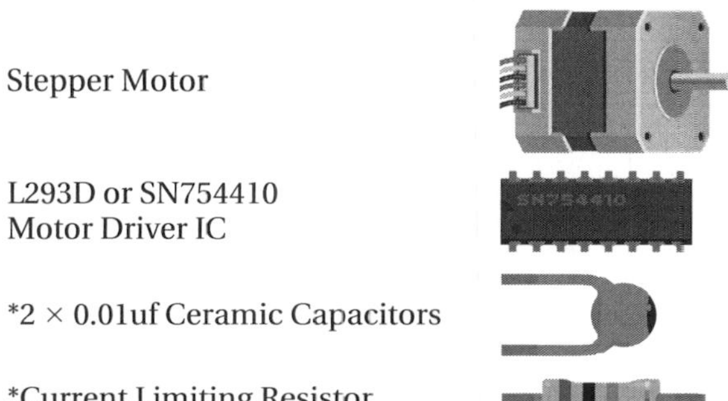

Connect It Up

Connect everything up as in Figure 10-1. See the variation for bipolar motors.

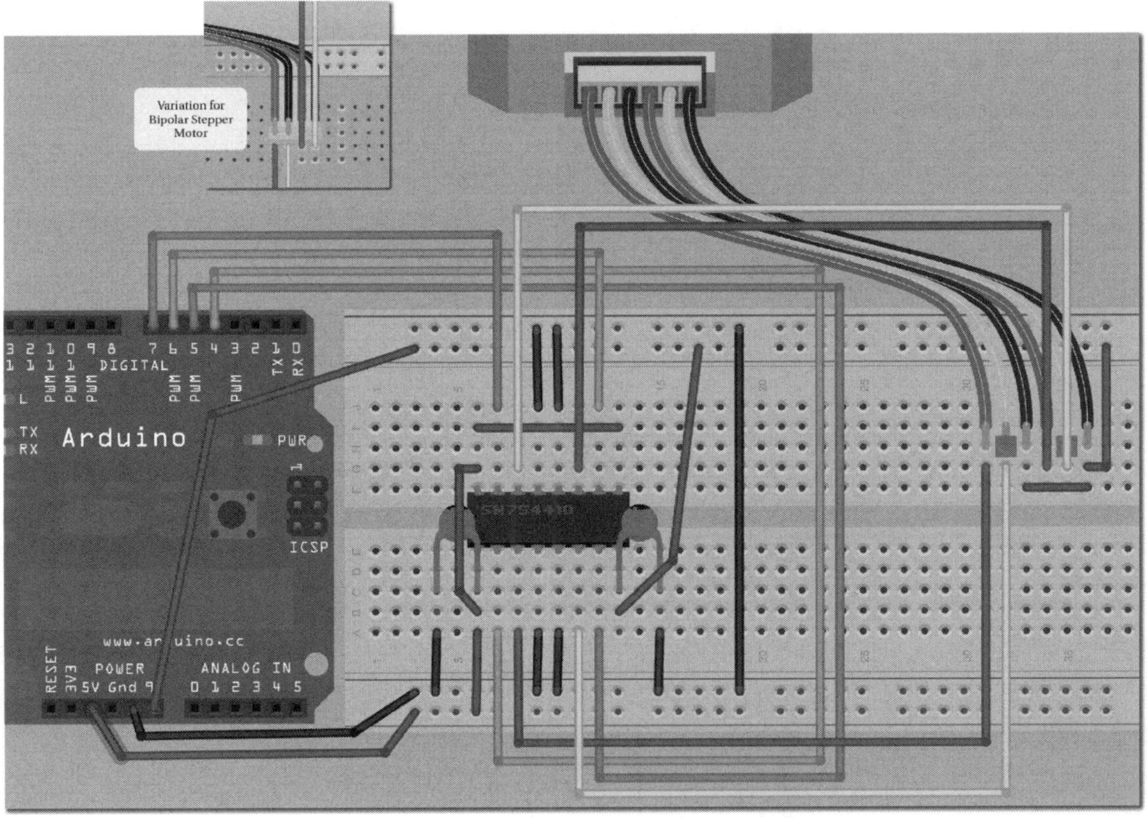

Figure 10-1. The circuit for Project 28 – Basic Stepper Control

Make sure the Arduino is connected to an external DC power supply so as not to overload it. The capacitors are optional and help to smooth out the current and prevent interference with the Arduino. These go between the +5v and Ground and the motor power supply and Ground. You can also use low value electrolytic capacitors, but make sure you connect them correctly as they are polarized. I found that without them the circuit did not work.

You may also require a current-limiting resistor between the Vin pin on the Arduino and the power rail supplying the SN754410 or L293D chip. The Vin pin will provide whatever voltage you provide from an external power supply so you may need to drop this voltage down to whatever the motor requires. Failure to do so may damage the motor.

Digital Pins 4, 5, 6 and 7 on the Arduino go to the Input 1, 2, 3 and 4 pins on the motor driver (see Figure 10-2). Output Pins 1 and 2 of the motor driver go across coil 1 of the motor and output Pins 3 and 4 to coil 2. You will need to check the datasheet of your specific motor to see which colored wires go to coil 1 and which go to coil 2. A unipolar motor will also have a 5th and/or a 6th wire that go to Ground.

The 5v pin on the Arduino goes to Pin 16 (VSS) of the motor driver pin and the 2 chip inhibit pins (1 and 9) are also tied to the 3.3v line to make them go HIGH.

The Vin pin on the Arduino goes to Pin 8 of the driver IC (VC). Pins 4, 5, 12, and 13 all go to Ground.

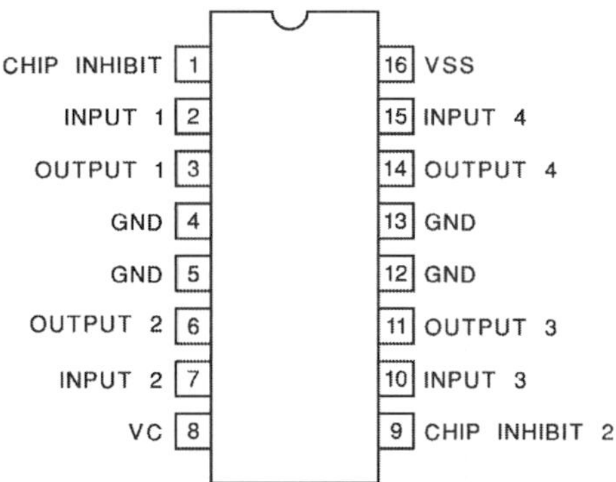

Figure 10-2. *Pin diagram for an L293D or SN754410 Motor Driver IC.*

Once you are happy that everything is connected up as it should be, enter the code below.

Enter the Code

Enter the code in Listing 10-1.

Listing 10-1. *Code for Project 28*

```
// Project 28
#include <Stepper.h>

// steps value is 360 / degree angle of motor
#define STEPS 200

// create a stepper object on pins 4, 5, 6 and 7
Stepper stepper(STEPS, 4, 5, 6, 7);

void setup()
{
}
```

```
void loop()
{
    stepper.setSpeed(60);
    stepper.step(200);
    delay(100);
    stepper.setSpeed(20);
    stepper.step(-50);
    delay(100);
}
```

Make sure that your Arduino is powered by an external DC power supply before running the code. When the sketch runs, you will see the stepper motor rotate a full rotation, stop for a short time, then rotate backwards for a quarter rotation, stop a short time, then repeat. It may help to put a small tab of tape to the spindle of the motor so you can see it rotating.

Project 28 – Basic Stepper Control – Code Overview

The code for this project is again nice and simple, thanks to the stepper.h library that does all of the hard work for us. First, you include the library in the sketch:

```
#include <Stepper.h>
```

Then you need to define how many steps the motor requires to do a full 360 degree rotation. Typically, stepper motors will come in either a 7.5 degree or a 1.8 degree variety but you may have a stepper motor with a different step angle. To work out the steps, just divide 360 by the step angle. In the case of the stepper motor I used, the step angle was 1.8 degrees, meaning 200 steps were required to carry out a full 360 degree rotation:

```
#define STEPS 200
```

Then you create a stepper motor object, call it `stepper` and assign the pins going to either side of the two coils:

```
Stepper stepper(STEPS, 4, 5, 6, 7);
```

The setup function does nothing at all, but must be included:

```
void setup()
{
}
```

In the main loop, you first set the speed of the motor in rpm (revolutions per minute). This is done with the `.setSpeed` command and the speed, in rpm, goes in the parenthesis:

```
stepper.setSpeed(60);
```

Then you tell the stepper how many steps it must carry out. You set this to 200 steps at 60 rpm, meaning it carries out a full revolution in one second:

```
stepper.step(200);
```

At the end of this revolution, a delay of 1/10th of a second is carried out:

```
delay(100);
```

Then the speed is slowed down to just 20 rpm:

```
stepper.setSpeed(20);
```

The motor is then made to rotate in the opposite direction (hence the negative value) for 50 steps, which on a 200 step motor is a quarter revolution:

```
stepper.step(-50);
```

Then another 100 millisecond delay is executed and the loop repeats.

As you can see, controlling a stepper motor is very easy and yet you have control over its speed, which direction it goes in, and exactly how much the shaft will rotate. You can therefore control exactly where the item attached to the shaft rotates and by how much. Using a stepper motor to control a robot wheel would give very precise control and rotating a robot head or camera would allow you to position it to point exactly where you want it.

Project 28 – Basic Stepper Control – Hardware Overview

The new piece of hardware you are using in this project is the stepper motor. A stepper motor is a DC motor in which the rotation can be divided up into a number of smaller steps. This is done by having an iron gear-shaped rotor attached to the shafts inside the motor. Around the outside of the motor are electromagnets with teeth. One coil is energized, causing the teeth of the iron rotor to align with the teeth of the electromagnet. The teeth on the next electromagnet are slightly offset from the first; when it is energized and the first coil is turned off, this causes the shaft to rotate slightly more to towards the next electromagnet. This process is repeated by however many electromagnets are inside until the teeth are almost aligned up with the first electromagnet and the process is repeated.

Each time an electromagnet is energized and the rotor moves slightly, it is carrying out one step. By reversing the sequence of electromagnets energizing the rotor, it turns in the opposite direction.

The job of the Arduino is to apply the appropriate HIGH and LOW commands to the coils in the correct sequence and speed to enable the shaft to rotate. This is what is going on behind the scenes in the stepper.h library.

A unipolar motor has five or six wires and these go to four coils. The center pins on the coils are tied together and go to the power supply. Bipolar motors usually have four wires and they have no common centre connections. See Figure 10-3 for different types and sizes of stepper motor.

Figure 10-3. Different kinds of stepper motors (image by Aki Korhonen)

The step sequence for a stepper motor can be seen in Table 10-1.

Table 10-1. Step Sequence for a Stepper Motor

Step	Wire 1	Wire 2	Wire 4	Wire 5
1 HIGH		LOW	HIGH	LOW
2 LOW		HIGH	HIGH	LOW
3 LOW		HIGH	LOW	HIGH
4 HIGH		LOW	LOW	HIGH

Figure 10-4 shows the diagram for a unipolar stepper motor. As you can see, there are four coils (there are actually two coils, but they are divided by the center wires into two smaller coils). The center wire goes to the power supply and the two other wires go to the outputs on one side of the H-Bridge driver IC and the other two wires for the second coil go to the last two outputs of the H-Bridge.

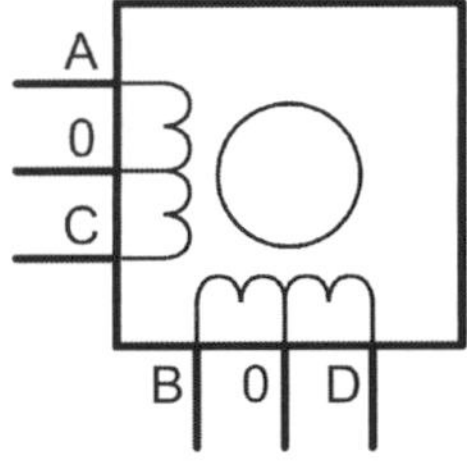

Figure 10-4. Circuit diagram for a unipolar stepper motor

Figure 10-5 shows the diagram for a bipolar stepper motor. This time there are just two coils with no centre pin. The step sequence for a bipolar motor is the same as for a unipolar. However, this time you reverse the current across the coils, i.e. a HIGH equates to a positive voltage and a LOW to a ground (or a pulled down connection).

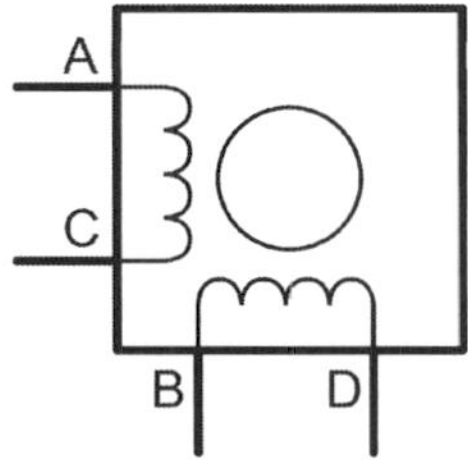

Figure 10-5. *Circuit diagram for a bipolar stepper motor*

It is possible to increase the resolution of the stepper motor by using special techniques for half stepping and microstepping. These can increase the resolution of the motor, but at the expense of reduced torque and reduced position reliability. The best way to increase resolution is through a gearing system.

Now that you know all about controlling a stepper motor, you'll go back to regular motor control, but this time you'll be using a motor shield and controlling two motors connected to wheel on a robot base.

Project 29 – Using a Motor Shield

You are now going to use a motor shield to control two motors separately. You'll learn how to control the speed and direction of each motor and apply that knowledge to control the wheels on a two-wheeled robot. When you move onto Project 30, these skills will be employed to make a line-following robot.

Parts Required

You can run this project just using two DC motors if that is all you have. However, that's not a lot of fun. So either obtain a two wheeled robot base or make one out of two geared motors with wheels. The rotation at half speed needs to be about 20cm or 6 inches of forward movement per second.

The battery pack will need to have enough voltage to run your Arduino, shield and motors. I used 6 × AA batteries in a holder with a jack plug soldered to the wire to power my setup for testing this project.

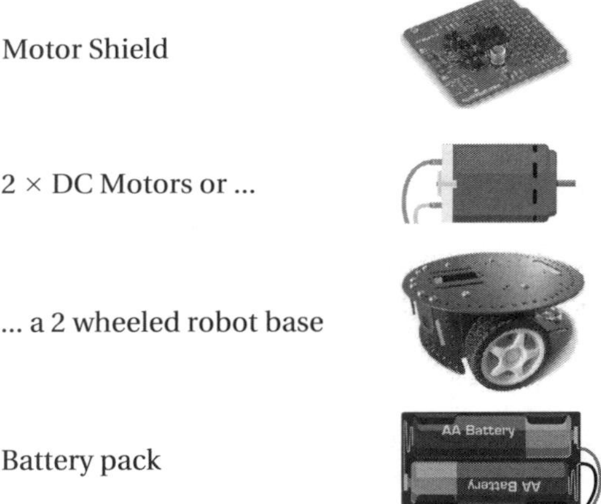

Connect It Up

As this project requires nothing more than a motor shield plugged into an Arduino and your two motors wires hooked up to the 4 outputs from the shield, there is no need for a circuit diagram. Instead, in Figure 10-6, you have a pretty picture of a motor shield plugged into an Arduino.

Figure 10-6. *A motor shield plugged into an Arduino (image courtesy of Sparkfun)*

For the testing of this project I used an Ardumoto motor shield from Sparkfun. This shield is designed to control two motors. There is also a shield available from Adafruit that will let you control up to four DC motors, two stepper motors, or two servos. The Adafruit shield also comes with the excellent AFMotor.h library that makes controlling the motors, steppers, or servos easy. The choice is up to you. However, the code for this project was designed with the Ardumoto in mind so if you use a different shield you will need to modify the code accordingly.

Each motor will need to be connected across the A (Output 1 and 2) and B (Output 3 and 4) port of the shield.

I also used a two wheeled robot base from DFRobot (see Figure 10-7). This is a nice inexpensive robot base that comes with attachments and mounting holes for fitting sensors. It's ideal for the line-following robot project that comes next. However, any robot base will do for this project; you could even use a four wheeled robot base if you just remember to control both sets of motors on each side instead of just the one. Of course, if you don't want to get a robot base, you can test just using two DC motors instead.

Figure 10-7. *A two wheeled robot base (image courtesy of DFRobot)*

Enter the Code

Enter the code from Listing 10-2.

Listing 10-2. *Code for Project 29*

```
// Project 29 - Using a motor shield

// Set the pins for speed and direction of each motor
int speed1 = 3;
int speed2 = 11;
int direction1 = 12;
int direction2 = 13;

void stopMotor() {
  // turn both motors off
  analogWrite(speed1, 0);
  analogWrite(speed2, 0);
}
```

```
void setup()
{
  // set all the pins to outputs
  pinMode(speed1, OUTPUT);
  pinMode(speed2, OUTPUT);
  pinMode(direction1, OUTPUT);
  pinMode(direction2, OUTPUT);
}

void loop()
{
  // Both motors forwaard at 50% speed for 2 seconds
  digitalWrite(direction1, HIGH);
  digitalWrite(direction2, HIGH);
  analogWrite(speed1,128);
  analogWrite(speed2,128);
  delay(2000);

  stopMotor(); delay(1000); // stop

  // Left turn for 1 second
  digitalWrite(direction1, LOW);
  digitalWrite(direction2, HIGH);
  analogWrite(speed1, 128);
  analogWrite(speed2, 128);
  delay(1000);

  stopMotor(); delay(1000); // stop

  // Both motors forward at 50% speed for 2 seconds
  digitalWrite(direction1, HIGH);
  digitalWrite(direction2, HIGH);
  analogWrite(speed1,128);
  analogWrite(speed2,128);
  delay(2000);

  stopMotor(); delay(1000); // stop

  // rotate right at 25% speed
  digitalWrite(direction1, HIGH);
  digitalWrite(direction2, LOW);
  analogWrite(speed1, 64);
  analogWrite(speed2, 64);
  delay(2000);

  stopMotor(); delay(1000); // stop

}
```

Project 29 – Using a Motor Shield – Code Overview

The first thing you need to do is assign which pins control the speed and direction. On the Ardumoto shield these are fixed at Pins 3, 11, 12, and 13:

```
int speed1 = 3;
int speed2 = 11;
int direction1 = 12;
int direction2 = 13;
```

Next, create a function to turn the motors off. The motor is turned off four times in the code so it makes sense to create a function to do this:

```
void stopMotor() {
  // turn both motors off
  analogWrite(speed1, 0);
  analogWrite(speed2, 0);
}
```

To turn the motors off you just need to set the speed of each motor to zero. Therefore, you write a value of zero to the speed1 (left motor) and speed2 (right motor) pins.

In the setup loop, the four pins are set to output mode:

```
pinMode(speed1, OUTPUT);
pinMode(speed2, OUTPUT);
pinMode(direction1, OUTPUT);
pinMode(direction2, OUTPUT);
```

In the main loop, you execute four separate movement routines. First, you move the robot forward at 50% speed for two seconds:

```
digitalWrite(direction1, HIGH);
digitalWrite(direction2, HIGH);
analogWrite(speed1,128);
analogWrite(speed2,128);
delay(2000);
```

This is done by first setting the direction pins to HIGH, which equates to forward (presuming your motors are wired the correct way around). The speed pins of both motors are then set to 128. The PWM values range from 0 to 255, so 128 is halfway between those. Therefore, the duty cycle is 50% and the motors will run at half speed. Whatever direction and speed you set the motors to run at, they will continue thusly until you change them. Therefore, the two second delay will ensure the robot moves forward at 50% speed for two seconds, which should be about a meter or 3 feet.

Next, you stop the motors from turning and wait one second:

```
stopMotor(); delay(1000); // stop
```

The next movement sequence changes the direction of the left hand motor to reverse and the right side motor to forward. To make a motor go forward, set its direction pin to HIGH; to make it go in reverse, set it to LOW. The speed remains at 50%, so the value of 128 is written to the speed pins of both motors (the lines for forward motion on the right wheel and the speeds are not strictly necessary but I have left them in so you can modify them as you wish to get different movements).

Making the right hand wheel go forward and the left hand wheel move in reverse causes the robot to rotate anti-clockwise (turn left). This movement is for one second, which should make it turn left by about 90 degrees. After this sequence, the motor is stopped for one second again:

```
digitalWrite(direction1, LOW);
digitalWrite(direction2, HIGH);
analogWrite(speed1, 128);
analogWrite(speed2, 128);
delay(1000);
```

The next sequence makes the robot move forward again at 50% speed for two seconds, followed by a one second stop:

```
digitalWrite(direction1, HIGH);
digitalWrite(direction2, HIGH);
analogWrite(speed1,128);
analogWrite(speed2,128);
delay(2000);
```

The final movement sequence changes the direction of the wheels so that the left hand wheel drives forward and the right hand wheel drives backwards. This will make the robot rotate clockwise (turn right). The speed this time is set at 64, which is 25% duty cycle, making it rotate slower than before. The rotation lasts for two seconds, which should be enough to turn the robot by 180 degrees.

```
digitalWrite(direction1, HIGH);
digitalWrite(direction2, LOW);
analogWrite(speed1, 64);
analogWrite(speed2, 64);
```

The four sequences together should make your robot go forward for two seconds, stop, turn left by 90 degrees, stop, go forward for two seconds again, stop, then turn at a slower rate by 180 degrees and repeat from the start.

You may well need to adjust the timings and speeds according to your own robot as you may be using a different voltage, faster or slower geared motors, etc. Play around with the movement sequences to get the robot to move quicker or slower or turn at different rates as you desire.

The whole idea behind Project 29 is to get you used to the necessary commands to move the two motors in different directions and different speeds. If you just have motors but no robot base, attach some tape to the spindle of the motors so you can see the speed and direction they are turning.

Project 29 – Using a Motor Shield – Hardware Overview

The new piece of hardware used in this project is the motor shield. A shield is simply a circuit board already made up and conveniently sized to fit over the Arduino. The shield has pins to connect itself to the pins on the Arduino; these have female sockets on the top so you can still access the pins through the shield. Of course, depending on what type of shield you have, some of the Arduino pins will be used by the shield and will therefore be out of bounds for use in your code. The Ardumoto shield, for example, uses Digital Pins 10, 11, 12, and 13.

Shields have the benefit of giving you added functionality to your Arduino by simply plugging it in and uploading the necessary code. You can get all kinds of shields to extend the function of the Arduino to include such things as Ethernet access, GPS, relay control, SD and Micro SD Card access, LCD displays, TV connectivity, wireless communications, touch screens, dot matrix displays, and DMX lighting control. See Figure 10-8 for examples of different kinds of shields.

Figure 10-8. *A proto shield, ethernet shield, data logger shield, and gps shield (courtesy of Adafruit Industries at `www.adafruit.com`)*

Project 30 – Line Following Robot

Now that you know how to control the two motors or your robot base using a motor shield, you are going to put those skills to good use! In this project, you are going to build a robot that is capable of detecting and following a black line drawn on a floor. This kind of robot is still used today in factories to ensure the robot keeps to a set path across the factory floor. They are known as Automated Guided Vehicles (AGVs).

Parts Required

For this project, you will need a small lightweight robot base. These can be purchased ready-made or in kit form. Or you can build one from scratch (much more fun). Make sure the wheels are geared so that they rotate much slower than the motor because the robot must be able to move fairly slowly to enable it to navigate the line.

As the robot will be autonomous, it will need its own battery pack. I found that a six-AA battery holder provided enough power for the Arduino, sensors, LEDs, shield, and motors. Larger batteries will give you a longer life but at the expense of greater weight, so it will depend on the load bearing capacity of your robot.

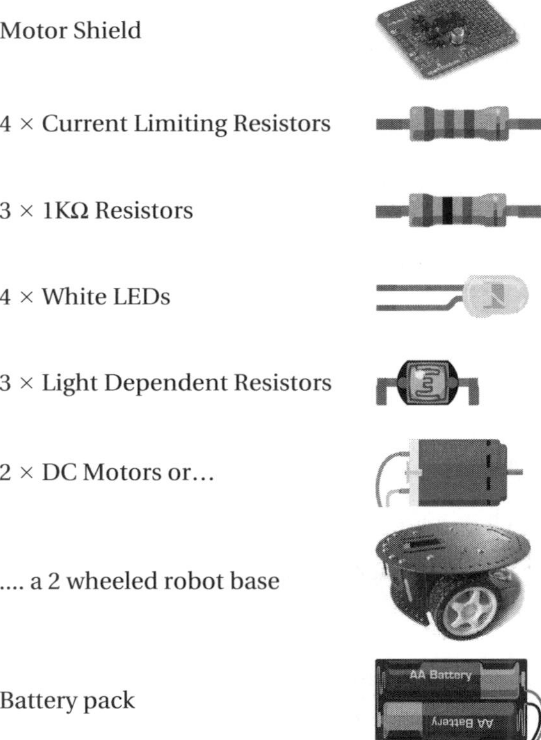

Motor Shield
4 × Current Limiting Resistors
3 × 1KΩ Resistors
4 × White LEDs
3 × Light Dependent Resistors
2 × DC Motors or…
…. a 2 wheeled robot base
Battery pack
AA Battery
AA Battery

Connect It Up

Connect the circuit up as in Figure 10-9. The shield is not shown, but the four outputs simply go to Motor A and Motor B.

The four LEDs can be any color as long as they have a reasonable enough brightness to illuminate the floor and create contrast between the floor and the black line for your sensor to detect. White LEDs are best as they output the greatest brightness for the lowest current. Four of these are connected in parallel with Pin 9. Make sure that you use the appropriate current limiting resistors for your LEDs.

Finally, connect up three light dependent resistors to Analog Pins 0, 1, and 2. One side of the LDR goes to ground, the other to +5v via a 1K ohm resistor. The wire from the analog pins goes between the resistor and the LDR pin (you used LDRs in Project 14).

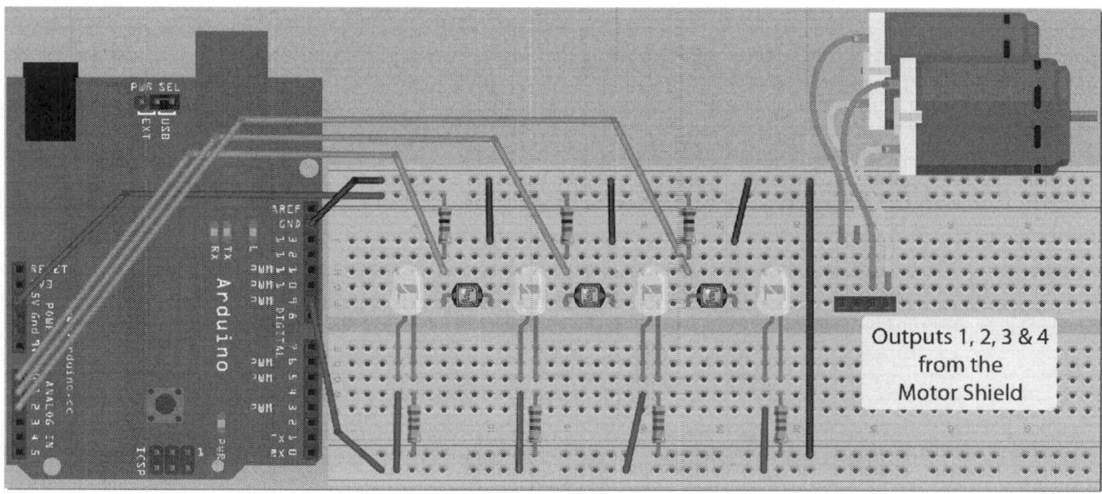

Figure 10-9. The circuit for Project 30 – Line Following Robot

The breadboard above can be used for testing purposes. However, for making the robot you will need to make up a sensor bar that houses the four LEDs and the three LDRs. These must be positioned so that they are all close together and pointing in the same direction. I soldered up the LED and sensor circuit onto a small piece of stripboard and placed the three LDRs in-between the four LEDs and just slightly higher than the LEDs so that the light from them did not shine onto the sensor. Figure 10-10 shows how I did it.

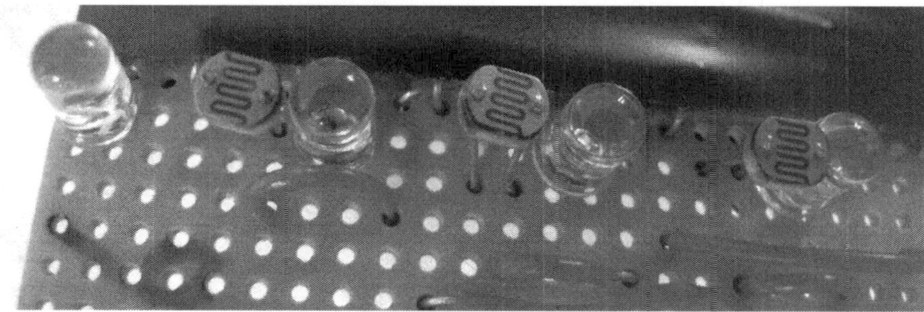

Figure 10-10. The sensor bar consisting of four LEDs and three LDRs.

The sensor bar is then attached to the front side of your robot in such a way that the LEDs and LDRs are about 1cm or half an inch above the floor (see Figure 10-11). I simply taped mine to the front of my robot, but for a more permanent solution the sensor bar could be bolted to the chassis.

***Figure 10-11.** The robot base fitted with the sensor bar.*

The battery pack should be placed centrally inside the robot base so as to not upset the load balance between the wheels. Fix the pack to the chassis with some Velcro so it cannot move around as the robot navigates the course.

As you can see from Figure 10-11, wires runs between the motor shield and the two motors and also down to the sensor bar. One wire provides +5v, one is for Ground, one is for +5v from Digital Pin 9, and the other three go to analog sensors 0, 1 and 2, with 0 being the left hand sensor (looking from the front of the robot), 1 being the center sensor, and 2 being the right hand one. It is critical that you get the order correct or the robot will not work as expected. See Figure 10-12 for an image of my robot in action on my kitchen floor (there is also a video of it in action on YouTube and Vimeo if you can find them).

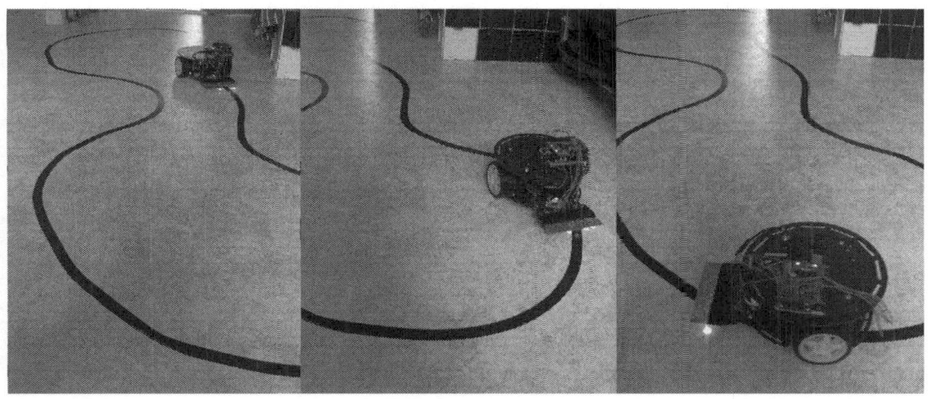

Figure 10-12. My own line-following robot in action.

Enter the Code

When you have built your robot and everything has been checked over, enter the code from Listing 10-3.

Listing 10-3. Code for Project 30

```
// Project 30 - Line Following Robot

#define lights 9
int LDR1, LDR2, LDR3; // sensor values

// calibration offsets
int leftOffset = 0, rightOffset = 0, centre = 0;
// pins for motor speed and direction
int speed1 = 3, speed2 = 11, direction1 = 12, direction2 = 13;
// starting speed and rotation offset
int startSpeed = 70, rotate = 30;
// sensor threshold
int threshhold = 5;
// initial speeds of left and right motors
int left = startSpeed, right = startSpeed;

// Sensor calibration routine
void calibrate() {

  for (int x=0; x<10; x++) { // run this 10 times to obtain average
  digitalWrite(lights, HIGH); // lights on
  delay(100);
  LDR1 = analogRead(0); // read the 3 sensors
  LDR2 = analogRead(1);
  LDR3 = analogRead(2);
```

```
  leftOffset = leftOffset + LDR1; // add value of left sensor to total
  centre = centre + LDR2; // add value of centre sensor to total
  rightOffset = rightOffset + LDR3; // add value of right sensor to total

  delay(100);
  digitalWrite(lights, LOW); // lights off
  delay(100);
  }
  // obtain average for each sensor
  leftOffset = leftOffset / 10;
  rightOffset = rightOffset / 10;
  centre = centre /10;
  // calculate offsets for left and right sensors
  leftOffset = centre - leftOffset;
  rightOffset = centre - rightOffset;
}

void setup()
{
    // set the motor pins to outputs
    pinMode(lights, OUTPUT); // lights
    pinMode(speed1, OUTPUT);
    pinMode(speed2, OUTPUT);
    pinMode(direction1, OUTPUT);
    pinMode(direction2, OUTPUT);
    // calibrate the sensors
    calibrate();
    delay(3000);

    digitalWrite(lights, HIGH); // lights on
    delay(100);

    // set motor direction to forward
    digitalWrite(direction1, HIGH);
    digitalWrite(direction2, HIGH);
    // set speed of both motors
    analogWrite(speed1,left);
    analogWrite(speed2,right);
}

void loop() {

  // make both motors same speed
  left = startSpeed;
  right = startSpeed;

  // read the sensors and add the offsets
  LDR1 = analogRead(0) + leftOffset;
  LDR2 = analogRead(1);
  LDR3 = analogRead(2) + rightOffset;
```

```
  // if LDR1 is greater than the centre sensor + threshold turn right
  if (LDR1 > (LDR2+threshhold)) {
    left = startSpeed + rotate;
    right = startSpeed - rotate;
  }

  // if LDR3 is greater than the centre sensor + threshold turn left
  if (LDR3 > (LDR2+threshhold)) {
    left = startSpeed - rotate;
    right = startSpeed + rotate;
  }

  // send the speed values to the motors
    analogWrite(speed1,left);
    analogWrite(speed2,right);
}
```

Lay out a course for your robot on a flat surface. I used the linoleum on my kitchen floor and made a course using black electrical tape. Turn the robot on, making sure it is sitting on a blank piece of floor next to, but not over, the back line. The calibration routine will run, making the LEDs flash ten times in quick succession. Once this stops, you have three seconds to pick up the robot and place it on the line. If all is well, the robot will now happily follow the line. Don't make the turns too sharp as this rapid transition will not be detected with only three LDRs. See Figure 10-12 for an example of a course made with black electrical tape.

Project 30 – Line Following Robot – Code Overview

First, you define the pin for the lights, and then three integers are declared that will hold the values read from the three light dependent resistors:

```
#define lights 9
int LDR1, LDR2, LDR3; // sensor values
```

Then another three integers are declared that will hold the offset values for the three sensors calculated in the calibration routine (this will be explained later):

```
int leftOffset = 0, rightOffset = 0, centre = 0;
```

Next, you define the pins that will control the speed and direction of the two motors:

```
int speed1 = 3, speed2 = 11, direction1 = 12, direction2 = 13;
```

Then two integers are created to hold the initial speed of the motors and the speed offset for each wheel that you add or subtract to make the robot rotate:

```
int startSpeed = 70, rotate = 30;
```

The default speed is set to 70, which is around 27% duty cycle. You may need to adjust this value to suit your own robot. Too high a value will make the robot overshoot the line and too low will prevent the motors from turning fast enough to turn the wheels to overcome friction.

The rotate value is how much you will speed up or slow down the wheels to cause the robot to turn. In my case, the required value is 30. So when turning left, for example, the right wheel spins at speed 100 and the left wheel at a speed of 40 (70+30 and 70-30). The rotate value is another setting you may need to adjust for your own setup.

Another integer is created to hold the sensor threshold:

```
int threshhold = 5;
```

This is the difference in values required between the center sensor and the left or right sensors before the robot decides to turn. In my case, a setting of 5 works well. This means that the left and right sensors would need to detect a value greater than the value read from the center sensor plus the threshold value before action is taken. In other words, if the center sensor is reading a value of 600 and the left sensor is reading 603, then the robot will keep going straight. However, a left sensor value of 612 (which is higher than the center value plus threshold) means that the left sensor is detecting the back line, indicating that the robot is too far over to the left. So the motors would adjust to make the robot turn to the right to compensate.

The threshold value will vary depending on the contrast between your floor (or whatever surface you use) and the black line. This may need to be adjusted to ensure the robot only turns when it has detected enough of a difference between floor and line to ascertain it had moved too far left or right.

The final set of variables will store the speed values for the left and right motors. These are initially set to the value in startSpeed:

```
int left = startSpeed, right = startSpeed;
```

After the variables are all declared and initialized, you come to your first and only function, which is the calibration routine:

```
void calibrate() {
```

The purpose of this routine is two-fold. First, it obtains an average value from each of the three sensors over a sequence of ten reads. Second, it flashes the lights 10 times (while reading values from the three sensors) to show you that the robot is calibrating and nearly ready to run.

The sensors require calibration, as each one will read different values to the next one. Every LDR will give a slightly different reading and this will be affected by manufacturing tolerances, the tolerance of the voltage divider resistors used, and the resistance in the wires. You want all three sensors to read (roughly) the same value, so you take ten readings from each, average them out, and calculate the difference that the left and right sensors are from the center sensor (which is used as the baseline).

You start off with creating a for loop that runs ten times:

```
for (int x=0; x<10; x++) {
```

The LEDs attached to Pin 9 are turned on, followed by a delay of 100 milliseconds:

```
digitalWrite(9, HIGH);
delay(100);
```

Next, the values from all three sensors are read in and stored in LDR1, LDR2, and LDR3:

```
LDR1 = analogRead(0);
LDR2 = analogRead(1);
LDR3 = analogRead(2);
```

Now you take those values and add them to the `leftOffset`, `center`, and `rightOffset` variables. These variables start off at zero, so after ten iterations they will contain a running total of all ten values read from the sensors.

```
leftOffset = leftOffset + LDR1;
centre = centre + LDR2;
rightOffset = rightOffset + LDR3;
```

Then you wait 100 milliseconds, turn the light off, wait another 100 milliseconds, and then repeat the process:

```
delay(100);
digitalWrite(9, LOW); // lights off
delay(100);
```

After this process has repeated ten times, you exit the `for` loop and then divide each of the running totals by ten. This gives you an average sensor reading for each of the three LDRs.

```
leftOffset = leftOffset / 10;
rightOffset = rightOffset / 10;
centre = centre /10;
```

You then calculate what the offset will be by deducting the left and right sensor values by the centre one:

```
leftOffset = centre - leftOffset;
rightOffset = centre - rightOffset;
```

These values will be added to the sensor readings from the left and right sensors so that all three sensors will be giving approximately the same readings. This will make ascertaining the difference between the three readings a lot easier when detecting the difference between the floor and the black line.

Next, you have the setup routine, which starts off by setting the pin for the LEDs and the pins for the motor speed and direction to OUTPUT:

```
pinMode(9, OUTPUT); // lights
pinMode(speed1, OUTPUT);
pinMode(speed2, OUTPUT);
pinMode(direction1, OUTPUT);
pinMode(direction2, OUTPUT);
```

The calibration routine is now run to ensure all three sensors issue similar readings, followed by a delay of three seconds. After the LEDs flash ten times during the calibration routine, you have three seconds to place the robot on the line it is to follow:

```
calibrate();
delay(3000);
```

The lights are turned on, followed by a brief delay:

```
digitalWrite(9, HIGH); // lights on
delay(100);
```

The direction of both motors is set to forward and the speeds are set to the values stored in the `right` and `left` variables (initially set to the value stored in `startSpeed`):

```
digitalWrite(direction1, HIGH);
digitalWrite(direction2, HIGH);
analogWrite(speed1,left);
analogWrite(speed2,right);
```

Now you move onto the main loop of the program. This starts off by setting the speed of the left and right motors to the value in `startSpeed`:

```
left = startSpeed;
right = startSpeed;
```

The motor speed is reset to these values at the start of each loop so that the robot is always going forward, unless the values are changed later in the loop to make the robot turn.

You now read the sensor values from each of the three LDRs and store the values in the LDR1, LDR2, and LDR3 integers. The offsets calculated for the left and right sensors are added to the value so that when all three sensors are looking at the same surface they will read approximately the same values.

```
LDR1 = analogRead(0) + leftOffset;
LDR2 = analogRead(1);
LDR3 = analogRead(2) + rightOffset;
```

Now you need to check those sensor values and see if the black line has moved to far from the center. You do this by checking the left and right sensors and seeing if the values read are greater than the value read from the center LDR plus the threshold offset.

If the value from the left sensor is greater than the reading-plus-threshold-offset, then the black line has shifted from the centerline and is too far to the right. The motor speeds are then adjusted so that the left wheel spins faster than the right, thus turning the robot to the right which will bring the black line back to the centre.

```
if (LDR1 > (LDR2+threshhold)) {
    left = startSpeed + rotate;
    right = startSpeed - rotate;
  }
```

The same is done for the right hand sensor, this time turning the robot to the left:

```
  if (LDR3 > (LDR2+threshhold)) {
    left = startSpeed - rotate;
    right = startSpeed + rotate;
  }
```

The speeds, which may or may not have been adjusted if the line was off center, are then sent out to the motors:

```
analogWrite(speed1,left);
analogWrite(speed2,right);
```

This whole process is repeated over and over many times per second and forms a feedback loop which makes the robot follow the line.

If your robot runs off the line, you may need to adjust the speed in `startSpeed` to a slower one. If it doesn't turn fast or far enough or if it turns too much, then the `rotate` value needs to be adjusted accordingly. The sensitivity of the LDRs can be adjusted by changing the value in the `threshold` variable. Play around with these values until you get the robot to follow the line successfully.

Summary

Chapter 10 started off with a simple introduction to stepper motors and how to control their speed and direction using a motor drive IC. You also learned the difference between a bipolar and a unipolar stepper motor and how they work. Then you moved onto using a simple motor shield to control two motors independently and ended up with connecting that shield to a robot base to make a two wheeled line-following robot.

You have also learned about shields and their different uses, and you've put a motor shied to a practical application. Knowing how to control stepper motors and standard motors, as well as servos (Chapter 9), means you are well on your way to making your own advanced robot or animatronics device!

Subjects and Concepts covered in Chapter 10

- The difference between unipolar and bipolar stepper motors
- How to connect a stepper to a motor driver IC
- Using capacitors to smooth a signal and reduce interference
- How to set up a stepper object in your code
- Setting the speed and number of steps of the motor
- Controlling the direction of the motor with positive or negative numbers
- How a stepper motor works
- The coil energizing sequence required to drive a stepper motor
- That resolution can be increased using half stepping and microstepping
- How to use a motor shield

- Using a motor shield to control the speed and/or direction of several motors
- What an Arduino shield is and the different kinds available
- How to detect contrast variations in light using several LDRs
- How to obtain an average sensor reading
- Using offset values to balance sensor readings
- How to make an awesome line-following robot

CHAPTER 11

Pressure Sensors

Now you are going to take a look at pressure sensors, in particular the SCP1000 absolute digital pressure sensor from VTI. This is a great sensor that is easily interfaced with an Arduino and provides accurate pressure and temperature readings. The device needs to be connected to the Arduino's SPI (Serial Peripheral Interface) bus for data to be exchanged. SPI is a new concept for you, and although this chapter will not cover it in great detail (SPI would need a chapter or two of its own), you will learn the basic concepts of SPI and how to use it to get data from the SCP1000 sensor.

Absolute pressure sensors are ideal for making your own weather station. You'll start off in this chapter by learning how to interface the SCP1000 to the Arduino and read data from it using the serial monitor. You will then use the sensor and an LCD to display a pressure graph over a 24-hour period. Along the way, you will also learn how to control a GLCD (Graphic LCD) display.

Project 31 – Digital Pressure Sensor

You are going to use an Arduino Mega for this project because Project 32 uses a GLCD and you'll need the extra pins the Mega provides. If you don't have a Mega, you can still use a standard Arduino—just change the SPI pins to match those of a Duemilanove.

Parts Required

The tiny SCP1000 sensor can be purchased from Sparkfun or their distributors pre-soldered to a breakout board (see Figure 11-1) to make it easy to interface with an Arduino (or other microcontroller). You will need to solder some header pins onto the board if you wish to push it into a breadboard. Otherwise, solder some wires to it so it can be connected to the Mega.

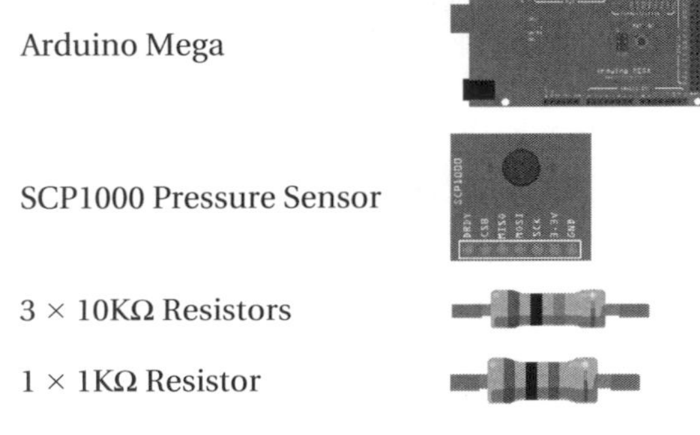

Arduino Mega

SCP1000 Pressure Sensor

3 × 10KΩ Resistors

1 × 1KΩ Resistor

Figure 11-1. *The SCP1000 on a Sparkfun breakout board*

Connect It Up

Connect everything as shown in Figure 11-2.

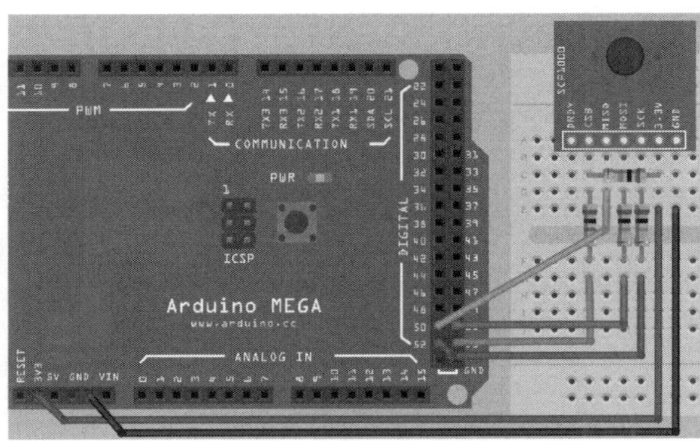

Figure 11-2. *The circuit for Project 31 – Digital Pressure Sensor*

The sensor has a TRIG and PD pins that will need to be connected to Ground, too. Make sure that everything is connected up correctly, especially the resistors as these will protect the SCP1000 from over voltage. Now enter the code.

Enter the Code

Enter the code from Listing 11-1.

***Listing 11-1.** Code for Project 31*

```
/*
SCP1000               Mega
DRDY                  N/A
CSB                   53 via Logic Level Convertor
MISO                  50 (straight through)
MOSI                  51 via Logic Level Convertor
SCK                   52 via Logic Level Convertor
3.3v                  3.3v
GND                   GND
TRIG                  GND
PD                    GND
*/

// SPI PINS
#define SLAVESELECT 53
#define SPICLOCK 52
#define DATAOUT 51  //MOSI
#define DATAIN 50   //MISO
#define UBLB(a,b)  ( ( (a) << 8) | (b) )
#define UBLB19(a,b) ( ( (a) << 16 ) | (b) )

//Addresses
#define PRESSURE 0x1F   //Pressure 3 MSB
#define PRESSURE_LSB 0x20 //Pressure 16 LSB
#define TEMP 0x21       //16 bit temp

char rev_in_byte;
int temp_in;
unsigned long pressure_lsb;
unsigned long pressure_msb;
unsigned long temp_pressure;
unsigned long pressure;
```

```
void setup()
{
        byte clr;
        pinMode(DATAOUT, OUTPUT);
        pinMode(DATAIN, INPUT);
        pinMode(SPICLOCK, OUTPUT);
        pinMode(SLAVESELECT, OUTPUT);
        digitalWrite(SLAVESELECT, HIGH); //disable device

        SPCR = B01010011; // SPi Control Register
        //MPIE=0, SPE=1 (on), DORD=0 (MSB first), MSTR=1 (master), CPOL=0 (clock idle when↵
 low), CPHA=0 (samples MOSI on rising edge), SPR1=0 & SPR0=0 (500kHz)
        clr=SPSR; // SPi Status Register
        clr=SPDR; // SPi Data Register
        delay(10);
        Serial.begin(38400);
        delay(500);

        write_register(0x03,0x09); // High Speed Read Mode
        write_register(0x03,0x0A); // High Resolution Measurement Mode
}

void loop()
{
        pressure_msb = read_register(PRESSURE);
        pressure_msb &= B00000111;
        pressure_lsb = read_register16(PRESSURE_LSB);
        pressure_lsb &= 0x0000FFFF;
        pressure = UBLB19(pressure_msb, pressure_lsb);
        pressure /= 4;

        Serial.print("Pressure (hPa): ");
        float hPa = float(pressure)/100;
        Serial.println(hPa);

        Serial.print("Pressure (Atm): ");
        float pAtm = float(pressure)/101325.0;
        Serial.println(pAtm, 3);

        temp_in = read_register16(TEMP);
        float tempC = float(temp_in)/20.0;
        Serial.print("Temp. C: ");
        Serial.println(tempC);
        float tempF = (tempC*1.8) + 32;
        Serial.print("Temp. F: ");
        Serial.println(tempF);
        Serial.println();
        delay(1000);
}
```

```
char spi_transfer(char data)
{
        SPDR = data;                      // Start transmission
        while (!(SPSR & (1<<SPIF))) { }; // Wait for transmission end
        return SPDR;                      // return the received byte
}

char read_register(char register_name)
{
        char in_byte;
        register_name <<= 2;
        register_name &= B11111100; //Read command

        digitalWrite(SLAVESELECT, LOW); //Enable SPI Device
        spi_transfer(register_name); //Write byte to device
        in_byte = spi_transfer(0x00); //Send nothing but get back register value
        digitalWrite(SLAVESELECT, HIGH); // Disable SPI Device
        delay(10);
        return(in_byte); // return value
}

unsigned long read_register16(char register_name)
{
        byte in_byte1;
        byte in_byte2;
        float in_word;

        register_name <<= 2;
        register_name &= B11111100; //Read command

        digitalWrite(SLAVESELECT, LOW); //Enable SPI Device
        spi_transfer(register_name); //Write byte to device
        in_byte1 = spi_transfer(0x00);
        in_byte2 = spi_transfer(0x00);
        digitalWrite(SLAVESELECT, HIGH); // Disable SPI Device
        in_word = UBLB(in_byte1,in_byte2);
        return(in_word); // return value
}

void write_register(char register_name, char register_value)
{
        register_name <<= 2;
        register_name |= B00000010; //Write command

        digitalWrite(SLAVESELECT, LOW); //Select SPI device
        spi_transfer(register_name); //Send register location
        spi_transfer(register_value); //Send value to record into register
        digitalWrite(SLAVESELECT, HIGH);
}
```

This code is based on work by Conor and a few others from the Arduino forums, so thanks to those involved. Also, version 0019 of the Arduino IDE came in an SPI example sketch for the SCP1000 using the SPI.h library by Tom Igoe.

The code above does things the hard way again so that you can see exactly how the SCP1000 communicates with the Arduino. Once you understand it, you can make life easier by using the SPI library.

After you have uploaded the code, open up the serial monitor window and ensure that your baud rate is set to 38400. You will see a stream of data from the sensor showing the pressure in hPa (hectopascals) and in atmospheres. Hectopascals are the unit of pressure commonly used in weather forecasts. You will also see the temperature in Celsius and Fahrenheit.

Project 31 – Digital Pressure Sensor – Code Overview

The code starts off with a set of defines for your pins on the Mega:

```
#define SLAVESELECT 53
#define SPICLOCK 52
#define DATAOUT 51  //MOSI
#define DATAIN 50   //MISO
```

If you are using a Duemilanove, the pins will be:

```
#define SLAVESELECT 10
#define SPICLOCK 13
#define DATAOUT 11  //MOSI
#define DATAIN 12   //MISO
```

Next are another two defines that are cleverly designed to do some bitshifting for you:

```
#define UBLB(a,b)  ( ( (a) << 8) | (b) )
#define UBLB19(a,b) ( ( (a) << 16 ) | (b) )
```

The first one will take two 8 bit digits and convert them to a 16 bit digit by using one as the LSB (least significant byte) and the other as the MSB (most significant byte). It does this with some bit shifting and some bitwise operations.

For example, if you had two 8 bit numbers (10010101 and 00111001) and you put them into the equation

```
UBLB(a,b)  ( ( (a) << 8) | (b) )
```

the calculation works out as

```
(((B10010101) << 8) | (B00111001))
```

So, the first digit is bit shifted left eight times to create

```
B1001010100000000
```

This number is then bitwise OR'ed with the second digit to create

```
B1001010100111001
```

So it has simply taken two 8 bit numbers and converted them into a 16 bit number using one set of 8 bits as the MSB and the other as the LSB.

The second define does something similar:

```
#define UBLB19(a,b) ( ( (a) << 16 ) | (b) )
```

This time it will create a 19 bit number, which is the resolution of the SCP1000 pressure sensor. It does this bit shifting the first 3 bits sixteen places to the left leaving 16 bits clear to add the 16 bit digit stored in b.

Next, you define the three registers inside the sensor that must be read in order to obtain the pressure data and the temperature:

```
#define PRESSURE 0x1F    //Pressure 3 MSB
#define PRESSURE_LSB 0x20 //Pressure 16 LSB
#define TEMP 0x21        //16 bit temp
```

The PRESSURE register at address 0x1F holds the three most significant bits of the 19 digit number that makes up the pressure reading. The PRESSURE_LSB register at address 0x20 holds the next 16 digits of the number. By using the calculation defined in UBLB19(a,b) the 16 bit and 3 bit numbers will be combined to create one 19 bit number.

Next, you declare some variables that will be used to store the values read from the pressure and temperature sensors:

```
char rev_in_byte;
int temp_in;
unsigned long pressure_lsb;
unsigned long pressure_msb;
unsigned long temp_pressure;
unsigned long pressure;
```

Next comes the setup routine. You start off by declaring a local variable of type byte (you will see how this is used soon):

```
byte clr;
```

Next, you set the four pins that make up the SPI bus to their respective INPUT and OUTPUT status:

```
pinMode(DATAOUT, OUTPUT);
pinMode(DATAIN, INPUT);
pinMode(SPICLOCK, OUTPUT);
pinMode(SLAVESELECT, OUTPUT);
```

Then you set the slave select pin to HIGH to disable the device as you don't want to exchange data with it while you are still setting up:

```
digitalWrite(SLAVESELECT, HIGH); //disable device
```

Next, you set SPCR to the binary value of B01010011:

```
SPCR = B01010011; // SPi Control Register
```

You may have noticed that this variable has not been declared yet, but the code will work. How can this be? Well, SPCR stands for SPI Control Register. It's one of three registers used in SPI communications that are hardcoded into the Arduino IDE. The other two are SPSR (SPI Status Register) and SPDR (SPI Data Register). Whenever you assign values to any of these registers, you will change what is going on with the SPI bus.

Let's take a little detour to look at SPI and how it works.

SPI – Serial Peripherals Interface

Before you look at the code any further, you need to understand what SPI is and how it works. SPI can be a complicated subject, so I am not going to go into it in any great depth. This is a beginner's book after all. Instead, I am going to give you just enough knowledge so that you understand what SPI is, how it works, and the parts that are relevant to the sketches in Projects 31 and 32 that use the SPI bus with the SCP1000 sensor. You will then be able to understand how to interface with other devices that also use SPI.

SPI is a way for two devices to exchange information. It has the benefits of needing only four pins from the Arduino and it's is fast. SPI is a synchronous protocol that allows a master device to communicate with a slave device. The data is controlled with a clock signal (CLK) which decides when data can change and when it is valid for reading. The clock rate can vary, unlike some other protocols in which the clock signal must be timed very accurately. This makes it ideal for microcontrollers that do not run particularly fast or whose internal oscillator is not clocked precisely.

SPI is a Master-Slave protocol (see Figure 11-3), meaning that a master device controls the clock signal. No data can be transmitted unless the clock is pulsed. SPI is also a data exchange protocol. This means that as data is clocked out, new data is being clocked in. Devices cannot simply transmit or receive data; they must exchange it, even if the data on one side is not being used in your program.

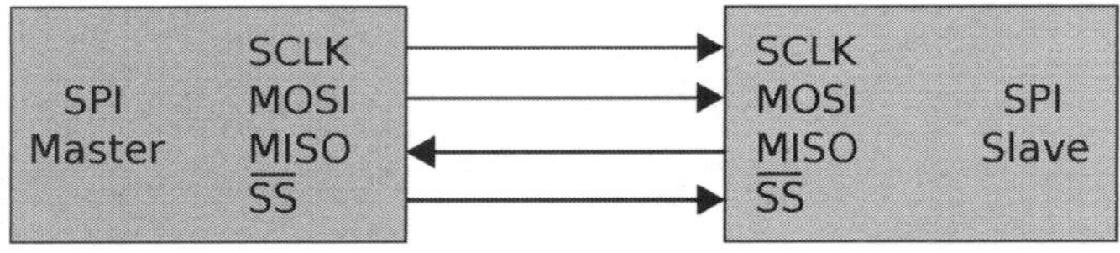

Figure 11-3. *SPU bus: single master and single slave (image courtesy of Colin M.L. Burnett)*

The slave select pin will control when a device can be accessed if more than one slave is attached to the master (see Figure 11-4). When there is only one slave device, as in your case, the SS (called CSB on the SCP1000) is optional. However, as a rule, it should be used regardless as it is also used as a reset for the slave to make it ready to receive the next byte. The slave select signal is sent out by the master to tell the slave that it wishes to start an SPI data exchange. This signal is active when LOW, so when held HIGH the slave device is not selected.

Data is only output during either the rising or falling edge of the clock signal on SCK. Data is latched during the opposite edge of SCK. The polarity of the clock is set by the master using one of the flags set in the SPCR register. The two data lines are known as MOSI (Master Output Slave Input) and MISO (Master

Input Slave Output). So, if the device is set to send data from the master on the rising edge of the clock pulse, data would be sent back from the slave on the falling edge of the clock pulse. Data is therefore both sent (MOSI) and input (MISO) from the master during one clock pulse.

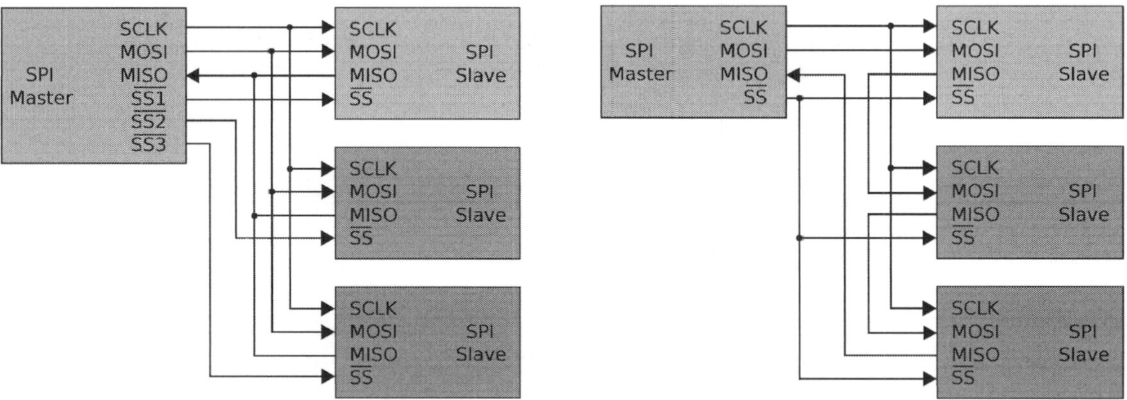

Figure 11-4. *Left: A master with three independent slaves. Right: daisy chained slaves. (Images courtesy of Colin M.L. Burnett)*

Remember that even if you only want to read data from a device (like you do with the SCP1000), you still need to send data both ways during one exchange.

The three registers used by the SPI bus are:

- SPCR – SPI Control Register
- SPDR – SPI Data Register
- SPSR – SPI Status Register

The Control Register has 8 bits and each bit controls a particular SPI setting. These bits are listed in Table 11-1.

Table 11-1. *The SPI Control Register Settings*

7	6	5	4	3	2	1	0
SPIE SPE		DORD	MSTR	CPOL	CPHA	SPR1	SPR0

- SPIE – SPI Interrupt Enable - Enables the SPI interrupt if 1.
- SPE – SPI Enable - SPI enabled when set to 1.
- DORD – Data Order - LSB transmitted first if 1 and MSB if 0.

- MSTR – Master/Slave Select – Sets Arduino in Master Mode if 1, Slave Mode when 0.
- CPOL – Clock Polarity – Sets Clock to be idle when high if set to 1, idle when low if set to 0.
- CPHA – Clock Phase – Determines if data is sampled on the leading or trailing edge of the clock.
- SPR1/0 – SPI Clock Rate Select 1 & 0 – These two bits control the clock rate of the master device.

The reason you can change these settings is that different SPI devices expect the clock polarity, clock phase, data order, speed, etc. to be different. This is mainly due to the fact that there is no standard for SPI, therefore manufacturers create devices with minor differences. In your code you set the SPCR thus:

```
SPCR = B01010011;
```

So you have disabled the interrupt (SPIE = 0), enabled the SPI (SPE = 1), set the data order to MSB first (DORD = 0), set the Arduino as master (MSTR = 1), set the clock polarity to be idle when low (CPOL = 0), set the clock phase to sample on the rising edge (CPHA = 0), and set the speed to be 250kHz (SPR1/2 = 11, which is 1/64th of the Arduino's oscillator frequency (16,000/64)).

The SPI Status Register (SPSR) uses 3 of its bits for setting the status of the SPI transfer. You are only interested in bit 7 (SPIF – SPI Interrupt Flag), which tells you if a serial transfer has been completed or not. If a transfer has been completed, it is set to 1. This bit is cleared (set to 0) by first reading the SPSR with bit 7 set to 1 and then the SPI Data Register (SPDR) is accessed.

The SPDR simply holds the byte that is going to be sent out of the MOSI line and read in from the MISO line.

All of the above sounds pretty complicated, but most of it you do not need to know (just yet). The SPI bus can be explained in layman's terms as having a master and slave device that want to talk to each other. The clock pulse ensures that data is sent from the master to the slave as the clock pulse rises (or falls, depending on how you have set the control register) and from the slave to the master as the clock falls (or rises). SPIF is set to 1 after the transfer is complete.

Now let's get back to the code.

Project 31 – Digital Pressure Sensor – Code Overview (cont.)

You now read in the SPSR and SPDR registers into clr. All this does is ensure that any junk data that may be in those registers is cleared out and the device is ready for you to use.

```
clr=SPSR; // SPi Status Register
clr=SPDR; // SPi Data Register
```

You then have a small delay, set the baud rate, followed by 500 millisecond delay to allow the serial line to set itself:

```
delay(10);
Serial.begin(38400);
delay(500);
```

You now use the `write_register` function (explained later) to write two values to the operation register address in the sensor, which is at Hexadecimal address 0x03. Writing a value of 0x09 to this register sets the sensor to high speed read mode and sending a value of 0x0A sets it to high resolution acquisition mode to ensure you get the most accurate value from the sensor.

```
write_register(0x03,0x09); // High Speed Read Mode
write_register(0x03,0x0A); // High Resolution Measurement Mode
```

Next comes your main loop. You start off by reading the value from the PRESSURE register (address 0x1F) and storing it in pressure_msb. This value will be the most significant byte of your 19 bit value (i.e. the 3 bits you need).

```
pressure_msb = read_register(PRESSURE);
```

Next you bit mask that value by carrying out a bitwise AND (&) with the value in pressure_msb and the binary number B00000111. Remember that the bitwise AND operator sets bits to 1 if both bits are 1 and to 0 if both bits are 0. Having the first three bits set to 1 (B00000111) means you will end up with only the first 3 bits, which is what you want.

```
pressure_msb &= B00000111;
```

You now want the remaining 16 bits of the pressure value so read the value stored in the PRESSURE_LSB register (address 0x20):

```
pressure_lsb = read_register16(PRESSURE_LSB);
```

Then you carry out a bitwise AND with this value and 0x0000FFFF, which is binary number B1111111111111111, meaning you only end up with the first 16 bits of any value read:

```
pressure_lsb &= 0x0000FFFF;
```

You then use the clever define trick in UBLB19 to take the 16 bits and the 3 bits and combine them into one 19 bit number:

```
pressure = UBLB19(pressure_msb, pressure_lsb);
```

The datasheet for the SCP1000 tells you that the pressure value is an integer; to convert it from a decimal integer to a value that represents Pascals (the measurement of pressure), you have to divide it by four:

pressure /= 4;

Now that you have your pressure data, you need to send it to the serial monitor so you can read it. You therefore print out the pressure value, first converting it to hPa (hectopascals) by dividing by 100, and storing that in a float called hPa. You must cast it to a float first to ensure that you get the two digits after the decimal point.

```
Serial.print("Pressure (hPa): ");
float hPa = float(pressure)/100;
Serial.println(hPa);
```

Next, you print out the pressure again but this time in atmospheres. You do this by dividing the value by 101325. One atmosphere equals 101325 Pascals. The number 3 after pAtm in the third line below tells the serial monitor to print out the value to three decimal places.

```
Serial.print("Pressure (Atm): ");
float pAtm = float(pressure)/101325.0;
Serial.println(pAtm, 3);
```

Next, you need to read the temperature data. This is done by calling the read_register16 function and passing it the TEMP register (address 0x21). The value returned from this function is stored in the temp_in variable. The temperature is a 14 bit value.

```
temp_in = read_register16(TEMP);
```

That value is cast to a float and then divided by 20 to get the temperature in Celsius:

```
float tempC = float(temp_in)/20.0;
Serial.print("Temp. C: ");
Serial.println(tempC);
```

And you then multiply that value by 1.8 and add 32 to get the temperature in Fahrenheit instead, and output that as well:

```
float tempF = (tempC*1.8) + 32;
Serial.print("Temp. F: ");
Serial.println(tempF);
```

You now have four functions that allow you to read data from the sensor over the SPI bus. The first is the `spi_transfer` function. You will be passing a char (one byte) to the function and getting a char back so the function is of type char. The data passed to the function is of type char also.

```
char spi_transfer(char data)
```

The byte sent to this function is passed to the SPI Data Register:

```
SPDR = data;
```

You then wait until the SPIF flag is set to signify the data has been successfully sent:

```
while (!(SPSR & (1<<SPIF))) { };
```

Nothing is inside the code block so it just sits and does nothing until SPIF is set. It works this out by doing a bitwise operation on SPSR and the value in the SPIF flag:

```
!(SPSR & (1<<SPIF))
```

So let's break this down into its constituent parts. First you have

```
(1<<SPIF)
```

All this is doing is ensuring that you move a 1 bit into the seventh bit position ready for it to be a bitmask. SPIF will have been defined in a macro somewhere as 7 (for the Atmega chips).

You then AND that bitmask with the value in SPSR

```
(SPSR & (1<<SPIF))
```

which will result in a non-zero value if the SPIF flag is set to 1. So if SPSR was, for example, B01010101, and the SPIF flag was 1, then the calculation would be (B01010101 & (1<<7)), which would equate to (B01010101 & B10000000), which would result in B00000000, as the AND operator will only leave a 1 in any bit if that bit in both numbers is a 1.

But if SPSR was B11010101 and the SPIF flag was 1 then you have (B11010101) & (B10000000) which would result in B10000000, which is a non-zero value. The whole calculation is then checked with the logical operator NOT '!'

```
!(SPSR & (1<<SPIF))
```

In other words, if the SPIF flag is NOT set to 1, do nothing and keep doing nothing until the SPIF flag is set to a 1, which then exits the `while` loop and executes the next command which is

```
return SPDR;
```

which returns the value in the SPDR register. So, the whole function sends a byte from the master to the slave, waits till that has been done, and then returns a byte from the slave to the master.

The next function is for reading an 8 bit value from a register in the SCP1000. It takes a char as a parameter and returns a char so is of that type.

```
char read_register(char register_name)
```

A variable of type char is declared and called `in_byte`. This will hold the value read back from the pressure register.

```
char in_byte;
```

Next, the register address is bitshifted left two places:

```
register_name <<= 2;
```

Now you enable the SPI device by pulling the Slave Select (CSB) line LOW:

```
digitalWrite(SLAVESELECT, LOW); //Enable SPI Device
```

Then transfer the register name to the device:

```
spi_transfer(register_name); //Write byte to device
```

Next, you send another byte, but this time you send nothing so you get the register value back:

```
in_byte = spi_transfer(0x00); //Send nothing but get back register value
```

in_byte now holds the MSB value of the pressure reading. Next, the SPI line is disabled, and you return the MSB of the pressure reading to the main loop:

```
digitalWrite(SLAVESELECT, HIGH); // Disable SPI Device
delay(10);
return(in_byte); // return value
```

The next function is read_register16() and it does pretty much the same thing, except this time instead of returning an 8 bit byte, it will return a 16 bit word. Again, the register address is passed to the function.

```
unsigned long read_register16(char register_name)
```

Then you declare two bytes and a float:

```
byte in_byte1;
byte in_byte2;
float in_word;
```

The two bytes will hold 8 bits each of the 16 bit word and the float will hold the final 16 bit word that is passed back from the function. The rest of the function is the same as the one before, except this time you receive back two sets of 8 bit bytes instead of just one.

```
register_name <<= 2;
digitalWrite(SLAVESELECT, LOW); //Enable SPI Device
spi_transfer(register_name); //Write byte to device
in_byte1 = spi_transfer(0x00);
in_byte2 = spi_transfer(0x00);
digitalWrite(SLAVESELECT, HIGH); // Disable SPI Device
```

The UBLB command takes the two bytes and bit shifts them into one 16 bit word and then the result is returned from the function:

```
in_word = UBLB(in_byte1,in_byte2);
return(in_word); // return value
```

The final functions job is to write a value to a register in the SCP1000. The function does not return anything so is of type void and has two a parameters, the register address and value to be written:

```
void write_register(char register_name, char register_value)
```

The register address is bitshifted left two places and then bitwise ORed with B00000010 to create the write command:

```
register_name <<= 2;
register_name |= B00000010; //Write command
```

The SPI line is enabled, the register address and its value is then transferred to the device, and the SPI line closed again before the function exits:

```
digitalWrite(SLAVESELECT, LOW); //Select SPI device
spi_transfer(register_name); //Send register location
spi_transfer(register_value); //Send value to record into register
digitalWrite(SLAVESELECT, HIGH);
```

This project is simply reading (OK, so using SPI is not exactly simple, but hopefully you understand it by now) the temperature and pressure readings and sending them out to the serial monitor. As the SCP1000 is a closed device, I am not going to do a hardware overview. All you need to know is that it senses pressure and temperature and transmits that data over the serial SPI line.

Let's do something useful with the pressure readings.

Project 32 – Digital Barograph

Now that you can hook up the SCP1000 and obtain data from it, you are going to put it to some use. This project is to make a digital barograph, which is a graph of pressure over time. To display the graph, you are going to use a GLCD (Graphic LCD). You'll learn how to display graphics as well as text.

Parts Required

The parts list is identical to Project 31, with the addition of a 128×64 GLCD, an extra resistor, and a potentiometer. You are going to use the glcd.h library so the GLCD must have a KS0108 (or equivalent) driver chip. Check the datasheet before purchase.

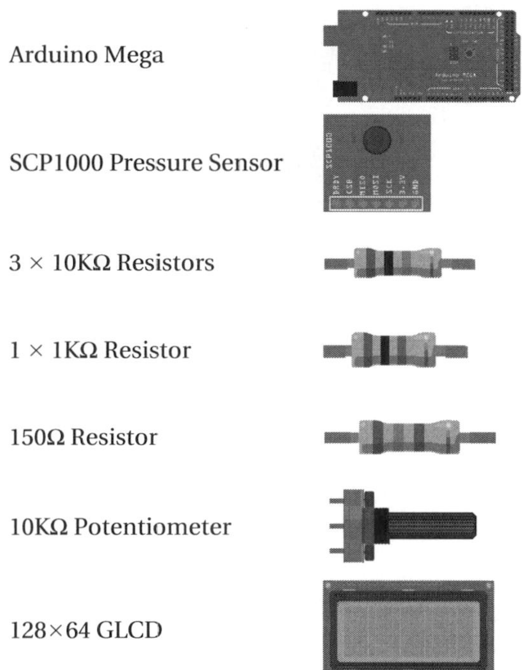

Connect It Up

Connect everything as shown in Figure 11-5.

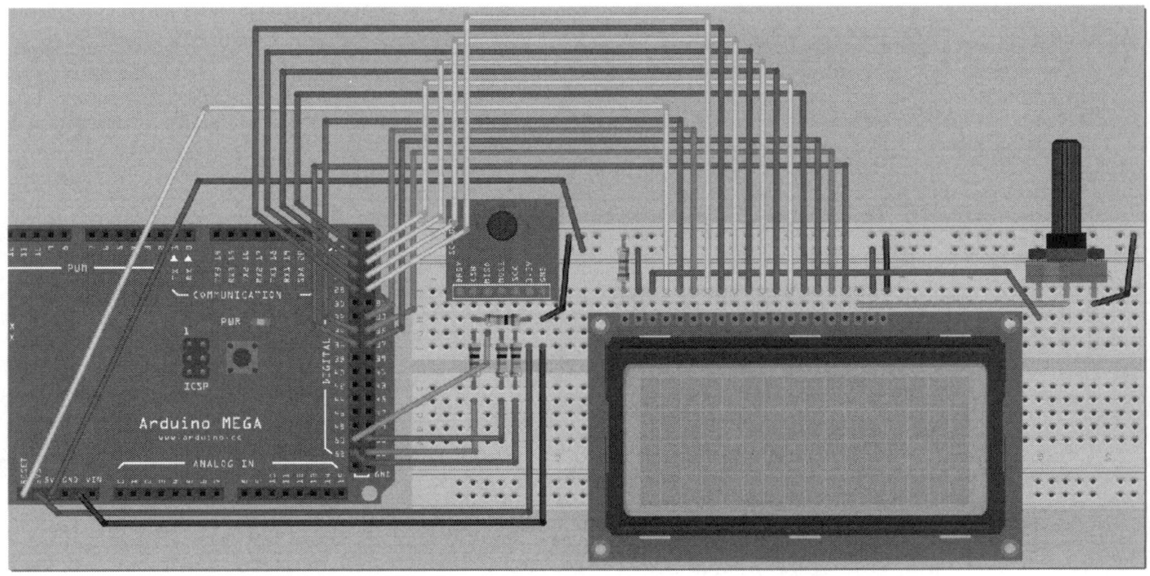

Figure 11-5. *The circuit for Project 32 – Digital Barograph*

The SCP1000 part of the circuit hasn't changed from Project 31. You are simply adding some extra components to that circuit. The GLCD you use may have different pinouts to the one from this project. Read the datasheet and make sure the pins match those in Table 11-2 below.

Table 11-2. *Pinouts between the Mega and the GLCD*

Mega	GLCD	Other
GND GND		
+5v +5v		
	LCD Contrast	Centre pot pin
36 D/I		
35 R/W		
37 Enab	le	

Mega	GLCD	Other
22 DB0		
23 DB1		
24 DB2		
25 DB3		
26 DB4		
27 DB5		
28 DB6		
29 DB7		
33 C	S1	
34 C	S2	
Reset Res	et	
	VEE	Positive side of pot
Back	light +5v	+5v
Back	light +0v	GND via 150Ω Resistor

Do not power up the circuit until everything is connected up and you have double-checked the wiring. It is very easy to damage a GLCD by having it wired incorrectly. In particular, make sure that the potentiometer has one side ground to Ground, the center pin is going to the LCD's contrast adjustment pin, and the other pin to VEE (LCD Voltage). The 150 ohm resistor is to limit the current going to the LCD backlight; you may need to experiment with this value to get the correct brightness, but make sure you do not exceed the voltage in the datasheet for your LCD. The potentiometer is used to adjust the contrast on the display to get it so it can be viewed easily.

Once you are confident everything is connected properly, power up your Arduino. You should see the GLCD light up ready to receive data. Now enter the code.

Enter the Code

Before you enter the code, you will need to download and install the GLCD.h library. This great library, written by Michael Margolis, is currently on its third version. It comes with a great document that shows how to connect up different types of GLCDs and full instructions for all of the commands in the library. Look on the Arduino Playground under LCDs to find it. Once you have downloaded the library, unzip it, and place the entire folder into the "libraries" folder inside your Arduino installation. The next time you fire up the Arduino IDE, it will be loaded and ready for use.

Enter the code from Listing 11-2.

Listing 11-2. Code for Project 32

```
/*
SCP1000              Mega
DRDY                 N/A
CSB                  53 via Logic Level Convertor
MISO                 50 (straight through)
MOSI                 51 via Logic Level Convertor
SCK                  52 via Logic Level Convertor
3.3v                 3.3v
GND                  GND
TRIG                 GND
PD                   GND
*/

#include <glcd.h>

#include "fonts/allFonts.h"

// SPI PINS
#define SLAVESELECT 53
#define SPICLOCK 52
#define DATAOUT 51       //MOSI
#define DATAIN 50        //MISO
#define UBLB(a,b)  ( ( (a) << 8) | (b) )
#define UBLB19(a,b) ( ( (a) << 16 ) | (b) )

//Addresses
#define PRESSURE 0x1F    //Pressure 3 MSB
#define PRESSURE_LSB 0x20 //Pressure 16 LSB
#define TEMP 0x21        //16 bit temp
#define INTERVAL 900  // Time interval in seconds (approx.)

int dots[124], dotCursor = 0, counter = 0;;
char rev_in_byte;
int temp_in;
float hPa;
unsigned long pressure_lsb;
unsigned long pressure_msb;
unsigned long temp_pressure;
unsigned long pressure;
```

```
void setup()
{
  GLCD.Init();   // initialise the library
  GLCD.ClearScreen();
  GLCD.SelectFont(System5x7, BLACK); // load the font

  byte clr;
  pinMode(DATAOUT, OUTPUT);
  pinMode(DATAIN, INPUT);
  pinMode(SPICLOCK,OUTPUT);
  pinMode(SLAVESELECT,OUTPUT);
  digitalWrite(SLAVESELECT,HIGH); //disable device

  SPCR = B01010011; // SPi Control Register
  //MPIE=0, SPE=1 (on), DORD=0 (MSB first), MSTR=1 (master), CPOL=0 (clock idle when low),↵
 CPHA=0 (samples MOSI on rising edge), SPR1=1 & SPR0=1 (250kHz)
  clr=SPSR;// SPi Status Register
  clr=SPDR; // SPi Data Register
  delay(10);

  write_register(0x03,0x09); // High Speed Read Mode
  write_register(0x03,0x0A); // High Resolution Measurement Mode

  GLCD.DrawRect(1,1,125,44); // Draw a rectangle
  for (int x=0; x<46; x+=11) { // Draw vertical scale
    GLCD.SetDot(0,1+x, BLACK);
    GLCD.SetDot(127,1+x, BLACK);
  }
    for (int x=0; x<128; x+=5) { // Draw horizontal scale
    GLCD.SetDot(1+x,0, BLACK);
  }

  for (int x; x<124; x++) {dots[x]=1023;} // clear the array
  getPressure();
  drawPoints(dotCursor);
}

void loop()
{
  getPressure();

  GLCD.CursorToXY(0, 49); // print pressure
  GLCD.print("hPa:");
  GLCD.CursorToXY(24,49);
  GLCD.print(hPa);

  temp_in = read_register16(TEMP);
  float tempC = float(temp_in)/20.0;
  float tempF = (tempC*1.8) + 32;
```

```
  GLCD.CursorToXY(0,57); // print temperature
  GLCD.print("Temp:");
  GLCD.CursorToXY(28, 57);
  GLCD.print(tempC); // change to tempF for Fahrenheit

  delay(1000);

  GLCD.CursorToXY(84,49); // print trend
  GLCD.print("TREND:");
  GLCD.CursorToXY(84,57);
  printTrend();

   counter++;
  if (counter==INTERVAL) {drawPoints(dotCursor);}

}

void drawPoints(int position) {
  counter=0;
  dots[dotCursor] = int(hPa);
  GLCD.FillRect(2, 2, 123, 40, WHITE); // clear graph area
  for (int x=0; x<124; x++) {
    GLCD.SetDot(125-x,44-((dots[position]-980)), BLACK);
    position--;
    if (position<0) {position=123;}
  }
  dotCursor++;
  if (dotCursor>123) {dotCursor=0;}
  }

void getPressure() {
  pressure_msb = read_register(PRESSURE);
  pressure_msb &= B00000111;
  pressure_lsb = read_register16(PRESSURE_LSB);
  pressure_lsb &= 0x0000FFFF;
  pressure = UBLB19(pressure_msb, pressure_lsb);
  pressure /= 4;
  hPa = float(pressure)/100;
}

void printTrend() { // calculate trend since last data point and print
  int dotCursor2=dotCursor-1;
  if (dotCursor2<0) {dotCursor2=123;}
  int val1=dots[dotCursor2];
  int dotCursor3=dotCursor2-1;
  if (dotCursor3<0) {dotCursor3=123;}
  int val2=dots[dotCursor3];
  if (val1>val2) {GLCD.print("RISING ");}
  if (val1==val2) {GLCD.print("STEADY ");}
  if (val1<val2) {GLCD.print("FALLING");}
}
```

```
char spi_transfer(char data)
{
  SPDR = data;                    // Start the transmission
  while (!(SPSR & (1<<SPIF)))     // Wait for the end of the transmission
  {
  };
  return SPDR;   // return the received byte
}

char read_register(char register_name)
{
    char in_byte;
    register_name <<= 2;

    digitalWrite(SLAVESELECT,LOW); //Enable SPI Device
    spi_transfer(register_name); //Write byte to device
    in_byte = spi_transfer(0x00); //Send nothing but get back register value
    digitalWrite(SLAVESELECT,HIGH); // Disable SPI Device
    delay(10);
    return(in_byte); // return value
}

unsigned long read_register16(char register_name)
{
    byte in_byte1;
    byte in_byte2;
    float in_word;

    register_name <<= 2;

    digitalWrite(SLAVESELECT,LOW); //Enable SPI Device
    spi_transfer(register_name); //Write byte to device
    in_byte1 = spi_transfer(0x00);
    in_byte2 = spi_transfer(0x00);
    digitalWrite(SLAVESELECT,HIGH); // Disable SPI Device
    in_word = UBLB(in_byte1,in_byte2);
    return(in_word); // return value
}

void write_register(char register_name, char register_value)
{
    register_name <<= 2;
    register_name |= B00000010; //Write command

    digitalWrite(SLAVESELECT,LOW); //Select SPI device
    spi_transfer(register_name); //Send register location
    spi_transfer(register_value); //Send value to record into register
    digitalWrite(SLAVESELECT,HIGH);
}
```

When you run the code, you will see a graph of pressure over time as well as the current pressure and temperature. This isn't very exciting at first, as it needs over 24 hours to show the pressure changes. Each dot represents 15 minutes of time and the horizontal scale is hours. If you want to speed things up and fill the graph up more quickly, change the value in the INTERVAL define to something smaller.

Project 32 – Digital Barograph – Code Overview

Most of the code for Project 32 is identical to Project 31. However, there are new sections to control the GLCD, and the parts for sending data to the serial monitor have been removed. I shall therefore gloss over code that is repeated from Project 31 and concentrate on the additions.

First, you need to include the GLCD.h library in your code, as well as the fonts you are going to use:

```
#include <glcd.h>
#include "fonts/allFonts.h"
```

In the addresses section, there is a new define for `INTERVAL`. This defines the interval, in seconds, in between data points stored and displayed on the graph. The interval is 900 seconds, which is 15 minutes in between points.

```
#define INTERVAL 900  // Time interval in seconds (approx.)
```

Three new integers are declared and initialized. One is the `dots[]` array that holds the pressure measurements read at fifteen minute intervals. The next is the `dotCursor` variable that stores the index of the array you are currently on. Finally, the `counter` variable will be incremented every time the main loop is repeated and will be used to see how many seconds (roughly) have passed since the last data point was stored.

```
int dots[124], dotCursor = 0, counter = 0;;
```

In the setup routine, you first initialize the GLCD device:

```
GLCD.Init();
```

The commands to control the GLCD all come after the dot, such as the next command to clear the screen:

```
GLCD.ClearScreen();
```

Next, you choose which font you are going to use and if it is to be displayed as black or white pixels:

```
GLCD.SelectFont(System5x7, BLACK); // load the font
```

There are many different types and sizes of fonts that can be used. Also, the library includes a cool piece of free software called FontCreator2 that can be used to create a font header file to include in your sketch. This program can convert PC fonts for use with the library.

Next, the box for the graph is displayed. This is done with the `DrawRect` command:

```
GLCD.DrawRect(1,1,125,44);
```

The coordinate system for the 128×64 display is 128 pixels wide and 64 pixels high with pixel 0 for both axis being in the top left corner. The X coordinate then stretches across from 0 to 127. The Y coordinates go from 0 to 63 at the bottom. The DrawRect draws a rectangle from the X and Y coordinates that form the first two parameters. These are the upper left corner of the box. The next two parameters are the height and width extending from the X and Y co-ordinates. Your box goes from point 1,1 and stretches 125 pixels wide and 44 pixels high.

You can also create a filled rectangle with the FillRect() command, so

```
GLCD.FillRect(1,1,125,44, BLACK);
```

would create a solid black rectangle of the same dimensions. Next, you need the vertical and horizontal scale. You use a for loop to create dots at 0 pixels and 127 pixels across and at 11 pixel intervals starting at 1 pixel down:

```
  for (int x=0; x<46; x+=11) {
    GLCD.SetDot(0,1+x, BLACK);
    GLCD.SetDot(127,1+x, BLACK);
  }
```

You do this with the SetDot command that simply puts a single pixel at the X and Y co-ordinates in either BLACK or WHITE. White pixels will simply erase any black pixels already displayed.

Next, the vertical scale (hours) is drawn at 5 pixel intervals from pixel 1 across to the right hand side:

```
    for (int x=0; x<128; x+=5) {
    GLCD.SetDot(1+x,0, BLACK);
  }
```

Next, the array of pressure measurements is initialized with the value of 1023. This is because the graph will display all points stored right from the start. As you don't want to display all of the points and only those you have actually stored since the Arduino was powered up, the value of 1023 will ensure that those measurements coincide with the top line of the graph and will therefore be hidden from view. This will be explained further in the drawPoints() function.

```
for (int x; x<124; x++) {dots[x]=1023;}
```

Next, you call the getPressure() function. The code from the main loop in Project 31 has simply been placed into the getPressure() function as it is called a few times in the code. The parts from Project 31 that sent the data out to the serial monitor have all been removed as the data is now displayed on the GLCD instead.

```
getPressure();
```

You now call the drawPoints() function:

```
drawPoints(dotCursor);
```

This is a function to draw the points on the graph and will be explained shortly. You get the pressure and draw the graph prior to running the main loop so that there is already one measurement stored in the first index of the dots[] array. This is vital to ensure the printTrend() function (explained shortly also) works correctly.

In the main program loop, you find out the current pressure:

```
getPressure();
```

Then you print that pressure on the display. To print text, the cursor first needs to be moved into position. This is done by putting an X and Y coordinate into the CursorToXY(x,y) command and then printing the appropriate text. You do that twice to print the words "hPa:" and then the pressure value.

```
GLCD.CursorToXY(0, 49);
GLCD.print("hPa:");
GLCD.CursorToXY(24,49);
GLCD.print(hPa);
```

You do the same to print the temperature below the pressure:

```
GLCD.CursorToXY(0,57);
GLCD.print("Temp:");
GLCD.CursorToXY(28, 57);
GLCD.print(tempC);
```

If you wish to display Fahrenheit instead of Celsius, change tempC to tempF.

Next, you have a delay of 1000 milliseconds, meaning the pressure is obtained and displayed approximately every second:

```
delay(1000);
```

Next, you print the pressure trend. You obtain the trend value by calling the `printTrend()` function (explained shortly):

```
GLCD.CursorToXY(84,49);
GLCD.print("TREND:");
GLCD.CursorToXY(84,57);
printTrend();
```

You only want to store the current pressure value every INTERVAL seconds. So, after each 1000 millisecond delay, you increase the counter by 1

```
counter++;
```

and then check if the counter value has reached the INTERVAL value. If it does, you call the `drawPoints()` function:

```
if (counter==INTERVAL) {drawPoints(dotCursor);}
```

Next, you have added two new functions to draw the graph and print the current pressure trend. The first is the `drawPoints()` function. You pass it the dotCursor value as a parameter:

```
void drawPoints(int position) {
```

The counter value has reached the INTERVAL value, so you now reset it back to zero:

```
counter=0;
```

The current pressure reading is stored in the dots[] array at the current position. As you are only interested in a dot on a low resolution display, you don't need any numbers after the decimal point, so cast hPa to an integer. This also saves memory as an array of ints takes up less space than an array of floats.

```
dots[dotCursor] = int(hPa);
```

Now you need to clear the graph for the new data. This is done with a FillRect command, creating a white rectangle just inside the borders of the graph box:

```
  GLCD.FillRect(2, 2, 123, 40, WHITE); // clear graph area
```

You now iterate through the 124 elements of the array with a `for` loop:

```
for (int x=0; x<124; x++) {
```

Then place a dot at the appropriate position on the graph using the `SetDot()` command:

```
GLCD.SetDot(125-x,44-((dots[position]-980)), BLACK);
```

You want the graph to draw from right to left so that the most current reading is in the right hand side and the graph scrolls to the left. So you start off with drawing the first point at the X coordinate of 125-x, which will move the points to the left as the value of x increases. The Y co-ordinate is determined by taking the pressure in hPa and subtracting 980. The vertical scale of the graph is 40 pixels high and ranges from hPa value 980 to 1020.

These are typical hPa values for most locations. If you live in an area with generally higher or lower pressure, you can adjust the 980 value accordingly. You then deduct that number from 44 to give you the Y position of the dot for that particular pressure reading in the array.

The value of position, which was originally set as the current value of `dotCursor`, is then decremented

```
position--;
```

and, in case it goes below zero, is set back to 123

```
if (position<0) {position=123;}
```

Once all 124 dots have been drawn, the value of `dotCursor` is incremented, ready to store the next pressure measurement in the array

```
dotCursor++;
```

and, in case it goes above the value of 123 (the maximum element of the array), is set back to zero

```
if (dotCursor>123) {dotCursor=0;}
```

The next new function is the `printTrend()` function. The job of this function is to simply find out if the current pressure measurement stored is higher, lower, or the same as the last reading stored and to print RISING, STEADY, or FALLING accordingly.

You start by storing the last position of `dotCursor` in `dotCursor2`. You deduct one from its value as it was incremented after the measurement was stored in the `drawPoints()` function.

```
int dotCursor2=dotCursor-1;
```

You check if that value is less than zero, and if so, set it back to 123:

```
if (dotCursor2<0) {dotCursor2=123;}
```

`dotCursor2` now stores the position in the array of the last measurement taken. You now declare an integer called `val1` and store the last pressure measurement taken in it.

```
int val1=dots[dotCursor2];
```

You now want the measurement taken BEFORE the last one, so you create another variable called `dotCursor3` that will store the position in the array before the last one taken:

```
int dotCursor3=dotCursor2-1;
if (dotCursor3<0) {dotCursor3=123;}
int val2=dots[dotCursor3];
```

You now have `val1` with the last pressure reading and `val2` with the pressure reading before that one. All that is left to do is to decide if the last pressure reading taken is higher, lower, or the same as the one before that and print the relevant trend accordingly.

```
if (val1>val2) {GLCD.print("RISING ");}
if (val1==val2) {GLCD.print("STEADY ");}
if (val1<val2) {GLCD.print("FALLING");}
```

The rest of the code is the same as in Project 31. When you run this program, you will end up with a display similar to Figure 11-6. If the pressure has changed considerably over the last 24 hours, you will see a greatly varying line.

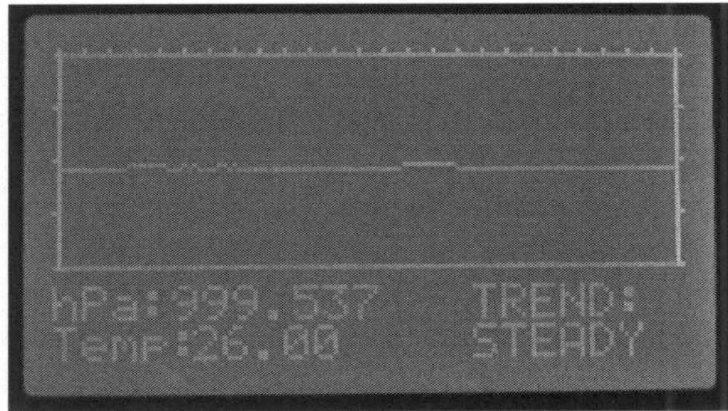

Figure 11-6. *The display for Project 32 – Digital Barograph*

The main purpose of Chapter 32 was to show you a practical use for the SCP1000 sensor and how to use a GLCD display. The commands for the GLCD introduced were just a taste for what you can do with a GLCD. You can display rectangles, circles, and lines, set dots, and even draw bitmaps. The screen can be divided up into text and graphics areas and you can access and print to them independently. The library comes with very good documentation by Michael Margolis and is very easy to use. Have a good read of the documentation and you will see there is a lot you can do with it. The library also comes with a whole set of example sketches including Conway's Game of Life and a great little rocket game.

Summary

Chapter 11 has shown you how to use a digital pressure sensor and communicate with it over a Serial Peripheral Interface. You have been introduced to the basic concepts of SPI and how it works. Now that you know roughly how SPI works, you can use the great SPI library bundled with version 0019 of the Arduino library. This will do all of the hard work for you when communicating with any other SPI devices. You have learned how to use SPI to read data from the great little SCP1000 pressure sensor. If you wish to make your own weather station, this inexpensive sensor is an ideal choice. I chose this sensor for an amateur attempt at a high altitude balloon project, as it is small, accurate, and easy to use. It also gives pressure readings well below the range specified in the datasheet, so it's therefore ideal for HAB (High Altitude Balloon) experiments.

You have also learned how to connect a graphic LCD to the Arduino and how easy it is to print text and basic graphics on it using the GLCD.h library. By reading the documentation further, you can learn how to do cool things like display bitmaps or create your own games. An Arduino with a GLCD could easily be placed into a small box to make your own handheld game console.

In the next chapter, you'll learn how to use a touch screen.

Subjects and Concepts covered in Chapter 11

- How to connect an SCP1000 pressure sensor to an Arduino
- How to use a #define to carry out bitwise operations on a set of numbers
- How to create larger bit length numbers by combining smaller bit length numbers together
- How an SPI interface works
- That SPI devices can be controlled separately or daisy chained
- That an SPI device comprises a master and a slave
- How data is clocked in and out of an SPI device with the clock pulse
- The purpose and usage of the three SPI bus registers
- Converting pressure in Pascals to Hectopascals and Atmospheres
- Using bitwise operators to check if a single bit is set or not
- How to connect a Graphic LCD to an Arduino
- Using the basic commands in the glcd.h library to draw lines, dots, and print text

CHAPTER 12

■ ■ ■

Touch Screens

You are now going to take a look at a cool gadget that you can use easily with an Arduino—a touch screen. Since the advent of smart phones and handheld game consoles, touch screens are now inexpensive and readily available. A touch screen allows you to make an easy touch interface for a device or it can be overlaid onto an LCD screen to give a touch interface. Companies such as Sparkfun make it easy to interface with these devices by providing connectors and breakout units. A breakout unit allows you to take what would normally be a tiny set of connectors or a non-standard connector and "break it out" to something more user-friendly, such as some header pins that you can use to push the unit into a breadboard. In this project, you're going to use the readily available Nintendo DS touch screen with a breakout unit from Sparkfun. You'll start off with a simple project that shows how to obtain readings from the touch screen before putting it to use.

Project 33 – Basic Touch Screen

For this project, you will need a Nintendo DS touch screen as well as a breakout module. The latter is essential as the output from the touch screen is a very thin and fragile ribbon connector, and it will be impossible to interface to the Arduino without additional components.

Parts Required

Nintendo DS touch screens are inexpensive and can be obtained from many suppliers. The XL version is about twice the size of the standard version; this is the recommended unit, if you can obtain one. The breakout module is from Sparkfun or their distributors.

Nintendo DS touch screen	
Touch screen breakout	

Connect It Up

Connect everything as shown in Figure 12-1.

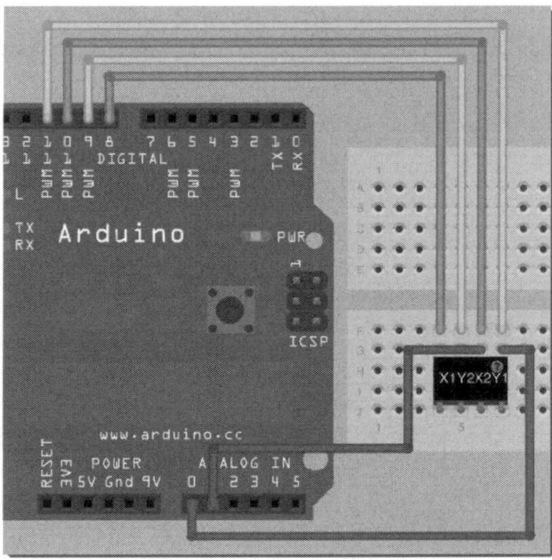

Figure 12-1. *The circuit for Project 33 – Basic Touch Screen*

The breakout unit has pins marked as X1, Y2, X2, and Y1. Connect the pins as described in Table 12-1.

Table 12-1. *Pin Connections for Project 33*

Arduino	Breakout
Digital Pin 8	X1
Digital Pin 9	Y2
Digital Pin 10	X2
Digital Pin 11	Y1
Analog Pin 0	Y1
Analog Pin 1	X2

You will need to solder some header pins to the breakout unit. The pins are soldered such that the Sparkfun logo is facing upward. The screen is connected to the breakout unit via the small connector. Pull back the tab and push the tiny ribbon cable into the connector, then push the tab closed to lock it in place. The screen goes with the ribbon connector at the top right when connecting. From now on, be very careful with the unit is it is very fragile and easily broken! I broke three screens and two breakouts in testing. If you can find a way of fixing the breadboard, breakout, and touch screen in place to prevent it from moving, you should do so.

Enter the Code

Enter the code in Listing 12-1.

Listing 12-1. *Code for Project 33*

```
// Project 33

// Power connections
#define Left 8      // Left (X1) to digital pin 8
#define Bottom 9    // Bottom (Y2) to digital pin 9
#define Right 10    // Right (X2) to digital pin 10
#define Top 11      // Top (Y1) to digital pin 11

// Analog connections
#define topInput 0   // Top (Y1) to analog pin 0
#define rightInput 1 // Right (X2) to analog pin 1

int coordX = 0, coordY = 0;

void setup()
{
        Serial.begin(38400);
}

void loop()
{
        if (touch())  // If screen touched, print co-ordinates
        {
                Serial.print(coordX);
                Serial.print("  ");
                Serial.println(coordY);
                delay(250);
        }
}
```

```
// return TRUE if touched, and set coordinates to touchX and touchY
boolean touch()
{
        boolean touch = false;

        // get horizontal co-ordinates
        pinMode(Left, OUTPUT);
        digitalWrite(Left, LOW); // Set Left to Gnd

        pinMode(Right, OUTPUT); // Set right to +5v
        digitalWrite(Right, HIGH);

        pinMode(Top, INPUT); // Top and Bottom to high impedance
        pinMode(Bottom, INPUT);

        delay(3);
        coordX = analogRead(topInput);

        // get vertical co-ordinates
        pinMode(Bottom, OUTPUT); // set Bottom to Gnd
        digitalWrite(Bottom, LOW);

        pinMode(Top, OUTPUT); // set Top to +5v
        digitalWrite(Top, HIGH);

        pinMode(Right, INPUT); // left and right to high impedance
        pinMode(Left, INPUT);

        delay(3);
        coordY = analogRead(rightInput);

        // if co-ordinates read are less than 1000 and greater than 0 then the screen↵
 has been touched
        if(coordX < 1000 && coordX > 0 && coordY < 1000 && coordY > 0) {touch = true;}

          return touch;
}
```

Enter the code and upload it to your Arduino. Once it is running, open up the serial monitor, and then touch the touch screen. Whenever the screen is touched, the coordinates of your finger will be displayed on the serial monitor. The coordinates are X across the horizontal plane going from left to right and Y across the vertical plane going from top to bottom.

Before you take a look at the code, it will help if you know how a touch screen works. I will therefore take a look at the hardware before examining the code.

Project 33 – Basic Touch Screen – Hardware Overview

The touch screen that you are using, from a Nintendo DS, is known as a *resistive touch screen.* It is a relatively simple construction made up of different layers. The bottom layer of the screen is made of glass that has been coated with a transparent film of metal oxide. This makes the coating both conductive and resistive. A voltage applied across the film has a gradient. On top of the rigid glass layer is a flexible top layer that is also covered in the transparent resistive film. These two layers are separated by a very thin gap kept apart by a grid of tiny insulating dots. These dots have the job of holding the two conductive layers apart so they don't touch.

If you examine your touch screen, you will see four connectors on the ribbon cable that lead to four metallic strips on the edges of the screen. Two of the metal strips are at the top and bottom of the screen, and if you flip the screen over, you will see the other two on the second layer and on the left and right hand sides of the screen.

When a finger or stylus is pressed against the top flexible layer, the layer bends down to touch the rigid layer, closing the circuit and creating a switch (see Figure 12-2).

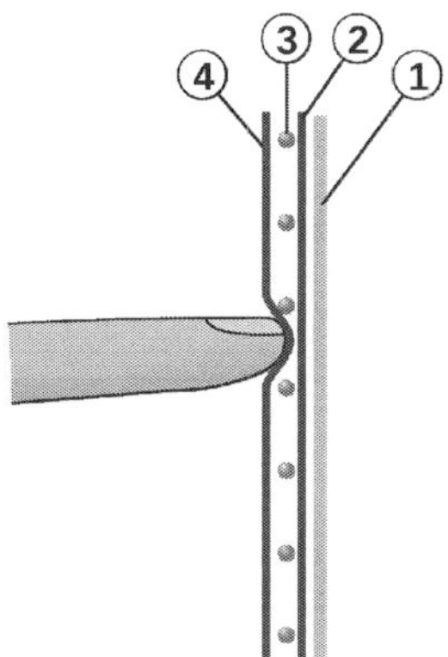

Figure 12-2. *How a touch screen works (courtesy of Mercury13 from Wikimedia Commons). 1: Rigid layer. 2: Metal oxide layer. 3: Insulating dots. 4: Flexible layer with metal oxide film.*

To find the coordinates of the touched point, a voltage is first applied across the gradient from left to right. Making one side Ground and the other 5v accomplishes this. Then, one of the strips on the opposite layer is read using an analog input to measure the voltage. The voltage when a point is pressed close to the five volts side will measure close to five volts; likewise, the voltage when pressed close to the ground side will measure close to zero.

Next, the voltage is applied across the opposing layer and read from the other. This is done in quick succession hundreds of times a second so by reading first the X and then the Y axis quickly, you can obtain a voltage for each layer. This gives you an X and Y coordinate for the point on the screen that has been touched. If you touch two points on the screen at the same time, you get a reading equal to the halfway point in-between the two touched points.

There are other technologies used in touch screens, but the resistive type is cheap to manufacture and it's very easy to interface to the Arduino without needing other circuitry to make it work. Now that you know how the screen works, let's take a look at the code to see how to measure the voltages and obtain the coordinates.

Project 33 – Basic Touch Screen – Code Overview

The code for reading a touch screen is actually very simple. You start off by defining the four digital pins you will use for applying the power across the layers and the two analog pins you will use to measure the voltages:

```
// Power connections
#define Left 8      // Left (X1) to digital pin 8
#define Bottom 9    // Bottom (Y2) to digital pin 9
#define Right 10    // Right (X2) to digital pin 10
#define Top 11      // Top (Y1) to digital pin 11

// Analog connections
#define topInput 0   // Top (Y1) to analog pin 0
#define rightInput 1 // Right (X2) to analog pin 1
```

Then you declare and initialize the X and Y integers that will hold the coordinates, which are both initially set to zero:

```
int coordX = 0, coordY = 0;
```

As you are going to read the coordinates using the serial monitor, in the setup procedure all you need to do is begin serial communication and set the baud rate. In this case, you'll use 38400 baud:

```
Serial.begin(38400);
```

The main program loop comprises nothing more than an `if` statement to determine of the screen has been touched or not:

```
if (touch())  // If screen touched, print co-ordinates
```

`touch()` is next. If the screen has been touched, you simply print out the X and Y coordinates to the serial monitor with a space in between, using the `Serial.print` commands:

```
Serial.print(coordX);
Serial.print("  ");
Serial.println(coordY);
```

After you have printed the coordinates, you wait a quarter of a second so the coordinates are readable if you keep your finger pressed down on the screen:

```
delay(250);
```

Next comes the function that does all of the hard work. The function will be returning a Boolean true or false, so it is of data type boolean. You do not pass any parameters to the function, so the parameter list is empty.

```
boolean touch()
```

You declare a variable of type boolean and initialise it to false. This will hold a true or false value depending if the screen is touched or not.

```
boolean touch = false;
```

Next, you need to put a voltage across the left-right layer and read the voltage using the top input pin on the second layer. To do this, you set the left and right pins to outputs and then make the left pin LOW so it becomes Ground and the right pin HIGH so it has five volts across it:

```
pinMode(Left, OUTPUT);
digitalWrite(Left, LOW); // Set Left to Gnd

pinMode(Right, OUTPUT); // Set right to +5v
digitalWrite(Right, HIGH);
```

The top and bottom digital pins are then set to INPUT so that they become high impedance:

```
pinMode(Top, INPUT);
pinMode(Bottom, INPUT);
```

High impedance simply means that the pins are not driven by the circuit and are therefore *floating*, i.e. they are neither HIGH nor LOW. You do not want these pins to have a voltage across them or to be at ground, hence the high impedance state is perfect as you will want to read an analog voltage using one of these pins.

Next, you wait a short delay to allow the above state changes to occur and then read the analog value from the top input pin. This value is then stored in `coordX` to give you the X coordinate.

```
delay(3);
coordX = analogRead(topInput);
```

You now have your X coordinate. So next you do exactly the same thing but this time you set the voltage across the top-bottom layer and read it using the `rightInput` pin on the opposing layer:

```
pinMode(Bottom, OUTPUT); // set Bottom to Gnd
digitalWrite(Bottom, LOW);

pinMode(Top, OUTPUT); // set Top to +5v
digitalWrite(Top, HIGH);

pinMode(Right, INPUT); // left and right to high impedance
pinMode(Left, INPUT);

delay(3);
coordY = analogRead(rightInput);
```

You set the Boolean variable `touch` to true only if the values read are greater than zero and less than one thousand. This is to ensure you only return a true value if the readings are within acceptable values.

```
if(coordX < 1000 && coordX > 0 && coordY < 1000 && coordY > 0) {touch = true;}
```

You will find the values range from approximately 100 at the lowest scale to around 900 at the top end. Finally, you return the value of `touch`, which will be false if the screen is not pressed and true if it is:

```
return touch;
```

As you can see, reading values from the touch screen is very simple and allows for all kinds of uses. You can put a picture or diagram behind the screen relating to buttons or other controls or overlay the screen onto an LCD display, as in the Nintendo DS, which will allow you to change the user interface below the screens as required.

You'll now move onto a simple demonstration of this by printing out a keypad that can be placed underneath the touch screen and reading the appropriate values to work out which key has been pressed.

Project 34 – Touch Screen Keypad

You'll now place a user interface underneath the touch screen in the form of a printed keypad and determine from the touch locations which key has been pressed. Once you understand the basics of doing this, you can go on to replace the printed keypad with one displayed on an LCD or OLED display.

You will output the key pressed on an LCD display so you'll need to add one to the parts list for this project.

Parts Required

You'll be using the exact same parts and circuit as in Project 33 with the addition of a 16×2 LCD display.

Nintendo DS touch screen

Touch screen breakout

16×2 LCD Display

The other difference is that you will create and print out a keypad to place underneath the touch screen. The standard DS touch screen is 70mm × 55mm (2.75" × 2.16") so you will need to create a template of this size using an art or word processing package and then place a set of evenly spaced keys on the rectangle so it resembles a phone keypad. Figure 12-3 shows the keypad I created. Feel free to use it.

Figure 12-3. The keypad diagram for Project 34

Connect It Up

Connect everything as shown in Figure 12-4.

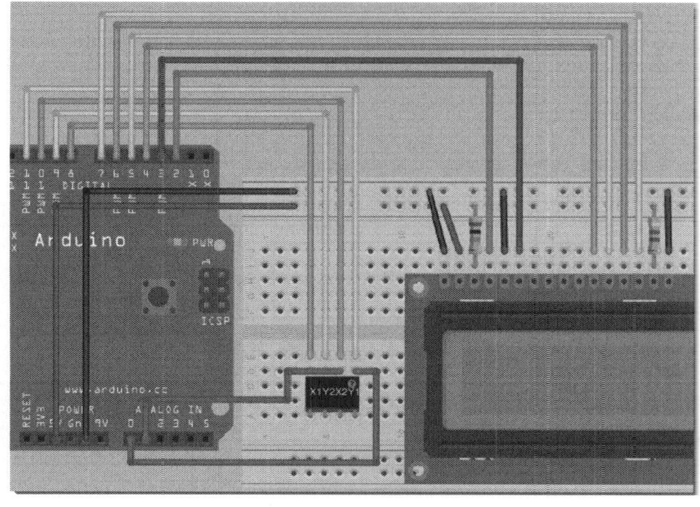

Figure 12-4. The circuit for Project 34 – Touch Screen Keypad

Refer to Table 12-2 for the pin outs for the LCD.

***Table 12-2.** Pinouts for the LCD in Project 34*

Arduino	Other	Matrix
Digital 2		Enable
Digital 3		RS (Register Select)
Digital 4		DB4 (Data Pin 4)
Digital 5		DB5 (Data Pin 5)
Digital 6		DB6 (Data Pin 6)
Digital 7		DB7 (Data Pin 7)
Gnd		Vss (GND)
Gnd		R/W (Read/Write)
+5v		Vdd
	+5v via resistor	Vo (Contrast)
	+5v via resistor	A/Vee (Power for LED)
	Gnd	Gnd for LED

Enter the Code

Enter the code in Listing 12-2.

***Listing 12-2.** Code for Project 34*

```
// Project 34

#include <LiquidCrystal.h>

LiquidCrystal lcd(2, 3, 4, 5, 6, 7); // create an lcd object and assign the pins
```

```
// Power connections
#define Left 8      // Left (X1) to digital pin 8
#define Bottom 9    // Bottom (Y2) to digital pin 9
#define Right 10    // Right (X2) to digital pin 10
#define Top 11      // Top (Y1) to digital pin 11

// Analog connections
#define topInput 0   // Top (Y1) to analog pin 0
#define rightInput 1 // Right (X2) to analog pin 1

int coordX = 0, coordY = 0;
char buffer[16];

void setup()
{
  lcd.begin(16, 2); // Set the display to 16 columns and 2 rows
  lcd.clear();
}

void loop()
{
  if (touch())
  {
    if ((coordX>110 && coordX<300) && (coordY>170 && coordY<360)) {lcd.print("3");}
    if ((coordX>110 && coordX<300) && (coordY>410 && coordY<610)) {lcd.print("2");}
    if ((coordX>110 && coordX<300) && (coordY>640 && coordY<860)) {lcd.print("1");}
    if ((coordX>330 && coordX<470) && (coordY>170 && coordY<360)) {lcd.print("6");}
    if ((coordX>330 && coordX<470) && (coordY>410 && coordY<610)) {lcd.print("5");}
    if ((coordX>330 && coordX<470) && (coordY>640 && coordY<860)) {lcd.print("4");}
    if ((coordX>490 && coordX<710) && (coordY>170 && coordY<360)) {lcd.print("9");}
    if ((coordX>490 && coordX<710) && (coordY>410 && coordY<610)) {lcd.print("8");}
    if ((coordX>490 && coordX<710) && (coordY>640 && coordY<860)) {lcd.print("7");}
    if ((coordX>760 && coordX<940) && (coordY>170 && coordY<360)) {scrollLCD();}
    if ((coordX>760 && coordX<940) && (coordY>410 && coordY<610)) {lcd.print("0");}
    if ((coordX>760 && coordX<940) && (coordY>640 && coordY<860)) {lcd.clear();}
    delay(250);
  }
}

// return TRUE if touched, and set coordinates to touchX and touchY
boolean touch()
{
  boolean touch = false;

  // get horizontal co-ordinates
  pinMode(Left, OUTPUT);
  digitalWrite(Left, LOW); // Set Left to Gnd

  pinMode(Right, OUTPUT); // Set right to +5v
  digitalWrite(Right, HIGH);
```

```
  pinMode(Top, INPUT); // Top and Bottom to high impedance
  pinMode(Bottom, INPUT);

  delay(3); // short delay
  coordX = analogRead(topInput);

  // get vertical co-ordinates
  pinMode(Bottom, OUTPUT); // set Bottom to Gnd
  digitalWrite(Bottom, LOW);

  pinMode(Top, OUTPUT); // set Top to +5v
  digitalWrite(Top, HIGH);

  pinMode(Right, INPUT); // left and right to high impedance
  pinMode(Left, INPUT);

  delay(3); // short delay
  coordY = analogRead(rightInput);

  // if co-ordinates read are less than 1000 and greater than 0 then the screen has↩
 been touched
  if(coordX < 1000 && coordX > 0 && coordY < 1000 && coordY > 0) {touch = true;}

    return touch;
}

void scrollLCD() {
  for (int scrollNum=0; scrollNum<16; scrollNum++) {
    lcd.scrollDisplayLeft();
    delay(100);
  }
  lcd.clear();
}
```

Enter the code and upload it to your Arduino. Slide the keypad template underneath the keypad with the ribbon cable at the bottom right (next to the E). You can now press the keys on the touch screen and what you press is displayed on the LCD. When you press the C (for Clear) button, the display will clear. When you press the E (for Enter) key, the numbers displayed will scroll to the left until they disappear.

You already know how the LCD screen and the touch screen work so I will skip the hardware overview in this project and just look at the code.

Project 34 –Touch Screen Keypad – Code Overview

You start off by including the LiquidCrystal library and creating an `lcd` object:

```
#include <LiquidCrystal.h>

LiquidCrystal lcd(2, 3, 4, 5, 6, 7); // create an lcd object and assign the pins
```

This time you are using Pins 2 and 3 for the RS and Enable on the LCD and Pins 4 to 7 for the data lines. Next, the pins for the touch screens are defined and the X and Y variables initialized:

```
// Power connections
#define Left 8      // Left (X1) to digital pin 8
#define Bottom 9    // Bottom (Y2) to digital pin 9
#define Right 10    // Right (X2) to digital pin 10
#define Top 11      // Top (Y1) to digital pin 11

// Analog connections
#define topInput 0   // Top (Y1) to analog pin 0
#define rightInput 1 // Right (X2) to analog pin 1

int coordX = 0, coordY = 0;
```

In the setup routine, you begin the LCD object and set it to 16 columns, 2 rows, then clear the display so you're ready to begin:

```
lcd.begin(16, 2); // Set the display to 16 columns and 2 rows
lcd.clear();
```

In the main loop, you have an `if` statement as you did in Project 33, but this time you need to check that the coordinates touched are within a rectangle that defines the boundary of each button. If the coordinate is within the relevant button boundary, the appropriate number is displayed on the LCD. If the C button is pressed, the display is cleared; if the E button is pressed, the `scrollLCD` function is called.

```
if (touch())
  {
    if ((coordX>110 && coordX<300) && (coordY>170 && coordY<360)) {lcd.print("3");}
    if ((coordX>110 && coordX<300) && (coordY>410 && coordY<610)) {lcd.print("2");}
    if ((coordX>110 && coordX<300) && (coordY>640 && coordY<860)) {lcd.print("1");}
    if ((coordX>330 && coordX<470) && (coordY>170 && coordY<360)) {lcd.print("6");}
    if ((coordX>330 && coordX<470) && (coordY>410 && coordY<610)) {lcd.print("5");}
    if ((coordX>330 && coordX<470) && (coordY>640 && coordY<860)) {lcd.print("4");}
    if ((coordX>490 && coordX<710) && (coordY>170 && coordY<360)) {lcd.print("9");}
    if ((coordX>490 && coordX<710) && (coordY>410 && coordY<610)) {lcd.print("8");}
    if ((coordX>490 && coordX<710) && (coordY>640 && coordY<860)) {lcd.print("7");}
    if ((coordX>760 && coordX<940) && (coordY>170 && coordY<360)) {scrollLCD();}
    if ((coordX>760 && coordX<940) && (coordY>410 && coordY<610)) {lcd.print("0");}
    if ((coordX>760 && coordX<940) && (coordY>640 && coordY<860)) {lcd.clear();}
    delay(250);
  }
```

Each `if` statement is a set of conditional and logical operators. If you look at the statement for button three

```
if ((coordX>110 && coordX<300) && (coordY>170 && coordY<360)) {lcd.print("3");}
```

you can see that the first logical AND condition is checking that the touched position is within position 110 and 300 from the left and the second is within position 170 and 360 from the top. All conditions must be met for the button to be pressed, hence the AND (&&) logical operators are used.

To find out your button coordinates, simply press gently using a pointed stylus on the left and right hand side of the button to get the X coordinates. Then repeat with the top and bottom sides to get the Y coordinates. If you use Project 33 to print out the coordinates to the serial monitor, you can use it to determine the exact coordinates for your button locations if you need to adjust the code or if you want to make your own button layout.

Next is the touch function; you already know how it works. Finally, there's the `scrollLCD` function that does not return any data nor takes any parameters and so is of type void:

```
void scrollLCD() {
```

Then you have a `for` loop that repeats 16 times, which is the maximum number of characters that can be entered and displayed:

```
for (int scrollNum=0; scrollNum<16; scrollNum++) {
```

Inside the `for` loop, you use the `scrollDisplayLeft()` function from the LiquidCrystal library to scroll the displayed characters one space to the left. This is followed by a 100 millisecond delay.

```
lcd.scrollDisplayLeft();
delay(100);
```

Once this has been done 16 times, the numbers entered will slide off to the left, giving the impression they have been entered into the system. You can write your own routines to do whatever you want with the data once entered.

Finally, you clear the display to ensure it is ready for new data before exiting the function back to the main loop:

```
lcd.clear();
```

This project gives you an idea how to zone off parts of a touch screen so that you can select areas for buttons, etc. The paper can be substituted with a Graphic LCD or an OLED display on which you can draw buttons. The advantage of this is that different menus and different buttons can be drawn depending on what the user has selected. Using this technique, you could create a really fancy touch screen user interface for your project.

You'll now move on to controlling an RGB LED and sliding the touch screen instead of pressing it to control the colors.

Project 35 – Touch Screen Light Controller

In this project, you will use the touch screen to turn an RGB LED lamp on and off and to control the color of the LED.

Parts Required

You will be using the exact same parts and circuit as in Project 33 with the addition of an RGB LED. The RGB LED needs to be of the common cathode type. This means that one of the pins is connected to ground (the cathode) and the other three pins go separately to the control pins for the red, green, and blue voltages.

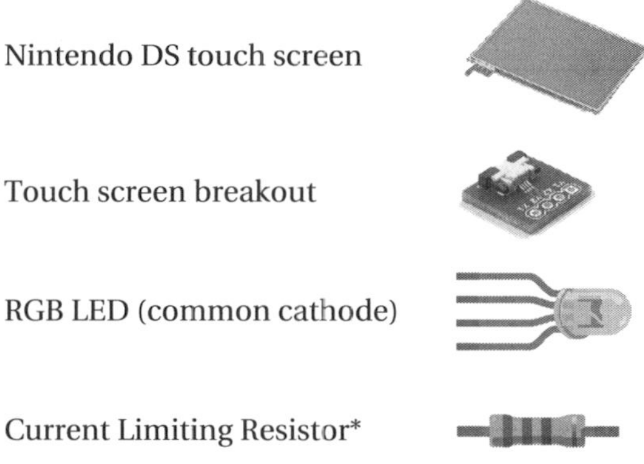

Nintendo DS touch screen

Touch screen breakout

RGB LED (common cathode)

Current Limiting Resistor*

**if needed*

You will also need a keypad template as in Project 34. This time it needs to have areas for the colour sliders and the on/off buttons. Feel free to use the image in Figure 12-5.

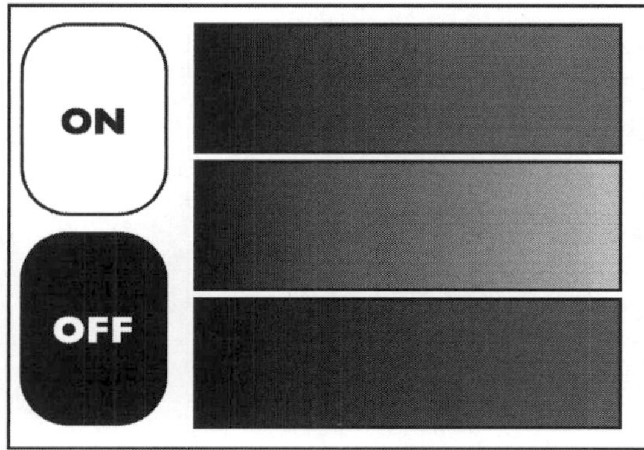

Figure 12-5. *The keypad diagram for Project 35*

Connect It Up

Connect everything up as in Figure 12-6.

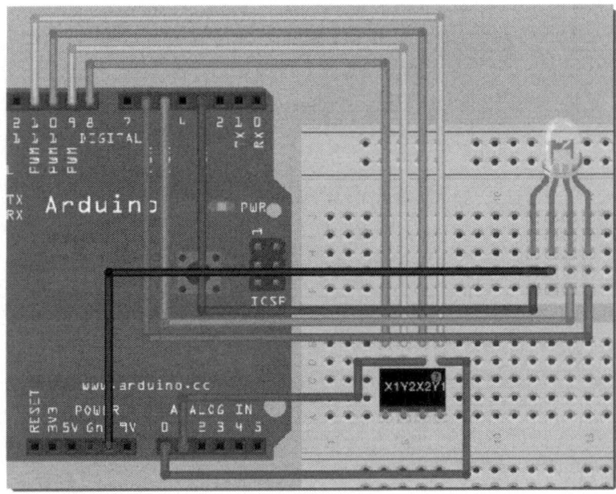

Figure 12-6. *The circuit for Project 35 – Touch Screen Light Controller*

The ground wire goes to the common cathode pin of the LED. PWM Pin 3 goes to the red anode, PWM Pin 5 to the green anode, and PWM Pin 6 to the blue anode. Place current limiting resistors on the color pins if necessary. I used a Piranha RGB LED which is rated at 5v so it did not need any resistors, in my opinion. However, this is considered bad practice. Using LEDs without current limiting resistors will reduce their life.

Enter the Code

Enter the code in Listing 12-3.

Listing 12-3. *Code for Project 35*

```
// Project 35

// Power connections
#define Left 8      // Left (X1) to digital pin 8
#define Bottom 9    // Bottom (Y2) to digital pin 9
#define Right 10    // Right (X2) to digital pin 10
#define Top 11      // Top (Y1) to digital pin 11

// Analog connections
#define topInput 0   // Top (Y1) to analog pin 0
#define rightInput 1 // Right (X2) to analog pin 1
```

```
// RGB pins
#define pinR 3
#define pinG 5
#define pinB 6

int coordX = 0, coordY = 0;
boolean ledState = true;
int red = 100, green = 100, blue = 100;

void setup()
{
  pinMode(pinR, OUTPUT);
  pinMode(pinG, OUTPUT);
  pinMode(pinB, OUTPUT);
}

void loop()
{
        if (touch()) {
                if ((coordX>0 && coordX<270) && (coordY>0 && coordY<460)) {ledState =↵
 true; delay(50);}
                if ((coordX>0 && coordX<270) && (coordY>510 && coordY< 880)) {ledState =↵
 false; delay(50);}
                if ((coordX>380 && coordX<930) && (coordY>0 && coordY<300)) {red=↵
map(coordX, 380, 930, 0, 255);}
                if ((coordX>380 && coordX<930) && (coordY>350 && coordY<590))↵
 {green=map(coordX, 380, 930, 0, 255);}
                if ((coordX>380 && coordX<930) && (coordY>640 && coordY<880))↵
 {blue=map(coordX, 380, 930, 0, 255);}
                delay(10);
}

        if (ledState) {
                analogWrite(pinR, red);
                analogWrite(pinG, green);
                analogWrite(pinB, blue);
        }
        else {
                analogWrite(pinR, 0);
                analogWrite(pinG, 0);
                analogWrite(pinB, 0);
        }
}

// return TRUE if touched, and set coordinates to touchX and touchY
boolean touch()
{
  boolean touch = false;
```

```
  // get horizontal co-ordinates
  pinMode(Left, OUTPUT);
  digitalWrite(Left, LOW); // Set Left to Gnd

  pinMode(Right, OUTPUT); // Set right to +5v
  digitalWrite(Right, HIGH);

  pinMode(Top, INPUT); // Top and Bottom to high impedance
  pinMode(Bottom, INPUT);

  delay(3); // short delay
  coordX = analogRead(topInput);

  // get vertical co-ordinates
  pinMode(Bottom, OUTPUT); // set Bottom to Gnd
  digitalWrite(Bottom, LOW);

  pinMode(Top, OUTPUT); // set Top to +5v
  digitalWrite(Top, HIGH);

  pinMode(Right, INPUT); // left and right to high impedance
  pinMode(Left, INPUT);

  delay(3); // short delay
  coordY = analogRead(rightInput);

  // if co-ordinates read are less than 1000 and greater than 0 then the screen has↩
 been touched
  if(coordX < 1000 && coordX > 0 && coordY < 1000 && coordY > 0) {touch = true;}

    return touch;
}
```

Project 35 – Touch Screen Controller – Code Overview

The initial defines are the same as in Projects 33 and 34 with the addition of a set of defines for the three PWM pins used to control the R, G, and B components of the RGB LED:

```
// RGB pins
#define pinR 3
#define pinG 5
#define pinB 6
```

You add a Boolean called `ledState` and set it to true. This Boolean will hold the state of the LEDs, i.e. true = on and false = off.

```
boolean ledState = true;
```

A set of three integers are declared and initialized with the value of 100 each:

```
int red = 100, green = 100, blue = 100;
```

These three integers will hold the separate colour values for the LED. These will equate to the PWM values output from pins 3, 5, and 6.

In the main setup routine, the three LED pins you have defined are all set to outputs:

```
pinMode(pinR, OUTPUT);
pinMode(pinG, OUTPUT);
pinMode(pinB, OUTPUT);
```

In the main loop, you have an `if` statement again to check if the value returned from `touch()` is true. Inside it are more `if` statements to decide which parts of the touch screen have been pressed. The first two define the borders of the ON and OFF buttons and change the `ledState` to true if a touch is detected within the border of the ON button and to false if it is within the borders of the OFF button. A short delay is included after this to prevent false readings from the buttons.

```
if ((coordX>0 && coordX<270) && (coordY>0 && coordY<460)) {ledState = true; delay(50);}
if ((coordX>0 && coordX<270) && (coordY>510 && coordY< 880)) {ledState = false; delay(50);}
```

Next, you check if a touch has been detected within the borders of the slider areas for the red, green, and blue controls. If a touch has been detected, then the value in the red, green, or blue integer is changed to match which part of the slider has been touched.

```
if ((coordX>380 && coordX<930) && (coordY>0 && coordY<300)) {red=map(coordX, 380, 930,↩
 0, 255);}
if ((coordX>380 && coordX<930) && (coordY>350 && coordY<590)) {green=map(coordX, 380, 930,↩
 0, 255);}
if ((coordX>380 && coordX<930) && (coordY>640 && coordY<880)) {blue=map(coordX, 380, 930,↩
 0, 255);}
```

You accomplish this using a `map()` function, which takes five parameters. The first is the variable you are checking followed by the upper and lower ranges of the variable (all others are ignored). The final two parameters are the upper and lower ranges you wish to map the values to. In other words, you take the X coordinates within the slider area and map that value to go from 0 at the far left of the slider to 255 at the far right. By sliding your finger from left to right, you can make the relevant colour component change from 0 at its dimmest, which is off, to 255 at its maximum brightness.

Finally, you have another `if` statement to set the PWM values of the R, G, and B pins to the appropriate values stored in red, green, and blue, but only if `ledState` is true. An `else` statement sets the PWM values all to 0, or off, if `ledState` is false.

```
if (ledState) {
        analogWrite(pinR, red);
        analogWrite(pinG, green);
        analogWrite(pinB, blue);
}
```

```
else {
        analogWrite(pinR, 0);
        analogWrite(pinG, 0);
        analogWrite(pinB, 0);
}
```

The remainder of the program is the `touch()` function which has already been covered.

Summary

Project 35 has introduced the concepts of buttons and slider controls controlling a touch screen. Again, using a GLCD or OLED display would give you greater control over the lighting system. Project 35 could, relatively easily, be extended to control mains powered RGB lighting around a house with the standard light switches replaced with colour OLED displays and touch screens for versatile lighting control.

Chapter 12 has shown that resistive touch screens are very easy to interface with the Arduino and use. With only a short and simple program, a touch screen and an Arduino can give provide flexibility for user control. Coupled with graphic displays, a touch screen becomes a very useful tool for controlling systems.

Subjects and Concepts covered in Chapter 12

- How to use a breakout module to make interfacing with non-standard connectors easier
- How a resistive touch screen works
- The correct power and voltage measurement cycle to obtain the X & Y co-ordinates
- The meaning of *high impedance*
- That touch screens can be overlaid onto graphic displays to create interactive buttons
- How to define a button area using coordinates and logical AND operators
- How touch screen areas can be zoned into buttons or sliders

CHAPTER 13

Temperature Sensors

The two projects in this chapter will demonstrate how to hook up analog and digital temperature sensors to an Arduino and how to get readings from them. Temperature sensors are used a lot in Arduino projects, from weather stations to brewing beer to high altitude balloon projects. You are going to take a look at two sensors, the analog LM335 sensor and the digital DS18B20.

Project 36 – Serial Temperature Sensor

This project uses the LM335 analog temperature sensor. This sensor is part of the LM135 range of sensors from National Semiconductors. It has a range from -40°C to +100°C (-40°F to +212°F) and so is ideal for using in a weather station, for example.

Parts Required

The circuit and code is designed for an LM335 sensor, but you can just as easily substitute an LM135 or LM235 if you wish. You will need to adjust your code accordingly to the relevant sensor. The 5K ohm trim pot can be substituted with a standard rotary potentiometer of a similar value. Any value trimmer or potentiometer with a value between 5K ohm and 10K ohm will do.

LM335 Temperature Sensor

5K ohm Trim Pot

2.2K ohm Resistor

A trim pot, or trimmer potentiometer, is simply a small potentiometer designed to adjust, or trim, part of a circuit and then, once calibrated, be left alone.

Connect It Up

Connect everything as shown Figure 13-1.

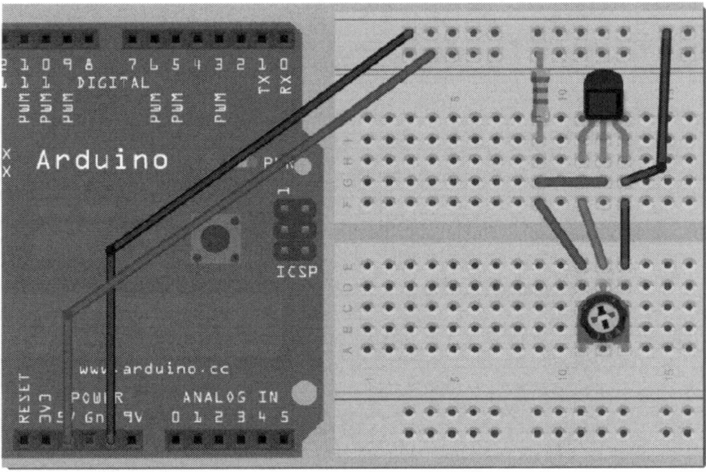

Figure 13-1. The circuit for Project 36 – Serial Temperature Sensor

If you have the flat side of the LM335 temperature sensor facing you, the left hand leg is the adjustment pin that goes to the center pin of the pot, the middle leg is the positive supply pin, and the right hand leg is the ground pin. See Figure 13-2 for the diagram from the National Semiconductors datasheet.

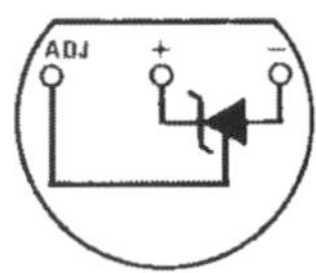

Bottom View

Figure 13-2. Pin diagram for the LM335 temperature sensor

Enter the Code

Enter the code in Listing 13-1.

Listing 13-1. Code for Project 36

```
// Project 36

#define sensorPin 0

float Celsius, Fahrenheit, Kelvin;
int sensorValue;

void setup() {
Serial.begin(9600);
Serial.println("Initialising.....");
}

void loop() {

  GetTemp();
  Serial.print("Celsius: ");
  Serial.println(Celsius);
  Serial.print("Fahrenheit: ");
  Serial.println(Fahrenheit);
  Serial.println();

  delay(2000);
}

void GetTemp()
{
  sensorValue = analogRead(sensorPin); // read the sensor
  Kelvin = (((float(sensorValue) / 1023) * 5) * 100); // convert to Kelvin
  Celsius = Kelvin - 273.15; // convert to Celsius
  Fahrenheit = (Celsius * 1.8) +32;  // convert to Fahrenheit
}
```

Enter the code and upload it to your Arduino. Once the code is running, open the serial monitor and make sure your baud rate is set to 9600. You will see the temperature displayed in both Fahrenheit and Celsius. The temperature may look incorrect to you. This is where the trimmer comes in; you must first calibrate your sensor. The easiest way to do this is with some ice. Get an ice cube and put it inside a thin plastic bag. Alternatively, you can put the sensor inside some heat shrink tubing with a small overlap at the end of the sensor; once you heat seal the sensor, it will be waterproof and can be held directly against a block of ice. So go ahead and hold the ice cube to your sensor for around 30 seconds to allow it to get down to zero degrees Celsius (or 32°F). Now turn your trimmer or pot until the reading in the serial monitor shows the correct temperature. Your sensor is now calibrated.

You can remove the trimmer part of the circuit and it will run just fine. However, the temperature will be a close approximation, within 1°C . How the sensor works is not important (and is in fact pretty complicated) so I will simply look at how the code works for this project. If you do want to learn more about how this kind of sensor works, read "The Art of Electronics" by Horowitz and Hill. This book is often referred to as "The Electronics Bible."

Project 36 – Serial Temperature Sensor – Code Overview

The code for this project is short and simple. You start off by defining the sensor pin. In this case, you are using Analog Pin 0.

```
#define sensorPin 0
```

You then need some variables to store the temperatures in Celsius, Fahrenheit, and Kelvin. As you want accuracy, you use variables of type float.

```
float Celsius, Fahrenheit, Kelvin;
```

Then you create an integer to hold the value read from the analog pin:

```
int sensorValue;
```

The setup loop begins serial communication at a baud rate of 9600:

```
Serial.begin(9600);
```

Then you display "Initialising….." to show the program is about to start:

```
Serial.println("Initialising.....");
```

In the main program loop, you call the `GetTemp()` function that reads the temperature from the sensor and converts it to Celsius and Fahrenheit. Then it prints out the temperatures in the serial monitor window.

```
GetTemp();
Serial.print("Celsius: ");
Serial.println(Celsius);
Serial.print("Fahrenheit: ");
Serial.println(Fahrenheit);
Serial.println();
```

Now you create the `GetTemp()` function:

```
void GetTemp()
```

First, the sensor is read and the value stored in `sensorValue`:

```
sensorValue = analogRead(sensorPin); // read the sensor
```

The output from the sensor is in Kelvin, with every 10mV being one K. Kelvin starts at zero degrees K when the temperature is at absolute zero, or the lowest possible temperature in the universe. So at absolute zero, the sensor will be outputting 0 volts. According to the datasheet, the sensor can be calibrated by checking that the voltage from the sensor is 2.98 volts at 25°C. To convert from Kelvin to Celsius, you simply subtract 273.15 from the Kelvin temperature to get the Celsius temperature. So 25°C in Kelvin is 298.15 and if every degree is 10mV, then you simply move the decimal point two places to the left to get the voltage at that temperature, which is indeed 2.98 volts.

So, to get the temperature in Kelvin, you read the value from the sensor, which will range from 0 to 1023, and then divide it by 1023, and multiply that result by 5. This will effectively map the range from 0 to 5 volts. As each degree K is 10mV, you then multiply that result by 100 to get degrees K.

```
Kelvin = (((float(sensorValue) / 1023) * 5) * 100); // convert to Kelvin
```

The sensor value is an integer so it is cast to a float to ensure the result is a float, too.

Now that you have your reading in K, it's easy to convert to Celsius and Fahrenheit. To convert to Celsius, subtract 273.15 from the temperature in K:

```
Celsius = Kelvin - 273.15; // convert to Celsius
```

And to convert to Fahrenheit, multiply the Celsius value by 1.8 and add 32:

```
Fahrenheit = (Celsius * 1.8) +32;  // convert to Fahrenheit
```

The LM135 range of sensors is nice in that they can be easily calibrated so you can ensure an accurate reading every time. They are also cheap so you can purchase a whole bunch of them and obtain readings from different areas of your house or the internal and external temperatures from a high altitude balloon project.

Other analog sensors can be used. You may find that the third pin on some sensors, which is the adj (adjustment) pin in the LM335, is the temperature output pin. Therefore, you should use this third pin to read the temperature instead of the supply voltage pin. Calibrating these types of sensors can be done easily in software.

You will next look at a digital temperature sensor. By far the most popular of these types is the DS18B20 from Dallas Semiconductor (Maxim).

Project 37 – 1-Wire Digital Temperature Sensor

You are now going to take a look at the DS18B20 digital temperature sensor. These sensors send the temperature as a serial data stream over a single wire, which is why the protocol is called 1-Wire. Each sensor also has a unique serial number, allowing you to query different sensors using its ID number. As a result, you can connect many sensors on the same data line. This makes them very popular to use with an Arduino because an almost unlimited amount of temperature sensors can be daisy chained together and all connected to just one pin on the Arduino. The temperature range is also wide at -55°C to +125°C.

You'll use two sensors in this project to demonstrate not only how to connect and use this type of sensor but also how to daisy chain two or more together.

Parts Required

You will need two DS18B20 sensors in the TO-92 format (this just means it has three pins and so can easily be inserted into a breadboard or soldered onto a PCB). Some are marked DS18B20+, which means they are lead free.

2 × DS18B20 Temperature Sensor

4.7K ohm Resistor

Connect It Up

Connect everything as shown in Figure 13-3.

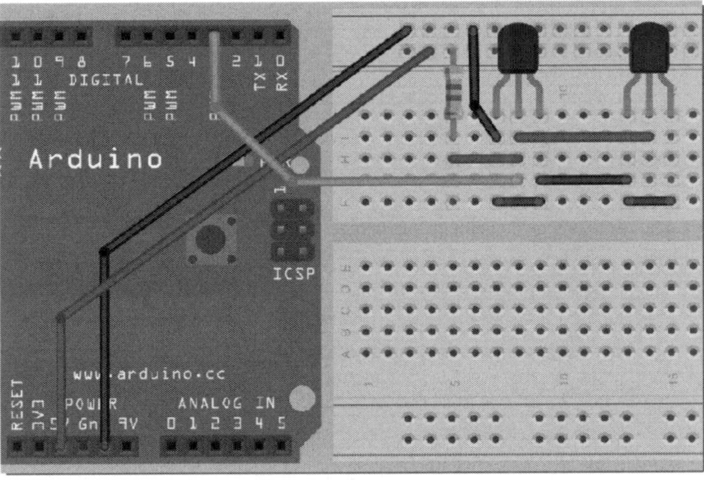

Figure 13-3. *The circuit for Project 37 – 1-Wire Digital Temperature Sensor*

I am going to do the code in two parts. The first part will find out the addresses of the two sensors. Once you know those addresses, you will move onto part 2, where the addresses will be used to obtain the temperatures directly from the sensors.

Enter the Code

Before you enter the code, you need to download and install two libraries. The first is the OneWire library. Download it from `www.pjrc.com/teensy/td_libs_OneWire.html` and unzip it. The OneWire library was first written by Jim Studt with further improvements by Robin James, Paul Stoffregen, and Tom Pollard. This library can be used to communicate with any 1-Wire device. Place it in the "libraries" folder of your Arduino installation.

Next, download and install the DallasTemperature library from `http://milesburton.com/index.php?title=Dallas_Temperature_Control_Library` and again install it in the "libraries" folder. This library is an offshoot of the OneWire library and was developed by Miles Burton with improvements by Tim Newsome and James Whiddon. This project is based on code from the examples included with this library.

Once you have installed both libraries, restart your Arduino IDE and then enter the code from the program in Listing 13-2.

Listing 13-2. *Code for Project 37 (Part 1)*

```
// Project 37 - Part 1

#include <OneWire.h>
#include <DallasTemperature.h>

// Data line goes to digital pin 3
#define ONE_WIRE_BUS 3

// Setup a oneWire instance to communicate with any OneWire devices (not just Maxim/Dallas↵
 temperature ICs)
OneWire oneWire(ONE_WIRE_BUS);

// Pass our oneWire reference to Dallas Temperature.
DallasTemperature sensors(&oneWire);

// arrays to hold device addresses
DeviceAddress insideThermometer, outsideThermometer;

void setup()
{
  // start serial port
  Serial.begin(9600);

  // Start up the library
  sensors.begin();

  // locate devices on the bus
  Serial.print("Locating devices...");
  Serial.print("Found ");
  Serial.print(sensors.getDeviceCount(), DEC);
  Serial.println(" devices.");

  if (!sensors.getAddress(insideThermometer, 0)) Serial.println("Unable to find address↵
 for Device 0");
  if (!sensors.getAddress(outsideThermometer, 1)) Serial.println("Unable to find address↵
 for Device 1");
```

```
  // print the addresses of both devices
  Serial.print("Device 0 Address: ");
  printAddress(insideThermometer);
  Serial.println();

  Serial.print("Device 1 Address: ");
  printAddress(outsideThermometer);
  Serial.println();
  Serial.println();
}

// function to print a device address
void printAddress(DeviceAddress deviceAddress)
{
  for (int i = 0; i < 8; i++)
  {
    // zero pad the address if necessary
    if (deviceAddress[i] < 16) Serial.print("0");
    Serial.print(deviceAddress[i], HEX);
  }
}

// function to print the temperature for a device
void printTemperature(DeviceAddress deviceAddress)
{
  float tempC = sensors.getTempC(deviceAddress);
  Serial.print("Temp C: ");
  Serial.print(tempC);
  Serial.print(" Temp F: ");
  Serial.print(DallasTemperature::toFahrenheit(tempC));
}

// main function to print information about a device
void printData(DeviceAddress deviceAddress)
{
  Serial.print("Device Address: ");
  printAddress(deviceAddress);
  Serial.print(" ");
  printTemperature(deviceAddress);
  Serial.println();
}

void loop()
{
  // call sensors.requestTemperatures() to issue a global temperature
  // request to all devices on the bus
  Serial.print("Requesting temperatures...");
  sensors.requestTemperatures();
  Serial.println("DONE");
```

```
  // print the device information
  printData(insideThermometer);
  printData(outsideThermometer);
  Serial.println();
  delay(1000);
}
```

Once the code has been uploaded, open up the serial monitor. You will have a display similar to this:

```
Locating devices...Found 2 devices.

Device 0 Address: 28CA90C202000088
Device 1 Address: 283B40C202000093

Requesting temperatures...DONE
Device Address: 28CA90C202000088 Temp C: 31.00 Temp F: 87.80
Device Address: 283B40C202000093 Temp C: 25.31 Temp F: 77.56
```

The program gives you the two unique ID numbers of the DS18B20 sensors you are using. You can find out which sensor is which by varying the temperature between the two. I held onto the right hand sensor for a few seconds and, as you can see, the temperature increased on that one. This tells me that the right sensor has address 28CA90C202000088 and the left one has address 283B40C202000093. The addresses of your sensors will obviously differ. Write them down or copy and paste them into your text editor.

Now that you know the ID numbers of the two devices you can move onto part 2. Enter the code from Listing 13-3.

Listing 13-3. *Code for Project 37 (Part 2)*

```
// Project 37 - Part 2

#include <OneWire.h>
#include <DallasTemperature.h>

// Data wire is plugged into pin 3 on the Arduino
#define ONE_WIRE_BUS 3
#define TEMPERATURE_PRECISION 12

// Setup a oneWire instance to communicate with any OneWire devices (not just Maxim/Dallas↵
 temperature ICs)
OneWire oneWire(ONE_WIRE_BUS);

// Pass our oneWire reference to Dallas Temperature.
DallasTemperature sensors(&oneWire);

// arrays to hold device addresses - replace with your sensors addresses
DeviceAddress insideThermometer = { 0x28, 0xCA, 0x90, 0xC2, 0x2, 0x00, 0x00, 0x88 };
DeviceAddress outsideThermometer = { 0x28, 0x3B, 0x40, 0xC2, 0x02, 0x00, 0x00, 0x93 };
```

```
void setup()
{
  // start serial port
  Serial.begin(9600);

  // Start up the library
  sensors.begin();

  Serial.println("Initialising...");
  Serial.println();

// set the resolution
  sensors.setResolution(insideThermometer, TEMPERATURE_PRECISION);
  sensors.setResolution(outsideThermometer, TEMPERATURE_PRECISION);
}

// function to print the temperature for a device
void printTemperature(DeviceAddress deviceAddress)
{
  float tempC = sensors.getTempC(deviceAddress);
  Serial.print(" Temp C: ");
  Serial.print(tempC);
  Serial.print("  Temp F: ");
  Serial.println(DallasTemperature::toFahrenheit(tempC));
}

void loop()
{
  // print the temperatures
  Serial.print("Inside Temp:");
  printTemperature(insideThermometer);
  Serial.print("Outside Temp:");
  printTemperature(outsideThermometer);
  Serial.println();
  delay(3000);
}
```

Replace the two sensor addresses with those you discovered using the code from part 1 and then upload this code. Open the serial monitor and you will get a readout like this:

```
Initialising...

Inside Temp: Temp C: 24.25  Temp F: 75.65
Outside Temp: Temp C: 19.50  Temp F: 67.10

Inside Temp: Temp C: 24.37  Temp F: 75.87
Outside Temp: Temp C: 19.44  Temp F: 66.99

Inside Temp: Temp C: 24.44  Temp F: 75.99
Outside Temp: Temp C: 19.37  Temp F: 66.87
```

If you solder the outside sensor to a long twin wire (solder Pins 1 and 3 together for one wire and Pin 2 for the second wire) and then waterproof it by sealing it in heatshrink tubing, it can be placed outside to gather external temperatures. The other sensor can obtain the internal temperature.

Project 37 – 1-Wire Digital Temperature Sensor – Code Overview

First the two libraries are included:

```
#include <OneWire.h>
#include <DallasTemperature.h>
```

Then the digital pin you will be using for reading the data from the sensors is defined

```
#define ONE_WIRE_BUS 3
```

followed by a definition for the precision required, in bits

```
#define TEMPERATURE_PRECISION 12
```

The precision can be set between 9 and 12 bits resolution. This corresponds to increments of 0.5°C, 0.25°C, 0.125°C, and 0.0625°C, respectively. The default resolution is 12 bit. The maximum resolution of 12 bit gives the smallest temperature increment, but at the expense of speed. At maximum resolution, the sensor takes 750ms to convert the temperature. At 11 bit, it is half that at 385ms, 10 bit is half again at 187.5ms, and finally 9 bit is half again at 93.75ms. 750ms is fast enough for most purposes. However, if you need to take several temperature readings a second for any reason, then 9 bit resolution would give the fastest conversion time.

Next, you create an instance of a OneWire object and call it `oneWire`:

```
OneWire oneWire(ONE_WIRE_BUS);
```

You also create an instance of a DallasTemperature object, call it `sensors`, and pass it a reference to the object called `oneWire`:

```
DallasTemperature sensors(&oneWire);
```

Next, you need to create the arrays that will hold the sensor addresses. The DallasTemperature library defines variables of type DeviceAddress (which are just byte arrays of eight elements). We create two variables of type DeviceAddress, call them `insideThermometer` and `outsideThermometer` and assign the addresses found in part 1 to the arrays.

Simply take the addresses you found in part 1, break them up into units of 2 hexadecimal digits and add 0x (to tell the compiler it is a hexadecimal number and not standard decimal), and separate each one by a comma. The address will be broken up into eight units of two digits each.

```
DeviceAddress insideThermometer = { 0x28, 0xCA, 0x90, 0xC2, 0x2, 0x00, 0x00, 0x88 };
DeviceAddress outsideThermometer = { 0x28, 0x3B, 0x40, 0xC2, 0x02, 0x00, 0x00, 0x93 };
```

In the setup loop, you begin serial communications at 9600 baud:

```
Serial.begin(9600);
```

Next, the communication with the sensors object is started using the `.begin()` command:

```
sensors.begin();
```

You print "Initialising..." to show the program has started, followed by an empty line:

```
Serial.println("Initialising...");
Serial.println();
```

Next, you set the resolution of each sensor using the .setResolution command. This command requires two parameters with the first being the device address and the second being the resolution. You have already set the resolution at the start of the program to 12 bits.

```
sensors.setResolution(insideThermometer, TEMPERATURE_PRECISION);
sensors.setResolution(outsideThermometer, TEMPERATURE_PRECISION);
```

Next, you create a function called `printTemperature()` that will print out the temperature in both degrees C and F from the sensor address set in its single parameter:

```
void printTemperature(DeviceAddress deviceAddress)
```

Next, you use the `.getTempC()` command to obtain the temperature in Celsius from the device address specified. You store the result in a float called `tempC`.

```
float tempC = sensors.getTempC(deviceAddress);
```

You then print that temperature

```
Serial.print(" Temp C: ");
Serial.print(tempC);
```

followed by the temperature in Fahrenheit

```
Serial.print("  Temp F: ");
Serial.println(DallasTemperature::toFahrenheit(tempC));
```

You use :: to access the `toFahrenheit` function that is inside the DallasTemperature library. This converts the value in `tempC` to Fahrenheit.

In the main loop, you simply call the `printTemperature()` function twice, passing the address of the inside and then the outside sensor each time followed by a three second delay:

```
Serial.print("Inside Temp:");
printTemperature(insideThermometer);
Serial.print("Outside Temp:");
printTemperature(outsideThermometer);
Serial.println();
delay(3000);
```

I recommend you try out the various examples that come with the DallasTemperature library as these will give a greater understanding of the various functions available within the library. I also recommend that you read the datasheet for the DS18B20. This sensor can also have alarms set inside it to trigger when certain temperature conditions are met that could be useful for sensing conditions that are too hot or cold.

The DS18B20 is a very versatile sensor that has a wide temperature sensing range and has the advantage over an analog sensor in that many can be daisy chained along the same data line so that only one pin is needed no matter how many sensors you have.

Next, you are going to take a look at a totally different kind of sensor that uses sound waves.

Summary

In this chapter, you have worked through two simple projects that showed you how to connect analog and digital temperature sensors to your Arduino. The projects showed you the basics of reading data from each sensor and displaying it in the serial monitor. Once you know how to do that, it's a relatively easy step to get that data displayed on an LCD or LED dot matrix display.

Knowing how to obtain temperature readings from sensors opens up a whole new range of projects to the Arduino enthusiast. You will revisit temperature sensors later in the book when they are put to practical use in Chapter 17.

Subjects and Concepts covered in Chapter 13

- How to wire up an analog temperature sensor to an Arduino
- How to use a trimmer to calibrate an LM135 series sensor
- How to convert the voltage from the sensor to Kelvin
- How to convert Kelvin to Celsius and Celsius to Fahrenheit
- How to waterproof sensors using heat shrink tubing
- How to wire up a 1-wire temperature sensor to an Arduino
- That 1-wire devices can be daisy chained
- That 1-wire devices have unique ID numbers
- How to set the resolution of a DS18B20 sensor
- That higher resolutions equal slower conversion speeds

CHAPTER 14

■ ■ ■

Ultrasonic Rangefinders

You are now going to take a look at a different kind of sensor, one that is used a lot in robotics and industrial applications. The ultrasonic rangefinder is designed to detect a distance to an object by bouncing an ultrasonic sound pulse off the object and listening for the time it takes for the pulse to return. You are going to use a popular ultrasonic range finder, the Maxbotix LV-MaxSonar range of sensors, but the concepts learned in this chapter can be applied to any other make of ultrasonic range finder. You'll learn the basics of connecting the sensor to the Arduino first, then move on to putting the sensor to use.

Project 38 – Simple Ultrasonic Rangefinder

The LV-MaxSonar ultrasonic range finder comes in EZ1, EZ2, EZ3, and EZ4 models. All have the same range, but they come in progressively narrower beam angles to allow you to match your sensor to your particular application. I used an EZ3 in the creation of this chapter, but you can choose any model.

Parts Required

LV-MaxSonar EZ3* 

100µF Electrolytic Capacitor 

100 ohm Resistor 

**or any from the LV range (image courtesy of Sparkfun)*

Connect It Up

Connect everything as shown in Figure 14-1.

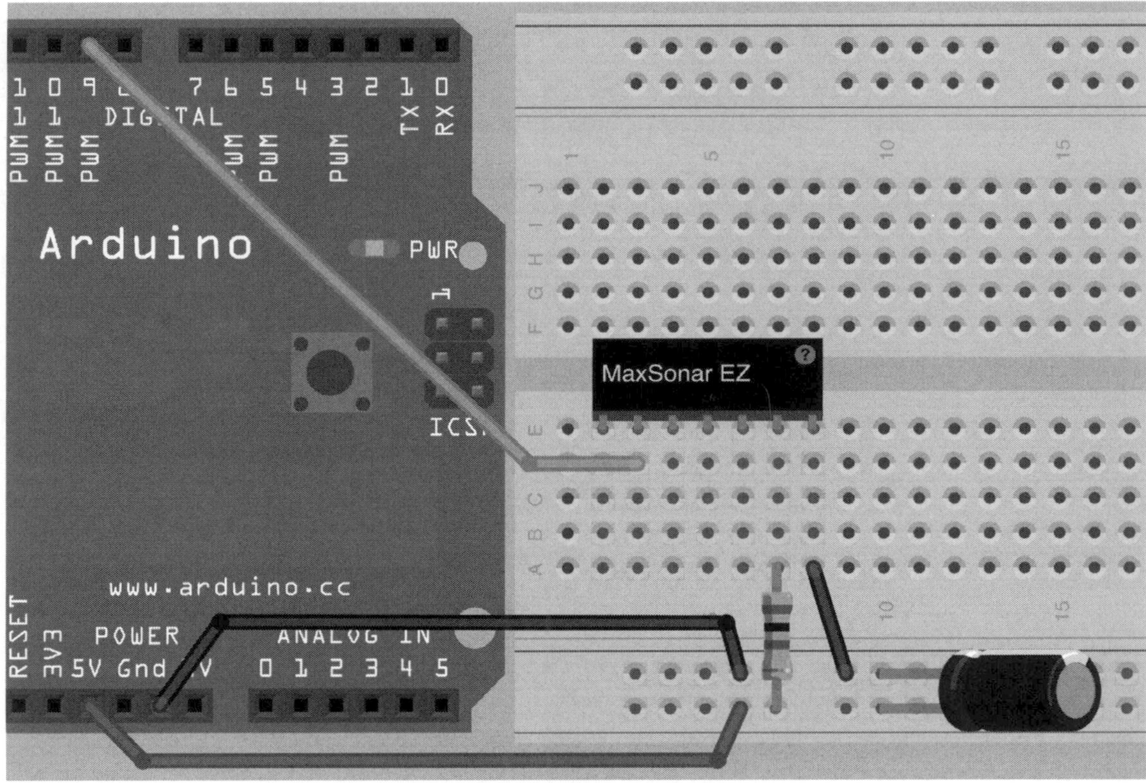

Figure 14-1. *The circuit for Project 38 – Simple Ultrasonic Rangefinder*

As Fritzing (the software used to create the breadboard diagrams in this book) does not have a LV-MaxSonar in its parts library, I have used a “mystery part” as a substitute. Connect the +5v and Ground to the two power rails on the breadboard. Place a 100µF electrolytic capacitor across the power rails, ensuring you get the longer leg connected to the +5v and the shorter leg (also with a white band and minus signs across it) to the ground rail. Then connect a jumper wire between ground and the Gnd pin on the sensor. It is essential you get the polarity correct as they can explode if connected the wrong way around! Then connect a 100 ohm resistor between the +5v rail and the +5v pin on the sensor. Finally, connect a wire between the PW pin on the sensor and Digital Pin 9.

Enter the Code

Once you have checked that your wiring is correct, enter the code in Listing 14-1 and upload it to your Arduino.

Listing 14-1. Code for Project 38

```
// Project 38

#define sensorPin 9

long pwmRange, inch, cm;

void setup() {
  // Start serial communications
  Serial.begin(115200);
  pinMode(sensorPin, INPUT);
}

void loop() {
pwmRange = pulseIn(sensorPin, HIGH);

  // 147uS per inch according to datasheet
  inch = pwmRange / 147;
  // convert inch to cm
  cm = inch * 2.54;

  Serial.print(inch);
  Serial.print(" inches    ");
  Serial.print(cm);
  Serial.println(" cm");
}
```

Once you have uploaded the code, power the Arduino down for a second. Then make sure that your ultrasonic sensor is still and pointing at something that is not moving. Putting it flat on a table and pointing it at your ceiling will work best. Make sure that nothing is near the sensor when you power the Arduino back up. When the device is first powered up, it runs through a calibration routine for the first read cycle. Make sure nothing is moving around in its beam while this takes place, otherwise you will get inaccurate readings. This information is then used to determine the range to objects in the line of sight of the sensor. Measure the distance between the sensor and the ceiling, and this distance (roughly) will be output from the serial monitor when you open it up. If the distance is inaccurate, power the Arduino down and back up, allowing the device to calibrate without obstacles. By moving the sensor around or by raising and lowering your hand over the sensor, the distance to the object placed in its path will be displayed on the serial monitor.

Project 38 – Simple Ultrasonic Range Finder – Code Overview

Again, you have a short and simple piece of code to use this sensor. First, you start of by defining the pin you will use to detect the pulse. You are using Digital Pin 9:

```
#define sensorPin 9
```

Then three variables of type long are declared:

```
long pwmRange, inch, cm;
```

These will be used to store the range read back from the sensor, the range converted into inches, and then into centimeters, respectively.

In the setup routine, you simply begin serial communications at 115200 baud and set the sensor pin to an input:

```
Serial.begin(115200);
pinMode(sensorPin, INPUT);
```

In the main loop, you start by reading the pulse from the sensor pin and storing it in pwmRange:

```
pwmRange = pulseIn(sensorPin, HIGH);
```

To accomplish this, you use the new command, `pulseIn`. This new command is tailor made for this use as it is designed to measure the length of a pulse, in microseconds, on a pin. The PW pin of the sensor sends a HIGH signal when the ultrasonic pulse is sent from the device, and then a LOW signal once that pulse is received back. The time in-between the pin going high and low will give you the distance, after conversion. The `pulseIn` command requires two parameters. The first is the pin you want to listen to and the second is either a HIGH or a LOW to define at what state the `pulseIn` command will commence timing the pulse. In your case, you have this set to HIGH, so as soon as the sensor pin goes HIGH, the `pulseIn` command will start timing; once it goes LOW, it will stop timing and then return the time in microseconds.

According to the datasheet for the LV-MaxSonar range of sensors, the device will detect distances from 0 inches to 254 inches (6.45 meters) with distances below 6 inches being output as 6 inches. Each 147µS (micro-seconds) equates to one inch. So, to convert the value returned from the `pulseIn` command to inches, you simply need to divide it by 147. This value is then stored in `inch`.

```
inch = pwmRange / 147;
```

Next, that value is multiplied by 2.54 to give you the distance in centimeters:

```
cm = inch * 2.54;
```

Finally, the values in inches and centimeters are printed to the serial monitor:

```
Serial.print(inch);
Serial.print(" inches    ");
Serial.print(cm);
Serial.println(" cm");
```

Project 38 – Simple Ultrasonic Range Finder – Hardware Overview

The new component introduced in this project is the ultrasonic range finder. This device uses ultrasound, which is a very high frequency sound above the upper limit of human hearing. In the case of the MaxSonar, it sends a pulse at 42KHz. The average human has an upper hearing limit of around 20KHz, so the sensor is way above the range of human hearing. A pulse of ultrasonic sound is sent out by the device from a transducer and is then picked up again, by the same transducer, when it reflects off an object. By calculating the time it takes for the pulse to return, you can work out the distance to the reflected object (See Figure 14-2). Sound waves travel at the speed of sound which, in dry air at 20 °C (68 °F) is 343 meters per second, or 1125 feet per second. Knowing this, you can work out the speed, in microseconds, that the sound wave takes to return to the sensor. As it happens, the datasheet tells you that every inch takes 147µS for the pulse to return. So taking the time in microseconds and dividing it by 147 gives us the distance in inches, and then you can convert that to centimeters if necessary.

This principle is also called SONAR (sound navigation and ranging) and is used in submarines to detect distances to other marine craft or nearby hazards. It is also used by bats to detect their prey.

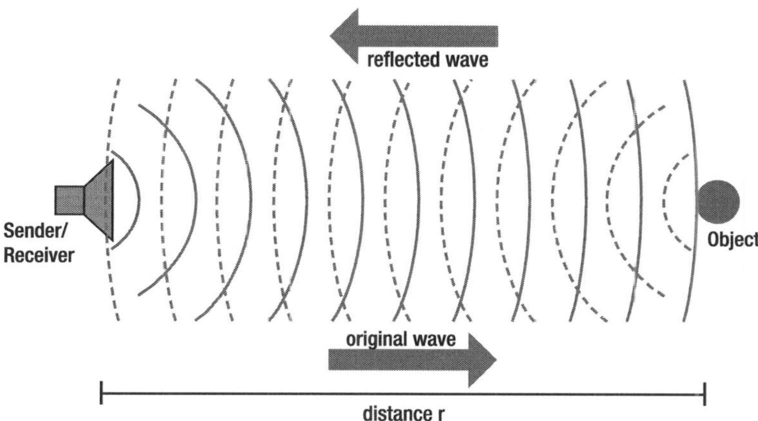

Figure 14-2. The principle of sonar or radar distance measurement (Image by Georg Wiora)

The MaxSonar devices have three ways to read the data from the sensor. One is an analog input, the second is a PWM input, and the final one is a serial interface. The PWM input is probably the easiest to use with the most reliable data, hence this is what I have used here. Feel free to research and use the other two pins if you wish, although there will be no real benefit from doing so unless you specifically need to have an analog or serial data stream.

Now you know how the sensor works, let's put it to a practical use and make an ultrasonic tape measure or distance display.

Project 39 – Ultrasonic Distance Display

Now you're going to use the ultrasonic sensor to create a (fairly) accurate distance display. You are going to use the MAX7219 LED driver IC used back in Chapter 7 to display the distance measured. Instead of a dot matrix display, however, you're going to use what the MAX7219 was designed for, a set of 7-segment LED displays.

Parts Required

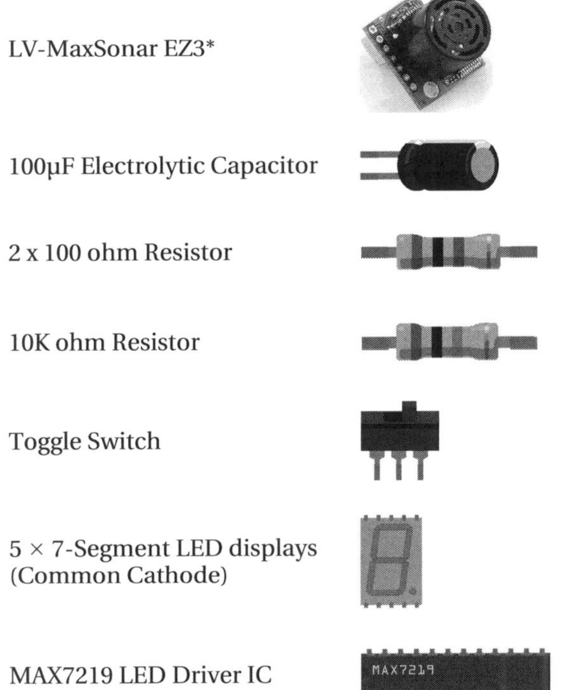

LV-MaxSonar EZ3*

100µF Electrolytic Capacitor

2 x 100 ohm Resistor

10K ohm Resistor

Toggle Switch

5 × 7-Segment LED displays (Common Cathode)

MAX7219 LED Driver IC

**or any from the LV range (image courtesy of Sparkfun)*

The toggle switch must be the single pole, double throw type (SPDT). These switches have a sliding switch that stays in one of two positions. You will use one of those positions to switch the display between inches and centimeters. The 7-segment LED displays must be the common cathode type. Make sure to get the datasheet for the type you purchase so that you can ascertain how to connect it, as it may differ from mine.

Connect It Up

Connect everything as shown in Figure 14-3.

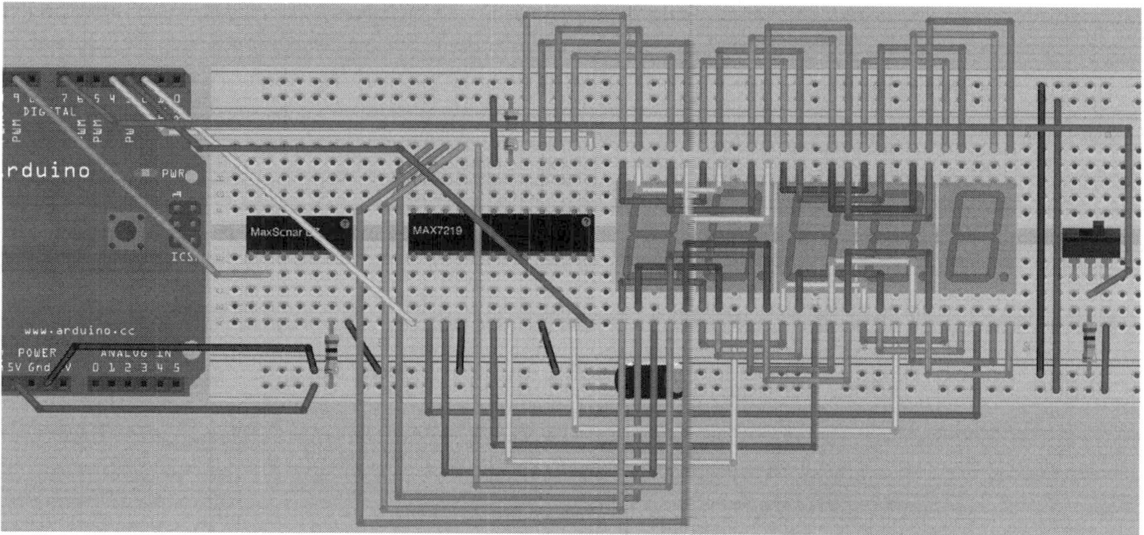

Figure 14-3. *The circuit for Project 39 – Ultrasonic Distance Display*

This circuit is pretty complex so I below I have also provided a table of pins (Table 14-1) for the Arduino, Max7219, and 7-Segment display so you can match them to the diagram. The displays I used had the code 5101AB, but any common cathode 7-segment display will work. Make sure the pins are across the top and bottom of the display and not along the sides, otherwise you will not be able to insert them into a breadboard.

Table 14-1. Pin Outs Required for Project 39

Arduino	MaxSonar	MAX7219	7-Segment	Other
Digital Pin 2		Pin 1 (DIN)		
Digital Pin 3		Pin 12 (LOAD)		
Digital Pin 4		Pin 13 (CLK)		
Digital Pin 7				Switch
Digital Pin 9	PW	Pin 4 (Gnd)		Gnd
		Pin 9 (Gnd)		Gnd
		Pin 18 (ISET)		Gnd via 10KΩ Resistor
		Pin 19 (VDD)		+5 volts
		Pin 2 (DIG 0)	Gnd on Display 0	
		Pin 11 (DIG 1)	Gnd on Display 1	
		Pin 6 (DIG 2)	Gnd on Display 2	
		Pin 7 (DIG 3)	Gnd on Display 3	
		Pin 3 (DIG 4)	Gnd on Display 4	
		Pin 14	SEG A	
		Pin 16	SEG B	
		Pin 20	SEG C	
		Pin 23	SEG D	
		Pin 21	SEG E	
		Pin 15	SEG F	
		Pin 17	SEG G	
		Pin 22	SEG DP	

Once you have connected the MAX7219 to the SEG A-G and DP pins of the first 7-segment display, i.e. the one nearest the chip (see Figure 14-4), connect the SEG pins on the first display to the second, and then the second to the third, and so on. All of the SEG pins are tied together on each display with the ground pins being separate and going to the relevant DIG pins on the MAX7219. Make sure you read the datasheet for your 7-segment display as its pins may differ from mine.

The MaxSonar is connected the same as before, except for the PW pin going to Digital Pin 9 instead of 3. Finally, Digital Pin 7 goes to the toggle switch.

Note that you may need to use an external power supply for this project if you find it is erratic—it may draw too much power from the USB port.

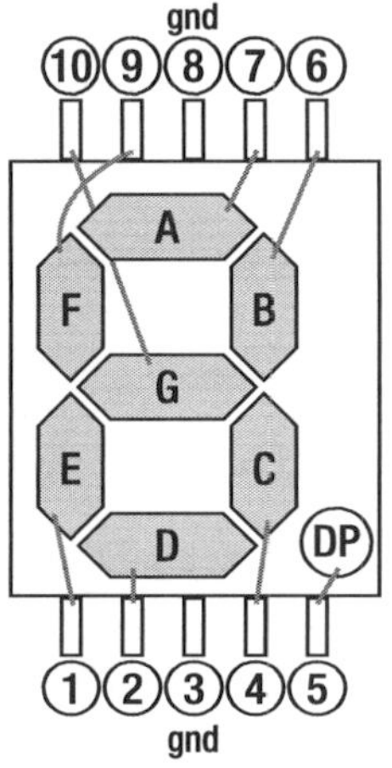

Figure 14-4. *A typical common cathode 7-segment LED display with pin assignments (image courtesy of Jan-Piet Mens)*

Enter the Code

Once you have checked that your wiring is correct, power up the Arduino and enter the code in Listing 14-2, then upload it to your Arduino. Make sure you have LedControl.h in your libraries folder (see Chapter 7 for instructions).

Listing 14-2. *Code for Project 39*

```
// Project 39

#include "LedControl.h"

#define sensorPin 9
#define switchPin 7
#define DataIn 2
#define CLK 4
#define LOAD 3
```

```
#define NumChips 1
#define samples 5.0

float pwmRange, averageReading, inch, cm;
LedControl lc=LedControl(DataIn,CLK,LOAD,NumChips);

void setup() {
        // Wakeup the MAX7219
        lc.shutdown(0,false);
        // Set it to medium brightness
        lc.setIntensity(0,8);
        // clear the display
        lc.clearDisplay(0);
        pinMode(sensorPin, INPUT);
        pinMode(switchPin, INPUT);
}

void loop() {
        averageReading = 0;
        for (int i = 0; i<samples; i++) {
                pwmRange = pulseIn(sensorPin, HIGH);
                averageReading += pwmRange;
        }

        averageReading /= samples;
        // 147uS per inch according to datasheet
        inch = averageReading / 147;
        // convert inch to cm
        cm = inch * 2.54;

        if (digitalRead(switchPin)) {
                displayDigit(inch);
        }
        else {
                displayDigit(cm);
        }
}

void displayDigit(float value) {
        int number = value*100;
        lc.setDigit(0,4,number/10000,false); // 100s digit
        lc.setDigit(0,3,(number%10000)/1000,false); // 10s digit
        lc.setDigit(0,2,(number%1000)/100,true); // first digit with DP on
        lc.setDigit(0,1,(number%100)/10,false); // 10th digit
        lc.setDigit(0,0,number%10,false); // 100th digit
}
```

Project 39 – Ultrasonic Distance Display – Code Overview

The project starts by including the LedControl.h library:

```
#include "LedControl.h"
```

You then define the pins you will require for the sensor and the MAX7219 chip:

```
#define sensorPin 9
#define switchPin 7
#define DataIn 2
#define CLK 4
#define LOAD 3
#define NumChips 1
```

The sensor readings are smoothed out using a simple running average algorithm, so you need to define how many samples you take to do that:

```
#define samples 5.0
```

You will be using this number with floats later, so to avoid errors, the number is defined as 5.0 rather than a 5 to make sure it is forced as a float and not an int.

Next, the floats for the sensor are declared as in Project 38, but with the addition of **averageReading**, which you will use later on in the program:

```
float pwmRange, averageReading, inch, cm;
```

You create an **LedControl** object and set the pins used and the number of chips:

```
LedControl lc=LedControl(DataIn,CLK,LOAD,NumChips);
```

As in Project 21, you ensure the display is enabled, the intensity is set to medium, and the display is cleared and ready for use:

```
lc.shutdown(0,false);
lc.setIntensity(0,8);
lc.clearDisplay(0);
```

The pins for the sensor and the switch are both set to INPUT:

```
pinMode(sensorPin, INPUT);
pinMode(switchPin, INPUT);
```

Then you reach the main loop. First the variable **averageReading** is set to zero:

```
averageReading = 0;
```

Next, a **for** loop runs to collect the samples from the sensor. The sensor value is read into **pwmRange** as before, but it is then added to **averageReading** each time the loop runs. The **for** loop will reiterate the number of times defined in samples at the start of the program

```
for (int i = 0; i<samples; i++) {
        pwmRange = pulseIn(sensorPin, HIGH);
        averageReading += pwmRange;
}
```

Then you take the value in averageReading and divide it by the number in samples. In your case, the sample number is set to 5, so five samples are taken, added to averageReading, which is initially zero, and then divide by five to give you an average reading. This ensures you have a more accurate reading and averages out any noise in the readings or other changes in the timings that may be due to temperature or air pressure changes.

```
averageReading /= samples;
```

As before, the timing of the pulse is converted into inches and centimeters:

```
inch = averageReading / 147;
cm = inch * 2.54;
```

Next, you use an if statement to check if the toggle switch is HIGH or LOW. If it is HIGH, then the displayDigit() function (explained shortly) is run and the value in inches is passed to it. If the switch is LOW, the else statement runs the function but using centimeters instead.

```
if (digitalRead(switchPin)) {
        displayDigit(inch);
}
else {
        displayDigit(cm);
}
```

This if-else statement ensures that either inches or centimeters are displayed depending on the position of the toggle switch.

Finally, you define the displayDigit() function. This function simply prints the number passed to it on the 7-segment LED display. A floating point number must be passed to the function as a parameter. This will be either inches or centimeters.

```
void displayDigit(float value) {
```

The number passed to this function is a floating point number and will have digits after the decimal point. You are only interested in the first two digits after the decimal point, so it is multiplied by 100 to shift those two digits two places to the left:

```
int number = value*100;
```

This is because you will be using the modulo % operator, which requires integer numbers, and so must convert the floating point number to an integer. Multiplying it by 100 ensures that the two digits after the decimal point are preserved and anything else is lost. You now have the original number but without the decimal point. This does not matter as you know there are two digits after the decimal point.

Next, you need to take that number and display it one digit at a time on the 7-segment displays. Each digit is displayed using the setDigit command, which requires four parameters. These are

```
setDigit(int addr, int digit, byte value, boolean dp);
```

with addr being the address of the MAX7219 chip. You have just one chip so this value is zero. If a second chip was added, its address would be 1, and so on. Digit is the index of the 7-segment display being controlled. In your case the right hand display is digit 0, the one to its left is 1, and so on. Value is the actual digit, from 0 to 9, that you wish to display on the 7-segment LED. Finally, a Boolean value of false or true decides if the decimal point on that display is on or off.

So, using the setDigit command, you take the value stored in the integer called number and do division and modulo operations on it to get each digit separately and then display them on the LED:

```
lc.setDigit(0,4,number/10000,false); // 100s digit
lc.setDigit(0,3,(number%10000)/1000,false); // 10s digit
lc.setDigit(0,2,(number%1000)/100,true); // first digit with DP on
lc.setDigit(0,1,(number%100)/10,false); // 10th digit
lc.setDigit(0,0,number%10,false); // 100th digit
```

Digit 2 has its decimal point turned on as you want two digits after the decimal point, so the DP flag is true.

You can see how the above works with the following example. Let's say the number to be displayed was 543.21. Remember that the number is multiplied by 100, so you then have 54321. For Digit 0, you take the number and do a modulo 10 operation on it. This leaves you with the first digit (the rightmost) which is 1.

543.21 * 100 = 54321
54321 % 10 = 1

Remember that the modulo % operator divides an integer by the number after it, but only leaves you with the remainder. 54321 divided by 10 would be 5432.1 and the remainder is 1. This gives you the first digit (rightmost) to be displayed.

The second digit (the 10s column) is modulo 100 and then divided by 10 to give you the second digit.

54321 % 100 = 21
21 / 10 = 2 (remember this is integer arithmetic and so anything after the decimal point is lost)

and so on.......

If you follow the calculations using 543.21 as your original number, you will see that the set of modulo and division operations leave you with each individual digit of the original number. The addition of the decimal point on digit 2 (third from right) makes sure the number is displayed with two digits after the decimal point.

You end up with an ultrasonic tape measure that is pretty accurate and to 100th of an inch or centimeter. Be aware that the results may not be exactly spot on as the sound waves will move faster or slower due to different temperatures or air pressures. Also, sound waves are reflected off different surfaces differently. A perfectly flat surface perpendicular to the plane of the sensor will reflect the sound well and will give the most accurate reading. A surface with bumps on it or one that absorbs sound or one that is at an angle will give an inaccurate reading. Experiment with different surfaces and compare the readings with a real tape measure.

Let's use the ultrasonic sensor for something different now.

Project 40 – Ultrasonic Alarm

You will now build upon the circuit from the last project and turn it into an alarm system.

Parts Required

LV-MaxSonar EZ3*

100μF Electrolytic Capacitor

2 × 100 ohm Resistor

2 × 10K ohm Resistor

Toggle Switch

5 × 7-Segment LED displays (Common Cathode)

MAX7219 LED Driver IC

5-10K ohm Potentiometer

Piezo Sounder or 8 ohm Speaker

**or any from the LV range (image courtesy of Sparkfun)*

Connect It Up

Connect everything as shown in Figure 14-5.

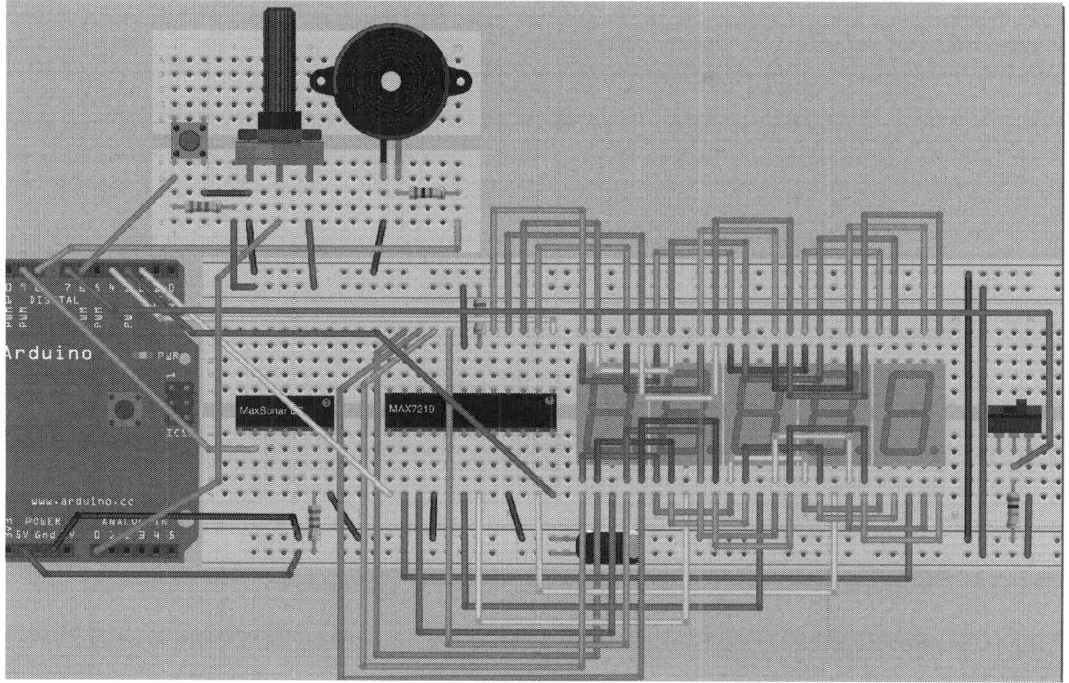

Figure 14-5. The circuit for Project 40 – Ultrasonic Alarm

The circuit is the same as for Project 39 but with the addition of a pushbutton, a potentiometer, and a piezo sounder (or speaker). The button has both terminals connected to +5v and Ground, with the +5v pin connected to +5v via a 10K ohm resistor. A wire goes from this same pin to Digital Pin 6. The potentiometer has +5v and Ground connected to its outer pins and the center pin goes to Analog Pin 0. The speaker has its negative terminal connected to ground and the positive terminal, via a 100 ohm resistor, to Digital Pin 8. The potentiometer will be used to adjust the alarm sensor range and the button will reset the system after an alarm activation. The piezo will obviously sound the alarm.

Enter the Code

After checking your wiring is correct, power up the Arduino and upload the code from Listing 14-3.

Listing 14-3. Code for Project 40

```
// Project 40

#include "LedControl.h"

#define sensorPin 9
#define switchPin 7
```

```
#define buttonPin 6
#define potPin 0
#define DataIn 2
#define CLK 4
#define LOAD 3
#define NumChips 1
#define samples 5.0

float pwmRange, averageReading, inch, cm, alarmRange;
LedControl lc=LedControl(DataIn,CLK,LOAD,NumChips);

void setup() {

 // Wakeup the MAX7219
  lc.shutdown(0,false);
  // Set it to medium brightness
  lc.setIntensity(0,8);
  // clear the display
  lc.clearDisplay(0);
  pinMode(sensorPin, INPUT);
  pinMode(switchPin, INPUT);
}


void loop() {
  readPot();
  averageReading = 0;
  for (int i = 0; i<samples; i++) {
   pwmRange = pulseIn(sensorPin, HIGH);
  averageReading += pwmRange;
  }

  averageReading /= samples;
  // 147uS per inch according to datasheet
  inch = averageReading / 147;
  // convert inch to cm
  cm = inch * 2.54;

  if (digitalRead(switchPin)) {
  displayDigit(inch);
  }
  else {
    displayDigit(cm);
  }

        // if current range smaller than alarmRange, set off alarm
        if (inch<=alarmRange) {startAlarm();}
}
```

```
void displayDigit(float value) {
    int number = value*100;
    lc.setDigit(0,4,number/10000,false); // 100s digit
    lc.setDigit(0,3,(number%10000)/1000,false); // 10s digit
    lc.setDigit(0,2,(number%1000)/100,true); // first digit
    lc.setDigit(0,1,(number%100)/10,false); // 10th digit
    lc.setDigit(0,0,number%10,false); // 100th digit
}

// read the potentiometer
float readPot()  {
  float potValue = analogRead(potPin);
  alarmRange = 254 * (potValue/1024);
  return alarmRange;
}

// set off the alarm sound till reset pressed
void startAlarm() {
  while(1) {
    for (int freq=800; freq<2500;freq++) {
      tone(8, freq);
      if (digitalRead(buttonPin)) {
        noTone(8);
        return;
      }
    }
  }
}
```

Once the code is entered, upload it to your Arduino, and then power down the device. Power back up, making sure the sensor is able to calibrate properly. Now you can turn the potentiometer to adjust the range of the alarm. Put a hand into the beam and steadily move closer until the alarm goes off. The reading once the alarm is activated will remain still and show you the last distance measured. This is your alarm range. Press the reset button to silence the alarm, reset the system, and then keep adjusting the potentiometer until you get a range you are happy with. Your alarm is now ready to protect whatever it is near. Anything that comes within the range of the sensor that you have set will activate the alarm until reset.

Project 40 – Ultrasonic Alarm – Code Overview

Most of the code is the same as explained in Project 39, so I will skip over explaining those sections. The LedControl library is loaded in:

```
#include "LedControl.h"
```

Then the pins used are defined as well as the number of chips and samples as before:

```
#define sensorPin 9
#define switchPin 7
#define buttonPin 6
#define potPin 0
#define DataIn 2
#define CLK 4
#define LOAD 3
#define NumChips 1
#define samples 5.0
```

You add a definition for the `buttonPin` and `potPin`. The variables are declared including the new variable called `alarmRange` that will hold the distance threshold after which the alarm will sound if a person moves closer than the range set:

```
float pwmRange, averageReading, inch, cm, alarmRange;
```

You create an `LedControl` object called `lc` and define the pins:

```
LedControl lc=LedControl(DataIn,CLK,LOAD,NumChips);
```

The `setup()` loop is the same as before with the addition of setting the `pinMode` of the `buttonPin` to `INPUT`:

```
lc.shutdown(0,false);
lc.setIntensity(0,8);
lc.clearDisplay(0);
pinMode(sensorPin, INPUT);
pinMode(switchPin, INPUT);
pinMode(buttonPin, INPUT);
```

The main loop starts with calling a new function called `readPot()`. This function reads the value from the potentiometer that you will use to adjust the alarm range (discussed later):

```
readPot();
```

The rest of the main loop is the same as in project 39

```
averageReading = 0;
for (int i = 0; i<samples; i++) {
        pwmRange = pulseIn(sensorPin, HIGH);
        averageReading += pwmRange;
 }

averageReading /= samples;
inch = averageReading / 147;
cm = inch * 2.54;
```

```
if (digitalRead(switchPin)) {
        displayDigit(inch);
}
else {
        displayDigit(cm);
}
```

until you reach the next `if` statement

```
if (inch<=alarmRange) {startAlarm();}
```

which simply checks if the current measurement from the sensor is smaller or equal to the value in **alarmRange** that has been set by the user and if so, calls the **startAlarm()** function.

The **displayDigit()** function is the same as in Project 39:

```
void displayDigit(float value) {
    int number = value*100;
    lc.setDigit(0,4,number/10000,false); // 100s digit
    lc.setDigit(0,3,(number%10000)/1000,false); // 10s digit
    lc.setDigit(0,2,(number%1000)/100,true); // first digit
    lc.setDigit(0,1,(number%100)/10,false); // 10th digit
    lc.setDigit(0,0,number%10,false); // 100th digit
}
```

Next is the first of the two new functions. This one is designed to read the potentiometer and convert its value into inches to set the range of the alarm. The function has no parameters but is of type float as it will be returning a float value in alarmRange.

```
float readPot()
```

Next, you read the analog value from the potPin and store it in **potValue**:

```
float potValue = analogRead(potPin);
```

You then carry out a calculation on this value to convert the values from 0 to 1023 that is read in from the potentiometer and converts it to the maximum and minimum range of the sensor, i.e. 0 to 254 inches.

```
alarmRange = 254 * (potValue/1024);
```

Then you return that value to the point where the function was called:

```
return alarmRange;
```

The next function is responsible for setting off the alarm sound. This is the **startAlarm()** function:

```
void startAlarm() {
```

Next you have a while loop. You came across the while loop in Chapter 3. The loop will run while the statement in the brackets is true. The parameter for the while loop is 1. This simply means that while the value being checked is true, the loop will run. In this case, the value being checked is a constant value of 1, so the loop always runs forever. You will use a return command to exit the loop.

```
while(1) {
```

Now you have a for loop that will sweep up through the frequencies from 800 to 2500Hz:

```
for (int freq=800; freq<2500;freq++) {
```

You play a tone on pin 8, where the piezo sounder is, and play the frequency stored in freq:

```
tone(8, freq);
```

Now you check the buttonPin using digitalRead to see if the button has been pressed or not:

```
if (digitalRead(buttonPin)) {
```

If the button has been pressed, the code inside the brackets is run. This starts with a noTone() command to cease the alarm sound and then a return to exit out of the function and back to the main loop of the program:

```
noTone(8);
return;
```

In the next project, you will keep the same circuit, but upload some slightly different code to use the sensor for a different purpose.

Project 41 – Ultrasonic Theremin

For this project, you are going to use the same circuit. Although you won't be using the potentiometer, switch, or reset button in this project I am leaving them in to give you the flexibility to modify the project if you wish—plus it means you can jump back to using Project 40 if you wish later.

This time you are going to use the sensor to create a Theremin that uses the sensor ranging instead of the electrical field that a real Theremin uses. If you don't know what a Theremin is, look it up on Wikipedia. It is basically an electronic instrument that is played without touching it by placing your hands inside an electrical field and by moving your hands inside that field. The device senses changes in the field and plays a note that relates to the distance to the coil. It is difficult to explain, so check out some videos of it being used on YouTube. As the circuit is the same, I will jump right to the code.

Enter the Code

Enter the code in Listing 14-4.

Listing 14-4. Code for Project 41

```
// Project 41

#define sensorPin 9

#define lowerFreq 123 // C3
#define upperFreq 2093 // C7
#define playHeight 36

float pwmRange, inch, cm, note;

void setup() {
        pinMode(sensorPin, INPUT);
}

void loop() {
        pwmRange = pulseIn(sensorPin, HIGH);

        inch = pwmRange / 147;
        // convert inch to cm
        cm = inch * 2.54;

        // map the playHeight range to the upper and lower frequencies
        note = map(inch, 0, playHeight, lowerFreq, upperFreq);
        if (inch<playHeight) {tone(8, note); }
        else {noTone(8);}
}
```

Once you upload it to the Arduino, you can now enter your hand into the sensor's beam and it will play the note mapped to that height from the sensor. Move your hand up and down in the beam and the tones played will also move up and down the scale. You can adjust the upper and lower frequency ranges in the code if you wish.

Project 41 – Ultrasonic Theremin – Code Overview

This code is a stripped down version of Project 40 with some code to turn the sensor range into a tone to be played on the piezo sounder or speaker. You start off by defining the sensor pin as before.

```
#define sensorPin 9
```

Then you have some new definitions for the upper and lower notes to be played and the `playHeight` in inches. The `playHeight` is the range between the sensor and as far as your arm will reach while playing the instrument within. You can adjust this range to something more or less if you wish.

```
#define lowerFreq 123 // C3
#define upperFreq 2093 // C7
#define playHeight 36
```

The variables are declared with one for note, which will be the note played through the speaker:

```
float pwmRange, inch, cm, note;
```

The setup routine simply sets the sensor pin to be an input:

```
pinMode(sensorPin, INPUT);
```

In the main loop, the code is just the essentials. The value from the sensor is read and converted to inches:

```
pwmRange = pulseIn(sensorPin, HIGH);
inch = pwmRange / 147;
```

Next, the inch values from zero to the value stored in playHeight are mapped to the upper and lower frequencies defined at the start of the program:

```
note = map(inch, 0, playHeight, lowerFreq, upperFreq);
```

You only want the tone to play when your hand is inside the beam, so you check if the value from the sensor is less than or equal to the play height. If so, a hand must be within the play area, and therefore a tone is played.

```
if (inch<=playHeight) {tone(8, note); }
```

If the hand is not in the beam or removed from the beam the tone is stopped:

```
else {noTone(8);}
```

Play around with the playHeight, upperFreq, and lowerFreq values to get the sound you want.

Summary

In this chapter you have learnt how to interface an ultrasonic sensor. I have also introduced a few uses of the sensor to give you a feel for how it can be used in your own projects. Sensors such as these are often used in hobby robotics projects for the robot to sense if it is near a wall or other obstacle. I have also seen them used in gyrocopter projects to ensure the craft does not bump into any walls or people. Another common use is to detect the height of a liquid inside a tank or a tube. I am sure you will think of other great uses for these kinds of sensors.

Subjects and Concepts covered in Chapter 14

- How an ultrasonic sensor works
- How to read the PW output from the MaxSonar devices
- Using a capacitor to smooth the power line
- How to use the pulseIn command to measure pulse widths

- Various potential uses for an ultrasonic range finder
- How to use the MAX7219 to control 7-segment displays
- How to wire up a common cathode 7-segment display
- Using a running average algorithm to smooth data readings
- How to use the `setDigit()` command to display digits on 7-segment LEDs
- Using division and modulo operators to pick out digits from a long number
- How to make an infinite loop with a `while(1)` command

CHAPTER 15

■ ■ ■

Reading and Writing to an SD Card

Now you are going to learn the basics of writing to and reading from an SD Card. SD Cards are a small and cheap method of storing data, and an Arduino can communicate relatively easily with one using its SPI interface. You will learn enough to be able to create a new file, append to an existing file, timestamp a file, and write data to that file. This will allow you to use an SD Card and an Arduino as a data-logging device to store whatever data you wish. Once you know the basics, you will put that knowledge to use to create a time-stamped temperature data logger.

Project 42 – Simple SD Card/Read Write

You will need an SD Card and some way of connecting it to an Arduino. The easiest way is get an SD/MMC Card Breakout Board from various electronics hobbyist suppliers. I used one from Sparkfun.

Parts Required

SD Card & Breakout*

3 × 3.3K ohm Resistors

3 × 1.8K ohm Resistors

**image courtesy of Sparkfun*

The resistors are to create a voltage divider and to drop the 5v logic levels down to 3.3v. (Note that a safer way would be to use a dedicated logic level converter, though resistors are easier.)

Connect It Up

Connect everything as shown in Figure 15-1.

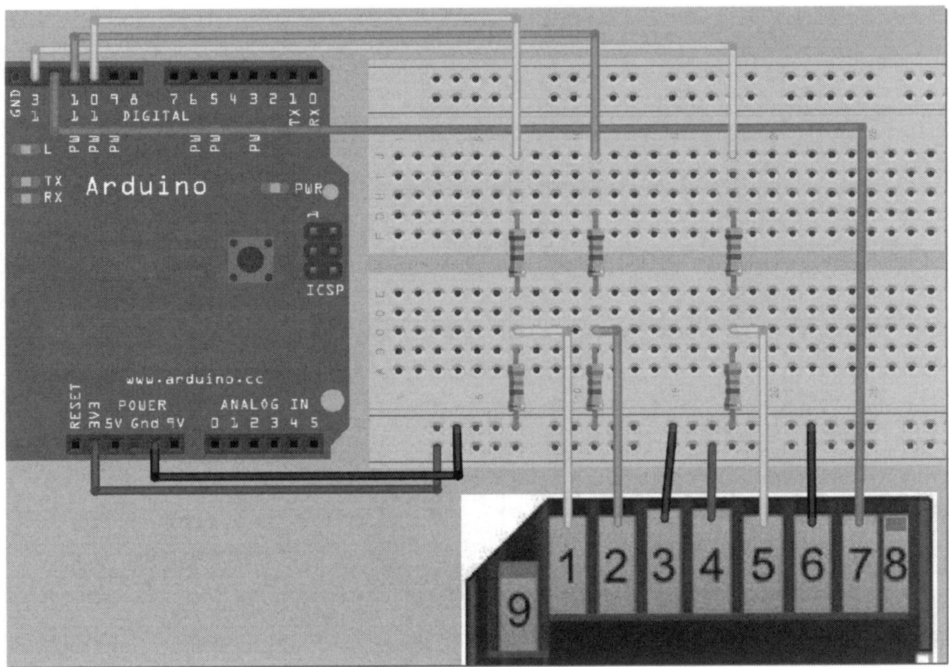

***Figure 15-1.** The circuit for Project 42 – Simple SD Card Read/Write*

Refer to Table 15-1 for the correct pin outs. Digital Pin 12 on the Arduino goes straight into Pin 7 (DO) on the SD Card. Digital Pins 13, 11, and 10 go via the resistors to drop the logic levels to 3.3v.

Table 15-1. Pin Connections between the Arduino and SD Card

Arduino	SD Card
+3.3v	Pin 4 (VCC)
Gnd	Pins 3 & 6 (GND)
Digital Pin 13 (SCK)	Pin 5 (CLK)
Digital Pin 12 (MISO)	Pin 7 (DO)
Digital Pin 11 (MOSI)	Pin 2 (DI)
Digital Pin 10 (SS)	Pin 1 (CS)

Enter the Code

First, you will need to install the SdFat.h and SdFatUtil.h libraries by Bill Greiman. This can currently be found at `http://code.google.com/p/sdfatlib/`. Download the library, unzip it, and install the sdfat folder in your Arduino libraries folder. Once the libraries are installed and you have checked your wiring is correct, enter the code in Listing 15-1 and upload it to your Arduino.

Listing 15-1. Code for Project 42

```
// Project 42
// Based on the SD Fat examples by Bill Greiman from sdfatlib

#include <SdFat.h>
#include <SdFatUtil.h>

Sd2Card card;
SdVolume volume;
SdFile root;
SdFile file;

// store error strings in flash to save RAM
#define error(s) error_P(PSTR(s))
```

```
void error_P(const char* str) {
  PgmPrint("error: ");
  SerialPrintln_P(str);
  if (card.errorCode()) {
    PgmPrint("SD error: ");
    Serial.print(card.errorCode(), HEX);
    Serial.print(',');
    Serial.println(card.errorData(), HEX);
  }
  while(1);
}

// Write a Carriage Return and Line Feed to the file
void writeCRLF(SdFile& f) {
  f.write((uint8_t*)"\r\n", 2);
}

// Write an unsigned number to file
void writeNumber(SdFile& f, uint32_t n) {
  uint8_t buf[10];
  uint8_t i = 0;
  do {
    i++;
    buf[sizeof(buf) - i] = n%10 + '0';
    n /= 10;
  } while (n);
  f.write(&buf[sizeof(buf) - i], i);
}

// Write a string to file
void writeString(SdFile& f, char *str) {
  uint8_t n;
  for (n = 0; str[n]; n++);
  f.write((uint8_t *)str, n);
}

void setup() {
  Serial.begin(9600);
  Serial.println();
  Serial.println("Type any character to start");
  while (!Serial.available());

  // initialize the SD card at SPI_HALF_SPEED to avoid bus errors with breadboards.
  // Use SPI_FULL_SPEED for better performance if your card an take it.
  if (!card.init(SPI_HALF_SPEED)) error("card.init failed");

  // initialize a FAT volume
  if (!volume.init(&card)) error("volume.init failed");
```

```
  // open the root directory
  if (!root.openRoot(&volume)) error("openRoot failed");

  // create a new file
  char name[] = "TESTFILE.TXT";

  file.open(&root, name, O_CREAT | O_EXCL | O_WRITE);
  // Put todays date and time here
  file.timestamp(2, 2010, 12, 25, 12, 34, 56);

 // write 10 lines to the file
  for (uint8_t i = 0; i < 10; i++) {
    writeString(file, "Line: ");
    writeNumber(file, i);
    writeString(file, " Write test.");
    writeCRLF(file);
  }

  // close file and force write of all data to the SD card
  file.close();
  Serial.println("File Created");

  // open a file
  if (file.open(&root, name, O_READ)) {
    Serial.println(name);
  }
  else{
    error("file.open failed");
  }
  Serial.println();

  int16_t character;
  while ((character = file.read()) > 0) Serial.print((char)character);

  Serial.println("\nDone");
}

void loop() { }
```

Make sure that your SD card has been freshly formatted in the FAT format. Run the program and open the serial monitor. You will be prompted to enter a character and then press SEND. The program will now attempt to write a file to the SD card, and then read back the filename and its contents to the serial monitor window. If everything goes well, you will get a readout like this:

```
Type any character to start
File Created
TESTFILE.TXT

        Line: 0 Write test.
        Line: 1 Write test.
        Line: 2 Write test.
```

```
Line: 3 Write test.
Line: 4 Write test.
Line: 5 Write test.
Line: 6 Write test.
Line: 7 Write test.
Line: 8 Write test.
Line: 9 Write test.

Done
```

Be warned that SD cards that work well on your PC or Mac may not work well with an Arduino. I had to work my way through six cards before I found one that worked (SD4/16Gb Kingston), so you may need to experiment yourself. Others users report success using Sandisk cards.

Once the program has finished, eject the card from your SD card connector and insert it in your PC and Mac. You will find a file called TESTFILE.TXT on it; if you open this file, it will contain the text in the output above. Let's see how the code works.

Project 42 – Simple SD Card Read/Write – Code Overview

You start off by including the two libraries from the sdfatlib library suite that will enable the code to work:

```
#include <SdFat.h>
#include <SdFatUtil.h>
```

Next, you need to create instances of Sd2Card, SdVolume, SdFile, and give them names:

```
Sd2Card card;
SdVolume volume;
SdFile root;
SdFile file;
```

The Sd2Card object gives you access to standard SD cards and SDHC cards, The SdVolume object supports FAT16 and FAT32 partitions. The Sdfile object give you file access functions, such as `open()`, `read()`, `remove()`, `write()`, `close()` and `sync()`. This will object gives you access to the root directory and its subdirectories.

Next, you have a definition to catch errors. You define `error(s)` and this reference the first function called `error_P`:

```
#define error(s) error_P(PSTR(s))
```

Next, you create a function called `error_P`. The purpose of this function is to simply print out any error messages that you pass to it and any relevant error codes generated. The parameter for the function is a reference to a character string. The character string has const before it. This is known as a variable qualifier and it modifies the behavior of the variable. In this case it makes it read-only. It can be used in the same way any other variable can be used, but its value cannot be changed.

```
void error_P(const char* str) {
```

Next comes a `PGMPrint()` command. This is a command from the sdfatlib library, and it stores and prints the string in its brackets in flash memory.

```
PgmPrint("error: ");
```

Then comes a `SerialPrintln_P` command. Again, this is from the library and prints a string in flash memory to the serial port followed by a CR/LF (Carriage Return and Line Feed).

```
SerialPrintln_P(str);
```

Next, the function checks if any error codes have been generated using the `.errorCode()` command. The library documentation will give you a list of the error codes.

```
if (card.errorCode()) {
```

If an error is generated, the code within the brackets is executed that displays the error code and the error data:

```
PgmPrint("SD error: ");
Serial.print(card.errorCode(), HEX);
Serial.print(',');
Serial.println(card.errorData(), HEX);
```

Finally, if an error has occurred, a `while(1)` creates an infinite loop to cease the sketch from doing anything else:

```
while(1);
```

The next function is called `writeCRLF()` and is designed to simply write a carriage return and line feed to the file. The parameter passed to it is a reference to a file.

```
void writeCRLF(SdFile& f) {
```

The code in its brackets uses the `write()` command to write 2 bytes to the file. These are \r and \n, which are the codes for a carriage return and line feed. The `write()` command is what is known as an overloaded function, which means it is a function that has been defined several times to accept different data types. The function has (uint8_t) to tell it that you wish to call the unsigned 8-bit integer version of the function.

```
f.write((uint8_t*)"\r\n", 2);
```

The next function is designed to write numbers to the file. It accepts the file reference and an unsigned 32-bit integer number.

```
void writeNumber(SdFile& f, uint32_t n) {
```

An array of length 10 of unsigned 8-bit integers is created as well as a variable called `i` which is initialized to 0:

```
uint8_t buf[10];
uint8_t i = 0;
```

Next comes a do-while loop that does the clever job of turning the integer number into a string one digit at a time:

```
do {
    i++;
    buf[sizeof(buf) - i] = n%10 + '0';
    n /= 10;
} while (n);
```

The do-while loop is something you haven't come across before. It works in the same manner as a while loop. However, in this case the condition is tested at the end of the loop instead of at the beginning. Where the while loop will not run if the condition is not met, the do-while loop will always run the code in its brackets at least once. The loop will only repeat if the condition is met.

The loop increments i, then uses the sizeof command to find out the size of the array. This returns the number of bytes in the array. You know it is 10 and that i starts off as 1, so it will access 10-1 or the ninth element of the array first, i.e. the last element in the array. Next, it will be 10-2 or the eighth element, and so on working from right to left. It then stores in that element the result of n%10, which will always be the rightmost digit of any number you give it. Next, n is divided by 10, which has the result of lopping off the rightmost digit. Then the process repeats. This has the effect of obtaining the rightmost digit of the number, storing it in the last element of the array, losing the rightmost digit, then repeating the process. By doing so, the number is chopped up into individual digits and then stored in the array as a string. The number is converted to its ASCII equivalent by the +'0' on the end.

```
buf[sizeof(buf) - i] = n%10 + '0';
```

This has the effect of putting the ASCII digit "0" in, but adding to it the value of n%10. In other words, if the number was 123, then 123%10 = 3, so the ASCII code for "0", which is 48, has 3 added to it to create 51, which is the ASCII code for "3". In doing so, the digit is converted into its ASCII equivalent. Once the loop is exited, the contents of the buf[] array are written to the file using

```
f.write(&buf[sizeof(buf) - i], i);
```

which takes a pointer to the location of the data being written, followed by the number of bytes to write. This is yet another version of the overloaded write() function. Next comes a function to write a text string to the file. The parameters are the file and a pointer to the string.

```
void writeString(SdFile& f, char *str) {
```

Again, you simply use a for loop to look at each element of the string array character by character, and write it to the file.

```
uint8_t n;
for (n = 0; str[n]; n++);
f.write((uint8_t *)str, n);
```

Next comes the setup routine, which does all of the work. As you only want this code to run once, you put it all in setup() and nothing in loop().

You start by initializing serial communications and then asking the user to enter a character to start:

```
Serial.begin(9600);
Serial.println();
Serial.println("Type any character to start");
```

Now the program waits until something is entered in the serial monitor by using a **while** loop to do nothing while there is NOT anything available on the serial line:

```
while (!Serial.available());
```

Next you run three if statements to run the error function if there are any errors initializing the card, the volume, or opening the root directory:

```
if (!card.init(SPI_HALF_SPEED)) error("card.init failed");
if (!volume.init(&card)) error("volume.init failed");
if (!root.openRoot(&volume)) error("openRoot failed");
```

You may change the speed to SPI_FULL_SPEED if you card can take it. I had errors when trying to run it at full speed so I left it at half speed. You may have more success at full speed.

You now need a name for the new file you are about to create, so you place this into a char array:

```
char name[] = "TESTFILE.TXT";
```

Next, you open a file in the root directory:

```
file.open(&root, name, O_CREAT | O_EXCL | O_WRITE);
```

The file being opened is that stored in name, which you just initialized as TESTFILE.TXT. As this file does not exist, it will create it at the same time. There are three flags in the command that tell it what to do. They are O_CREAT, O_EXCL and O_WRITE.

The O_CREAT flag tells the open command to create the file if it does not exist. The O_EXCL command will make the command fail if O_CREAT is also set (i.e. the file is exclusive, so if it already exists, do not create it again). The O_WRITE makes the file open for writing. So, in essence, this command will open the file; create it if it does not exist already; make sure a new file is not overwritten if the file already exists; and finally, open the file and make it ready for writing to.

Next, you use the timestamp command to make sure the file has the correct data and time when created. The command accepts seven parameters. These are a flag, the year, the month, the day, the hour, minutes, and seconds.

```
file.timestamp(2, 2010, 12, 25, 12, 34, 56);
```

In this case you pass it false data, but ideally you would obtain the time from a time source such as an RTC (Real Time Clock) chip or a GPS module and then use that data to timestamp the file correctly. The flag that makes up the first parameter is made up of:

```
T_ACCESS = 1
T_CREATE = 2
T_WRITE = 4
```

- T_ACCESS - Sets the file's last access date.
- T_CREATE - Sets the file's creation date and time.
- T_WRITE - Sets the file's last write/modification date and time.

In your case, you just use the value of 2, which means you set the files creation date and time. If you wanted to set all three at the same time, the value would be 7 (4+2+1).

Next, a `for` loop runs ten times to write the line number and some test data to the file, followed by a carriage return and line feed. The three functions for writing numbers, strings, and CRLF are called to accomplish this.

```
for (uint8_t i = 0; i < 10; i++) {
    writeString(file, "Line: ");
    writeNumber(file, i);
    writeString(file, " Write test.");
    writeCRLF(file);
}
```

Any action that is carried out on the file is not written until the file is closed. You use the `.close()` command to do this. This closes the file and writes all of the data you set in your code to it.

```
file.close();
```

Then you let the user know that the file has been created:

```
Serial.println("File Created");
```

Now that you have created a new file and written data to it, you move onto the part of the program that opens the file and reads data from it. You use the `open()` command, which needs three parameters: the directory the file is on, the name of the file, and the appropriate flag for file operation. You use &root to ensure you look in the root directory, and the flag is `O_READ` which opens a file for reading. The command is the condition of an `if` statement so that you can print the name of the file if the file is opened successfully and run the error routine if it is not.

```
if (file.open(&root, name, O_READ)) {
    Serial.println(name);
  }
  else{
    error("file.open failed");
  }
  Serial.println();
```

Then you read the file one character at a time using a `while` loop and a `.read()` command, and print the result to the serial monitor:

```
int16_t character;
while ((character = file.read()) > 0) Serial.print((char)character);
```

Finally, if all is successful, you print "Done":

```
  Serial.println("\nDone");
}
```

The main loop of the program contains no code at all. You only want the code to run once, so it makes sense to put it all in the `setup()` routine and nothing in the loop. The code will run once only, then the loop will be executed, and as it contains no code, nothing will happen until the Arduino is powered off or reset:

```
void loop() { }
```

The above example shows you the basic method of creating a file, writing basic numbers and strings to the file, closing the file, and then reading it. You shall now expand on that knowledge and put it to a practical use by using the SD Card to log some sensor data.

Project 43 – Temperature SD Datalogger

Now you'll add some DS18B20 temperature sensors to the circuit along with a DS1307 RTC (Real Time Clock) chip. The readings from the temperature sensors will be logged onto the SD Card, and you'll use the RTC chip to read the date and time so that the sensor readings and the file modification can all be time stamped.

Parts Required

SD Card & Breakout*
3 × 3.3K ohm Resistors
3 × 1.8K ohm Resistors
4.7K ohm Resistor
2 × 1K ohm Resistors
DS1307 RTC IC

32.768khz 12.5pF Watch Crystal

2 × DS18B20 Temp. Sensors

*Coin Cell Holder**

**images courtesy of Sparkfun*
***Optional*

The coin cell holder is optional. Having a coin cell as a battery backup will allow you to retain the time and date in the RTC even when you power down your project.

Connect It Up

Connect everything as shown in Figure 15-2.

***Figure 15-2.** The circuit for Project 43 – Temperature SD Datalogger*

Refer to Table 15-2 for the correct pin outs. Connect the DS18B20s exactly as in Project 37. If you are using the coin cell battery backup, do not install the wire between Pins 3 and 4 on the RTC as in the diagram. Instead, connect the positive terminal of the battery to Pin 3 of the chip and the negative to Pin 4.

Table 15-2. Pin Connections between the Arduino, SD Card, and RTC

Arduino	SD Card	RTC
+5v -		Pin 5
+3.3v	Pin 4 (VCC)	
Gnd	Pins 3 & 6 (GND)	Pins 3 & 4
Digital Pin 13 (SCK)	Pin 5 (CLK)	
Digital Pin 12 (MISO)	Pin 7 (DO)	
Digital Pin 11 (MOSI)	Pin 2 (DI)	
Digital Pin 10 (SS)	Pin 1 (CS)	
Analog Pin 4		Pin 5
Analog Pin 5		Pin 6

Place 1K ohm resistors between Pin 8 and Pins 5 and 6 on the RTC.

Enter the Code

Make sure that the OneWire.h and DallasTemperature.h libraries used in Project 37 are installed for this project. You will also be using the DS1307.h library by Matt Joyce and D. Sjunnesson to control the DS1307 chip.

Listing 15-2. Code for Project 43

```
// Project 43
// Based on the SD Fat examples by Bill Greiman from sdfatlib
// DS1307 library by Matt Joyce with enhancements by D. Sjunnesson

#include <SdFat.h>
#include <SdFatUtil.h>
#include <OneWire.h>
#include <DallasTemperature.h>
#include <WProgram.h>
#include <Wire.h>
#include <DS1307.h> // written by  mattt on the Arduino forum and modified by D. Sjunnesson
```

```
// store error strings in flash to save RAM
#define error(s) error_P(PSTR(s))
// Data wire is plugged into pin 3 on the Arduino
#define ONE_WIRE_BUS 3
#define TEMPERATURE_PRECISION 12

Sd2Card card;
SdVolume volume;
SdFile root;
SdFile file;

// Setup a oneWire instance to communicate with any OneWire devices (not just Maxim/Dallas↩
 temperature ICs)
OneWire oneWire(ONE_WIRE_BUS);
// Pass our oneWire reference to Dallas Temperature.
DallasTemperature sensors(&oneWire);

// arrays to hold device addresses
  DeviceAddress insideThermometer = { 0x10, 0x20, 0x2C, 0xA9, 0x01, 0x08, 0x00, 0x73 };
  DeviceAddress outsideThermometer = { 0x10, 0x22, 0x5B, 0xA9, 0x01, 0x08, 0x00, 0x21 };

  float tempC, tempF;
  int hour, minute, seconds, day, month, year;

// create a new file name
char name[] = "TEMPLOG.TXT";

void error_P(const char* str) {
  PgmPrint("error: ");
  SerialPrintln_P(str);
  if (card.errorCode()) {
    PgmPrint("SD error: ");
    Serial.print(card.errorCode(), HEX);
    Serial.print(',');
    Serial.println(card.errorData(), HEX);
  }
  while(1);
}

void writeCRLF(SdFile& f) {
  f.write((uint8_t*)"\r\n", 2);
}
```

```
// Write an unsigned number to file
void writeNumber(SdFile& f, uint32_t n) {
  uint8_t buf[10];
  uint8_t i = 0;
  do {
    i++;
    buf[sizeof(buf) - i] = n%10 + '0';
    n /= 10;
  } while (n);
  f.write(&buf[sizeof(buf) - i], i);
}

// Write a string to file
void writeString(SdFile& f, char *str) {
  uint8_t n;
  for (n = 0; str[n]; n++);
  f.write((uint8_t *)str, n);
}

void getTemperature(DeviceAddress deviceAddress)
{
  sensors.requestTemperatures();
  tempC = sensors.getTempC(deviceAddress);
  tempF = DallasTemperature::toFahrenheit(tempC);
}

void getTimeDate() {
  hour = RTC.get(DS1307_HR,true); //read the hour and also update all the values by↵
 pushing in true
  minute = RTC.get(DS1307_MIN,false);//read minutes without update (false)
  seconds = RTC.get(DS1307_SEC,false);//read seconds
  day = RTC.get(DS1307_DATE,false);//read date
  month = RTC.get(DS1307_MTH,false);//read month
  year = RTC.get(DS1307_YR,false); //read year
}

void setup() {
  Serial.begin(9600);
  Serial.println("Type any character to start");
  while (!Serial.available());
  Serial.println();

  // Start up the sensors library
  sensors.begin();
  Serial.println("Initialising Sensors.");

  // set the resolution
  sensors.setResolution(insideThermometer, TEMPERATURE_PRECISION);
  sensors.setResolution(outsideThermometer, TEMPERATURE_PRECISION);
  delay(100);
```

```
  // Set the time on the RTC.
  // Comment out this section if you have already set the time and have a battery backup
  RTC.stop();
  RTC.set(DS1307_SEC,0);         //set the seconds
  RTC.set(DS1307_MIN,15);      //set the minutes
  RTC.set(DS1307_HR,14);        //set the hours
  RTC.set(DS1307_DOW,7);        //set the day of the week
  RTC.set(DS1307_DATE,3);        //set the date
  RTC.set(DS1307_MTH,10);         //set the month
  RTC.set(DS1307_YR,10);          //set the year
  RTC.start();

  Serial.println("Initialising SD Card...");

  // initialize the SD card at SPI_HALF_SPEED to avoid bus errors with breadboards.
  // Use SPI_FULL_SPEED for better performance if your card an take it.
  if (!card.init(SPI_HALF_SPEED)) error("card.init failed");

  // initialize a FAT volume
  if (!volume.init(&card)) error("volume.init failed");

  // open the root directory
  if (!root.openRoot(&volume)) error("openRoot failed");
  Serial.println("SD Card initialised successfully.");
  Serial.println();
}

void loop() {

  Serial.println("File Opened.");
  file.open(&root, name, O_CREAT | O_APPEND | O_WRITE);
  getTimeDate();
  file.timestamp(7, year, month, day, hour, minute, seconds);

   getTemperature(insideThermometer);
    Serial.print("Inside: ");
    Serial.print(tempC);
    Serial.print(" C  ");
    Serial.print(tempF);
    Serial.println(" F");
    writeNumber(file, year);
    writeString(file, "/");
    writeNumber(file, month);
    writeString(file, "/");
    writeNumber(file, day);
    writeString(file, "  ");
    writeNumber(file, hour);
    writeString(file, ":");
    writeNumber(file, minute);
    writeString(file, ":");
    writeNumber(file, seconds);
    writeCRLF(file);
```

```
    writeString(file, "Internal Sensor: ");
    writeNumber(file, tempC);
    writeString(file, " C   ");
    writeNumber(file, tempF);
    writeString(file, " F");
    writeCRLF(file);

    getTemperature(outsideThermometer);
    Serial.print("Outside: ");
    Serial.print(tempC);
    Serial.print(" C  ");
    Serial.print(tempF);
    Serial.println(" F");
    writeString(file, "External Sensor: ");
    writeNumber(file, tempC);
    writeString(file, " C   ");
    writeNumber(file, tempF);
    writeString(file, " F");
    writeCRLF(file);
    writeCRLF(file);

  Serial.println("Data written.");
  // close file and force write of all data to the SD card
  file.close();
  Serial.println("File Closed.");
  Serial.println();
  delay(10000);
}
```

Open the serial monitor and the program will ask you to enter a character to start the code. You will then get an output similar to this:

```
Type any character to start

Initialising Sensors.
Initialising SD Card...
SD Card initialised successfully.

File Opened.
Inside: 27.25 C  81.05 F
Outside: 15.19 C  59.34 F
Data written.
File Closed.

File Opened.
Inside: 28.31 C  82.96 F
Outside: 15.25 C  59.45 F
Data written.
File Closed.
```

```
File Opened.
Inside: 28.62 C  83.52 F
Outside: 15.31 C  59.56 F
Data written.
File Closed.
```

If you power off the Arduino and eject the SD Card, then insert it into your PC or Mac, you will see a file called TEMPLOG.TXT. Open up this file in a text editor and you will see the time stamped sensor readings looking like:

```
2010/10/3  17:29:9
Internal Sensor: 27 C   81 F
External Sensor: 15 C   59 F

2010/10/3  17:29:21
Internal Sensor: 28 C   82 F
External Sensor: 15 C   59 F

2010/10/3  17:29:32
Internal Sensor: 28 C   83 F
External Sensor: 15 C   59 F
```

Let's see how the program works.

Project 43 – Temperature SD Datalogger – Code Overview

As a lot of this code is covered in Project 37 and 42, I will concentrate on the new bits.

First, the appropriate libraries are included:

```
#include <SdFat.h>
#include <SdFatUtil.h>
#include <OneWire.h>
#include <DallasTemperature.h>
#include <WProgram.h>
#include <Wire.h>
#include <DS1307.h>
```

The last three libraries are new and are required to run the DS1307 code. The WProgram.h and Wire.h libraries come as part of the core Arduino program.

The definitions for error catching and the one wire bus are created:

```
#define error(s) error_P(PSTR(s))
#define ONE_WIRE_BUS 3
#define TEMPERATURE_PRECISION 12
```

Objects for the SDcard are created:

```
Sd2Card card;
SdVolume volume;
SdFile root;
SdFile file;
```

You also create instances for the one wire and Dallas temperature sensor:

```
OneWire oneWire(ONE_WIRE_BUS);
DallasTemperature sensors(&oneWire);
```

You then define the addresses for the DS18B20 sensors. Use Project 37, Part 1, to find out the addresses of your own sensors.

```
DeviceAddress insideThermometer = { 0x10, 0x20, 0x2C, 0xA9, 0x01, 0x08, 0x00, 0x73 };
DeviceAddress outsideThermometer = { 0x10, 0x22, 0x5B, 0xA9, 0x01, 0x08, 0x00, 0x21 };
```

You now create some variables that will store the temperature readings and the date and time from the RTC, plus the array that will hold the file name you will log data to:

```
float tempC, tempF;
int hour, minute, seconds, day, month, year;
char name[] = "TEMPLOG.TXT";
```

Next come the functions for error catching, writing a CR and LF to the file, and writing numbers and strings:

```
void error_P(const char* str) {
  PgmPrint("error: ");
  SerialPrintln_P(str);
  if (card.errorCode()) {
    PgmPrint("SD error: ");
    Serial.print(card.errorCode(), HEX);
    Serial.print(',');
    Serial.println(card.errorData(), HEX);
  }
  while(1);
}

void writeCRLF(SdFile& f) {
  f.write((uint8_t*)"\r\n", 2);
}

// Write an unsigned number to file
void writeNumber(SdFile& f, uint32_t n) {
  uint8_t buf[10];
  uint8_t i = 0;
```

```
  do {
    i++;
    buf[sizeof(buf) - i] = n%10 + '0';
    n /= 10;
  } while (n);
  f.write(&buf[sizeof(buf) - i], i);
}

// Write a string to file
void writeString(SdFile& f, char *str) {
  uint8_t n;
  for (n = 0; str[n]; n++);
  f.write((uint8_t *)str, n);
}
```

You now create a new function to obtain the temperatures from the sensor. The address of the device is passed as a parameter.

```
void getTemperature(DeviceAddress deviceAddress)
{
  sensors.requestTemperatures();
  tempC = sensors.getTempC(deviceAddress);
  tempF = DallasTemperature::toFahrenheit(tempC);
}
```

Next, you create another new function to obtain the time and date from the DS1307 real time clock chip. This function is called `getTimeDate()`.

```
void getTimeDate() {
```

To obtain data for the hours, minutes, seconds, day, month, and year from the RTC, you use the `.get()` command. First, you obtain the hour from the device and store it in the hour variable.

```
hour = RTC.get(DS1307_HR,true); //read the hour and also update all the values by pushing↩
 in true
```

The command requires two parameters. The first is a flag to state what data piece you want. Their names make it pretty obvious what they are. The second is either false or true. If true, the time constants (DS1307_HR, DS1307_YR, etc.) will all be updated to the current time and date. If false, they will simply read the last time that was updated. As you want to update this only once at the start of the time/date read, you have a true flag on the first `.get()` command and a false on the remainder.

```
minute = RTC.get(DS1307_MIN,false);//read minutes without update (false)
seconds = RTC.get(DS1307_SEC,false);//read seconds
day = RTC.get(DS1307_DATE,false);//read date
month = RTC.get(DS1307_MTH,false);//read month
year = RTC.get(DS1307_YR,false); //read year
```

Next comes the setup routine:

```
void setup() {
Serial.begin(9600);
Serial.println("Type any character to start");
while (!Serial.available());
Serial.println();
```

The DS18B20 sensors are initialized and their resolution is set:

```
sensors.begin();
Serial.println("Initialising Sensors.");
sensors.setResolution(insideThermometer, TEMPERATURE_PRECISION);
sensors.setResolution(outsideThermometer, TEMPERATURE_PRECISION);
```

Next comes the part that sets the data and time on the RTC. You use the `.set()` command, which is essentially the reverse of the `.get()` command. Before you set the device, you need to use the `.stop()` command to stop it first. Once the time is set, the `.start()` command is used to start the RTC with its new time and date.

```
RTC.stop();
RTC.set(DS1307_SEC,0);        //set the seconds
RTC.set(DS1307_MIN,15);     //set the minutes
RTC.set(DS1307_HR,14);       //set the hours
RTC.set(DS1307_DOW,7);       //set the day of the week
RTC.set(DS1307_DATE,3);       //set the date
RTC.set(DS1307_MTH,10);        //set the month
RTC.set(DS1307_YR,10);         //set the year
RTC.start();
```

The SD Card is initialized:

```
Serial.println("Initialising SD Card...");

// initialize the SD card at SPI_HALF_SPEED to avoid bus errors with breadboards.
// Use SPI_FULL_SPEED for better performance if your card an take it.
if (!card.init(SPI_HALF_SPEED)) error("card.init failed");

// initialize a FAT volume
if (!volume.init(&card)) error("volume.init failed");

// open the root directory
if (!root.openRoot(&volume)) error("openRoot failed");
Serial.println("SD Card initialised successfully.");
Serial.println();
```

Next comes the main loop. The file is opened. This time you use the `O_APPEND` flag.

```
file.open(&root, name, O_CREAT | O_APPEND | O_WRITE);
```

Next, you call the `getTimeDate()` function to obtain the time and date settings from the RTC:

```
getTimeDate();
```

Those values are used for the file timestamp:

```
file.timestamp(7, year, month, day, hour, minute, seconds);
```

Next, you call the `getTemperature()` function to obtain the temperature from the first device:

```
getTemperature(insideThermometer);
```

The temperatures are printed on the serial monitor and then the timestamp, and then the temperatures are written to the file:

```
Serial.print("Inside: ");
Serial.print(tempC);
Serial.print(" C  ");
Serial.print(tempF);
Serial.println(" F");
writeNumber(file, year);
writeString(file, "/");
writeNumber(file, month);
writeString(file, "/");
writeNumber(file, day);
writeString(file, "  ");
writeNumber(file, hour);
writeString(file, ":");
writeNumber(file, minute);
writeString(file, ":");
writeNumber(file, seconds);
writeCRLF(file);
writeString(file, "Internal Sensor: ");
writeNumber(file, tempC);
writeString(file, " C   ");
writeNumber(file, tempF);
writeString(file, " F");
writeCRLF(file);
```

Then you obtain the temperature from the second device and do the same (minus the timestamp):

```
getTemperature(outsideThermometer);
Serial.print("Outside: ");
Serial.print(tempC);
Serial.print(" C  ");
Serial.print(tempF);
Serial.println(" F");
writeString(file, "External Sensor: ");
writeNumber(file, tempC);
writeString(file, " C   ");
writeNumber(file, tempF);
```

```
writeString(file, " F");
writeCRLF(file);
writeCRLF(file);
```

Finally, the file is closed and you inform the user of this, followed by a ten second delay for the next reading:

```
Serial.println("Data written.");
// close file and force write of all data to the SD card
file.close();
Serial.println("File Closed.");
Serial.println();
delay(10000);
```

You now have the basic idea of how to write sensor or other data to an SD card. For more advanced functionality, read the documentation that comes with the SDfat library. You will now take a quick look at the RTC chip before moving onto the next chapter.

Project 43 – Temperature SD Datalogger – Hardware Overview

In Project 43, you were introduced to a new IC, the DS1307 real time clock chip. This is a great little IC that allows you to easily add a clock to your projects. With the addition of the coin cell battery backup, you can disconnect your Arduino from the power and the chip will automatically switch over to the battery backup and keep its data and time updated using the battery. With a good quality crystal, the device will keep reasonably accurate time. The device even adjusts itself for leap years and for months with days less than 31. It can also be set to operate in either 24-hour or 12-hour modes. Communication with the device is via an I^2C interface, which I will explain shortly.

The chip is interesting in that it also has a square wave output on Pin 7. This can be 1Hz, 4.096kHz, 8.192kHz, or 32.768kHz. You could therefore also use it as an oscillator for generating sound or other purposes that require a pulse. You could easily add an LED to this pin to indicate the seconds as they go by if set at 1Hz.

The communication with the chip is over a protocol called I^2C. You have come across one-wire and SPI so far, but this is a new protocol. To use the I^2C protocol, you need to include the Wire.h library in your code.

The I^2C (or Inter-IC) protocol (sometimes also called TWI or Two Wire Interface) was developed by Philips Semiconductors (now known as NXP) to create a simple bidirectional bus using just two wires for inter-IC control. The protocol uses just two wires: the serial data line (SDA) and the serial clock line (SCL). On the Arduino, these pins are Analog Pin 4 (SDA) and Analog Pin 5 (SCL). The only other external hardware required is a pull-up resistor on each of the bus lines. You can have up to 128 I^2C devices (or nodes) connected on the same two wires. Some I^2C devices use +5v and others +3.3v, so this is something to watch out for when using them. Make sure you read the datasheet and use the correct voltage before wiring up an I^2C device. If you ever wanted two Arduinos to talk to each other then I^2C would be a good protocol to use.

The I^2C protocol is similar to SPI in that there are master and slave devices. The Arduino is the master and the I^2C device is the slave. Each device has its own I^2C address. Each bit of the data is sent on each clock pulse. Communication commences when the master issues a START condition on the bus and is terminated when the master issues a STOP condition.

To start I^2C communication on an Arduino, you issue the **Wire.begin()** command. This will initialize the Wire library and the Arduino as the master I^2C device. It also reconfigures the Analog Pin 4 and 5 to be the I^2C pins. To initiate communications as a slave (i.e. for two Arduinos connected via I^2C), the address of the slave device must be included in the parenthesis. In other words,

```
Wire.begin(5);
```

will cause the Arduino to join the I^2C bus as the slave device on address 5. A byte can be received from an I^2C device using

```
Int x = Wire. Receive();
```

Before doing so you must request the number of bytes using **Wire.requestFrom(address, quantity)**

so

```
Wire.requestFrom(5,10);
```

would request 10 bytes from device 5. Sending to the device is just as easy with

```
Wire.beginTransmission(5);
```

which sets the device to transmit to device number 5 and then

```
Wire.send(x);
```

to send one byte or

```
Wire.send("Wire test.");
```

to send 10 bytes.

You can learn more about the Wire library at **www.arduino.cc/en/Reference/Wire** and about I^2C from Wikipedia or by reading the excellent explanation of I^2C in the Atmega datasheets on the Atmel website.

Summary

In Chapter 15 you have learned the basics of reading and writing to an SD Card. There are many more concepts you can learn about using the SD Card with the SDFat library by reading the documentation that comes with it. You have just scratched the surface with the projects in this chapter! Along the way, you have been introduced to the I^2C protocol. You have also learned how to connect a DS1307 real time clock chip, which will be very useful for your own clock based projects in future. Another great way of obtaining a very accurate time signal is using a cheap GPS device with a serial output.

Knowing how to read and write to an SD card is a vital piece of knowledge for making data loggers, especially for remote battery operated devices. Many of the High Altitude Balloon (HAB) projects based on the Arduino or AVR chips use SD cards for logging GPS and sensor data for retrieval once the balloon is on the ground.

Subjects and Concepts covered in Chapter 15

- How to connect an SD card to an Arduino
- Using voltage divider circuits with resistors to drop voltage levels from +5v to +3.3v
- How to use the SDfat library
- Writing strings and numbers to files
- Opening and closing files
- Naming files
- Creating file timestamps
- Catching file errors
- The concept of the `do-while` loop
- Using modulo and division to strip out individual digits from a long number
- How to connect a DS1307 real time clock chip to an Arduino
- How to use the DS1307.h library to set and get time and date
- Using a battery backup on the DS1307 to retain data after power loss
- An introduction to the I^2C protocol

CHAPTER 16

Making an RFID Reader

RFID (Radio Frequency Identification) readers are quite common today. They are the method of choice for controlling access in office blocks and for entry systems for public transport. Small RFID tags are injected into animals for identification if they get lost. Vehicles have tags on them for toll collection. They are even used in hospitals to tag disposable equipment in operating rooms to ensure that no foreign objects are left inside patients. The cost of the technology has come down drastically over the years to the point where readers can now be purchased for less than $10. They are easy to connect to an Arduino and easy to use. As a result, all kinds of cool projects can be created out of them.

You will be using the easily obtainable and cheap ID-12 reader from Innovations. These readers use 125KHz technology to read tags and cards up to 180mm away from the reader. There are other readers in the same range that give greater range, and with the addition of an external antenna you can increase the range further still.

You'll start off by connecting one up and learning how easy it is to obtain serial data from it. You'll then make a simple access control system.

Project 44 – Simple RFID Reader

The pins on the ID12 readers are non-standard spacing so they will not fit into a breadboard. You will need to obtain a breakout board from a supplier such as Sparkfun. The cards or tags can be purchased from all kinds of sources and are very cheap; I got a bag of small keyfob style tags on eBay for a few dollars. Make sure the tag or card is of 125KHz technology, otherwise it will not work with this reader.

Parts Required

ID-12 RFID Reader

ID-12 Breakout Board*

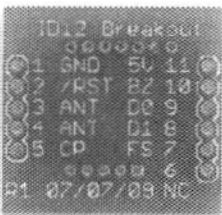

Current Limiting Resistor

5mm LED

125KHz RFID tags or cards*
(At least 4)

**image courtesy of Sparkfun*

Connect It Up

Connect everything as shown in Figure 16-1.

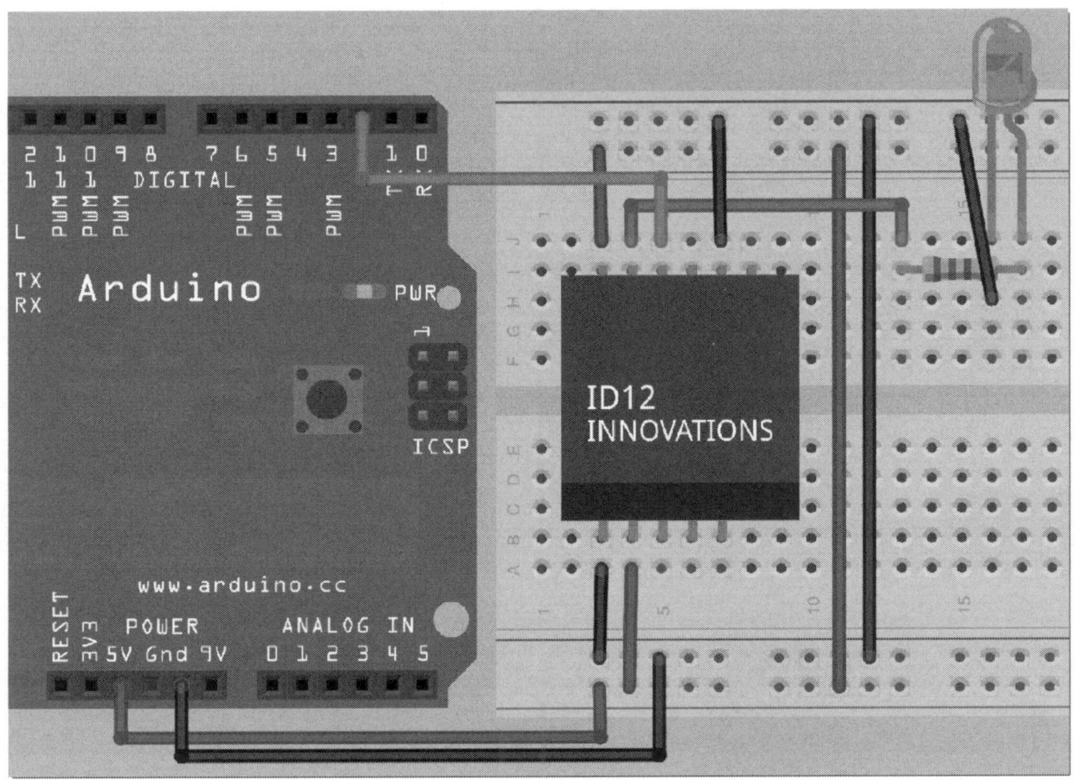

***Figure 16-1.** The circuit for Project 44 – Simple RFID Reader*

Connect an LED via a current limiting resistor to Pin 10 (BZ) on the reader.

Enter the Code

Enter the code in Listing 16-1.

Listing 16-1. *Code for Project 44.*

```
// Project 44

char val = 0; // value read for serial port

void setup() {
    Serial.begin(9600);
}

void loop () {

  if(Serial.available() > 0) {
  val = Serial.read(); // read from the serial port
  Serial.print(val, BYTE); // and print it to the monitor
  }
}
```

Run the code, open up the serial monitor, and hold your RFID tag or card up to the reader. The LED will flash to show it has read the card, and the serial monitor window will show you a 12 digit number which makes up the unique ID of the card. Make a note of the IDs of your tags as you will need them in the next project.

The code is nothing more than a simple read of the data present on the serial port. By now, you should know enough to work out how this program works. I shall therefore skip over the code overview and look at the hardware instead.

Project 44 – Simple RFID Reader – Hardware Overview

RFID is everywhere from your bus pass to the doors that let you into your office or college, and so on. The tags or cards come in all kinds of shapes and sizes (see Figure 16-2) and can be made so small that scientists have even attached RFID tags to ants to monitor their movements. They are simple devices that do nothing but transmit a unique serial code via radio waves to the reader. Most of the time, the cards or tags are *passive*, meaning they have no battery and need power from an external source. Other options include *passive RFID*, which has its own power source, and *battery assisted passive* (BAP), which waits for an external source to wake it up and then uses its own power source to transmit, giving greater range.

The kind you are using are the passive type that have no battery. They get their power from a magnetic field transmitted by the reader. As the tag passes into the magnetic field, it inducts a current in the wires inside the tag. This current is used to wake up a tiny chip, which transmits the serial number of the tag. The reader then sends that data in serial format to the PC or microcontroller connected to it. The format of the data sent from the ID12 reader is as follows:

STX (02h)	DATA (10 ASCII)	CHECKSUM (2 ASCII)	CR	LF	ETX (03H)

An STX or transmission start character is sent first (ASCII 02), followed by 10 bytes that make up the individual HEX (Hexadecimal) digits of the number. The next two HEX digits are the checksum of the number (this will be explained in the next project), then there's have a Carriage Return (CR) and Line Feed (LF), followed by an ETX or transmission end code.

Only the 12 ASCII digits will show up on the serial monitor as the rest are non-printable characters. In the next project, you'll use the checksum to ensure the received string is correct and the STX code to tell you that a string is being sent.

Figure 16-2. RFID tags and cards come in all shapes and sizes (image courtesy of Timo Arnall)

Project 45 – Access Control System

You're now going to create an access control system. You'll read tags using the RFID reader and validate select tags to allow them to open a door. The Arduino, via a transistor, will then operate an electric strike lock.

Parts Required

ID-12 RFID Reader

ID-12 Breakout Board*

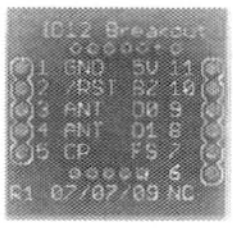

Current Limiting Resistor

5mm LED

125KHz RFID tags or cards*
(At least 4)

1N4001 Diode

TIP-120 NPN Transistor

2.1mm Power Jack

12v DC Power Supply

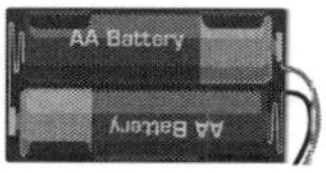

8 ohm Speaker or a piezo sounder

12v Electric Strike Lock

**image courtesy of Sparkfun*

Connect It Up

Connect everything as shown in Figure 16-3.

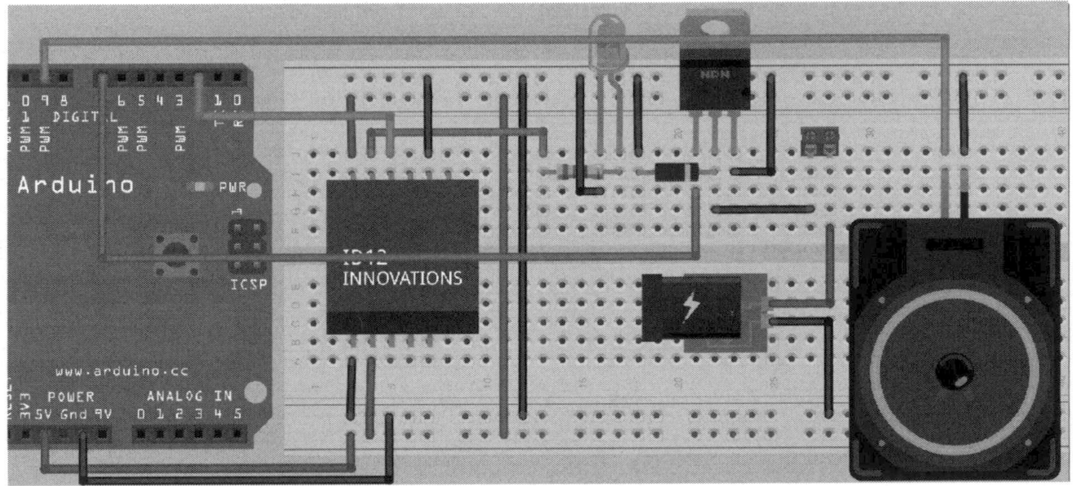

Figure 16-3. *The circuit for Project 45 – Access Control System*

If you are not using the TIP120, make sure you read the datasheet for your transistor to ensure you have the pins wired correctly. From left to right on the TIP120, you have the base, collector, and emitter. The base goes to Digital Pin 7, the collector goes to Ground via the diode and also to the negative terminal of the piezo or speaker. The emitter goes to Ground. An 8 ohm speaker makes a nicer and louder sound than a piezo if you can get hold of one.

The power for the lock must come from an external 12v DC power supply with a rating of at least 500mA.

Enter the Code

Enter the code in Listing 16-2.

Listing 16-2. *Code for Project 45*

```
// Project 45

#define lockPin 7
#define speakerPin 9
#define tx 3
#define rx 2
#define unlockLength 2000
```

```
#include <SoftwareSerial.h>

SoftwareSerial rfidReader = SoftwareSerial(rx, tx);

int users = 3;

char* cards[] = { // valid cards
  "3D00768B53",
  "3D00251C27",
  "3D0029E6BF",
};

char* names[] = { // cardholder names
  "Tom Smith",
  "Dick Jones",
  "Harry Roberts"
};

void setup() {
  pinMode (lockPin, OUTPUT);
  pinMode (speakerPin, OUTPUT);
  digitalWrite(lockPin, LOW);
  Serial.begin(9600);
  rfidReader.begin(9600);
}

void loop() {
  char cardNum[10]; // array to hold card number
  byte cardBytes[6]; // byte version of card number + checksum
  int index=0; // current digit
  byte byteIn=0; // byte read from RFID
  byte lastByte=0; // the last byte read
  byte checksum = 0; // checksum result stored here

  if (rfidReader.read()==2) { // read the RFID reader
      while(index<12) { // 12 digits in unique serial number
          byteIn = rfidReader.read(); // store value in byteIn
          if ((byteIn==1) || (byteIn==2) || (byteIn==10) || (byteIn==13)) {return;}↩
 // if STX, ETX, CR or LF break
          if (index<10) {cardNum[index]=byteIn;} // store first 10 HEX digits only↩
 (last 2 are checksum)
          // convert ascii hex to integer hex value
          if ((byteIn>='0') && (byteIn<='9')) {
          byteIn -= '0';
          }
          else if ((byteIn>='A') && (byteIn<='F')) {
          byteIn = (byteIn+10)-'A';
          }
```

```
        if ((index & 1) == 1) { // if odd number merge 2 4 bit digits into 8 bit byte
            cardBytes[index/2]= (byteIn | (lastByte<<4)); // move the last digit 4 bits➥
left and add new digit
            if (index<10) {checksum ^= cardBytes[index/2];} // tot up the checksum value
        }
        lastByte=byteIn; // store the last byte read
        index++; // increment the index
        if (index==12) {cardNum[10] = '\0';} // if we have reached the end of all digits➥
add a null terminator
    }

    Serial.println(cardNum); // print the card number
    int cardIndex =checkCard(cardNum); // check if card is valid and return index number
    if(cardIndex>=0 && (cardBytes[5]==checksum)) { // if card number and checksum are valid
        Serial.println("Card Validated");
        Serial.print("User: ");
        Serial.println(names[cardIndex]); // print the relevant name
        unlock(); // unlock the door
        Serial.println();
    }
    else {
        Serial.println("Card INVALID");
        tone(speakerPin, 250, 250);
        delay(250);
        tone(speakerPin, 150, 250);
        Serial.println();
    }
  }
}

int checkCard(char cardNum[10]) {
    for (int x=0; x<=users; x++) { // check all valid cards
        if(strcmp(cardNum, cards[x])==0) { // compare with last read card number
            return (x); // return index of card number
        }
    }
  return (-1); // negative value indicates no match
}

void unlock() {
    tone(speakerPin, 1000, 500);
    digitalWrite(lockPin, HIGH);
    delay(unlockLength);
    digitalWrite(lockPin, LOW);
}
```

Make sure that the code numbers for three of your tags are entered into the `cards[]` array at the start of the program. Use Project 44 to find out the code numbers, if necessary (run the code and open the serial monitor). Now, present your four cards to the reader. The reader will flash its LED to show it has read the card and you will then get an output similar to this:

```
3D00251C27
Card Validated
User: Dick Jones

3D0029E6BF
Card Validated
User: Harry Roberts

3D002A7C6C
Card INVALID

3D00768B53
Card Validated
User: Tom Smith
```

The card number will be displayed and then either "Card INVALID" or "Card Validated", followed by the name of the user. If the card is valid, a high-pitched tone will sound and the lock will open for two seconds. If the card is not valid, a low-pitched two-tone beep will sound and the door will not unlock. The 12v electric strike is powered using a transistor to power a higher voltage and current than the Arduino can provide. You used this same principle in Chapter 5 when you drove a DC Motor. Let's see how this project works.

Project 45 – Access Control System – Code Overview

First, you have some definitions for the pins you will be using for the lock and the speaker. Also, you are using the SoftwareSerial.h library instead of the normal serial pins on Digital Pins 0 and 1, so you must define the rx and tx pins. You also have a length, in microseconds, that the lock will open for.

```
#define lockPin 7
#define speakerPin 9
#define tx 3
#define rx 2
#define unlockLength 2000
```

You are using the SoftwareSerial.h library (now a core part of the Arduino IDE) for convenience. If you were using the standard rx and tx pins, you would have to disconnect whatever was connected to those pins every time you wanted to upload any code to the Arduino. By using the SoftwareSerial.h library, you can use any pin you want.

```
#include <SoftwareSerial.h>
```

Next, you create an instance of a SoftwareSerial object and call it rfidReader. You pass to it the rx and tx pins you have defined.

```
SoftwareSerial rfidReader = SoftwareSerial(rx, tx);
```

Next comes a variable to hold the number of users in the database:

```
int users = 3;
```

Next are two arrays to hold the card ID numbers and the names of the cardholders. Change the card numbers those of your own (first 10 digits only).

```
char* cards[] = { // valid cards
  "3D00768B53",
  "3D00251C27",
  "3D0029E6BF",
};

char* names[] = { // cardholder names
  "Tom Smith",
  "Dick Jones",
  "Harry Roberts"
};
```

The setup routine sets the lock and speaker pins as outputs

```
pinMode (lockPin, OUTPUT);
pinMode (speakerPin, OUTPUT);
```

then sets the lock pin to LOW to ensure the lock does not unlock at the start

```
digitalWrite(lockPin, LOW);
```

Then you begin serial communications on the serial port and the SoftwareSerial port:

```
Serial.begin(9600);
rfidReader.begin(9600);
```

Next comes the main loop. You start off by defining the variables that you will use in the loop:

```
char cardNum[10]; // array to hold card number
byte cardBytes[6]; // byte version of card number + checksum
int index=0; // current digit
byte byteIn=0; // byte read from RFID
byte lastByte=0; // the last byte read
byte checksum = 0; // checksum result stored here
```

Next, you check if there is any data coming into the RFID readers serial port. If so, and the first character is ASCII character 2, which is a transmission start code, then you know an ID string is about to be transmitted and can start reading in the digits.

```
if (rfidReader.read()==2) { // read the RFID reader
```

Then comes a whole loop that will run while the index is less than 12:

```
while(index<12) { // 12 digits in unique serial number
```

The `index` variable will hold the value of your current place in the digit you are reading in. As you are reading in a digit of 12 characters in length, you will only read in the first 12 digits.

Next, the value from the serial port is read in and stored in `byteIn`:

```
byteIn = rfidReader.read(); // store value in byteIn
```

Just in case some characters have been missed for any reason, you next check for an occurrence of a transmission start, transmission end, carriage return, or line feed codes. If they are detected, the loop is exited.

```
if ((byteIn==1) || (byteIn==2) || (byteIn==10) || (byteIn==13)) {return;} // if STX, ETX,↩
 CR or LF break
```

The last two digits of the 12 digit string are the checksum. You don't wish to store this in the cardNum array so you only store the first 10 digits:

```
if (index<10) {cardNum[index]=byteIn;} // store first 10 HEX digits only (last 2 are↩
 checksum)
```

Next, you need to convert the ASCII characters you are reading into their hexadecimal number equivalents, so you run an `if-else` statement to determine if the characters are between 0 and 9 and A and Z. If so, they are converted to their hexadecimal equivalents

```
if ((byteIn>='0') && (byteIn<='9')) {
        byteIn -= '0';
}
else if ((byteIn>='A') && (byteIn<='F')) {
        byteIn = (byteIn+10)-'A';
}
```

Logical AND (&&) operators are used to ensure the characters fall between 0 and 9 or between A and Z. Next, you convert the two last hexadecimal digits into a byte. A hexadecimal digit is base sixteen. The number system we normally use is base ten, with digits ranging from 0 to 9. In hexadecimal, the digits go from 0 to 15. The letters A to F are used for numbers 10 to 15. So, the number FF in hex is 255 in decimal:

F = 15
(F * 16) + F = (15 * 16) + 15 = 255

You therefore need to convert the last two ASCII digits into a single byte and the decimal equivalent. You have already declared a variable called `lastByte` which stores the last digit you processed on the last run of the `while` loop. This is initially set to zero. You only need to do this for every second digit as each of the two HEX digits make up a single byte. So you check that the index is an odd number by carrying out bitwise AND (&) operation on the value stored in index with 1 and seeing if the result is also 1. Remember that index starts off as zero, so the second digit has an index of 1.

```
if ((index & 1) == 1) { // if odd number merge 2 4 bit digits into 8 bit byte
```

Any odd number ANDed with 1 will result in 1 and any even number will result in 0:

```
        12 (even) & 1 = 0
        00001100
        00000001 &
=       00000000
```

```
        11 (odd) & 1 = 1
        00001011
        00000001 &
=       00000001
```

If the result determines you are on the second, fourth, sixth, eighth, or twelfth digit, then you store in cardBytes the result of the following calculation:

```
cardBytes[index/2]= (byteIn | (lastByte<<4)); // move the last digit 4 bits left and add↩
 new digit
```

You use index/2 to determine the index number. As index is an integer, only the value before the decimal point will be retained. So for every two digits that the index increments the index for, the cardBytes array will increase by one.

The calculation takes the last byte value and bitshifts it four places to the left. It then takes this number and carries out a bitwise OR (|) operation on it with the current value read. This has the effect of taking the first HEX value, which makes up the first four bits of the number and bit shifting it four places to the left. It then merges this number with the second HEX digit to give us the complete byte. So, if the first digit was 9 and the second was E, the calculation would do this:

```
Lastbyte = 9 =  00001001
00001001 << 4 = 10010000
E = 14 =        00001110
                10010000 OR
=               10011110
```

The checksum is a number you use to ensure that the entire string was read in correctly. Checksums are used a lot in data transmission; they're simply the result of each of the bytes of the entire data string XORed together.

```
if (index<10) {checksum ^= cardBytes[index/2];} // tot up the checksum value
```

The ID number of your first card is:

3D00768B53

Therefore, its checksum will be:

```
3D XOR 00 XOR 76 XOR 8B XOR 53

3D = 00111101
00 = 00000000
76 = 01110110
8B = 10001011
53 = 01010011
```

If you XOR (Exclusive OR) each of these digits to each other, you end up with 93. So 93 is the checksum for that ID number. If any of the digits were transmitted incorrectly due to interference, the checksum will come out as a value different than 93, so you know that the card was not read correctly and you discount it.

Outside of that loop, you set lastByte to the current value so next time around you have a copy of it:

```
lastByte=byteIn; // store the last byte read
```

The index number is incremented:

```
index++; // increment the index
```

If you have reached the end of the string, you must make sure that the tenth digit in the cardNum array is set to the ASCII code for \0 or the null terminator. This is necessary for later on when you need to determine if the end of the string has been reached or not. The null terminator shows that you are at the end of the string.

```
if (index==12) {cardNum[10] = '\0';}
```

Then you print the card number you have read in from the RFID reader:

```
Serial.println(cardNum); // print the card number
```

Next, an integer called cardIndex is created and set to the value returned from the checkCard() function (explained shortly). The checkCard() function will return a positive value if the card number is a valid one from the database and a negative number if it is not.

```
int cardIndex =checkCard(cardNum); // check if card is valid and return index number
```

You then check that the number returned is positive and also that the checksum is correct. If so, the card was read correctly and is valid, so you can unlock the door.

```
if(cardIndex>=0 && (cardBytes[5]==checksum)) { // if card number and checksum are valid
        Serial.println("Card Validated");
        Serial.print("User: ");
        Serial.println(names[cardIndex]); // print the relevant name
        unlock(); // unlock the door
        Serial.println();
    }
```

If the card is not valid or the checksum is incorrect, the card is ascertained to be invalid and the user is informed:

```
else {
        Serial.println("Card INVALID");
        tone(speakerPin, 250, 250);
        delay(250);
        tone(speakerPin, 150, 250);
        Serial.println();
    }
```

Next comes the checkCard() function. It will be returning an integer so this is its type and its parameter is the card number you pass to it.

```
int checkCard(char cardNum[10]) {
```

Next, you cycle through each of the cards in the database to see if it matches the card number you have read in:

```
for (int x=0; x<=users; x++) { // check all valid cards
```

You use a strcmp, or String Compare function, to ascertain if the card number passed to the checkCard() function and the card number in the current location of the database match each other. This is why you need a null terminator at the end of your card number as the strcmp function requires it.

```
if(strcmp(cardNum, cards[x])==0) { // compare with last read card number
```

The strcmp function requires two parameters. These are the two strings you wish to compare. The number returned from the function is a zero if both strings are identical. A non-zero number indicates they don't match. If they do match, you return the value of x, which will be the index in the card and name database of the valid card.

```
return (x); // return index of card number
```

If the cards do not match, you return a -1.

```
return (-1); // negative value indicates no match
}
```

The final function is unlock() which plays a high pitched tone, unlocks the door, waits for a preset length of time, and then relocks the door:

```
void unlock() {
    tone(speakerPin, 1000, 500);
    digitalWrite(lockPin, HIGH);
    delay(unlockLength);
    digitalWrite(lockPin, LOW);
}
```

The next step up from this project would be to add more readers and locks in order to secure your entire home. Authorized users would carry a card or tag to allow them into the relevant rooms. Individual access rights could be given to each user so that they have different access to different parts of the building, only allowing valid users into separate areas.

Now onto the final chapter of this book where you connect your Arduino to the Internet!

Summary

In this chapter you have seen how easy it is to read data from an RFID card or tag and then to use that data to unlock an electric strike lock or to take another kind of action. I have seen projects where an RFID keyfob is attached to a bunch of keys. The RFID reader is in a bowl and when the user gets home they throw their keys into the bowl. The house reacts to that person coming home, e.g. setting their chosen temperature and light levels, playing their favorite music, turning a shower on, etc. When it comes to using an RFID reader, you are only limited by your own imagination.

Subjects and Concepts covered in Chapter 16

- How RFID technology works
- How to connect an ID12 RFID reader to an Arduino
- Reading serial data from an RFID reader
- Using a transistor to control a higher powered device
- Using the SoftwareSerial library
- Converting ASCII to hexadecimal values
- Using bitwise AND to ascertain if a number is odd or even
- Merging two HEX digits using bitshifts and bitwise OR to create a byte
- Creating checksums using XOR (Exclusive OR)
- Using strcmp to compare two strings

CHAPTER 17

■ ■ ■

Communicating over Ethernet

For this final chapter, you are going to take a look at how to connect your Arduino to your router so that data can be sent over an Ethernet cable. By doing this, you can read it from elsewhere on your network. You can also send data out to the Internet so it's viewable via a web browser. You will be using the official Arduino Ethernet Shield to accomplish this.

The ability to connect your Arduino to a network or the internet opens up a whole new list of potential projects. You can send data to websites, like posting Twitter updates. You can also control the Arduino over the Internet or use the Arduino as a web server to serve simple web pages containing sensor data and so on. This chapter will give you the basic knowledge to create your own Ethernet or Internet Arduino-based projects.

Project 46 – Ethernet Shield

You'll now use the Ethernet Shield and a couple of temperature sensors to demonstrate accessing the Arduino over Ethernet.

Parts Required

Arduino Ethernet Shield	
2 × DS18B20 Temperature Sensors	
4.7K ohm Resistor	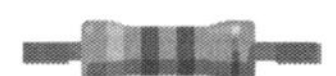

Connect It Up

Insert the Ethernet Shield on top of the Arduino, then connect everything as shown in Figure 17-1 with the wires going into the Ethernet Shield in the same place as they would on an Arduino.

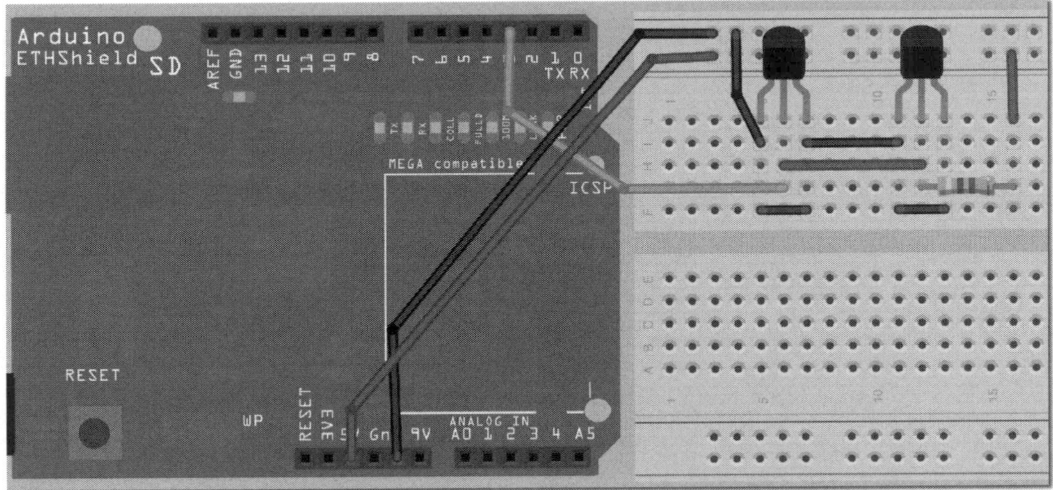

Figure 17-1. The circuit for Project 46 – Ethernet Shield

Enter the Code

Enter the code from Listing 17-1.

Listing 17-1. Code for Project 46

```
// Project 46 - Based on the Arduino Webserver example by David A. Mellis and Tom Igoe

#include <SPI.h>
#include <Ethernet.h>
#include <OneWire.h>
#include <DallasTemperature.h>

// Data wire is plugged into pin 3 on the Arduino
#define ONE_WIRE_BUS 3
#define TEMPERATURE_PRECISION 12

float tempC, tempF;

// Setup a oneWire instance to communicate with any OneWire devices (not just Maxim/Dallas
temperature ICs)
OneWire oneWire(ONE_WIRE_BUS);
```

```
// Pass our oneWire reference to Dallas Temperature.
DallasTemperature sensors(&oneWire);

// arrays to hold device addresses
DeviceAddress insideThermometer = { 0x10, 0x7A, 0x3B, 0xA9, 0x01, 0x08, 0x00, 0xBF };
DeviceAddress outsideThermometer = { 0x10, 0xCD, 0x39, 0xA9, 0x01, 0x08, 0x00, 0xBE};

byte mac[] = { 0x48, 0xC2, 0xA1, 0xF3, 0x8D, 0xB7 };
byte ip[] = { 192,168,0, 104 };

// Start the server on port 80
Server server(80);

void setup()
{
  // Begin ethernet and server
  Ethernet.begin(mac, ip);
  server.begin();
    // Start up the sensors library
  sensors.begin();
    // set the resolution
  sensors.setResolution(insideThermometer, TEMPERATURE_PRECISION);
  sensors.setResolution(outsideThermometer, TEMPERATURE_PRECISION);
}

// function to get the temperature for a device
void getTemperature(DeviceAddress deviceAddress)
{
  tempC = sensors.getTempC(deviceAddress);
  tempF = DallasTemperature::toFahrenheit(tempC);
}
void loop()
{
  sensors.requestTemperatures();

  // listen for incoming clients
  Client client = server.available();
  if (client) {
    // an http request ends with a blank line
    boolean BlankLine = true;
    while (client.connected()) {
      if (client.available()) {
        char c = client.read();

        // If line is blank and end of line is newline character '\n' = end of HTTP request
        if (c == '\n' && BlankLine) {
          getTemperature(insideThermometer);
  client.println("HTTP/1.1 200 OK"); // Standard HTTP response
          client.println("Content-Type: text/html\n");
          client.println("<html><head><META HTTP-EQUIV=""refresh""CONTENT=""5"">\n");
          client.println("<title>Arduino Web Server</title></head>");
          client.println("<body>\n");
```

```
          client.println("<h1>Arduino Web Server</h1>");
          client.println("<h3>Internal Temperature</h3>");
          client.println("Temp C:");
          client.println(tempC);
          client.println("<br/>");
          client.println("Temp F:");
          client.println(tempF);
          client.println("<br/>");
          getTemperature(outsideThermometer);
          client.println("<h3>External Temperature</h3>");
          client.println("Temp C:");
          client.println(tempC);
          client.println("<br/>");
          client.println("Temp F:");
          client.println(tempF);
          client.println("<br/>");

          break;
        }
          if (c == '\n') {
          // Starting a new line
          BlankLine = true;
        }
        else if (c != '\r') {
          // Current line has a character in it
          BlankLine = false;
        }
      }
    }
    // Allow time for the browser to receive data
    delay(10);
    // Close connection
    client.stop();
  }
}
```

You will need to enter the two address numbers of the temperature sensors (See Project 37) in this line:

```
byte ip[] = { 192,168,0, 104 };
```

You will also need to change the IP address to one of your own. To do this, you will need to find out from your router what IP address range has been set aside for devices on your computer. Usually, the address will start off as 192.168.0 or 192.168.1—then you just add another number higher than about 100 to make sure it does not interfere with existing devices. You may also need to go into your router settings to ensure that any HTTP requests to port 80 are forwarded to the IP address of the Ethernet Shield. Look under "Port Forwarding" in your router manual. It may also be necessary to open port 80 in your firewall.

Now, open up your web browser and type in the IP address and port, e.g.

```
192.168.0.104:80
```

If everything is working correctly, you will get the web page shown in Figure 17-2 in your browser.

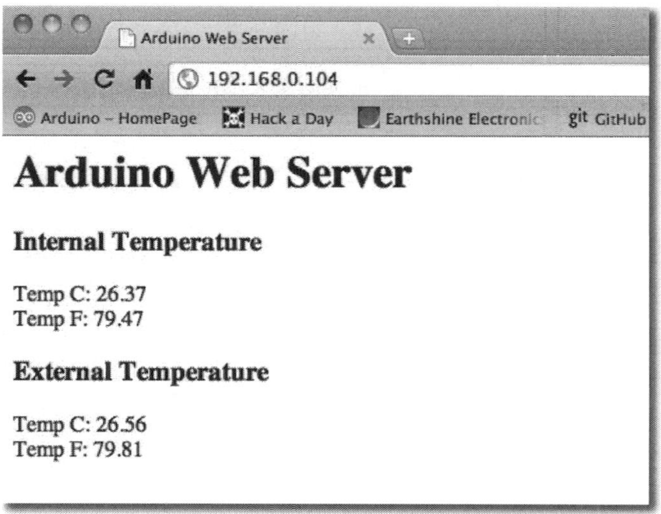

Figure 17-2. The web browser output from the Arduino web server

The page will auto refresh every five seconds to show any changes in the temperatures. If you have set up the port forwarding and firewall correctly in your router, you will also be able to access the page from anywhere that has Internet access. You will need to know the IP address of the router, which can be found from the routers administration page. Type it, followed by the port number, into any web browser, e.g.

```
95.121.118.204:80
```

The above web page will now show up in the browser and you can check the temperature readings from anywhere you have Internet access.

Project 46 – Ethernet Shield – Code Overview

Some parts of this code are repeated from Project 37, so I will gloss over those sections and instead concentrate on the parts relating to the Ethernet Shield. First, you load in the libraries. Make sure you have the libraries for the temperature sensors in your libraries folder first (see Project 37). Note that as of Arduino IDE version 0019, it has been necessary to include the SPI.h library in any project that requires the Ethernet.h library.

```
#include <SPI.h>
#include <Ethernet.h>
#include <OneWire.h>
#include <DallasTemperature.h>
```

Next, the pin and precision for the sensors is set

```
#define ONE_WIRE_BUS 3
#define TEMPERATURE_PRECISION 12
```

along with the two floats you will use to store the temperature in Celsius and Fahrenheit.

```
float tempC, tempF;
```

An instance of the oneWire object is created and you pass a reference to the Dallas Temperature library:

```
OneWire oneWire(ONE_WIRE_BUS);

DallasTemperature sensors(&oneWire);
```

The addresses for the two temperature sensors are set. Remember to find out what these are using the code in Project 37 if necessary.

```
DeviceAddress insideThermometer = { 0x10, 0x7A, 0x3B, 0xA9, 0x01, 0x08, 0x00, 0xBF };
DeviceAddress outsideThermometer = { 0x10, 0xCD, 0x39, 0xA9, 0x01, 0x08, 0x00, 0xBE};
```

Next, you need to define the MAC and IP address of the device:

```
byte mac[] = { 0x48, 0xC2, 0xA1, 0xF3, 0x8D, 0xB7 };
byte ip[] = { 192,168,0, 104 };
```

The MAC (Media Access Control) address is a unique identifier for network interfaces. The network card in your PC or Mac will have had its MAC address set buy the manufacturer. In your case, you are deciding what the MAC address is. It is simply a 48 bit number, so just put any six hexadecimal digits into the address, although leaving it as it is in the code will be fine. The IP address will need to be a manually set and it must be one from the range allowed by your router.

Next, an instance of a server object is created along with the port number for the device:

```
Server server(80);
```

The server will listen for incoming connections on the specified port. A port number is simply a pathway for data. You only have one Ethernet cable going into your device but the port number decides where that data will go. Imagine the MAC address as being the building address of a large apartment block and the port number the individual number of the apartment.

Next comes the setup routine. You start by initializing the Ethernet communications and passing the MAC and IP address of the device to the instance:

```
Ethernet.begin(mac, ip);
```

Now you need to tell your server to start listening to incoming connections using the begin() command:

```
server.begin();
```

You also need to start your sensors and set their resolution:

```
sensors.begin();
sensors.setResolution(insideThermometer, TEMPERATURE_PRECISION);
sensors.setResolution(outsideThermometer, TEMPERATURE_PRECISION);
```

Next, you create the function to obtain the temperatures from the sensor (as done in Project 37):

```
void getTemperature(DeviceAddress deviceAddress)
{
  tempC = sensors.getTempC(deviceAddress);
  tempF = DallasTemperature::toFahrenheit(tempC);
}
```

Next comes the main program loop. First, you request the temperatures from the two sensors:

```
sensors.requestTemperatures();
```

You need to listen for any incoming clients, i.e. web pages requesting to view the web page served by the Arduino. To do this, you create an instance of type Client and use it to check that there is data available for reading from the server. The client is the web browser that will connect to the Arduino. The server is the Arduino.

```
Client client = server.available();
```

Next, you check if a client has connected and if any data is available for it. If true, the `if` statement is executed.

```
if (client) {
```

First, the `if` statement creates a Boolean variable called `BlankLine` and sets it to true:

```
boolean BlankLine = true;
```

A HTTP request from the client will end with a blank line, terminated with a newline character. So you use the `BlankLine` variable to determine if you have reached the end of the data or not.

Next, you check if the client is still connected or not, and if so, run the code within the `while` loop:

```
while (client.connected()) {
```

Next, you check if data is available for the client or not. If data is available, the code within the next `if` statement is executed. The `available()` command returns the number of bytes that have been written to the client by the server it is connected to. If this value is above zero, then the `if` statement runs.

```
if (client.available()) {
```

Then a variable of type char is created to store the next byte received from the server. Use the client.read() command to obtain the byte.

```
char c = client.read();
```

If the character read is a newline ('\n') character, you also need to check if `BlankLine` is true or not. If so, you have reached the end of the HTTP request and so can serve the HTML code to the client (the user's web browser).

```
if (c == '\n' && BlankLine) {
```

Next comes the data you will send out from your server. You start by obtaining the temperature from the internal sensor.

```
getTemperature(insideThermometer);
```

Next comes the HTML code you have to issue to the client. Every page is made up of code called HTML (or HyperText Markup Language). Explaining HTML is beyond the scope of this book, so I will just give some basic information only. If you wish to learn more about HTML, check out the HTML entry on Wikipedia at `http://en.wikipedia.org/wiki/HTML`. There are also plenty of HTML tutorials available on the internet. You use the client.println() command to issue data to the client. Basically, you send out the code to create a web page. If you right click in a web page in most browsers, you will be given the option to view the source code. Try this and you will see the HTML code that makes up the web page you have just been viewing. The code tells the browser what to display and how to display it.

First, you tell the client that you are using HTTP version 1.1, which is the standard protocol used for issuing web pages, and that the content you are about to send is HTML:

```
client.println("HTTP/1.1 200 OK"); // Standard HTTP response
client.println("Content-Type: text/html\n");
```

Next, you have the HTML tag to say that everything from now on will be HTML code and the head tag of the HTML code. The head contains any commands you wish to issue to the browser, scripts you want to run, etc. before the main body of the code. The first command tells the browser that you want the page to automatically refresh every five seconds.

```
client.println("<html><head><META HTTP-EQUIV=""refresh""CONTENT=""5"">\n");
```

Then you give the page a title. It will appear at the top of the browser and in any tabs you have for that page.

```
client.println("<title>Arduino Web Server</title></head>\n");
```

You end the head section by inserting a </head> tag. Next is the body of the HTML. This is the part that will be visible to the user.

```
client.println("<body>\n");
```

You display a <h1> heading saying "Arduino Web Server". H1 is the largest heading, followed by H2, H3, etc.

```
client.println("<h1>Arduino Web Server</h1>");
```

followed by the title of the next section, which is "Internal Temperature" as an h3 heading

```
client.println("<h3>Internal Temperature</h3>");
```

Then, you print the temperature in C and F followed by line breaks <br/>:

```
client.println("Temp C:");
client.println(tempC);
client.println("<br/>");
client.println("Temp F:");
client.println(tempF);
client.println("<br/>");
```

Next, the external temperatures are requested and displayed:

```
getTemperature(outsideThermometer);
client.println("<h3>External Temperature</h3>");
client.println("Temp C:");
client.println(tempC);
client.println("<br/>");
client.println("Temp F:");
client.println(tempF);
client.println("<br/>");
```

Then the `while` loop is exited with a break command:

```
break;
```

You now set `BlankLine` to true if a \n (newline) character is read and false if it is not a \r (Carriage Return), i.e. there are still characters to be read from the server.

```
if (c == '\n') {
        // Starting a new line
BlankLine = true;
}
else if (c != '\r') {
        // Current line has a character in it
BlankLine = false;
}
```

You wait a short delay to allow the browser time to receive the data and then stop the client with a `stop()` command. This disconnects the client from the server.

```
delay(10);
client.stop();
```

This project is a basic introduction to serving a webpage with sensor data embedded in it via the Ethernet Shield. There are nicer ways of presenting data over the Internet and you will look at one of those methods next.

Project 47 – Internet Weather Display

You are now going to use the same parts and circuit, but this time you'll send the temperature data for the two sensors to Pachube. Pachube is an online database service that allows users to connect sensor data to the web (See Figure 17-3). Data can be sent in a variety of formats and shows up in a feed on the website in the form of a graph. The graphs are real-time and can be embedded into a website. You can also view historical data pulled from a feed as well as send alerts to control scripts, devices, etc. There is a series of tutorials on the website dedicated to the Arduino.

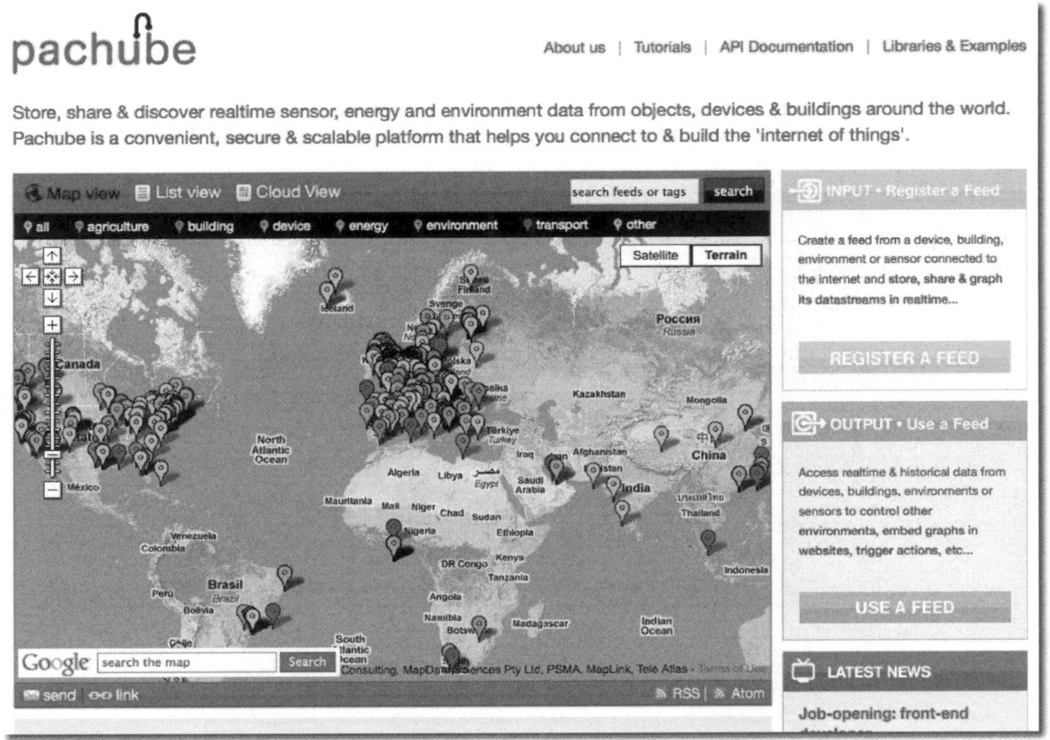

Figure 17-3. The Pachube website

To use the service, you must sign up for a Pachube account. It is an ideal way of displaying data from sensors, home energy monitors, building monitor systems, and so on. There are several levels—from a free service (10 datastreams, 10 updates per minute, and 30 days history stored) through four paid service levels that allow more datastreams, refresh rates, and history lengths.

An account must be created before you can upload data, so start by going to the website at `www.pachube.com` and click the "SIGN UP" button. Pick a plan (you can try any of the services for free for seven days). For this project, use the free service, which is the first option. If you like the service and require more datastreams, you can upgrade to one of the paid services at a later date.

The next page asks you to supply a username, e-mail address, and password. Fill these in and press the "SIGN UP" button. Once you have successfully signed up, you will be logged in and taken back to the main page. Now you need to create a feed. Click the "Register a Feed" button. You now have a feed form to fill out (See Figure 17-4).

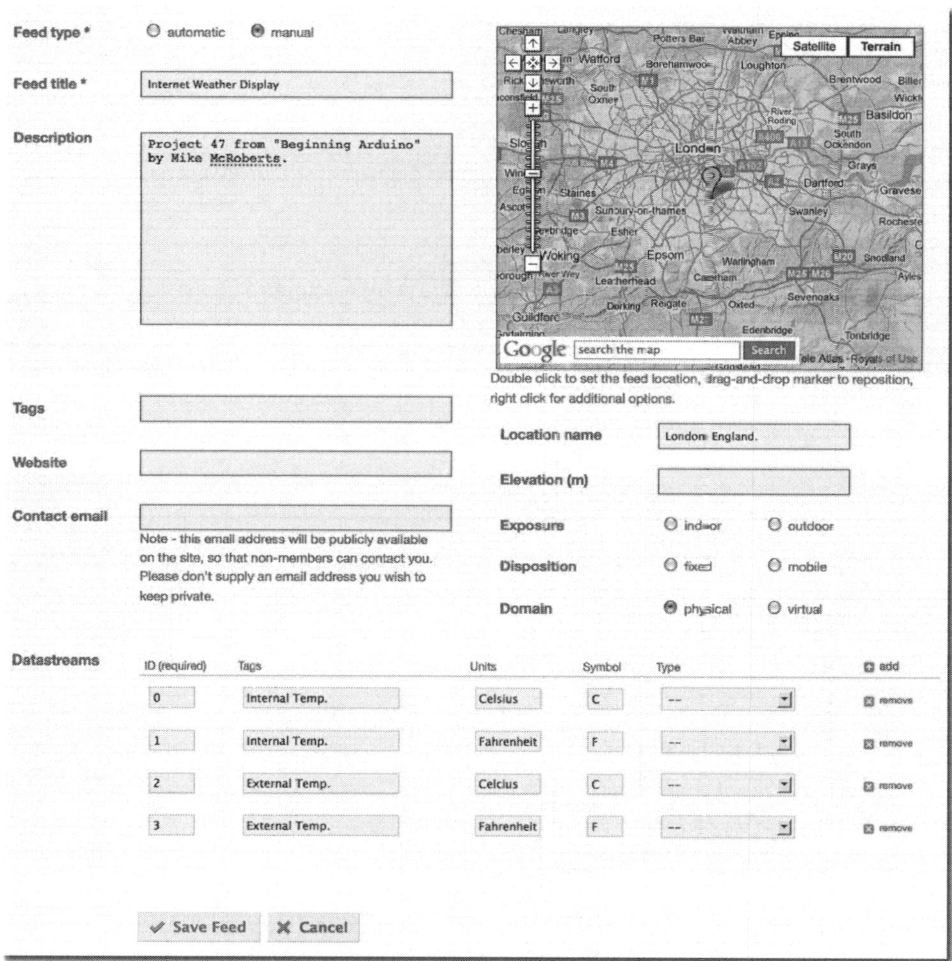

Figure 17-4. The Pachube feed registration page

Choose a manual feed type and enter the title of the feed. You can also chose a location for the feed and enter some data into the description box if you wish. All feeds for the free Pachube service are public, so do not enter any information into the feed registration page that you don't want to be viewed by anyone.

Next, add four feeds. These will be the data feeds from your temperature sensors displaying the internal temperature in both Celsius and Fahrenheit and the external temperatures, too. Leave the ID fields as they are and enter the names of the feeds as well as the units and symbol used as in Figure 17-4.

Once you have entered all of the data successfully, click the "Save Feed" button. This will take you to the feed page you have just created where you will see the names of the datastreams you entered on the registration page.

You now need to obtain some information for the code. First, you need the feed number. Look at the top left of your feed page, underneath the title, at the URL ending in .XML; the number at the end of this URL is your feed number (See Figure 17-5). Write it down.

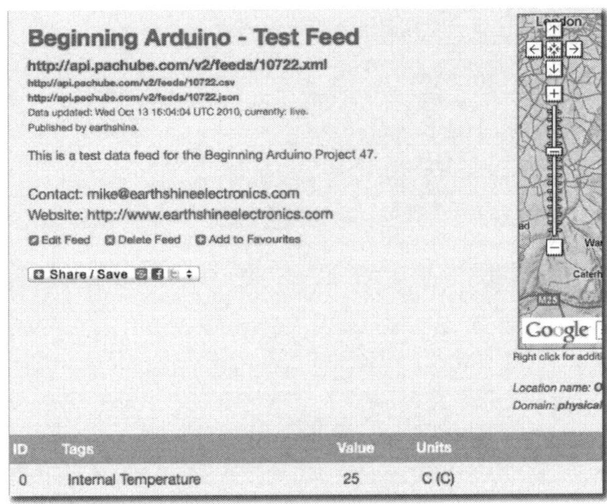

Figure 17-5. The feed number underneath the title

Next, you need your Master API Key. To obtain this click "My Settings" at the top of the page. A long number titled "Your Master API Key" will be displayed (See Figure 17-6). Copy and paste this key into the code.

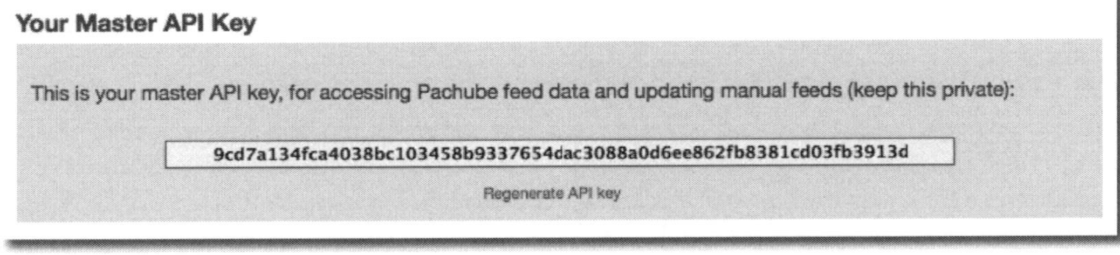

Figure 17-6. The Master API Key

Now that you have these vital pieces of information, you can enter the code.

Enter the Code

Enter the code from Listing 17-2. Thanks to Usman Hague at Pachube for assistance with this project.

Listing 17-2. *Code for Project 47*

```
// Project 47 - Based on the Pachube Arduino examples
#include <SPI.h>
#include <Ethernet.h>
#include <OneWire.h>
#include <DallasTemperature.h>

#define SHARE_FEED_ID  10722     // this is your Pachube feed ID
#define UPDATE_INTERVAL  10000    // if the connection is good wait 10 seconds before
updating again - should not be less than 5
#define RESET_INTERVAL  10000    // if connection fails/resets wait 10 seconds before trying
again - should not be less than 5
#define PACHUBE_API_KEY  "066ed6ea1d1073600e5b44b35e8a399697d66532c3e736c77dc11123dfbfe12f"
// fill in your API key

// Data wire is plugged into pin 3 on the Arduino
#define ONE_WIRE_BUS 3
#define TEMPERATURE_PRECISION 12

// Setup a oneWire instance to communicate with any OneWire devices (not just Maxim/Dallas
temperature ICs)
OneWire oneWire(ONE_WIRE_BUS);

// Pass our oneWire reference to Dallas Temperature.
DallasTemperature sensors(&oneWire);

// arrays to hold device addresses
DeviceAddress insideThermometer = { 0x10, 0x7A, 0x3B, 0xA9, 0x01, 0x08, 0x00, 0xBF };
DeviceAddress outsideThermometer = { 0x10, 0xCD, 0x39, 0xA9, 0x01, 0x08, 0x00, 0xBE};

byte mac[] = { 0xCC, 0xAC, 0xBE, 0xEF, 0xFE, 0x91 }; // make sure this is unique on your
network
byte ip[] = { 192, 168, 0, 104   };                  // no DHCP so we set our own IP address
byte remoteServer[] = { 173, 203, 98, 29 };           // pachube.com

Client localClient(remoteServer, 80);

unsigned int interval;
char buff[64];
int pointer = 0;
char pachube_data[70];
char *found;
boolean ready_to_update = true;
```

```
boolean reading_pachube = false;
boolean request_pause = false;
boolean found_content = false;
unsigned long last_connect;
int content_length;
int itempC, itempF, etempC, etempF;

void setupEthernet(){
  resetEthernetShield();
  delay(500);
  interval = UPDATE_INTERVAL;
  Serial.println("setup complete");
}

void clean_buffer() {
  pointer = 0;
  memset(buff,0,sizeof(buff));
}

void resetEthernetShield(){
  Serial.println("reset ethernet");
  Ethernet.begin(mac, ip);
}

void pachube_out(){
  getTemperatures();
  if (millis() < last_connect) last_connect = millis();

  if (request_pause){
    if ((millis() - last_connect) > interval){
      ready_to_update = true;
      reading_pachube = false;
      request_pause = false;
    }
  }

  if (ready_to_update){
    Serial.println("Connecting...");
    if (localClient.connect()) {

      sprintf(pachube_data,"%d,%d,%d,%d",itempC, itempF, etempC, etempF);
      Serial.print("Sending: ");
      Serial.println(pachube_data);
      content_length = strlen(pachube_data);

      Serial.println("Updating.");

      localClient.print("PUT /v1/feeds/");
      localClient.print(SHARE_FEED_ID);
      localClient.print(".csv HTTP/1.1\nHost: api.pachube.com\nX-PachubeApiKey: ");
      localClient.print(PACHUBE_API_KEY);
      localClient.print("\nUser-Agent: Beginning Arduino - Project 47");
```

```
      localClient.print("\nContent-Type: text/csv\nContent-Length: ");
      localClient.print(content_length);
      localClient.print("\nConnection: close\n\n");
      localClient.print(pachube_data);
      localClient.print("\n");

      ready_to_update = false;
      reading_pachube = true;
      request_pause = false;
      interval = UPDATE_INTERVAL;

    }
    else {
      Serial.print("connection failed!");
      ready_to_update = false;
      reading_pachube = false;
      request_pause = true;
      last_connect = millis();
      interval = RESET_INTERVAL;
      setupEthernet();
    }
  }

  while (reading_pachube){
      while (localClient.available()) {
        checkForResponse();
      }
      if (!localClient.connected()) {
        disconnect_pachube();
      }
  }
}

void disconnect_pachube(){
    Serial.println("disconnecting.\n===============\n\n");
    localClient.stop();
    ready_to_update = false;
    reading_pachube = false;
    request_pause = true;
    last_connect = millis();
    resetEthernetShield();
}

void checkForResponse(){
  char c = localClient.read();
  buff[pointer] = c;
  if (pointer < 64) pointer++;
```

```
  if (c == '\n') {
    found = strstr(buff, "200 OK");
    buff[pointer]=0;
    clean_buffer();
  }
}

// function to get the temperature for a device
void getTemperatures()
{
  sensors.requestTemperatures();
  itempC = sensors.getTempC(insideThermometer);
  itempF = DallasTemperature::toFahrenheit(itempC);
  etempC = sensors.getTempC(outsideThermometer);
  etempF = DallasTemperature::toFahrenheit(etempC);
}

void setup()
{
  Serial.begin(57600);
  setupEthernet();
      // Start up the sensors library
  sensors.begin();
    // set the resolution
  sensors.setResolution(insideThermometer, TEMPERATURE_PRECISION);
  sensors.setResolution(outsideThermometer, TEMPERATURE_PRECISION);
}

void loop()
{
pachube_out();
}
```

Upload the code and then open up the serial monitor. If everything is working correctly and you are successfully sending data to Pachube, the output will look something like:

```
reset ethernet
setup complete
Connecting...
Sending: 25,77,25,77
Updating.
disconnecting.
===============
```

Now open your web browser and go to www.Pachube.com. Navigate to your feed and view the page. The date and time the feed was last updated should be shown below the title along with a green "live" button to show the feed is currently live and receiving data (See Figure 17-7). The graphs should also be showing the temperatures over time. If you leave this for a considerable length of time, you should see the temperature changes throughout the day.

Clicking the buttons above the graphs will give you data for the last hour, last 24 hours, last 4 days, and last 3 months. If you click the graph, it will open a new page showing the graph at full resolution. These graph images can be embedded into your own web page to provide live feed data. There are other graph types in the Pachube app repository as well as apps to let you view the data from your mobile phone. The graphs can also be customized in terms of size, color, grid type, etc.

You can modify the code to add other temperature sensors such as the pressure sensor we used in Project 31, light sensors to measure ambient light, humidity sensors, and wind speed sensors to make a fully fledged weather station with your data logged and accessible over the Internet on Pachube.

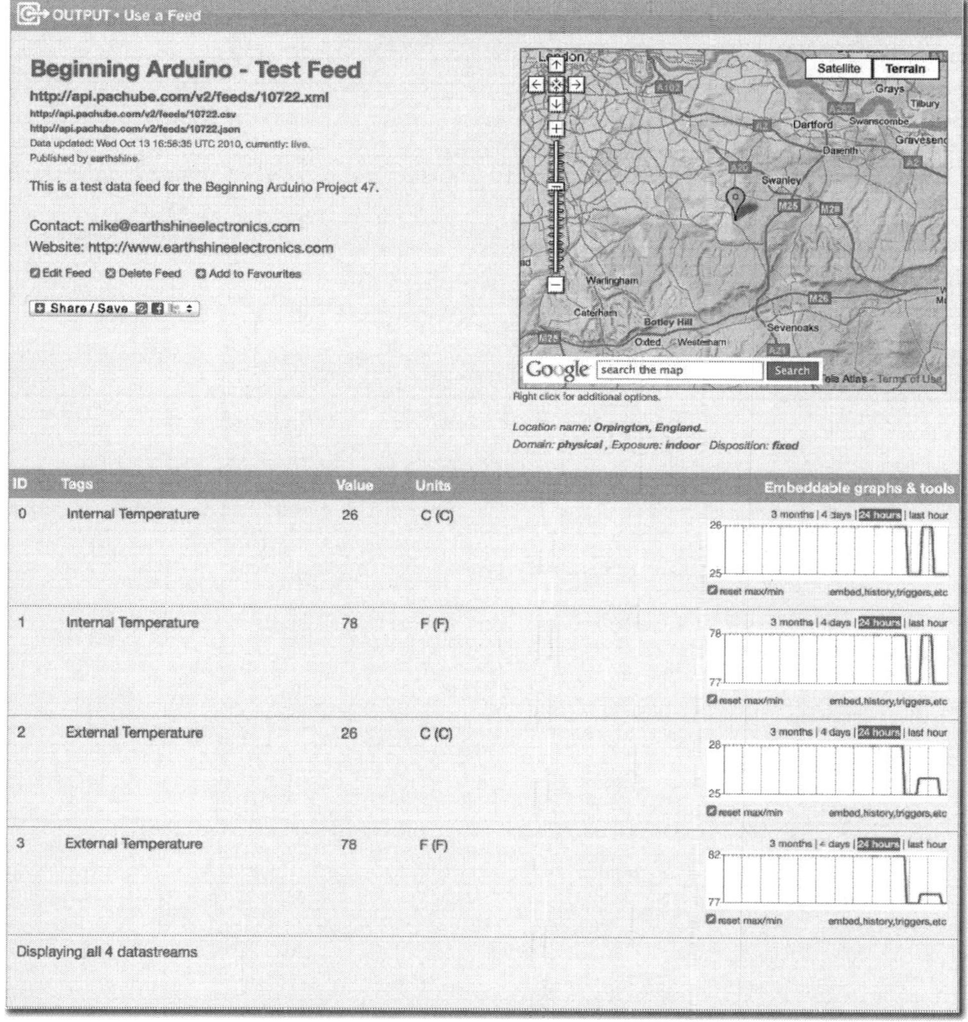

Figure 17-7. *A live Pachube feed page*

Now let's look at the code for this project to see how it works.

Project 47 – Internet Weather Display – Code Overview

The code starts off with the includes for the Ethernet Shield and the one wire temperature sensors:

```
#include <SPI.h>
#include <Ethernet.h>
#include <OneWire.h>
#include <DallasTemperature.h>
```

Next the feed number is defined. You will need to change this number so it matches your own feed ID.

```
#define SHARE_FEED_ID  10722
```

Next you define, in milliseconds, the interval length between data updates to Pachube and also how long to wait in-between connection fails. Make sure these are not below five seconds or you will get an "API key rate-limit warning." If you need more speed for the updates, you can purchase one of the paid subscriptions.

```
#define UPDATE_INTERVAL  10000
#define RESET_INTERVAL  10000
```

Next, you need to define your API key. This is the key from the "my settings" page. Copy and paste it from the page into the code.

```
#define PACHUBE_API_KEY  "066ed6eb e5b449c77dc1d13d66532c3e736073605e8a3a
0969711123dfbfe12f"
```

Then the two defines for the temperature sensors pin and precision are set

```
#define ONE_WIRE_BUS 3
#define TEMPERATURE_PRECISION 12
```

followed by the creation of an instance of a one-wire bus and a DallasTemperature object

```
OneWire oneWire(ONE_WIRE_BUS);

DallasTemperature sensors(&oneWire);
```

Then the serial numbers of the two DS17B20 sensors is set:

```
DeviceAddress insideThermometer = { 0x10, 0x7A, 0x3B, 0xA9, 0x01, 0x08, 0x00, 0xBF };
DeviceAddress outsideThermometer = { 0x10, 0xCD, 0x39, 0xA9, 0x01, 0x08, 0x00, 0xBE};
```

Then you need to enter the MAC and IP address of your Ethernet Shield:

```
byte mac[] = { 0xCC, 0xAC, 0xBE, 0xEF, 0xFE, 0x91 }; // make sure this is unique on your
network
byte ip[] = { 192, 168, 0, 104   };                      // no DHCP so we set our own IP address
```

Then the IP address of the remote server is set (this is the IP address of Pachube.com):

```
byte remoteServer[] = { 173, 203, 98, 29 };
```

Next, you create a Client instance passing the address of Pachube and port 80 to it:

```
Client localClient(remoteServer, 80);
```

Next are all of the variables you will use throughout the program, starting with the interval, in milliseconds, between updates or connection attempts,

```
unsigned int interval;
```

an array to hold characters read back from Pachube,

```
char buff[64];
```

a pointer, or index for the above array,

```
int pointer = 0;
```

an array to hold the string you will send to Pachube (make this longer if you are sending long data strings),

```
char pachube_data[70];
```

a variable to hold the result of a string compare function later on when you check to see that the data has been received by the feed correctly,

```
char *found;
```

a series of self-explanatory Booleans,

```
boolean ready_to_update = true;
boolean reading_pachube = false;
boolean request_pause = false;
boolean found_content = false;
```

the time, in milliseconds, since the last connection, which will be compared with the interval time you have set and the value in `millis()` to decide of you need to do another update or not,

```
unsigned long last_connect;
```

the length of the data string you will send to Pachube,

```
int content_length;
```

and finally, the temperatures in C and F from your sensors.

```
int itempC, itempF, etempC, etempF;
```

Next comes the first in a series of functions used throughout the sketch. The first function is `setupEthernet()`, which resets the Ethernet connection and updates the interval setting:

```
void setupEthernet(){
  resetEthernetShield();
  delay(500);
  interval = UPDATE_INTERVAL;
  Serial.println("setup complete");
}
```

Next comes the `clean_buffer()` function to clear the buffer and fill it with the value of zero:

```
void clean_buffer() {
```

First, the pointer (array index) is set to zero:

```
pointer = 0;
```

Then you use a memset command to fill the buffers memory space with the value zero:

```
memset(buff,0,sizeof(buff));
```

The memset command is something new. Its job is to set a certain number of bytes in memory to a specified value. It requires three parameters: a pointer to the block of memory to fill, the value to be set, and the number of bytes to set.

In your case, you pass it buff as the first parameter, so it points to the first byte in memory where buff is stored. It then writes the value 0 to that memory block and every block up to `sizeof(buff)`. The sizeof() command returns the size of the array in bytes.

The job of memset has been to fill the memory taken up by the buff array with 0 so it is cleaned of all data that may have been written previously.

Next comes the `resetEthernetShield()` function, which does exactly that by simply carrying out an Ethernet.begin command to reset the shield each time it's called:

```
void resetEthernetShield(){
  Serial.println("reset ethernet");
  Ethernet.begin(mac, ip);
}
```

Next comes the large function that has the job of sending the sensor data out to the internet and to the Pachube feed page:

```
void pachube_out(){
```

You start off by calling the getTemperatures() function so you have the readings from both sensors stored:

```
getTemperatures();
```

Then you check if the current value in millis() is smaller than the value stored in last_connect. If it is, then last_connect is updated to the current value of millis(). The value in last_connect will be updated to the value in millis() every time you disconnect from Pachube. You will use this value to see how many milliseconds have passed since you last connected.

```
if (millis() < last_connect) last_connect = millis();
```

Next is an if statement that runs if request_pause is true. This variable is only set to true if the connection has failed or if you have just disconnected from Pachube.

```
  if (request_pause){
```

Inside it you check if the current value in last_connect subtracted from the value in mills() is greater than the interval value. If it is, then the interval period has passed and the three flags are set to true or false respectively.

```
if ((millis() - last_connect) > interval){
      ready_to_update = true;
      reading_pachube = false;
      request_pause = false;
}
```

These flags tell the pachube_out() function that the interval has passed since your last connection or connection attempt and you are therefore ready to attempt the next update. If you are ready to update, the next if statement runs.

```
if (ready_to_update){
```

It starts off by informing the user you are connecting

```
Serial.println("Connecting...");
```

then checks that you have successfully connected to the client

```
if (localClient.connect()) {
```

and if so, runs the rest of the code to update the feed. First, you use a sprintf command to print to a string your formatted data. The sprintf (string print formatted) command is an excellent way of packing lots of different bits of information into one string.

```
sprintf(pachube_data,"%d,%d,%d,%d",itempC, itempF, etempC, etempF);
```

It takes three parameters: variable where you will store the formatted data (in this case, pachube_data), the contents of the string with specifiers, then the variables. What this does is insert the first variable into the string where the first %d appears, the second variable where the next %d appears, and so on. The four specifiers are separated by commas so the numbers will be separated by commas in the final string. So, if the values of the variables were

```
itempC          25
itempF          77
etempC          14
tempF           52
```

then, after running the sprintf command, the contents of pachube_data will be

```
"25,77,14,52"
```

If the sprintf command was

```
sprintf(pachube_data,"Internal Temps: %d,%d External Temps: %d,%d",itempC, itempF, etempC,
etempF);
```

then pachube_data will store

```
"Internal Temps: 25,77 External Temps: 14,52"
```

As you can see, the sprintf command is a powerful tool for converting longs mixes of strings and numbers into one string.

Next, you inform the user of what data you are sending

```
Serial.print("Sending: ");
Serial.println(pachube_data);
```

then work out the length of the string in pachube_data using the `strlen()` function

```
content_length = strlen(pachube_data);
```

and inform the user that you are about to update the feed.

```
Serial.println("Updating.");
```

Then you print data to the localCient. To do this, you build up a string that is sent to the URL of your feed. The first part of the string is the URL of the feed, including the feed ID, followed by the API key

```
localClient.print("PUT /v1/feeds/");
localClient.print(SHARE_FEED_ID);
localClient.print(".csv HTTP/1.1\nHost: api.pachube.com\nX-PachubeApiKey: ");
localClient.print(PACHUBE_API_KEY);
```

followed by the name of the user agent, the length of the data you are about to send, followed by the string of sensor data to the .csv (comma separated values) file.

Next, you send the user agent. This is an HTTP command that usually identifies what software is being used as a part of the client-server conversation. The User-Agent request-header field contains information about the user agent originating the request. It isn't necessary at all but it is considered good behavior to identify the client code.

```
localClient.print("\nUser-Agent: Beginning Arduino - Project 47");
```

Then you tell the client what type the content is and its length. In your case, it's a text file of the .csv file type.

```
localClient.print("\nContent-Type: text/csv\nContent-Length: ");
localClient.print(content_length);
localClient.print("\nConnection: close\n\n");
```

Finally, there's the string of comma separated sensor values:

```
localClient.print(pachube_data);
localClient.print("\n");
```

The flags are all set back to their default values:

```
ready_to_update = false;
reading_pachube = true;
request_pause = false;
interval = UPDATE_INTERVAL;
}
```

If you were unable to connect, you tell the user and set the appropriate flags, then resets the Ethernet connection:

```
else {
      Serial.print("connection failed!");
      ready_to_update = false;
      reading_pachube = false;
      request_pause = true;
      last_connect = millis();
      interval = RESET_INTERVAL;
      setupEthernet();
}
```

Next is a `while` statement to check of reading_pachube is true; if so, it checks if the localClient has data available, i.e. a response has been sent back from Pachube and if so, it calls the `checkForResponse()` function. If the localClient is not connected, it disconnects from Pachube by running the `disconnect_pachube()` function.

```
while (reading_pachube){
      while (localClient.available()) {
        checkForResponse();
      }
```

```
        if (!localClient.connected()) {
          disconnect_pachube();
        }
    }
}
```

The disconnect_pachube() function informs the user you are disconnecting, stops the localClient, sets the flags to their default values, and resets the Ethernet shield:

```
void disconnect_pachube(){
    Serial.println("disconnecting.\n===============\n\n");
    localClient.stop();
    ready_to_update = false;
    reading_pachube = false;
    request_pause = true;
    last_connect = millis();
    resetEthernetShield();
}
```

The checkForResponse() function has the job of checking that the client (Pachube) has sent back a "200 OK" command, which tells you that the sending of the data was successful. Then it checks you are at the end of the string being sent back (\n) and if so, clears the buffer ready for next time.

```
void checkForResponse(){
```

The read() command is used to receive a byte from the client and store it in c:

```
char c = localClient.read();
```

The byte received is stored in the buff array:

```
buff[pointer] = c;
```

If you have not gone over 64 bytes in length (the size of the array), the index is incremented:

```
if (pointer < 64) pointer++;
```

The value in c is checked to see if you have received the end of the string

```
if (c == '\n') {
```

and if so, you use the strstr command to see if "200 OK" appears somewhere in the string and returns a pointer to its location, which is stored in found.

```
found = strstr(buff, "200 OK");
```

The strstr command finds a sub-string inside another string. It requires two parameters: the first is the string you are checking and the second is the sub-string you wish to locate. If the sub-string is found, it returns the location of the sub-string and if not, it returns a null pointer.

The buffer is then reset and cleaned:

```
buff[pointer]=0;
clean_buffer();
```

Next is the final function to obtain the temperatures from the DS18B20s:

```
void getTemperatures()
{
  sensors.requestTemperatures();
  itempC = sensors.getTempC(insideThermometer);
  itempF = DallasTemperature::toFahrenheit(itempC);
  etempC = sensors.getTempC(outsideThermometer);
  etempF = DallasTemperature::toFahrenheit(etempC);
}
```

After you have defined all of your functions, you arrive at the setup routine

```
void setup()
```

that starts off by beginning serial communications at 57600 baud

```
Serial.begin(57600);
```

then calls the `setupEthernet()` function.

```
setupEthernet();
```

The one-wire sensors are started and their resolution is set:

```
sensors.begin();
sensors.setResolution(insideThermometer, TEMPERATURE_PRECISION);
sensors.setResolution(outsideThermometer, TEMPERATURE_PRECISION);
```

All that is left is for the main loop to simply do nothing else except call the `pachube_out` function over and over:

```
void loop()
{
        pachube_out();
}
```

Now that you know the basic methods of sending sensor data to Pachube to be stored and viewed, it will be a relatively easy task for you to modify the code to add further sensors or other data.

So far, you have learned how to send data over Ethernet to a web browser on the network, to a web browser over the Internet, and to the Pachube data storage and graphing service. Next, you will learn how to make the Arduino send an e-mail to alert you when the temperatures get too hot or too cold.

EXERCISE

In the C programming language, you can use %f with sprintf to print floats. However, this does not work with the Arduino version of C; only integers are printed. Modify the code so that the temperatures are sent as floating point numbers. Hint: You have converted digits to strings manually elsewhere in the book.

Project 48 – Email Alert System

You are now going to look at a different method of sending data. In this project, you will get the Arduino with the Ethernet Shield to send an e-mail when a temperature is either too cold or too hot. This project is designed to show you the basics of sending an e-mail via the Ethernet Shield. You'll use the same circuit but with just one of the temperature sensors.

Enter the Code

Enter the code from Listing 17-3. You will need to obtain the IP address of your SMTP email server. To do this, open up a terminal window (command window, console, whatever you know it as on your system) and type in ping, followed by the web address you wish to obtain the IP address of. In other words, if you wanted to know the IP address of the Hotmail SMTP server at smtp.live.com , you would type

```
ping smtp.live.com
```

and you will get back a reply similar to

```
PING smtp.hot.glbdns.microsoft.com (65.55.162.200): 56 data bytes
```

This shows you that the IP address is 65.55.162.200. Do this for the SMTP server of your e-mail service and enter this into the server section of the code. If your SMTP server requires authentication, you will need to obtain the Base-64 version of your username and password. There are many websites that will do this for you, such as

```
www.motobit.com/util/base64-decoder-encoder.asp
```

Enter your username and encrypt it to Base-64 and then do the same with your password. Copy and paste the results into the relevant section in the code. Also, change the FROM and TO sections of the code to your own e-mail address and the e-mail address of the recipient.

Listing 17-3. Code for Project 48

```
// Project 48 - Email Alert System

#include <Ethernet.h>
#include <SPI.h>
#include <OneWire.h>
#include <DallasTemperature.h>
```

```
#define time 1000
#define emailInterval 60
#define HighThreshold 40 // Highest temperature allowed
#define LowThreshold 10 // Lowest temperature

// Data wire is plugged into pin 3 on the Arduino
#define ONE_WIRE_BUS 3
#define TEMPERATURE_PRECISION 12

float tempC, tempF;
char message1[35], message2[35];
char subject[] = "ARDUINO: TEMPERATURE ALERT!!\0";
unsigned long lastMessage;

// Setup a oneWire instance to communicate with any OneWire devices
OneWire oneWire(ONE_WIRE_BUS);

// Pass our oneWire reference to Dallas Temperature.
DallasTemperature sensors(&oneWire);

// arrays to hold device addresses
DeviceAddress insideThermometer = { 0x10, 0x7A, 0x3B, 0xA9, 0x01, 0x08, 0x00, 0xBF };

byte mac[] = { 0x64, 0xB9, 0xE8, 0xC3, 0xC7, 0xE2 };
byte ip[] = { 192,168,0, 105 };
byte server[] = { 62, 234, 219, 95 };  // Mail server address. Change this to your own mail
servers IP.

Client client(server, 25);

void sendEmail(char subject[], char message1[], char message2[], float temp) {
  Serial.println("connecting...");

 if (client.connect()) {
   Serial.println("connected");
   client.println("EHLO MYSERVER");  delay(time); // log in
   client.println("AUTH LOGIN"); delay(time); // authorise
   // enter your username here
   client.println("caFzLmNvbQaWNZXGluZWVsZWNOcm9uNAZW2FsydGhzd3");  delay(time);
   // and password here
   client.println("ZnZJh4TYZ2ds");  delay(time);
   client.println("MAIL FROM:<alert@bobsmith.org>");      delay(time);
   client.println("RCPT TO:<fred@bloggs.com>");      delay(time);
   client.println("DATA");       delay(time);
   client.println("From: <alert@bobsmith.org>");       delay(time);
   client.println("To: <fred@bloggs.com>");       delay(time);
   client.print("SUBJECT: ");
   client.println(subject);       delay(time);
   client.println();      delay(time);
   client.println(message1);      delay(time);
   client.println(message2);      delay(time);
   client.print("Temperature: ");
```

```
    client.println(temp);   delay(time);
    client.println(".");      delay(time);
    client.println("QUIT");      delay(time);
    Serial.println("Email sent.");
    lastMessage=millis();
  } else {
    Serial.println("connection failed");
  }

}

void checkEmail() { // see if any data is available from client
  while (client.available()) {
    char c = client.read();
    Serial.print(c);
  }

 if (!client.connected()) {
    Serial.println();
    Serial.println("disconnecting.");
    client.stop();
  }
}

// function to get the temperature for a device
void getTemperature(DeviceAddress deviceAddress)
{
  tempC = sensors.getTempC(deviceAddress);
  tempF = DallasTemperature::toFahrenheit(tempC);
}

void setup()
{
 lastMessage = 0;
 Ethernet.begin(mac, ip);
 Serial.begin(9600);

     // Start up the sensors library
  sensors.begin();
    // set the resolution
  sensors.setResolution(insideThermometer, TEMPERATURE_PRECISION);

 delay(1000);
}

void loop()
{
  sensors.requestTemperatures();
  getTemperature(insideThermometer);
  Serial.println(tempC);
```

```
// Is it too hot?
if (tempC >= HighThreshold && (millis()>(lastMessage+(emailInterval*1000)))) {
    Serial.println("High Threshhold Exceeded");
    char message1[] = "Temperature Sensor\0";
    char message2[] = "High Threshold Exceeded\0";
    sendEmail(subject, message1, message2, tempC);
  } // too cold?
else if (tempC<= LowThreshold && (millis()>(lastMessage+(emailInterval*1000))))
    Serial.println("Low Threshhold Exceeded");
    char message1[] = "Temperature Sensor\0";
    char message2[] = "Low Threshold Exceeded\0";
    sendEmail(subject, message1, message2, tempC);
  }

    if (client.available()) {checkEmail();}
}
```

Upload the code and then open up the serial monitor window. The serial monitor will display the temperature from the first sensor over and over. If the temperature drops below the LowThreshold value, the serial monitor will display "Low Threshold Exceeded" and then send the relevant e-mail alert. If the temperature goes above the HighThreshold, it will displays "High Threshold Exceeded" and send the appropriate alert for a high temperature situation.

You can test this by setting the high threshold to be just above the ambient temperature and then holding the sensor until the temperature rises above the threshold. This will set the alert system into action.

Note that for the first 60 seconds the system will ignore any temperature alert situations. It will only start sending alerts once 60 seconds have passed. If the thresholds have been breached, the alert system will keep sending e-mails until the temperature drops to within acceptable levels. E-mails will be sent every `emailInterval` seconds while the thresholds have been breached. You can adjust this interval to your own settings.

After an e-mail is sent, the system will wait until a successful receipt has been received back from the client, and then it will display the response. You can use this data to debug the system if things do not work as planned.

Project 48 – Email Alert System – Code Overview

First, the libraries are included:

```
#include <Ethernet.h>
#include <SPI.h>
#include <OneWire.h>
#include <DallasTemperature.h>
```

Next, you define the delay, in milliseconds, when sending data to the server

```
#define time 1000
```

followed by a time, in seconds, in-between e-mails being sent.

```
#define emailInterval 60
```

Then you need to set the temperature high and low levels that will cause an alert:

```
#define HighThreshold 40 // Highest temperature allowed
#define LowThreshold 10 // Lowest temperature
```

Next, you set the pin and precision for the sensors

```
#define ONE_WIRE_BUS 3
#define TEMPERATURE_PRECISION 12
```

and the floats to store the temperatures,

```
float tempC, tempF;
```

then two character arrays that will store the message in the e-mail

```
char message1[35], message2[35];
```

plus another character array to store the subject of the e-mail. This is declared and initialized:

```
char subject[] = "ARDUINO: TEMPERATURE ALERT!!\0";
```

As you don't want to bombard the user with e-mail messages once the thresholds have been breached, you need to store the time the last e-mail was sent. This will be stored in an unsigned integer called lastMessage:

```
unsigned long lastMessage;
```

The instances for the sensor are set up along with the sensor address:

```
OneWire oneWire(ONE_WIRE_BUS);
DallasTemperature sensors(&oneWire);

DeviceAddress insideThermometer = { 0x10, 0x7A, 0x3B, 0xA9, 0x01, 0x08, 0x00, 0xBF };
```

The MAC and IP address of the Ethernet Shield is defined:

```
byte mac[] = { 0x64, 0xB9, 0xE8, 0xC3, 0xC7, 0xE2 };
byte ip[] = { 192,168,0, 105 };
```

Then you set the IP address of your e-mail SMTP server. This must be changed to your own one or the code will not work.

```
byte server[] = { 62, 234, 219, 95 };
```

A client instance is created and you pass it the server address and port number 25. If your SMTP server uses a different port, change this as required.

```
Client client(server, 25);
```

Next comes the first of your own functions. This one does the job of sending the e-mail to the server. The function requires four parameters: the e-mail subject, the first line of the message, the second line of the message, and finally, the temperature.

```
void sendEmail(char subject[], char message1[], char message2[], float temp) {
```

The user is advised that you are attempting to connect:

```
Serial.println("connecting...");
```

Then you check if the client has connected. If so, the code within the `if`-block is executed.

```
if (client.connect()) {
```

First, the user is informed that you have connected to the client. The client in this case is your e-mail SMTP server.

```
Serial.println("connected");
```

You now send commands to the server in pretty much the same way that you did in Project 46. First, you must introduce yourselves to the SMTP server. This is done with an EHLO command and the server details. After each command, you must wait a while to allow the command to be processed. I found 1000 milliseconds was required for my server; you may need to increase or decrease this number accordingly.

```
client.println("EHLO MYSERVER");  delay(time); // log in
```

This is like a shake hands procedure between the server and the client where they introduce themselves to each other. Next, you need to authorize the connection. If your SMTP server does not require authorization, you can comment out this line and the username and password lines.

```
client.println("AUTH LOGIN"); delay(time); // authorise
```

Sometimes the server requires an unencrypted login, in which case you would send AUTH PLAIN and the username and password in plain text.

Next, the Base-64 encrypted username and password must be sent to the server:

```
client.println("caFzLmNvbQaWNZXGluZWVsZWNOcm9uNAZW2FsydGhzd3");  delay(time);
client.println("ZnZJh4TYZ2ds");  delay(time);
```

Then you need to tell the server who the mail is coming from and who the mail is going to:

```
client.println("MAIL FROM:<alert@bobsmith.org>");      delay(time);
client.println("RCPT TO:<fred@bloggs.com>");      delay(time);
```

These must be changed to your own e-mail address and the address of the recipient. Most SMTP servers will only allow you to send e-mail using an e-mail address from its own domain (e.g. you cannot send an e-mail from a Hotmail account using a Yahoo server.)

Next is the DATA command to tell the server that what comes next is the e-mail data, i.e. the stuff that will be visible to the recipient.

```
client.println("DATA");       delay(time);
```

You want the recipient to see whom the e-mail is to and from, so these are included again for the recipient's benefit.

```
client.println("From: <alert@bobsmith.org>");       delay(time);
client.println("To: <fred@bloggs.com>");       delay(time);
```

Next, you send the e-mail subject. This is the word "SUBJECT:" followed by the subject passed to the function:

```
client.print("SUBJECT: ");
client.println(subject);      delay(time);
```

Before the body of the e-mail, you must send a blank line

```
client.println();      delay(time);
```

followed by the two lines of the message passed to the function.

```
client.println(message1);      delay(time);
client.println(message2);      delay(time);
```

Then you include the temperature:

```
client.print("Temperature: ");
client.println(temp);   delay(time);
```

All e-mails must end with a . on a line of its own to tell the server you have finished:

```
client.println(".");      delay(time);
```

Then you send a QUIT command to disconnect from the server:

```
client.println("QUIT");      delay(time);
```

Finally, the user is informed that the e-mail has been sent:

```
Serial.println("Email sent.");
```

Next, you store the current value of millis() in lastMessage as you will use that later to see if the specified interval has passed or not in-between message sends.

```
lastMessage=millis();
```

If the connection to the client was not successful, the e-mail is not sent and the user informed:

```
 } else {
   Serial.println("connection failed");
 }
```

Next comes the function to read the response back from the client:

```
void checkEmail() { // see if any data is available from client
```

While data is available to be read back from the client

```
while (client.available()) {
```

you store that byte in c

```
char c = client.read();
```

and then print it to the serial monitor window.

```
Serial.print(c);
```

If the client is NOT connected

```
if (!client.connected()) {
```

then the user is informed, the system is disconnecting, and the client connected is stopped.

```
Serial.println();
Serial.println("disconnecting.");
client.stop();
```

Next is the function you have used before to obtain the temperature from the one-wire sensor

```
void getTemperature(DeviceAddress deviceAddress)
{
  tempC = sensors.getTempC(deviceAddress);
  tempF = DallasTemperature::toFahrenheit(tempC);
}
```

followed by the setup routine that simply sets up the Ethernet and sensors.

```
void setup()
{
Ethernet.begin(mac, ip);
 Serial.begin(9600);

     // Start up the sensors library
  sensors.begin();
    // set the resolution
  sensors.setResolution(insideThermometer, TEMPERATURE_PRECISION);

 delay(1000);
}
```

Finally, there's the main program loop:

```
void loop()
```

You start off by requesting the temperatures from the DallasTemperature library

```
sensors.requestTemperatures();
```

then call your `getTemperature` function, passing it the address of the sensor

```
getTemperature(insideThermometer);
```

that is then displayed in the serial monitor window.

```
Serial.println(tempC);
```

Next you check that temperature to see if it has reached or exceeded your high threshold. If it has, then the appropriate e-mail is sent. However, you only want to send one e-mail every (`emailInterval*1000`) seconds so check also that `millis()` is greater than the last time the e-mail message was sent (`lastMessage`) plus the interval time. If true, the code is executed.

```
if (tempC >= HighThreshold && (millis()>(lastMessage+(emailInterval*1000)))) {
```

The user is informed and then the two lines that make up the e-mail message are sent:

```
Serial.println("High Threshhold Exceeded");
char message1[] = "Temperature Sensor\0";
char message2[] = "High Threshold Exceeded\0";
```

The `sendEmail` function is then called, passing it the parameters that make up the subject, message line one and two, and the current temperature:

```
    sendEmail(subject, message1, message2, tempC);
```

If the high teperature threshold has not been reached, you check if it has dropped below the low temperature threshold. If so, carry out the same procedure with the appropriate message.

```
else if (tempC<= LowThreshold && (millis()>(lastMessage+(emailInterval*1000))))
    Serial.println("Low Threshhold Exceeded");
    char message1[] = "Temperature Sensor\0";
    char message2[] = "Low Threshold Exceeded\0";
    sendEmail(subject, message1, message2, tempC);
  }
```

Finally, you check if there is any data ready to be received back from the client (after an e-mail has been sent) and display the results:

```
if (client.available()) {checkEmail();}
```

This data is useful for debugging purposes.

This project has given you the basic knowledge for sending an e-mail from an Arduino with Ethernet Shield. You can use this to send alerts or report whenever an action has occurred, such as a person has been detected entering a room or a box has been opened. The system can also take other actions, i.e. to open a window if the temperature in a room gets too hot or to top up a fish tank if the water level drops too low.

Next, you will learn how to send data from an Arduino to Twitter.

Project 49 – Twitterbot

Again you will use the circuit with the two temperature sensors. This time you will send regular updates about the status of the two sensors to Twitter. This will give you a simple system for checking on the status of any sensors you have connected to the Arduino.

Twitter is a microblogging service that allows you to send miniature blog posts or "tweets" of up to 140 characters in length. The tweets are publically accessible to anyone who does a search or to those persons who have chosen to subscribe to (or follow) your blog. Twitter is incredibly popular and can be accessed from any web browser or from one of the many Twitter clients that are available, including mobile phone apps. This makes it ideal for sending simple short pieces of information that you can check while on the move.

You will need to go to Twitter.com and create a new account. I recommend creating an account just for tweeting from your Arduino.

As of August 31,2010, Twitter changed its policy regarding third party apps accessing the website. An authentication method known as OAuth is now used that makes it very difficult to tweet directly from an Arduino; prior to this change it was an easy process. Tweeting, at the moment, can only be done via a third party. In other words, you sending the tweet to a website, or proxy, that will tweet on your behalf using the OAuth token (authorization code). The current Twitter library uses this method.

Once you have your account set up, enter the code below.

Enter the Code

At the time this book was written, the Ethernet libraries that the Twitter library relies on currently only work with the Arduino IDE version 0018. You will therefore need to visit the Arduino website, navigate to the download page, and obtain the IDE version 0018. Make sure you only run and upload the code from this version of the IDE. Keep it separate from your current version of the IDE. The EthernetDNS and EthernetDHCP libraries that are used by the Twitter library can be found at http://gkaindl.com/software/arduino-ethernet. Once this library has been updated to work with the latest IDE you can use it instead.

Before you upload the code, you will need a token for the Twitter account. The library you are using has been created by NeoCat and uses his website as a proxy for sending the tweet. This means you must first obtain a token, which is an encrypted version of your username and password, to access the Twitter website. To do this visit NeoCat's website at http://arduino-tweet.appspot.com and click on the "Step 1" link to obtain the token. Copy and paste this into the token section of the code.

Note that because you are using a proxy and have to give your Twitter username and password over to obtain the token, it is advisable to create a new twitter account and keep it anonymous (i.e. don't add any names or e-mail addresses into the Twitter profile of that account). I am sure that it is perfectly safe to use the library with your own account if you wish, but it is better to be safe than sorry.

Next, click the "Step 2" link and obtain the two sets of libraries that the code relies on. Install these in the libraries folder of the 0018 version of the Arduino IDE you downloaded and installed earlier. You will need to restart the IDE before you can use these. The Twitter library also comes with a few examples you can try out. If you wish to read up about the Twitter library you can find it on the Arduino playground at www.arduino.cc/playground/Code/TwitterLibrary.

Once you have your token and libraries installed, enter and upload the code in Listing 17-4.

Listing 17-4. *Code for Project 49*

```
// Project 49 - Twitterbot

#include <Ethernet.h>
#include <EthernetDHCP.h>
#include <EthernetDNS.h>
#include <Twitter.h>
#include <OneWire.h>
#include <DallasTemperature.h>

// Data wire is plugged into pin 3 on the Arduino
#define ONE_WIRE_BUS 3
#define TEMPERATURE_PRECISION 12

float itempC, itempF, etempC, etempF;
boolean firstTweet = true;
// Setup a oneWire instance to communicate with any OneWire devices (not just Maxim/Dallas
temperature ICs)
OneWire oneWire(ONE_WIRE_BUS);

// Pass our oneWire reference to Dallas Temperature.
DallasTemperature sensors(&oneWire);

// arrays to hold device addresses
DeviceAddress insideThermometer = { 0x10, 0x7A, 0x3B, 0xA9, 0x01, 0x08, 0x00, 0xBF };
DeviceAddress outsideThermometer = { 0x10, 0xCD, 0x39, 0xA9, 0x01, 0x08, 0x00, 0xBE};

byte mac[] = { 0x64, 0xB9, 0xE8, 0xC3, 0xC7, 0xE2 };

// Your Token to tweet (get it from http://arduino-tweet.appspot.com/)
Twitter twitter("608048201-CxY1yQi8ezhvjz6OZVfPHVdzIHbMOD1h2gvoaAIx");

unsigned long interval = 600000; // 10 minutes
unsigned long lastTime; // time since last tweet

// Message to post
char message[140], serialString[60];
```

```
// function to get the temperature for a device
void getTemperatures()
{
  itempC = sensors.getTempC(insideThermometer);
  itempF = DallasTemperature::toFahrenheit(itempC);
  etempC = sensors.getTempC(outsideThermometer);
  etempF = DallasTemperature::toFahrenheit(etempC);
}

void tweet(char msg[]) {
   Serial.println("connecting ...");
  if (twitter.post(msg)) {
    int status = twitter.wait();
    if (status == 200) {
      Serial.println("OK. Tweet sent.");
      Serial.println();
      lastTime = millis();
      firstTweet = false;
    } else {
      Serial.print("failed : code ");
      Serial.println(status);
    }
  } else {
    Serial.println("connection failed.");
  }
}

void setup()
{
  EthernetDHCP.begin(mac);
  Serial.begin(9600);
   sensors.begin();
    // set the resolution
  sensors.setResolution(insideThermometer, TEMPERATURE_PRECISION);
  sensors.setResolution(outsideThermometer, TEMPERATURE_PRECISION);

  sensors.requestTemperatures()

  getTemperatures();
  // compile the string to be tweeted
while (firstTweet) {
sprintf(message, "Int. Temp: %d C (%d F) Ext. Temp: %d C (%d F). Tweeted from Arduino. %ld",
int(itempC), int(itempF), int(etempC), int(etempF), millis());   tweet(message);
  }
}
```

```
void loop()
{
  EthernetDHCP.maintain();
  sensors.requestTemperatures();
  // compile the string to be printed to the serial monitor
  sprintf(serialString, "Internal Temp: %d C  %d F. External Temp: %d C %d F", int(itempC),
int(itempF), int(etempC), int(etempF));
  delay(500);
  Serial.println(serialString);
  Serial.println();

  if (millis() >= (lastTime + interval)) {
  // compile the string to be tweeted
sprintf(message, "Int. Temp: %d C (%d F) Ext. Temp: %d C (%d F). Tweeted from Arduino. %ld",
int(itempC), int(itempF), int(etempC), int(etempF), millis());   tweet(message);
    }
delay(10000); // 10 seconds
}
```

After you have uploaded the code to your Arduino, open the serial monitor window. The Arduino will attempt to connect to Twitter (actually NeoCat's website) and send the tweet. If the first tweet is successful, the output in the serial monitor window will be a bit like this:

```
connecting ...
OK. Tweet sent.

Internal Temp: 26 C  79 F. External Temp: 26 C 79 F

Internal Temp: 26 C  79 F. External Temp: 26 C 79 F

Internal Temp: 26 C  79 F. External Temp: 26 C 79 F
```

When the program first runs, it will obtain the temperature and then keep attempting to connect to Twitter in the setup routine before it moves onto the main loop. It will not stop until it successfully connects. If the program fails to connect, you will get a `failed : code 403` or `connection failed` message. If the tweet is successful, it will not tweet again until the interval period has passed. By default, this is set to 10 minutes, though you can change it. Twitter limits you to a maximum of 350 requests per hour, so don't overdo it. You can now access the Twitter website and view the account from anywhere to check up in the temperature readings.

Let's see how this code works.

Project 49 – Twitterbot – Code Overview

The program starts off by including the relevant libraries:

```
#include <Ethernet.h>
#include <EthernetDHCP.h>
#include <EthernetDNS.h>
```

```
#include <Twitter.h>
#include <OneWire.h>
#include <DallasTemperature.h>
```

The Twitter library needs the three Ethernet libraries to work so they are all included. Next, the defines for the sensors are set:

```
#define ONE_WIRE_BUS 3
#define TEMPERATURE_PRECISION 12
```

You create four floats for the temperatures, this time for internal and external temperatures in both C and F:

```
float itempC, itempF, etempC, etempF;
```

The first time the program attempts to make a tweet, you want it to keep on trying until it successfully connects and sends the message. Therefore, a Boolean is created and set to true, so you know if you have yet to make your first tweet or not:

```
boolean firstTweet = true;
```

As before, you create instances for the one-wire and temperature sensors as well as the addresses for the two sensors:

```
OneWire oneWire(ONE_WIRE_BUS);
DallasTemperature sensors(&oneWire);

DeviceAddress insideThermometer = { 0x10, 0x7A, 0x3B, 0xA9, 0x01, 0x08, 0x00, 0xBF };
DeviceAddress outsideThermometer = { 0x10, 0xCD, 0x39, 0xA9, 0x01, 0x08, 0x00, 0xBE};
```

You give the Ethernet shield a MAC address:

```
byte mac[] = { 0x64, 0xB9, 0xE8, 0xC3, 0xC7, 0xE2 };
```

Next, you create an instance of the Twitter library and pass it the token for your account:

```
Twitter twitter("608048201-CxY1yQi8ezhvjz60ZVfPHVdzIHbMOD1h2gvoaAIx");
```

The interval in-between tweets is set

```
unsigned long interval = 600000; // 10 minutes
```

as is a variable to store the time you last tweeted.

```
unsigned long lastTime; // time since last tweet
```

Two character arrays are created. These will store the message to be tweeted and the message you will output to the serial monitor window.

```
char message[140], serialString[60];
```

Now you create some functions. The first one is the function to obtain the temperatures from the two sensors and store them in your variables.

```
void getTemperatures()
{
  itempC = sensors.getTempC(insideThermometer);
  itempF = DallasTemperature::toFahrenheit(itempC);
  etempC = sensors.getTempC(outsideThermometer);
  etempF = DallasTemperature::toFahrenheit(etempC);
}
```

Next is the function that will do the tweeting for you. It requires one parameter, which is the character array that has your message in it.

```
void tweet(char msg[]) {
```

The user is informed that you are attempting to connect:

```
Serial.println("connecting ...");
```

Next, you use the `post()` method of the Twitter object to send the message. If the post is successful, the function returns true. If it fails to connect, it returns false.

```
  if (twitter.post(msg)) {
```

If you connect successfully, then you check the status of the post using the `wait()` method. This returns the HTTP status code in the response from Twitter.

```
int status = twitter.wait();
```

If the status code is 200, this is the HTTP code's way of saying everything is OK. In other words, if the tweet was successfully sent, then the code within the block will execute.

```
if (status == 200) {
```

If successful, you inform the user:

```
Serial.println("OK. Tweet sent.");
Serial.println();
```

Then set `lastTime` to the current value in millis(). This is so you can determine how long has passed since the last tweet.

```
lastTime = millis();
```

The first time you carry out a successful tweet, you want the program to jump out of the `while` loop in the setup routine and move onto the main loop, so you set the `firstTweet` flag to false.

```
firstTweet = false;
```

If the status is not 200, i.e. the post failed, then the user is informed and the code passed back for debugging purposes

```
} else {
      Serial.print("failed : code ");
      Serial.println(status);
}
```

and if you were not even able to connect in the first place, the user is informed of that instead.

```
} else {
    Serial.println("connection failed.");
}
```

The user functions out the way, you now come to the setup routine:

```
void setup()
```

First, you begin the EthernetDHCP library and pass it the MAC address:

```
EthernetDHCP.begin(mac);
```

DHCP (Dynamic Host Configuration Protocol) is an autoconfiguration protocol used on IP networks. It allows the Ethernet Shield to automatically be assigned an IP address from one that is available from the router. Previously, you manually set the IP address; this time you use the EthernetDHCP library to auto-assign one for you. The tradeoff is your code is much larger.

Next, you begin serial communications at 9600 baud and set up the sensors as before:

```
Serial.begin(9600);
sensors.begin();
sensors.setResolution(insideThermometer, TEMPERATURE_PRECISION);
sensors.setResolution(outsideThermometer, TEMPERATURE_PRECISION);
```

The temperatures are requested, as you are about to use them:

```
sensors.requestTemperatures()
getTemperatures();
```

You now attempt to send your first tweet. The `while` loop to do this will keep running as long as `firstTweet` is set to true:

```
while (firstTweet) {
```

Next, you use a `sprintf` command to compile the tweet into the message[] array. You pass it the four sets of temperatures as well as the value of millis(). As millis is an unsigned long number, you use the %ld specifier in `sprintf` to print a long integer.

```
sprintf(message, "Int. Temp: %d C (%d F) Ext. Temp: %d C (%d F). Tweeted from Arduino. %ld",
int(itempC), int(itempF), int(etempC), int(etempF), millis());
```

The reason you add the value of millis() onto the end of the tweet is that Twitter will not post a message that is the same as the last one sent. If the temperatures have not changed since the last tweet, the message will be the same and Twitter will return an error code instead. As you want regular updates every interval period, by adding the value of millis() to the end you will ensure that the message differs from the last one sent. Make sure that your tweet length does not go over 140 characters in total; otherwise, you will end up with weird messages appearing in your Twitter timeline.

Now that you have compiled your message, you pass it to the **tweet()** function:

```
tweet(message);
```

Next comes the main loop, which you will only reach if the first tweet in the setup routine is successful:

```
void loop()
```

First, you run a maintain command on the EthernetDHCP library. This keeps the auto-assigned IP address live and valid.

```
EthernetDHCP.maintain();
```

The temperatures are updated.

```
sensors.requestTemperatures();
```

Then you use a `sprintf` command to compile the output for the serial monitor. It's more convenient than a whole list of Serial.print() commands so you may as well use it, though it does increase the size of your code.

```
sprintf(serialString, "Internal Temp: %d C  %d F. External Temp: %d C %d F", int(itempC),
int(itempF), int(etempC), int(etempF));
```

Then the string is output to the serial monitor after a short delay:

```
delay(500);
Serial.println(serialString);
Serial.println();
```

Next you ascertain if the interval time has passed since the last tweet, and if so, send another one. You calculate the value of `lastTime` + interval and see if the current value in millis() is greater than it (i.e. the interval period has passed since the last tweet). If so, you compile the new message and tweet again.

```
if (millis() >= (lastTime + interval)) {
        sprintf(message, "Int. Temp: %d C (%d F) Ext. Temp: %d C (%d F). Tweeted from
        Arduino. %ld", int(itempC), int(itempF), int(etempC), int(etempF), millis());
        tweet(message);
}
```

Finally, you have a 10 second delay in-between the updates to the serial monitor so that you don't bombard the user with information:

```
delay(10000); // 10 seconds
```

Now that you know how to send tweets from your Arduino, you can use it for all kinds of purposes. How about a potted plant that tweets to let you know it needs watering? Or sensors around a house to tweet whenever anyone enters a room, a doorbell that tweets when someone is at the door, or a cat flap that tells you when your cat has left or entered the house? The possibilities are endless.

Now you've reached the final project in your journey. In this last project, you will use the Ethernet Shield to read some data from the Internet instead of sending data out.

Project 50 – RSS Weather Reader

The final project in this book will use the Ethernet Shield again, but instead of transmitting data out to a web service, you will use the Arduino and Ethernet Shield to fetch data from the Internet and then display it in the serial monitor window. The data you are going to use is an RSS (Really Simple Syndication) feed from the www.weather.gov website to obtain weather data for an area of your choosing in the U.S. This code will easily adapt to read an RSS weather feed from any other source if you are outside of the US.

RSS is a web format for publishing frequently updated information, such as weather, news, etc. The data is in XML (Extensible Markup Language) format, which is a set of rules for encoding documents in a machine-readable form. XML is a simple format and it's not really necessary to understand how it works. The Arduino will simply look for tags within the XML code where the temperature, humidity, and pressure data is stored and strip out that information for displaying.

You'll be using the XML feed for Edwards Air Force Base in California. If you wish to use a different feed, go to http://www.weather.gov/xml/current_obs/ and choose your area, then look for the full address of the XML data for that feed. Adjust the code accordingly to show the weather for that area.

As for hardware, this time you are using nothing more than an Ethernet Shield plugged into an Arduino.

Enter the Code

Plug the Ethernet shield into the Arduino (if it is not already there) and enter the code from Listing 17-5. Thanks to Bob S. (Xtalker) from the Arduino forums for the code.

Listing 17-5. Code for Project 50

```
// Project 50
// Thanks to  Bob S. for original code
// Get current weather observation for Edwards AFB from weather.gov in XML format

#include <Ethernet.h>
#include <SPI.h>

// Max string length may have to be adjusted depending on data to be extracted
#define MAX_STRING_LEN  20

// Setup vars
char tagStr[MAX_STRING_LEN] = "";
char dataStr[MAX_STRING_LEN] = "";
char tmpStr[MAX_STRING_LEN] = "";
char endTag[3] = {'<', '/', '\0'};
int len;
```

```
// Flags to differentiate XML tags from document elements (ie. data)
boolean tagFlag = false;
boolean dataFlag = false;

// Ethernet vars
byte mac[] = { 0xDE, 0xAD, 0xBE, 0xEF, 0xFE, 0xED };
byte ip[] = {172,31,24,232};
byte server[] = { 140, 90, 113, 200 }; // www.weather.gov

// Start ethernet client
Client client(server, 80);

void setup()
{
  Serial.begin(9600);
  Serial.println("Starting Weather RSS Reader");
  Serial.println("connecting...");
  Ethernet.begin(mac, ip);
  delay(1000);

  if (client.connect()) {
    Serial.println("connected");
    client.println("GET /xml/current_obs/KEDW.xml HTTP/1.0");
    client.println();
    delay(2000);
  } else {
    Serial.println("connection failed");
  }
}

void loop() {

  // Read serial data in from web:
  while (client.available()) {
    serialEvent();
  }

  if (!client.connected()) {

    client.stop();

  if (int t=0; t<15; t++) { // the feed is updated once every 15 mins
      delay(60000); // 1 minute
      }
```

```
    if (client.connect()) {
      client.println("GET /xml/current_obs/KEDW.xml HTTP/1.0");
      client.println();
      delay(2000);
    } else {
      Serial.println("Reconnection failed");
    }
  }
}

// Process each char from web
void serialEvent() {

   // Read a char
      char inChar = client.read();

   if (inChar == '<') {
      addChar(inChar, tmpStr);
      tagFlag = true;
      dataFlag = false;

   } else if (inChar == '>') {
      addChar(inChar, tmpStr);

      if (tagFlag) {
         strncpy(tagStr, tmpStr, strlen(tmpStr)+1);
      }

      // Clear tmp
      clearStr(tmpStr);

      tagFlag = false;
      dataFlag = true;

   } else if (inChar != 10) {
      if (tagFlag) {
         // Add tag char to string
         addChar(inChar, tmpStr);

         // Check for </XML> end tag, ignore it
         if ( tagFlag && strcmp(tmpStr, endTag) == 0 ) {
            clearStr(tmpStr);
            tagFlag = false;
            dataFlag = false;
         }
      }
```

```
      if (dataFlag) {
         // Add data char to string
         addChar(inChar, dataStr);
      }
   }

   // If a LF, process the line
   if (inChar == 10 ) {

      // Find specific tags and print data
      if (matchTag("<temp_f>")) {
            Serial.print("Temp: ");
         Serial.print(dataStr);
      }
      if (matchTag("<temp_c>")) {
            Serial.print(", TempC: ");
         Serial.print(dataStr);
      }
      if (matchTag("<relative_humidity>")) {
            Serial.print(", Humidity: ");
         Serial.print(dataStr);
      }
      if (matchTag("<pressure_in>")) {
            Serial.print(", Pressure: ");
         Serial.print(dataStr);
         Serial.println("");
      }

      // Clear all strings
      clearStr(tmpStr);
      clearStr(tagStr);
      clearStr(dataStr);

      // Clear Flags
      tagFlag = false;
      dataFlag = false;
   }
}

// Function to clear a string
void clearStr (char* str) {
   int len = strlen(str);
   for (int c = 0; c < len; c++) {
      str[c] = 0;
   }
}
```

```
//Function to add a char to a string and check its length
void addChar (char ch, char* str) {
   char *tagMsg  = "<TRUNCATED_TAG>";
   char *dataMsg = "-TRUNCATED_DATA-";

   // Check the max size of the string to make sure it doesn't grow too
   // big.  If string is beyond MAX_STRING_LEN assume it is unimportant
   // and replace it with a warning message.
   if (strlen(str) > MAX_STRING_LEN - 2) {
      if (tagFlag) {
         clearStr(tagStr);
         strcpy(tagStr,tagMsg);
      }
      if (dataFlag) {
         clearStr(dataStr);
         strcpy(dataStr,dataMsg);
      }

      // Clear the temp buffer and flags to stop current processing
      clearStr(tmpStr);
      tagFlag = false;
      dataFlag = false;

   } else {
      // Add char to string
      str[strlen(str)] = ch;
   }
}

// Function to check the current tag for a specific string
boolean matchTag (char* searchTag) {
   if ( strcmp(tagStr, searchTag) == 0 ) {
      return true;
   } else {
      return false;
   }
}
```

Upload the code and open up the serial monitor. If everything is working correctly, you will have an output similar to this:

```
Starting Weather RSS Reader
connecting...
connected
TempF: 60.0, TempC: 15.4, Humidity: 100, Pressure: 29.96
```

Every sixty seconds the display will update again with the latest data. Let's see how this code works.

Project 50 – RSS Weather Reader – Code Overview

The program starts off by including the relevant Ethernet libraries you will need:

```
#include <Ethernet.h>
#include <SPI.h>
```

Then you define the maximum length of the data string:

```
#define MAX_STRING_LEN  20
```

You may need to increase this if you are requesting further information from the feed. Next, you create three arrays that will store the various strings you will be processing (these all have the just the length defined).

```
char tagStr[MAX_STRING_LEN] = "";
char dataStr[MAX_STRING_LEN] = "";
char tmpStr[MAX_STRING_LEN] = "";
```

Then you create another array to store the possible end tags you will encounter in the XML feed:

```
char endTag[3] = {'<', '/', '\0'};
```

Then you create a variable that will store the length of the string you will be processing at the relevant section of the code:

```
int len;
```

Then you create two flags. These will be used to differentiate between the XML tags and the information after the tags that you wish to strip out of the XML code.

```
boolean tagFlag = false;
boolean dataFlag = false;
```

Next, you set up the MAC and IP address of the Ethernet Shield:

```
byte mac[] = { 0xDE, 0xAD, 0xBE, 0xEF, 0xFE, 0xED };
byte ip[] = {172,31,24,232};
```

Then the IP address of the www.weather.gov website:

```
byte server[] = { 140, 90, 113, 200 }; // www.weather.gov
```

If you are using a different website for your weather feed, change this IP address to the URL you are using. Next, you create a client object and pass it the address of the server and the port you are using:

```
Client client(server, 80);
```

Next comes the setup routine

```
void setup()
```

which starts off with beginning serial communications at 9600 baud so you can print data to the serial monitor.

```
Serial.begin(9600);
```

You inform the use of the name of the program and that you are attempting to connect:

```
Serial.println("Starting Weather RSS Reader");
Serial.println("connecting...");
```

Ethernet communications are started, passing the MAC and IP address of your device, followed by a short delay to allow it to connect:

```
Ethernet.begin(mac, ip);
delay(1000);
```

Next, you check if you have connected to your client (the www.weather.gov website) successfully:

```
if (client.connect()) {
```

If so, you inform the user

```
Serial.println("connected");
```

Then carry out a HTML GET command to access the XML data from the sub-directory that stores the relevant feed, followed by a delay to allow successful communications.

```
client.println("GET /xml/current_obs/KEDW.xml HTTP/1.0");
client.println();
delay(2000);
```

If the connection was not made, you inform the user of a failed connection:

```
  } else {
    Serial.println("connection failed");
  }
}
```

Next comes the main loop:

```
void loop() {
```

As you performed a GET command in the setup loop, the serial buffer should contain the contents of the XML feed returned from the server. So, while you have data available

```
while (client.available()) {
```

the `serialEvent()` function is called.

```
serialEvent();
```

This function will be explained shortly. If a connection has not been made

```
if (!client.connected()) {
```

the connection to the client is stopped

```
client.stop();
```

then you wait 15 minutes before you attempt another connection. The data feed is updated once every 15 minutes at most, so it is pointless updating the information any less than this:

```
if (int t=0; t<15; t++) { // the feed is updated once every 15 mins
      delay(60000); // 1 minute
      }
```

If you have made a successful connection to the client

```
if (client.connect()) {
```

then you perform another GET command to obtain the latest XML feed data

```
client.println("GET /xml/current_obs/KEDW.xml HTTP/1.0");
client.println();
delay(2000);
```

and if a connection fails, the user is informed.

```
} else {
      Serial.println("Reconnection failed");
    }
```

Next comes the `serialEvent()` function. The purpose of this function is to read the data from the XML feed and process it according to what it finds

```
void serialEvent() {
```

The function starts by reading in the first character and storing it in `inChar`:

```
char inChar = client.read();
```

Now you need to take a look at that character and decide if it is a tag or if it is data. If it is a tag, then we set the `tagFlag` to true. If it is data, we set the `dataFlag` to true. The other flag is set to false each time.

The raw data for the feed looks like:

```
<current_observation version="1.0"
        xmlns:xsd="http://www.w3.org/2001/XMLSchema"
        xmlns:xsi="http://www.w3.org/2001/XMLSchema-instance"
        xsi:noNamespaceSchemaLocation="http://www.weather.gov/view/current_observation.xsd">
        <credit>NOAA's National Weather Service</credit>
        <credit_URL>http://weather.gov/</credit_URL>
        <image><url>http://weather.gov/images/xml_logo.gif</url><title>NOAA's National
Weather Service</title><link>http://weather.gov</link></image>
        <suggested_pickup>15 minutes after the hour</suggested_pickup>
        <suggested_pickup_period>60</suggested_pickup_period>
        <location>Edwards AFB, CA</location>
        <station_id>KEDW</station_id>
        <latitude>34.91</latitude>
        <longitude>-117.87</longitude>
        <observation_time>Last Updated on Oct 19 2010, 9:55 am PDT</observation_time>
        <observation_time_rfc822>Tue, 19 Oct 2010 09:55:00 -0700</observation_time_rfc822>
        <weather>Mostly Cloudy</weather>
        <temperature_string>62.0 F (16.4 C)</temperature_string>
        <temp_f>62.0</temp_f>
        <temp_c>16.4</temp_c>
        <relative_humidity>100</relative_humidity>
```

As you can see, each piece of information is embedded inside a tag. For example, the temperature in Fahrenheit has the `<temp_f>` tag to start it off and a `</temp_f>` to end it. Everything in-between the tags are data.

First, you check if the character is a < character. If so, this is the start of a tag.

```
if (inChar == '<') {
```

If so, you call the `addChar` function, which will check if the string length is within the limits of MAX_STRING_LEN and if so, add the character to your tmpStr string. You will examine this function later on.

```
addChar(inChar, tmpStr);
```

As you have found a tag, the `tagFlag` is set to true and the `dataFlag` set to false:

```
tagFlag = true;
dataFlag = false;
```

If you reach the end of the tag by finding the > character

```
} else if (inChar == '>') {
```

then the character is added to the tmpStr string.

```
addChar(inChar, tmpStr);
```

If you are currently processing a tag and have reached the end of the tag, you can copy the entire tag from the tmpStr (temporary string) in the tag string (tgrStr). You use the strncpy command to do this.

```
if (tagFlag) {
        strncpy(tagStr, tmpStr, strlen(tmpStr)+1);
}
```

The strncpy command copies part of one string into another string. It requires three parameters: the string you are copying the data into, the string you are copying the data from, and the amount of characters to copy. For example, if you had

```
strncpy(firstString, secondString, 10);
```

then the first 10 characters of secondString are copied into firstString. In your case you copy the entire contents by finding the length of the temporary string (tmpStr)+1 and copying that amount of characters into the tag string.

Once the temporary string has been copied, you need to clear it so it's ready for the next piece of data. To do this, you call the **clearStr** function and pass it the string you wish to clear.

```
clearStr(tmpStr);
```

The two flags are set to false, ready for the next piece of information:

```
tagFlag = false;
dataFlag = true;
```

If the character read is a linefeed (ASCII 10)

```
} else if (inChar != 10) {
```

then you add the character to the string if you are currently processing a tag

```
if (tagFlag) {
      addChar(inChar, tmpStr);
```

You want to ignore the end tags so you check if you are currently processing a tag and have reached the end of the tag (by comparing with the endTag characters)

```
if ( tagFlag && strcmp(tmpStr, endTag) == 0 ) {
```

then the tag is ignored, the string is cleared, and the tags set to their defaults.

```
clearStr(tmpStr);
tagFlag = false;
dataFlag = false;
```

The strcmp command compares two strings. In your case, it compares the temporary string (tmpStr) with the characters in the endTag array:

```
strcmp(tmpStr, endTag)
```

The result will be 0 if the strings match and another value if they don't. By comparing it with the endTag array, you are checking that any of the three end tag characters are present.

If the current string is data

```
if (dataFlag) {
```

then you add the current character to the data string (dataStr).

```
addChar(inChar, dataStr);
```

The above code has basically decided if you are processing a tag, and if so, stores the characters in the tag string (tagStr) and if it is data, stores it in the data string (dataStr). You will end up with the tag and the data stored separately.

If you have reached a linefeed character, you are clearly at the end of the current string. So you now need to check the tags to see if they are the temperature, humidity, or pressure data that you want.

```
if (inChar == 10 ) {
```

To do this, you use the `matchTag` function (that you will come to shortly) which checks if the specified tag is within the tag string, and if, so returns a true value. You start with looking for the temperature in Fahrenheit tag

```
<temp_f>
```

```
if (matchTag("<temp_f>")) {
```

and if so, prints out the data string, which if the tag is <temp_f> will contain the temperature in Fahrenheit.

```
Serial.print("Temp: ");
Serial.print(dataStr);
```

Next you check for the temperature in Celsius,

```
if (matchTag("<temp_c>")) {
        Serial.print(", TempC: ");
        Serial.print(dataStr);
}
```

the humidity,

```
if (matchTag("<relative_humidity>")) {
        Serial.print(", Humidity: ");
        Serial.print(dataStr);
      }
```

and the pressure.

```
if (matchTag("<pressure_in>")) {
        Serial.print(", Pressure: ");
        Serial.print(dataStr);
        Serial.println("");
}
```

Then all of the strings are cleared ready for the next line

```
clearStr(tmpStr);
clearStr(tagStr);
clearStr(dataStr);
```

and the tags are cleared, too.

```
tagFlag = false;
dataFlag = false;
```

Next, you have your user functions, starting with the clear string (clearStr) function

```
void clearStr (char* str) {
```

that simply finds the length of the string passed to the function using the strLen() command

```
int len = strlen(str);
```

then uses a for-loop to fill each element of the array with an ASCII 0 (null) character.

```
for (int c = 0; c < len; c++) {
      str[c] = 0;
}
```

The next function is the `addChar` function. You pass the character currently read and the current string to it as parameters.

```
void addChar (char ch, char* str) {
```

You define two new character arrays and store error messages in them:

```
char *tagMsg  = "<TRUNCATED_TAG>";
char *dataMsg = "-TRUNCATED_DATA-";
```

If you find that the strings are over the length of MAX_STRING_LEN then you will replace them with these error messages.

You now check the length of the string to see if it has reached the maximum length:

```
if (strlen(str) > MAX_STRING_LEN - 2) {
```

If it has and you are currently processing a tag

```
if (tagFlag) {
```

then the tag string is cleared and you copy the error message into the tag string.

```
clearStr(tagStr);
strcpy(tagStr,tagMsg);
```

If you are processing data, then the data string is cleared and you copy the data error message into the data string.

```
if (dataFlag) {
        clearStr(dataStr);
        strcpy(dataStr,dataMsg);
}
```

The temporary string and tags are cleared

```
clearStr(tmpStr);
tagFlag = false;
dataFlag = false;
```

and if the length of the string has not exceeded the maximum length, you add the current character that has been read into the string. You use the length of the string to find out the last character, i.e. the next place you can add a character to.

```
} else {
      // Add char to string
      str[strlen(str)] = ch;
}
```

Finally, you come to the matchTag function that is used to check that the search tag passed to it as a parameter has been found or not, and if so, returns a true or false accordingly:

```
boolean matchTag (char* searchTag) {
```

The function is of type Boolean as it returns a Boolean value and requires a character array as a parameter:

```
if ( strcmp(tagStr, searchTag) == 0 ) {
      return true;
   } else {
      return false;
   }
}
```

By changing the XML feed URL and the tags found within that feed, you can use this code to look for pieces of data in any RSS feed you wish. For example, you could use the Yahoo weather feeds at http://weather.yahoo.com then navigate to the region you wish to view and click the RSS button. The URL of that feed can then be entered into the code. You can view the raw source of the feed by right clicking and choosing the right click menu option to view the source. You can then view the tags and modify the code to find the relevant piece of information.

This last project has showed you how to use your Ethernet Shield to obtain information from the Internet. Previously, you send data out from the shield to external sources. In this project, you read data back from the Internet instead. Rather than displaying the weather data in the serial monitor window, you can use the skills you have learned in the previous projects to display it on an LCD screen or on an LED dot matrix display.

Summary

This final chapter has showed how to connect your Arduino to the Internet, either for the purpose of sending data out in the form of a served webpage, a tweet to Twitter, an e-mail, or sensor data sent to Pachube, or for requesting a webpage and stripping data from that webpage for your own use. Having the ability to connect your Arduino to a LAN or the Internet opens up a whole new list of potential projects. Data can be sent anywhere around your house or office where an Ethernet port is available, or data can be read from the Internet for the Arduino to process, display, act upon, etc.

For example, you could use a current weather feed to determine if it is about to rain and warn you to bring your washing in from the clothesline or to close a skylight window. What you do with your Arduino once it's connected is only limited by your imagination.

Subjects and Concepts covered in Chapter 17:

- How to manually assign a MAC and IP address to your device
- The concept of client and server
- How to listen for client connections with the client.connected() command
- Sending HTML code by printing to a client
- Using your Arduino as a web server
- Connecting to the Arduino from a web browser
- Checking data is available with the client.available() command.
- Reading data with the client.read() command
- Sending data to Pachube, viewing the data as graphs, etc.
- Sending tweets to Twitter.com from the Arduino via a proxy
- Sending e-mails from the Arduino
- Fetching data from an RSS feed and parsing it for display
- Copying strings with the strcpy and strncpy commands
- Comparing strings with the strcmp command
- Filling memory locations with the memset command
- Finding the size of arrays with the sizeof command

- Processing strings with the sprintf command
- Finding lengths of strings with the strlen command
- Searching for sub-strings with the strstr command
- Finding IP address with the ping command
- Checking if a client has connected with the client.connect() command
- Creating an Ethernet connection with the Ethernet.begin(mac, ip) command
- Encrypting usernames and passwords to Base-64 with website utilities
- Using the EthernetDHCP.h library to automatically assign an IP address
- Using the Twitter library post and wait commands
- Looking for tags in an XML RSS feed

Index

Numbers & Symbols

A

B

C

D

E

M

N

O

P

T

U

V

W

X, Y, Z

Made in the USA
San Bernardino, CA
10 December 2012